Instant Pot

COOKBOOK FOR BEGINNERS

600 Easy and Delicious Instant Pot Recipes For Fast and Healthy Meals

Emilia Mitchell

TABLE OF CONTENTS

Introduction 1

Benefits of Pressure Cooking 2

Buttons and Time Settings 3

Pressure Releasing Methods 5

Parts of Instant Pot 6

Must Have Accessories 7

Useful Tips and Tricks 8

Breakfasts 9

Potatoes Breakfast Salad 9

Sweet Potato Mini Quiche 9

Creamy Sausage Frittata 10

Breakfast Millet Pilaf 10

Tofu & Potatoes Breakfast 10

Bacon, Egg & Cheese Muffins 11

Scrambled Eggs & Bacon 11

Cobbler Recipe 11

Pumpkin Butter Breakfast 12

Pomegranate Porridge 12

Apple Breakfast 12

Beef Roast 13

Poached Tomatoes and Eggs 13

Egg Side Dish 13

Spinach, Bacon & Eggs 14

Breakfast Bread Pudding 14

Potato Hash 15

Strawberry Oats 15

Carrot Oatmeal Breakfast 15

Millet Pudding 16

Vanilla Polenta 16

Tofu Scramble Recipe 16

Sweet Potato Poblano Hash 17

Breakfast Pudding 17

Cheesy Hash Brown 18

Easy and Cheesy Grits 18

Tasty Scotch Eggs 18

Breakfast Berries Jam 19

Breakfast Enchiladas 19

Easy Egg Muffins 20

Hard Boiled Eggs 20

Berry Toast Casserole 20

Blackberries Jam 21

Delicious Poached Eggs 21

Spinach & Tomato Breakfast 21

Banana Cake 22

Breakfast Hash 22

Blueberry Bliss Bowls 22

Quinoa and Granola Bowls 23

Tofu and Potato Casserole 23

French Toast Casserole 24

Tomato Spinach Quiche 24

Mushroom Oatmeal 25

Healthy Tasty Oats 25

Lemon Marmalade Recipe 26

Tasty Sausage 26

Pecan Sweet Potatoes 26

Mixed Mushroom Pate 27

Chocolate Steel Cut Oats 27

Breakfast Quiche 27

Eggs Breakfast 28

Chickpeas Spread 28

Maple Millet 29

Barbeque Tofu 29

Apple Porridge 29

Feta Spinach Egg Cups 30

Meat Recipes 31

Beef and Cabbage 31

Delicious Lamb Ragout......................................31

Pork Chops & Smashed Potatoes 31

Creamy Pork Chops 32

Braised Pork Recipe 32

Lamb & Beans Dish 32

Tasty Kalua Pork 33

Pork Tamales..33

Lamb Curry 34

Pork Carnitas...34

Feta & Lamb Meatballs......................................34

Easy and Tasty Meatloaf....................................35

Pork Chops & Brown Rice 35

Beef Curry..36

Meatball Delight...36

Red Beans & Sausage Dish 37

Collard with Bacon..37

Potatoes and Goat...37

Delicious Pork Chops 38

Tasty Beef Chili...38

Pork with Orange and Honey 39

Pork Sausages and Mashed Potatoes 39

Delicious Chili Con Carne 40

Pasta and Beef Casserole....................................40

Easy Veal Dish 40

Asian Short Ribs..41

Apple Cider Pork...41

Pulled Pork Dish...42

Pork Roast with Fennel......................................42

Chinese BBQ Pork...42

Spiced Pork 43

Beef & Broccoli Dish...43

Meatballs in Tomato Sauce.................................44

Meatloaf Dish...44

Hominy Dish 45

Awesome Beef Recipe...45

Rice & Beef Soup...46

Asian Ground Lamb...46

Hamburger Stew...47

Sausage and Kale Soup.......................................47

Beef with Cracked Wheat....................................47

Pulled Pork...48

Corned Beef Recipe..48

Chinese Steamed Ribs..49

Korean Beef Dish...49

Mexican Lamb Recipe..50

Wonton Meatballs...50

Sunday Brussels Sprouts.....................................51

Tasty Beef Dish...51

Pork Shoulder Tacos..52

Meatballs and Tomato Sauce...............................52

Pork Chile Verde...53

Korean Beef Stew..53

Pork Chops with Scallion Rice.............................54

Poultry Recipes **55**

Delicious Chicken Sandwiches.............................55

Simple Chicken Delight......................................55

Chickpea Chicken Masala...................................56

Delicious Chicken in Tomatillo Sauce 56

Moroccan Chicken...57

Chicken Curry 57

Cheering Chicken Wings.....................................58

Delicious Duck Chili..58

Chicken Salad 59

Creamy Chicken Dish...59

Potatoes and Chicken...59

Braised Duck and Potatoes Recipe.......................60

Barbeque Honey Chicken....................................60

Easy Turkey Chili..60

Three Cup Chicken...................................... 61

Italian Chicken... 61

Sesame Chicken Recipe............................. 62

Garlic Chicken.. 62

Stuffed Chicken Breast.............................. 63

Chicken with Rice...................................... 63

Chicken Dish.. 64

Teriyaki Chicken Delight............................ 64

Chicken Curry... 64

Chicken & Shrimp Recipe.......................... 65

Pepper Chicken Soup................................. 65

Crispy Chicken... 66

Chicken & Cabbage Dish........................... 66

Buffalo Chicken Recipe.............................. 67

Lemongrass Chicken Recipe...................... 67

Asian Chicken.. 67

Chicken and Corn Mix................................ 68

Chicken and Dumplings............................. 68

Turkey & Mashed Potatoes....................... 69

Delicious Chicken with Cumin-Chile Sauce.......... 69

Spiced Chicken and Rice Pilaf................... 70

Turkey Meatballs....................................... 70

Mushroom Chicken.................................... 71

Chicken & Broccoli Dish............................. 71

Easy Thai Chicken..................................... 72

Awesome Chicken Adobo........................... 72

Chicken Enchilada Casserole.................... 73

Sweet Corn Chicken Soup......................... 73

Soups and Stews.................................... 74

Chicken Stew Recipe................................. 74

Chorizo, Kale and Chicken Soup............... 74

Tomato Soup.. 75

Classic Cauliflower Soup........................... 75

Fish Chowder... 76

Chicken Noodle Soup.................................76

Chicken Meatball Soup Recipe..................76

Endive Soup...77

Sweet Potato and Turkey Soup.................77

Beef and Mushroom Stew..........................78

Chicken Chili Soup.....................................78

Cheese and Potato Soup...........................79

Zuppa Toscana Delight..............................79

Delicious Okra Stew...................................80

Minestrone Soup..80

Surprising Sweet Potato Stew...................81

White Bean and Swiss Chard Stew............81

Bacon and Broccoli Soup...........................82

Lasagna Soup..82

Delicious Beef Stew...................................83

Root and Beef Vegetables Stew................83

Spinach Stew...84

Broccoli Cream..84

Asparagus Cream......................................84

Turkey Stew...85

Butternut Squash Soup..............................85

Classic Lamb Stew....................................86

Simple Fennel Soup...................................86

Lamb Stew...86

Celery Soup...87

Cabbage Head Soup..................................87

Corn Soup..87

Double Bean Chili......................................88

Italian Sausage Stew.................................88

Chickpeas Stew...89

Artichoke Soup..89

Veggie Soup...89

Barley and Beef Soup................................90

Curried Squash Soup.................................90

Chestnut Soup Recipe 91

Veggie Noodle Soup 91

Chicken Soup 92

Easy Carrot Soup 92

White Bean Soup 92

Ginger Carrot Soup 93

Potato Leek Soup 93

Peanut Stew 94

Ham and White Bean Soup 94

Coconut Sweet Potato Stew 95

Minestrone Soup 95

Corn Chowder 96

Split Pea Soup 96

Italian Stew 97

Quinoa Butternut Chili 97

Taco Chili 98

Wild Rice Soup 99

Tomato Basil Soup 99

Mushroom Cream Soup 100

Chipotle Sweet Potato Chowder 100

Fish and Seafood 101

Surprising Shrimp Delight 101

Tuna & Pasta Casserole. 101

Almond Cod 101

Mussels and Spicy Sauce 102

Tasty Tomato Mussels 102

Cheesy Tuna Dish. 102

Poached Salmon Dish 103

Salmon and Veggies Dish 103

Salmon Dish 103

Crispy Salmon Fillet 104

Steamed Fish Recipe 104

Spicy Salmon Dish 104

Tuna and Noodle 105

Delicious Shrimp Paella 105

Crispy Skin Salmon Fillets. 105

Salmon Burger 106

Miso Mackerel 106

Shrimp with Herbs and Risotto 106

Fish with Orange Sauce 107

Simple Clams 107

Crab Legs and Garlic Butter Sauce. 107

Shrimp and Potatoes Dish 108

Shrimp and Fish 108

Shrimp and Sausage Boil 108

Tuna and Crushed Crackers Casserole. 109

Shrimp Coconut Soup 109

Shrimp Teriyaki Recipe 110

Instant Shrimp Boil 110

Cheesy Tilapia 110

Mediterranean Fish 111

Delicious Salmon and Raspberry Sauce 111

Sesame Honey Salmon 112

Crab Quiche 112

Shrimp with Tomatoes, Spinach 113

Seafood Stew 113

Fresh Catfish with Herbs. 114

Steamed Scallion Ginger Fish 114

Delicious Cod and Peas 115

Instant Pot Steamed Mussels 115

Vegetable Recipes 116

Tomatoes and Zucchinis 116

Savoy Cabbage & Cream 116

Maple Glazed Carrots Recipe 116

Instant Steamed Leeks 117

Wrapped Asparagus Canes 117

Braised Endives 117

Sausages and Cabbage 117

Turnips Dish 118

Stuffed Tomatoes Delight................................118

Corn and Okra 118

Tomato and Beet Salad................................119

Fennel Risotto Dish................................119

Collard Greens Delight................................120

Sweet & Spicy Cabbage 120

Eggplant Ratatouille Dish................................120

Cabbage Dish 121

Artichokes with Lemon Sauce 121

Eggplant Surprise 121

Carrots and Turnips 121

Shrimp and Asparagus 122

Instant Brussels Sprouts with Parmesan............122

Braised Fennel 122

Brussels Sprouts & Potatoes Dish................................123

Beet and Orange Salad................................123

Endives Dish 123

Roasted Potatoes 124

Stuffed Bell Peppers 124

Pasta and Cauliflower Recipe 124

Crispy Potatoes Recipe................................125

Brussels Sprouts with Pomegranate 125

Bacon and Kale 125

Lentil Swiss Chard Soup 126

Stuffed Bell Peppers 126

Cheesy Polenta................................127

Babaganoush 127

Collard Greens Dish 127

Sautéed Endives Recipe 128

Bacon and Collard Greens 128

Artichoke Hearts Recipe 128

Tasty Okra Pilaf 129

Eggplant Marinara Sauce Dish 129

Sweet Carrots Recipe................................129

Tomatoes and Okra 129

Bacon and Brussels Sprouts................................130

Braised Kale Recipe 130

Corn Pudding................................130

Pinto Bean Stew 131

Collard Greens 131

Mushroom Kale Stroganoff................................132

Tuscan Stew................................132

Hearts Of Palm Soup 133

Asian Coconut Rice and Veggies................................133

Moo Goo Gai Pan 134

Sweet Potato and Black Bean Tacos 134

Red Curry Cauliflower 135

Vegetable Salad 135

Cabbage Rolls 136

Black Eyed Peas 137

Mucho Burritos................................137

Barbecue Chickpea Tacos 138

Asian Gobi Masala 138

Sloppy Janes................................139

Polenta and Kale 139

Corn Chowder 140

Vegetable Soup................................140

Chickpea Kale Korma 140

Butternut Mac N Cheese 141

Layered Casserole 141

Vegetable Stock 142

Kimchi Pasta 143

Tomato Basil Pasta 143

Snacks and Appetizers................................ 144

Instant Chili Dip 144

Asian Squid Appetizer 144

Zucchini Rolls Recipe 144

Delicious Shrimp Appetizer 145

Spinach Dip Recipe 145

Prosciutto and Asparagus Appetizer...................145

Tuna Patties Appetizer 146

French Endives 146

Mushroom Dip...................146

English Chicken Wings 147

Spicy Mussels Recipe 147

Sausage and Shrimp Appetizer 147

Cauliflower Dip Recipe 148

Pumpkin and Cinnamon Muffins...................148

Tomatoes Appetizer 148

Stuffed Clams...................149

Stuffed Mushrooms and Shrimp...................149

Mussels and Clams 149

Chili Balls 150

Easy Mango Dip 150

Zucchini Dip Recipe 150

Shrimp Appetizer...................151

Artichoke Dip Recipe 151

Beet Hummus...................151

Italian Dip 152

Tasty Okra Bowls...................152

Instant Cod Puddings 152

Zucchini Appetizer Salad Recipe 153

Turkey Meatballs 153

Sweet Potato Slaw...................153

Baby Carrots 154

Tomato Dip Recipe...................154

Squash and Beets Dip...................154

Surprising Oysters...................155

Simple Baked Potatoes 155

Crab and Cheese Dip...................155

Shrimp Recipe...................156

Mussels Bowls...................156

Artichokes 156

Spicy Salsa 156

Avocado Dip Recipe...................157

Mushrooms and Mustard Dip...................157

Roasted Garlic...................157

Italian Mussels Appetizer...................158

Perfect Beets...................158

Appetizing Cranberry Dip...................158

Creamy Corn...................159

Lemon Broccoli 159

Salmon Patties 159

Eggplant Spread...................160

Side Dishes 161

Glazed Carrots...................161

Potato Casserole 161

Easy Veggies Dish...................162

Onions & Parsnips...................162

Artichokes Dish...................162

Potatoes Au Gratin...................163

Herbed Polenta...................163

Potatoes Side Dish...................163

Poached Fennel Dish...................164

Mashed Squash...................164

Black Beans Dish...................164

Cauliflower Mash Dish...................165

Mushrooms & Green Beans Side Dish...................165

Bok Choy Dish...................165

Eggplant Dish...................166

Brussels Sprouts Dish...................166

Mashed Turnips Dish...................166

Mushroom Risotto 166

Israeli Couscous Dish...................167

Quinoa Pilaf...................167

Green Beans Dish................................167

Fava Bean Sauté 168

Flavored Mashed Sweet Potatoes.................168

Pumpkin Risotto 168

Special Side Dish 169

Refried Beans 169

Tomato & Calamari Dish.........................169

Parmesan & Garlic Asparagus 170

Sweet Carrot Puree 170

Lemon Peas & Parmesan Risotto 170

Apple and Butternut Mash.......................171

Barley & Cauliflower Risotto 171

Saffron Risotto 171

Citrus and Cauliflower Dish 172

Broccoli dish 172

Mixed Beans Side Dish............................172

Garlic and Beet Dish 173

Delicious Almonds & Quinoa Side Dish 173

Goat Cheese & Spinach Risotto 174

Farro Side Dish 174

Rice Recipes **175**

Mexican Rice................................175

Chipotle Rice................................175

Fried Basmati Rice................................175

Wild Rice and Chicken Soup.....................176

Cajun Rice 176

Mix-Fruit Wild Rice................................176

Pink Rice................................177

Mexican Brown Rice Casserole.................177

Mexican Basmati Rice.............................177

Rice Bowl 178

Lentil & Rice................................178

Rice & Beef Soup 179

Pineapple Rice................................179

French Butter Rice................................179

Simple White Rice................................180

Rice and Peas................................180

Chickpea & Rice Stew.............................180

Dolma Casserole 181

Rice Pudding................................181

Salmon and Rice................................181

Rice and Chicken................................182

Steamed Eggs with Rice 182

Instant Brown Rice................................183

Coconut Sweet Rice................................183

Black Beans and Rice................................183

Arroz Con Pollo 184

Rice & Veggies Dish 184

Cauliflower & Pineapple Rice...................184

Grain Rice Millet Blend............................185

Veggie Rice Acorn Squash.......................185

Pumpkin Rice Pudding 185

Delicious Rice Pudding............................186

Tasty Green Rice................................186

Mix Rice Medley................................186

Easy Risotto................................187

Wild Rice & Farro Pilaf............................187

Artichokes Rice and Side Dish..................188

Ground Beef and Rice 188

Lentils and Rice 189

Sauce Recipes................................**190**

Carrot Sauce Recipe................................190

Fennel Sauce Recipe................................190

Apple sauce................................190

Asian Tomato Chutney............................190

Quince Sauce Recipe................................191

Rhubarb Sauce Recipe............................191

Leeks Sauce Recipe................................191

Corn Sauce Recipe 192

Orange Sauce 192

Cranberry Sauce 192

Cherry Sauce Recipe 193

Apricot Sauce Recipe 193

Bread Sauce recipe 193

Pineapple Sauce 193

Elderberry Sauce Recipe 194

Green Tomato Sauce 194

Chili Jam 194

Sauce Recipe 195

Grapes Sauce Recipe 195

Sriracha Sauce 195

Mushroom Gravy 196

Mustard Sauce Recipe 196

Clementine Sauce Recipe 196

Eggplant Sauce 197

Basil Red Sauce 197

Peach Sauce Recipe 197

Ginger and Orange Sauce 198

Plum Sauce Recipe 198

Tomato Sauce 198

Guava Sauce Recipe 199

Garden Salsa 199

Cilantro Sauce Recipe 199

Garlic Red Sauce 200

Poblano Sauce 200

Strawberry Sauce 201

Red Enchilada Sauce 201

Melon Sauce Recipe 201

Mango Sauce 202

Barbeque Sauce 202

Cashew Sour Cream 203

Beans and Grains 204

Mexican Cranberry Beans 204

Cheesy Barley Dish 204

Kidney Beans Curry Recipe 204

Asian Lentils Recipe 205

Classic Cranberry Bean Chili 205

Lentils and Tomato Sauce 206

Creamy White Beans 206

Black Eyed Peas with Peanuts 206

Marrow Beans & Lemon Dish 207

Garlic and Chickpeas 207

Veggie Risotto 207

Cracked Wheat and Jaggery 208

Delicious Frijoles 208

Cold Quinoa Salad with Pecans and Fruit 208

Orange & Bulgur Salad 209

Healthy Barley Salad 209

Bacon Butter Beans 209

Chickpeas Curry 210

Cranberry Beans Mix 210

Cabbage & Navy Beans 211

Mushroom & Barley Risotto 211

Hummus 211

Mung Beans 212

Classic Chili Lime Black Beans 212

Instant Wheat Berry Salad 213

Pasta & Cranberry Beans 213

Kidney Beans Dish 213

Lentils Tacos 214

Couscous with Veggies and Chicken 214

Mediterranean Lentils 214

Asian Rice 215

Black Beans 215

Cilantro Lime Brown Rice 216

Black Beans and Chorizo 216

Green Chile and Baked Beans 216

Green Chile Chickpeas 217

Red Beans and Rice 217

Spicy Lentils 218

Butternut Lentils 218

Shrimp and White Beans 219

Mushroom and Leek Risotto 219

Italian Lentils Dinner 220

Veggies Rice Pilaf 220

Black Bean Soup 220

Chickpea Basil Salad 221

Texas Roma Caviar 221

Re-fried Pinto Beans 222

Coconut Jasmine Rice 222

Pepper Lemon Quinoa 222

Chinese Fried Rice 223

Yogurt Recipes 224

Raspberry Yogurt. 224

Pumpkin Spice Yogurt. 224

Chocolate Yogurt. 224

White Chocolate Yogurt. 225

Vanilla Yogurt. 225

Strawberry Yogurt. 226

Blueberry Oats Yogurt. 226

Slow Cooked Fruity Yogurt. 227

Mango Yogurt. 227

Passionfruit Yogurt. 228

Vegan Soy Yogurt. 228

Cinnamon Yogurt. 229

Kiwi Yogurt. 229

Desserts 230

Ricotta Cake Recipe 230

Ginger and Pineapple Risotto 230

Instant Pot Key Lime Pie 230

Zucchini Nut Bread Recipe 231

Instant Pot Sweet Carrots 231

Mix Berries Compote 231

Poached Pears with Caramel Sauce 232

Instant Pot Baked Apples 232

Stuffed Peaches 232

Berry Jam Recipe 233

Banana Bread 233

Delicious Cobbler Recipe 233

Chocolate Cheese cake 234

Crème Brule 234

Pears Jam Recipe 235

Instant pot Banana Cake 235

Apple Bread 235

Holiday Pudding..236

Pina Colada Pudding 236

Pumpkin Chocolate Cake Recipe 237

Carrot Cake Recipe..237

Sticky Rice and Fruit 238

Delicious Apple Crisp..238

Quick Raspberry Curd 238

Candied Lemon Peel 239

Coconut Rice Pudding...239

Peach Jam Recipe..239

Peach Compote 240

Ruby Pears Delight 240

Brownie Cake Recipe 240

Lemon Crème Pots 241

Fruit Compote 241

Samoa Cheese Cake Recipe 241

Delicious Apple Cake...242

Chocolate Lava Cake Recipe 242

Tomato Jam Recipe 243

Caramel Sauce...243

Lemon Marmalade Recipe 243

Dulce De Leche 244

Bourbon Apple Crisp................................244

Poached Figs..244

Classic Rhubarb Compote 245

Vanilla Applesauce...................................245

Tapioca Pudding.......................................245

Chocolate Pudding....................................246

Chocolate Fondue Recipe.........................246

Introduction

The Instant Pot is revolutionary! You can cook virtually anything in your instant pot - from meats and main courses to rice, vegetables of every description, dessert to even yogurt. Better yet, pressure cooking allows you to prepare foods up to 70 % faster, on average, than conventional cooking methods do, which means you save energy in addition to your precious time!

If you are one of those "hurry-up" cooks who dreams of getting a delicious meal on the table in 30 minutes or less, you'll love this book. I love good meals, but I'm not patient about waiting a long time for it to be done.

For healthy, homemade fast food, the instant pot is the best option. We'll explore a wide variety of dishes, from pasta, fish, meatloafs, and cheesecakes, to all of the splendid soups, stews, and pot roasts, using wholesome and healthy ingredients in the process.

The pressure cooker makes potatoes creamy and tastier, just as when cooked right, and it does this every time. The pressure cooker works like charm with all potato varieties. In the case of rice, the pressure cooker only needs about ten minutes to make both brown and white rice

I love the Element of Surprise of the instant pot pressure cooker - you put everything in the pot, close the lid, and let it cook. It isn't until you've released the pressure and opened that lid, until you've dipped a spoon in and had that taste! is in that moment when you truly know what you have.

I invite you to experience the surprise and delight that awaits every cook who unlocks the lid of the instant pot and sees what magic has transpired within.

Pressure cooking is a very healthy way to cook food to preserve more nutrients and shorten the cooking time for beans, grains, and other foods. And so has the invention of the pressure cooker. It is best kitchen appliance that I know of, it always tops my list of kitchen appliances, whenever, and this is because of some of the fantastic functionalities of the instant pot. So here are some of the key functions

Time-saving: pressure cookers are time savers, and these features come in very handy for everyone, working-class parents, housewives, single parents, aging mothers etc. The pressure cooker has been manufactured with a great cooking speed that it becomes distinctive from every other kitchen appliance. The good news with pressure cookers is that as a cook, you get to spend less time in the kitchen, thereby having more time to achieve other things

Safe and Easy to Operate: the pressure cooker as it name goes cooks at a very high pressure because of heat level it is able to generate within a very short period of time. In order to prevent any sort of explosions, the modern pressure cookers are cooked with different layers of safety. Also, there are numerous other functions that can help to ensure end-user safety. For instance

Comfortability: the pressure cooker has some automated features like, keep warm, countdown, etc. The pressure cooker has a set of default setting with which a user could cook a specific type of meal without having to figure out the manual timing to set. For instance, the pressure cooker could help you cook your meat at a default setting and cook it fine.

You don't have to figure the manual timing to use for cooking that same meat. Apart from that, cooking with the pressure cooker leaves you with less to wash and less cleaning to do as there isn't room for spills or smell in the kitchen.

Energy Saver: the lesser time you have to cook your meal; the more electricity you get to save. It is been established that the pressure cook saves 70 % more energy than any other cooking appliance on the surface of the earth. This does not only save your time; it also saves your money.

Preserving Nutritional Value.: the more time your food spends on heat the more nutritious contents you get to loose from it. The fact that the pressure gives you less cooking time in a tightly enclosed environment, gives you the opportunity to lose fewer nutrients. I mean you don't get to go to your pot every single time in order to check if your meal is well cooked.

The pressure cooker cooks your food in a sealed environment giving no room for nutrients to escape unless you choose to let them. So with this, you have all your nutrients well preserved and waiting to be consumed. For example, steaming food like vegetables with the pressure cooker means that the vegetable gets to retain more nutrients

Delicious cooking: the fact that the pressure cooker cook at an extremely high heat which is extremely higher than what is obtainable with other cooking appliances and this enables it to draw out more flavors from the food and thereby helping to preserve the taste by making it taste a lot much better than usual

Manual / Pressure Buttons: This is probably going to be the buttons you use most on the Instant Pot. It will allow you to pressure cook and manually select the time you want – rather than the preset buttons (such as Soup/Stew or Meat buttons). You can adjust the pressure, temperature and time by selecting the "+/-"buttons.

Sauté Button: The "Saute" Button is the second most used function with my Instant Pot. You can do that and basically cook up anything as you would in a skillet or pan. You don't need the 1 cup of liquid. Just press the "Saute" button, add some cooking oil to the inner pot and add food you want to cook like a skillet or pan.

Meat / Stew: Make your favorite stew or meat dish in the Instant Pot. Adjust the settings depending on the texture you want. For instance, the "More" setting is better for fall-off-the-bone cooking. It will default to a High Pressure for 35 minutes. You can adjust for "More" to High Pressure for 45 minutes or "Less" for High Pressure for 20 minutes.

Bean / Chili: One of my favorite things to make in the Instant Pot is beans. It's so much faster (and tastier) with the Instant Pot. When you use the "Bean / Chili" button, it will default to a High Pressure for 30 minutes. You can adjust for "More" to High Pressure for 40 minutes or "Less" for High Pressure for 25 minutes.

Multigrain: The "Multigrain" button is best for cooking brown rice and wild rice, which typically takes longer than white rice to cook. Cook brown rice to a 1:1.25 ratio rice to water and wild rice to a 1:3 ratio rice to water for 22 - 30 minutes.

It will default at the "Normal" setting is 40 minutes of pressure cooking time. Adjust as needed for the "Less" setting is 20 minutes of pressure cooking time, or "More" at 45 minutes of warm water soaking and 60 minutes of pressure cooking.

Slow Cook Button: Use your Instant Pot like a slower cooker with this option. Just add food as you normally would to a slow cooker, close the lid and then press the "Slow Cook" button.

It will default to a 4-hour slow cook time. You can use "+/- "buttons to adjust the cook time.

Steam: Use the "Steam" button to steam vegetables, seafood or reheat food (it's a great alternative to the microwave). Be sure to use the steam rack included with the Instant Pot, otherwise food may burn and stick to the bottom of the inner pot.

Rice: You can cook rice in the Instant Pot in nearly half the time as a conventional rice cooker. White rice, short grain, Jasmine and Basmati rice can all be cooked on this setting in about 4 to 8 minutes. In general, you'll need a 1:1 ratio of rice to water (Basmati is a 1:1.5 ratio).

When you choose the "Rice" button, the cooking duration automatically adjusts depending on how much food you put into the unit and cook on low pressure.

Be sure to add about 10 - 12 minutes to the total cooking time to allow the Instant Pot to come to pressure.

Porridge: Use the "Porridge" button to make rice porridge (congee) and other grains (not regular white or brown rice). It will default to a High Pressure for 20 minutes, which is best for rice porridge. You can adjust for "More" to High Pressure for 30 minutes or "Less" for High Pressure for 15 minutes.

After the porridge is finished, do not use the Quick Release handle. Because it has a high starch content, using the Quick Release will splatter the porridge through the steam release vent. Use the Natural Release.

Poultry: Make your favorite chicken recipes with the "Poultry" button with the Instant Pot. It will default to a High Pressure for 15 minutes. You can adjust for "More" to High Pressure for 30 minutes or "Less" for High Pressure for 5 minutes.

Soup: Use the "Soup" button to make broth, stock or soup. The Instant Pot will control the pressure and temperature so that the liquid doesn't heavily boil. You can adjust the cooking time as needed, typically between 20 - 40 minutes, and the pressure to either low or high.

Egg: This button cooks at High Pressure for 5 minutes. Adjusted to more cooks for 6 minutes. Adjusted to less cooks for 4 minutes.

Cake: This button cooks at High Pressure for 30 minutes. Adjusted to more cooks for 40 minutes. Adjusted to less cooks for 25 minutes.

Central Dial: Unique to the Instant Pot Ultra, you turn this dial to scroll between menu options and push to select.

Delay Start: Select a cooking function and set adjustments, then press Delay Start and use the [+] and [-] buttons to set amount of time you'd like to wait before the Instant Pot starts cooking.

Cancel Button: At any time, you can cancel cooking and return to standby mode by pressing the "Keep Warm" / "Cancel" button. This is a great option if you selected the wrong time for pressure cooking and need to stop to make adjustments to the pressure or time.

Keep Warm Button: When pressure cooking is done, the Instant Pot will beep and automatically go into the "Keep Warm" function. It will display an "L" in front of a number to indicate how long it's been warm – e.g. "L0:30" for 30 minutes. It's a great feature to keep food warm for up to 99 hours, 50 minutes. It's perfect for pot lucks.

Timer Button: Use the Timer button to delay the cooking start time for the Instant Pot. This works for both pressure cooking and slow cook options.

To use this feature, just press the Timer button with 10 seconds of pressing either the Pressure / Manual button or Slow Cook button. Use "+/- "buttons to adjust the delayed hours, then wait a second and press Timer again to set delayed minutes. You can cancel the Timer anytime by pressing the Keep Warm / Cancel button.

Natural Release:

There's really nothing you have to depressurize your pressure cooker. Once the cooking is finished, the pressure will automatically slowly drop inside the electric pressure cooker. Because of this slow drop in pressure and heat, when using natural release, food continues cooking even though active cooking is complete. Your stocks and soups come out cleaner and food are more likely to stay intact.

After the cooking cycle ends, wait until the Floating Valve (metal pin) completely drops before opening the lid.

*(For Example, In our recipes, you may see "**Release the pressure naturally for 10 minutes**," – this means after the cooking cycle ends, wait for 10 minutes and then release remaining pressure by turning the valve to 'Venting')*

Use this method when cooking meat, foods that increase in volume or foam (like dried beans and legumes), soups, or any other foods that are primarily liquid.

Use Quick release when adding additional ingredients to the pot (like with a stew), or cooking eggs, vegetables, delicate foods, or ingredients that don't benefit from additional cook time.

Quick Release:

Quick release works by turning the valve once active cooking is complete. This process takes an extra degree of care, as a loud burst of steam is released from the valve. Rapid release takes no more than a minute or two, and works best with foods, like eggs, vegetables, or delicate ingredients that don't benefit from any extra cook time.

This method is also helpful when you need to check the doneness of food or add additional ingredients to the pressure cooker, as you might with a stew.

(*It's best to avoid using Quick release when cooking foods that increase in volume, froth, or foam, like legumes, or those that are mostly **liquid**, like **soup**, as the liquid can boil up and vent through the release valve.)

Silicone Sealing Ring: This is referred to and alluded to as the gasket in a few manuals. What's more, is a fixing ring inside the top of the cooker which keeps the steam inside. For security purposes, consider cleaning it in the wake of cooking, and get it supplanted once old

Cooker Lid: This is the upper piece of your instant pot used for fixing the cooker opening when cooking. To open/evacuate it subsequent to cooking, you should first discharge the pressure from pot using the brisk discharge strategy or using the common discharge technique

Pressure Indicator: The pressure pointer, is typically situated on the cooker top. It's a little stick arranged comfortable top and would regularly go up when the most extreme pressure point (HIGH Pressure) has been come to. A similar bind would drop when the pressure point is truly low showing that it's sheltered to open the cooker. The stick additionally bolts the cooker some of the time, so you can't open the pot when pressure is developed in the IP. A few books or manual may call it "bolt marker

Steam Release Valve: This is the valve used for discharging pressure from your Instant pot rapidly subsequent to cooking (QPR). Or, then again when time to add more fixing to pot/check sustenance for doneness. It's the handle situated on the cover and can be used essentially by swinging to either fixing or venting

Trivet and Steam Basket: Some electric pressure cooker has a trivet alongside a steam wicker bin. This trivet and the steam wicker bin help to keep the nourishment over the pressure cookers base. Individuals use the trivet to bubble eggs or steaming their vegetables to keep the supplement from draining into the fluid.

Steam Condensation Collector: This is a holder generally made of plastic which is situated in favor of the cooker. It helps gathers additional buildup

1. Seals: - the silicone sealing ring absorbs the smells of what you cook. As the Instant Pot heats the next batch of food, those smells from the sealing ring may filter into the new food. At least, you will want a sweet seal and a savory seal.

2. Silicone Baking Cups: - Useful for cakes, muffins, and smaller portions of just about any recipe you can cook in the IP, silicone baking cups are something that no kitchen should be without

3. Springform Pan: - Cheesecake recipes for the Instant Pot abound. For perfect cheesecake, a springform pan is essential. However, this pan is also great for other kinds of pies, lasagna, and meatloaf

4. Tempered Glass Lid: - The great thing about the Instant Pot is that while the pressure cooking options rock, you can also brown, simmer, and slow cook in it. For these types of meals, you do not need the heavier lid that comes with the unit. A tempered glass lid is easier for clean-up, and is a necessity if you plan to stir whatever you are cooking in your Instant Pot today

5. Steamer Basket: - The key to cooking great veggies in the Instant Pot is to steam them above the water rather than cooking them in the water. A steamer basket helps you do make perfect vegetables every time

6. Egg Bite Mold: - Egg bites are a great way to fix breakfast on the go in the Instant Pot. When cooled, egg bites can be put into containers making them easily portable

7. Stackable Steamer Rack: - A stackable steamer rack efficiently doubles the amount of food you can put into your Instant Pot, in some cases. With the addition of a steamer rack, you could cook two different types of food at the same time. Using the steamer rack also cuts down on food sticking to the insert

Experiment with the functions. Your instant pot does so many things, don't just use it for pressure cooking and get other pots and gadgets for the rest. Otherwise what's the point in having it? Use it to shallow fry, boil, steam, bake, etc. The possibilities are plentiful.

Measure your liquids carefully. Your instant pot has two different limits: the pressure limit and the slow cooker limit. Do not exceed the fluid amount for either! Always count things that liquefy, like gelatine or sugar, as a liquid.

Watch out about overfilling. Your instant pot should not be completely filled. Ever! You need space for pressure and/or steam to build up. Whether you are filling it with food or fluid, always make sure there is plenty of space from the top.

Be careful handling steam. Steam and pressure are nothing to joke around with! Never put your hand right in the steam, and always release the pressure according to the instructions manual. Always seal your instant pot properly before building pressure. Always open it when it is ready

Clean it well after each use. Your instant pot will not last if it ends up with a built up film of fat or layer of burnt and sticky food in it. Besides, that is unhealthy. Even if you have "only" used it to steam, remember that steam carries fat particles and creates a greasy film, so it still needs cleaning

Don't Use quick release unless specified. The pressure that can build up in your instant pot is intense. If you release it too fast you could get hurt. Only use quick release when a recipe specifically calls for it.

Don't Fill it with hot oil. This is not a deep fat fryer! Filling it with oil is dangerous and could cause a grease fire. At the very least, you will break your instant pot.

Don't Try and force it open. Again: intense pressure. Forcing it open could cause a seriously painful blast.

Don't Put things in in huge pieces. Even cooking is important, and big pieces do not respond as well to pressure or quick cooking. Leave the whole chickens for slow cooking only

Do not leave the house when it is on. Unlike with a traditional slow cooker, the instant pot reaches high temperatures, can carry a high voltage, and involves literal pressure

Breakfasts

Potatoes Breakfast Salad

(Prep + Cooking Time: 15 minutes | **Servings:** 4)

Ingredients:

- 6 potatoes, peeled and cubed
- 1 ½ cups water
- 1 cup homemade mayonnaise
- 1/4 cup onion; finely chopped
- 1 tbsp. dill pickle juice
- 2 tbsp. parsley; finely chopped
- 1 tbsp. mustard
- 4 eggs
- Salt and black pepper to the taste

Directions:

1. Put potatoes, eggs and the water in the steamer basket of your instant pot, close the lid and cook on High for 4 minutes
2. Quick release the pressure, transfer eggs to a bowl filled with ice water and leave them to cool down
3. In a bowl, mix mayo with pickle juice, onion, parsley and mustard and stir well
4. Add potatoes and toss to coat
5. Peel eggs, chop them, add them to salad and toss again.
6. Add salt and pepper to the taste; stir and serve your salad with toasted bread slices.

Sweet Potato Mini Quiche

(Prep + Cooking Time: 37 minutes | **Makes:** 7 Quiches)

Ingredients:

- 1 (14-ounce) package firm tofu, lightly pressed
- 1 cup plus 1 tbsp. water
- 1/2 cup shredded sweet potato
- 1/4 cup nutritional yeast
- 1 tbsp. cornstarch
- 1/4 cup nondairy milk
- 1 tsp sea salt or as your liking
- 1/2 tsp. garlic powder
- 1/2 tsp. onion powder
- 1/2 tsp. ground turmeric
- Handful kale leaves; chopped small
- Nonstick cooking spray; for preparing the mold
- Vegan-buttered toast; for serving
- Freshly ground black pepper

Directions:

1. Lightly coat an 8¼-inch silicone egg-bites mold with nonstick spray and set aside.
2. In a food processor, combine the tofu, milk, yeast, cornstarch, sea salt, garlic powder, onion powder and turmeric. Blend until smooth
3. Select the "Sauté" Low mode on your instant pot. When the display reads "Hot," add the sweet potato, kale and 1 tbsp. of water. Sauté for 1 to 2 minutes
4. Note: You may need to turn off the Instant Pot if the vegetables start to stick to the bottom, but that's okay because it stays hot
5. Stir the veggies into the tofu mixture and spoon the mixture into the prepared mold. Cover the mold tightly with aluminum foil and place on a trivet. Add the remaining 1 cup of water to the inner pot and use the trivet's handles to lower the trivet and mold into the pot.
6. Lock the lid and turn the steam release handle to Sealing. Using the Manual function, set the cooker to High Pressure for 18 minutes
7. After completing the cooking time, let the pressure release naturally for 10 minutes; quick release any remaining pressure
8. Remove the lid carefully. Remove the silicone mold from the Instant Pot and pull off the foil. Leave the mold on the trivet and let cool for a few minutes
9. The bites will continue to firm as they cool. When ready to eat, schmear the tofu bites onto a piece of vegan-buttered toast and top with a little salt and pepper.

Creamy Sausage Frittata.

(Prep + Cooking Time: 40 minutes | **Servings:** 4)

Ingredients:

- 4 beaten eggs
- 1/2 cup. cooked ground sausage
- 1 ½ cups. water
- 1/4 cup. grated sharp cheddar
- Black pepper to taste
- 2 tbsp. sour cream
- 1 tbsp. butter
- Salt to taste

Directions:

1. Pour water into the Instant Pot and lower in the steamer rack.
2. Grease a 6 - 7-inch soufflé dish
3. In a bowl, whisk the eggs and sour cream together
4. Add cheese, sausage, salt, and pepper. Stir
5. Pour into the dish and wrap tightly with foil all over
6. Lower into the steam rack and close the pot lid.
7. Hit "Manual" and then 17 minutes on "Low" pressure
8. Quick-release the pressure. Serve hot!

Breakfast Millet Pilaf

(Prep + Cooking Time: 20 minutes | **Servings:** 4)

Ingredients:

- 2 cups organic millet
- 1 bay leaf
- 1-inch cinnamon stick
- 1 white onion; chopped.
- 1 tbsp. ghee
- 1 tsp. cardamom; crushed.
- 3 cups water
- 3 tsp. cumin seeds
- Salt to the taste

Directions:

1. Set your instant pot on sauté mode; add ghee and heat it up
2. Add cumin, cinnamon, cardamom and bay leaf, stir and cook for 1 minute.
3. Add onion; stir and cook for 4 minutes
4. Add millet, salt and water; then stir well. seal the instant pot lid and cook at High for 1 minute
5. Release the pressure naturally, fluff the mix with a fork, transfer to bowls and serve

Tofu & Potatoes Breakfast.

(Prep + Cooking Time: 15 minutes | **Servings:** 4)

Ingredients:

- 3 purple potatoes; cubed
- 1 yellow onion; chopped.
- 1 ½ cups Brussels sprouts
- 2 garlic cloves; minced.
- 1 carrot; chopped.
- 1 ginger root; grated
- 1/2 lb. firm tofu; cubed
- 1 tbsp. tamari
- Mexican spice blend to the taste
- 3 tbsp. water

Directions:

1. Set your instant pot on sauté mode; add onion and brown it for 1 minute.
2. Add potatoes, ginger, garlic, tofu, carrots, tamari, spices, Brussels sprouts and water, close the lid and cook at High for 2 minutes
3. Quick release the pressure, open the instant pot lid; transfer to plates and serve

Bacon, Egg & Cheese Muffins.

(Prep + Cooking Time: 25 minutes | **Servings:** 8)

Ingredients:

- 4 eggs
- 1/4 tsp. lemon pepper seasoning
- 1 ½ cup. water, for the pot
- 4 tbsp. cheddar or pepper jack cheese, shredded.
- 4 slices bacon; cooked and crumbled.
- 1 green onion, diced.

Directions:

1. Pour the water into the Instant Pot container and then put a steamer basket into the pot. In a large-sized measuring bowl with a pour pout, break the eggs.
2. Add the lemon pepper and beat well. Divide the bacon, cheese, and green onion between 4 silicone muffin cups.
3. Pour the egg mix into each muffin cups; with a fork, stir using a fork to combine. Put the muffin cups. onto the steamer basket, close the lid.
4. Set the pressure on "High" pressure and the timer to 8 minutes
5. When the timer beeps, turn off the pot, wait for 2 minutes, and then turn the steam valve to quick release the pressure. Carefully open the pot lid, lift the steamer basket out from the container, and then remove the muffin cups.
6. Serve warm and enjoy!

Tips: These muffins can be stored in the refrigerator for more than 1 week. When ready to serve, just microwave for 30 seconds on "High" to reheat

Scrambled Eggs & Bacon.

(Prep + Cooking Time: 15 minutes | **Servings:** 4)

Ingredients:

- 7 eggs
- 1/2 cup. milk
- 1 tsp. basil
- 1/4 cup. fresh parsley
- 4 oz. bacon
- 1 tsp. salt
- 1 tsp. paprika
- 1 tbsp. butter
- 1 tbsp. cilantro

Directions:

1. Beat the eggs in the mixing bowl and whisk them well.
2. Then add milk, basil, salt, paprika, and cilantro. Stir the mixture. Chop the bacon and parsley.
3. Set the Instant Pot mode "Sauté" and transfer the chopped bacon. Cook it for 3 minutes
4. Then add whisked egg mixture and cook the dish for 5 minutes more.
5. After this, mix up the eggs carefully with the help of the wooden spoon
6. Then sprinkle the dish with the chopped parsley and cook it for 4 minutes more.
7. When the eggs are cooked - remove them from the Instant Pot.
8. Serve the dish immediately. Enjoy!

Cobbler Recipe

(Prep + Cooking Time: 25 minutes | **Servings:** 4)

Ingredients:

- 1 plum; chopped.
- 1/4 cup coconut; shredded.
- 1/2 tsp. cinnamon; ground.
- 3 tbsp. coconut oil
- 2 tbsp. sunflower seeds
- 1/4 cup pecans; chopped.
- 1 pear; chopped.
- 1 apple chopped
- 2 tbsp. honey

Directions:

1. Put all fruits in a heatproof dish, add coconut oil, cinnamon and honey and toss to coat
2. Place the dish in the steamer basket of your instant pot, close the lid and cook at High for 10 minutes
3. Release the pressure naturally, take out the dish and transfer all fruits to a bowl
4. In the same baking dish, mix coconut with sunflower seeds and pecans and stir.
5. Transfer these to your instant pot; set it on Sauté mode and toast them for 5 minutes
6. Add these to fruits in the bowl; toss to coat and serve.

Pumpkin Butter Breakfast

(Prep + Cooking Time: 25 minutes | Servings: 18)

Ingredients:

- 30 oz. pumpkin puree
- 3 apples; peeled; cored and chopped.
- 1/2 cup honey
- 12 oz. apple cider
- 1 tbsp. pumpkin spice
- 1 cup sugar
- A pinch of salt

Directions:

1. In your instant pot; mix pumpkin puree with pumpkin spice, apple pieces, sugar, honey, cider and a pinch of salt
2. Stir well, seal the instant pot lid and cook at High for 10 minutes.
3. Release the pressure naturally for 15 minutes, transfer the butter to small jars and keep it in the fridge until you serve it.

Pomegranate Porridge

(Prep + Cooking Time: 8 minutes | Servings: 2)

Ingredients:

- Seeds from 1 pomegranate
- 1 cup porridge oats
- 1 cup water
- 3/4 cup pomegranate juice
- A pinch of salt

Directions:

1. Put oats in your instant pot
2. Add water, a pinch of salt and pomegranate juice; then stir well. seal the instant pot lid and cook at High for 2 minutes
3. Release the pressure naturally; add pomegranate seeds, stir well; divide into bowls and serve.

Apple Breakfast

(Prep + Cooking Time: 35 minutes | Servings: 4)

Ingredients:

- 2 apples; diced
- 1 tbsp. cinnamon; ground.
- 1 cup red lentils; soaked for 4 hours and drained
- 1 tsp. cloves; ground.
- 3 cups rooibos tea
- 1 tsp. turmeric; ground.
- Maple syrup to the taste
- Coconut milk for serving

Directions:

1. Put lentils in your instant pot, add tea; then stir well. close the lid and cook at High for 15 minutes
2. Quick release the pressure, open the instant pot lid, add cinnamon, apples, turmeric, and cloves; then stir well. close the lid and cook at High for 15 more minutes
3. Quick release the pressure, divide lentils between bowls; add maple syrup to the taste and coconut milk

Beef Roast

(Prep + Cooking Time: 50 minutes | **Servings:** 8)

Ingredients:

- 4 lb. beef roast; cut into small chunks
- 2 tbsp. brown sugar
- 2 ½ tsp. garlic powder
- 2 tsp. mustard powder
- 2 tsp. onion flakes
- 2 tsp. paprika
- 2 tbsp. Worcestershire sauce
- 4 tbsp. butter; soft
- 8 hoagie rolls
- 1 tbsp. balsamic vinegar
- 8 slices provolone cheese
- 3 cups beef stock
- Salt and black pepper to the taste

Directions:

1. Put the meat in your instant pot.
2. Add salt, pepper, paprika, 2 teaspoon garlic powder, mustard powder, onion flakes, stock, vinegar and Worcestershire sauce, stir well, seal the instant pot lid and cook at High for 40 minutes
3. Quick release the pressure, transfer meat to a cutting board, strain the liquid and keep it in a bowl
4. Shred meat and divide among rolls after you've buttered them
5. Add provolone cheese on top, introduce sandwiches in preheated broiler and broil until cheese melts.
6. Dip sandwiches in the sauce from the pot and serve them.

Poached Tomatoes and Eggs.

(Prep + Cooking Time: 15 minutes | **Servings:** 4)

Ingredients:

- 4 eggs
- 1 tbsp. olive oil
- 1 tbsp. fresh dill
- 3 medium tomatoes
- 1/2 tsp. white pepper
- 1/2 tsp. paprika
- 1 red onion
- 1 tsp. salt

Directions:

1. Spray the ramekins with the olive oil inside
2. Beat the eggs in every ramekin.
3. Combine the paprika, white pepper, fresh dill, and salt together in the mixing bowl. Stir the mixture.
4. After this, chop the red onion.
5. Chop the tomatoes into the tiny pieces and combine them with the onion. Stir the mixture.
6. Then sprinkle the eggs with the tomato mixture.
7. Add spice mixture and transfer the eggs to the Instant Pot.
8. Close the lid and set the Instant Pot mode STEAM
9. Cook the dish for 5 minutes. Then remove the dish from the Instant Pot and chill it little.
10. Serve the dish immediately. Enjoy!

Egg Side Dish.

(Prep + Cooking Time: 20 minutes | **Servings:** 6)

Ingredients:

- 8 eggs
- 1 tbsp. mustard
- 1 tsp. minced garlic
- 1 tsp. salt
- 1 tsp. mayo sauce
- 1/4 cup. dill
- 1/4 cup. cream
- 1 tsp. ground white pepper

Directions:

1. Put the eggs in the Instant Pot and add water.
2. Cook the eggs at the high pressure for 5 minutes
3. Then remove the eggs from the Instant Pot and chill
4. Peel the eggs and cut them into 2 parts

5. Discard the egg yolks and mash them
6. Then add the mustard, cream, salt, mayo sauce, ground white pepper, and minced garlic in the mashed egg yolks
7. Chop the dill and sprinkle the egg yolk mixture with the chopped dill.
8. Mix up it carefully until you get smooth and homogenous mass
9. Then transfer the egg yolk mixture to the pastry bag.
10. Fill the egg whites with the yolk mixture
11. Serve the dish immediately. Enjoy!

Spinach, Bacon & Eggs.

(Prep + Cooking Time: 15 minutes | **Servings:** 4)

Ingredients:
- 7 oz. bacon
- 3 tbsp. cream
- 1/2 cup. spinach
- 2 tsp. butter
- 4 eggs, boiled
- 1 tsp. cilantro
- 1/2 tsp. ground white pepper

Directions:
1. Slice the bacon and sprinkle it with the ground white pepper, and cilantro. Stir the mixture
2. Peel eggs and wrap them in the spinach leaves
3. Then wrap the eggs in the sliced bacon
4. Set the Instant Pot mode MEAT/STEW and transfer the wrapped eggs
5. Add butter and cook the dish for 10 minutes.
6. When the time is over - remove the eggs from the Instant Pot and sprinkle them with the cream.
7. Serve the dish hot.

Breakfast Bread Pudding

(Prep + Cooking Time: 35 minutes | **Servings:** 6)

Ingredients:
- 14 oz. loaf and bread; cubed.
- 1 cup water
- 1 cup Swiss cheese; grated
- 1 cup mushrooms; sliced
- 4 tbsp. butter
- 1 cup onions; thinly sliced.
- 3 eggs; whisked.
- 2 cups half and half
- 1/2 tsp. thyme; dried.
- 1/2 tsp. mustard; dry
- Salt and black pepper to taste
- 1 cup ham; diced.
- 1/4 cup sugar
- Cooking spray

For the sauce:
- 1/2 cup mustard.
- 2 tbsp. maple syrup
- 1 ½ tsp. rice wine vinegar
- Salt and black pepper to taste

Directions:
1. Heat up a pan over medium heat; add butter and melt it.
2. Add onions, stir and cook for 2 minutes.
3. Add ham, stir again, cook for 2 minutes more, take off heat and leave aside
4. Spray a pan with some cooking oil
5. In a bowl; mix eggs with sugar, half and half, thyme, half of the Swiss cheese, salt, pepper, bread cubes, mushroom, ham and onions mix and stir well.
6. Pour this into greased pan, place it in the steamer basket of your instant pot, also add the water in the instant pot, cover with tin foil, close the instant pot lid and cook on High for 25 minutes
7. Meanwhile; heat up a small pot over medium heat, add dry mustard, salt, pepper, vinegar and maple syrup, stir well and cook for 2 - 3 minutes.
8. Release pressure from the pot; uncover, take the pan out, sprinkle the rest of the cheese, introduce in preheated broil and brown for a few minutes.
9. Divide bread pudding on plates; drizzle the sauce on top and serve

Potato Hash

(Prep + Cooking Time: 20 minutes | Servings: 4)

Ingredients:
- 6 potatoes; peeled and roughly chopped
- 6 eggs; whisked
- 1 cup ham; chopped.
- 1/4 cup water
- A drizzle of olive oil
- 1 cup cheddar cheese, shredded.
- Salt and black pepper to taste
- Toasted bread for serving

Directions:
1. Set your instant pot on Sauté; add the oil and heat it up
2. Add potatoes, stir and brown them for 3 minutes.
3. Add ham, eggs, cheese, salt, pepper and the water, stir, close the instant pot lid and cook at High for 5 minutes
4. Release the pressure; transfer hash to plates and serve with toasted bread.

Strawberry Oats

(Prep + Cooking Time: 45 minutes | Servings: 5)

Ingredients:

For Maple-Toasted Walnuts:
- 1/2 cup maple syrup
- 3 cups walnut halves
- 1/2 tsp. salt

For Oats:
- 2 cups strawberries; chopped or sliced
- 2 ½ cups unsweetened nondairy milk; divided
- 1/2 cup packed light brown sugar
- 2 ½ cups water
- 2 cups steel cut oats
- 2 tsp. vanilla extract
- 1/4 tsp. salt

Directions:

To Make Maple-Toasted Walnuts:
1. Cover a heat-resistant flat surface with parchment paper. On your stovetop, heat a skillet over medium-high heat.
2. Add the walnuts, maple syrup and salt. Cook for 3 to 4 minutes, stirring frequently; or until the maple syrup has caramelized and the walnuts are toasted
3. Pour the mixture onto the parchment-covered surface, spreading it out so it doesn't clump into one large piece. Let cool. Break into bite-size pieces.

To Make Oats:
1. In the Instant Pot, combine the oats, water, 2 cups of milk, the vanilla and salt. Stir well. Lock the lid and turn the steam release handle to Sealing. Using the Manual function, set the cooker to High Pressure for 12 minutes
2. After completing the cooking time, turn off the Instant Pot. Let the pressure release naturally for 10 minutes; quick release any remaining pressure
3. Remove the lid carefully and stir in the remaining ½ cup of milk, the strawberries and brown sugar. Top individual servings with the toasted walnuts.

Carrot Oatmeal Breakfast

(Prep + Cooking Time: 25 minutes | Servings: 6)

Ingredients:
- 1 cup steel cut oats
- 1 cup grated carrots
- 1/4 cup chia seeds
- 1 tbsp. butter
- 3 tbsp. maple syrup
- 4 cups water
- 2 tsp. cinnamon
- 3/4 cup raisins
- 1 tsp. pie spice
- A pinch of salt

Directions:

1. Select the Sauté mode on your instant pot, add butter and melt it
2. Add oats, stir for 3 minutes
3. Add carrots, water, maple syrup, cinnamon, spice and a pinch of salt; then stir well and seal the instant pot lid and cook at High for 10 minutes.
4. Release the pressure naturally for 10 minutes, then release remaining pressure by turning the valve to 'Venting', add raisins and chia seeds; then stir well and leave oatmeal aside for 10 minutes; divide it between bowls and serve right away.

Millet Pudding

(Prep + Cooking Time: 20 minutes | **Servings:** 4)

Ingredients:

- 1 ⅔ cup millet
- 14 oz. coconut milk
- 4 dates; pitted
- 7 oz. water
- A pinch of salt
- Honey for serving

Directions:

1. Put the millet in your instant pot.
2. Add milk; dates and a pinch of salt and stir
3. Add the water, stir again, seal the instant pot lid and cook at High for 10 minutes
4. Release the pressure naturally, open the instant pot lid, divide the pudding into bowls, top with honey and serve.

Vanilla Polenta

(Prep + Cooking Time: 40 minutes | **Servings:** 4)

Ingredients:

- ⅓ cup packed light brown sugar
- 2 cups nondairy milk; or more as needed
- 1 cup polenta
- 2 cups water
- 1 tsp. salt or as your liking
- 1 ½ tsp. vanilla extract
- Fresh fruit; for topping

Directions:

1. In the Instant Pot, combine the polenta, water, milk and salt, stirring well to break up any lumps.
2. Lock the lid and turn the steam release handle to Sealing. Using the Porridge function, set the cook time for 20 minutes
3. After completing the cooking time, turn off the pressure cooker and let the pressure release naturally until the pin drops, about 10 to 15 minutes
4. Remove the lid carefully. There will be liquid on top, but once you stir it in, the polenta will be beautifully creamy!
5. Stir in the brown sugar and vanilla. Taste and add another pinch of salt, if you like, as well as more milk if you want it creamier. Top with the fruit and enjoy.

Tofu Scramble Recipe.

(Prep + Cooking Time: 18 minutes | **Servings:** 4)

Ingredients:

- 12 oz. canned tomatoes, diced
- 1 yellow onion; thinly sliced
- 1 tsp. walnut oil
- 3 garlic cloves; minced.
- 1/4 cup veggie stock
- 1 cup carrot; chopped.
- 1 block firm tofu; drained
- 1 tsp. cumin
- 2 tbsp. red pepper; chopped.
- 1 tbsp. Italian seasoning
- 1 tsp. nutritional yeast
- Salt and black pepper to the taste

Directions:

1. Set your instant pot on Sauté mode; add oil and heat it up.
2. Add onion, carrot and garlic, stir and cook for 3 minutes.
3. Crumble tofu, add it to pot and stir
4. Add stock, red pepper, tomatoes, cumin, Italian seasoning, salt and pepper; then stir well. seal the instant pot lid and cook at High for 4 minutes
5. Quick release the pressure, transfer to bowls and serve with nutritional yeast on top.

Sweet Potato Poblano Hash

(Prep + Cooking Time: 2 hours 10 minutes | **Servings:** 5)

Ingredients:

- 1 (14-ounce) package extra-firm tofu, pressed for at least 2 hours, crumbled in a food processor
- 1 small onion; diced
- 1 bell pepper, any color; diced
- 2 poblano peppers, roasted; cut into large dice
- 2 garlic cloves; minced
- 2 sweet potatoes; cut into large dice
- 1 cup water
- 1 to 2 tbsp. oil
- 1 tsp. ground turmeric
- 1/2 tsp. smoked paprika
- 1/2 tsp. sea salt
- 1 ½ tsp. Montreal chicken seasoning

Directions:

1. In the Instant Pot, combine the sweet potatoes and water.
2. Lock the lid and turn the steam release handle to Sealing. Using the Manual function, set the cooker to High Pressure for 2 minutes
3. While the sweet potatoes cook, heat a skillet over medium heat on your stovetop.
4. Add the tofu crumbles, turmeric, paprika and sea salt. Cook for 4 to 5 minutes, stirring often, until the tofu gets a little crispy. Remove from the heat
5. When the cooking time is complete, quick release the pressure
6. Remove the lid carefully and pour the contents of the inner pot into a colander or steamer basket to drain. Return the inner pot to the Instant Pot and set the sweet potatoes aside.
7. Select the "Sauté" Low mode on your instant pot. When the display reads "Hot," add 1 tbsp. of oil. Heat the oil until it shimmers
8. Add the onion and bell pepper. Cook for 2 to 3 minutes. Add the poblanos, garlic and Montreal chicken seasoning and cook for 1 minute more
9. If the pot looks dry, add the remaining 1 tbsp. of oil. Add the sweet potatoes back to the pot. Cook for 2 to 3 minutes, stirring frequently. Turn off the Instant Pot and stir in the tofu. Mix well to combine and serve warm.

Breakfast Pudding

(Prep + Cooking Time: 15 minutes | **Servings:** 4)

Ingredients:

- 1/3 cup tapioca pearls
- 1/2 cup sugar
- 1 ¼ cup whole milk
- 1 ½ cups water
- Zest from 1/2 lemon

Directions:

1. Put 1 cup water in your instant pot
2. Put tapioca pearls in a heat proof bowl add milk, 1/2 cup water, lemon zest and sugar
3. Stir everything, place the bowl in the steamer basket of the pot, close the instant pot lid and cook at High for 10 minutes
4. Quick release the pressure; transfer pudding to cups and serve

Cheesy Hash Brown.

(Prep + Cooking Time: 10 minutes **| Servings:** 8)

Ingredients:
- 8 eggs
- 6 slices chopped bacon
- 1 cup. shredded cheddar cheese
- 1/4 cup. milk
- 1 tsp. salt
- 1/2 tsp. black pepper
- 2 cups. frozen hash browns

Directions:
1. Turn your Instant Pot to "Sauté" and cook the bacon until it becomes crispy.
2. Add hash browns and stir for 2 minutes, or until they start to thaw
3. In a bowl, whisk eggs, milk, cheese, and seasonings.
4. Pour over the hash browns in the pot, and lock and seal lid
5. Press "Manual" and adjust time to 5 minutes.
6. When time is up, hit "Cancel" and quick-release the pressure
7. Serve in slices.

Easy and Cheesy Grits

(Prep + Cooking Time: 20 minutes **| Servings:** 4)

Ingredients:
- 4 oz. cheddar cheese; grated
- 1 ¾ cup half and half
- 2 tbsp. coconut oil
- 1 cup stone ground grits
- 3 cups water
- 2 tsp. salt
- 3 tbsp. butter
- Butter for serving

Directions:
1. Set your instant pot on sauté mode; add grits, stir them for 3 minutes.
2. Add oil, half, and half, water, salt, butter and cheese; then stir well. close the instant pot lid and cook on High for 10 minutes.
3. Release the pressure naturally, leave cheesy grits aside for 15 minutes, transfer to breakfast bowls; add butter on top and serve

Tasty Scotch Eggs

(Prep + Cooking Time: 25 minutes **| Servings:** 4)

Ingredients:
- 1 lb. sausage; ground.
- 1 tbsp. vegetable oil
- 4 eggs
- 2 cups water

Directions:
1. Put the eggs in the instant pot, add 1 cup water, seal the instant pot lid and cook at High for 6 minutes
2. Release the pressure naturally for 6 minutes, then release remaining pressure by turning the valve to 'Venting', and carefully open the lid.
3. Remove the eggs and put them in a bowl filled with ice water
4. Peel the eggs and place them on a working surface
5. Divide sausage mix into 4 balls; flatten them, place 1 egg in the center of each sausage piece, wrap meat around each egg and put them all on a plate
6. Set your instant pot on Sauté mode; add the oil and heat it up
7. Add scotch eggs, brown them on each side and transfer them to a plate.
8. Add the rest of the water to your instant pot; arrange the eggs in the steamer basket of the pot, close the instant pot lid and cook at High for 6 minutes more
9. Quick release the pressure; divide the eggs among plates and serve.

Breakfast Berries Jam

(Prep + Cooking Time: 1 hour and 30 minutes | Servings: 12)

Ingredients:

- 16 oz. cranberries
- 4 oz. raisins
- 3 oz. water
- 2 ½ lb. sugar
- 16 oz. strawberries; chopped.
- Zest from 1 lemon
- A pinch of salt

Directions:

1. In your instant pot; mix strawberries with cranberries, lemon zest, and raisins.
2. Add sugar, stir and leave pot aside to 1 hour
3. Add water and a pinch of salt, seal the instant pot lid and cook at High for 15 minutes
4. Quick release the pressure, leave jam aside for 5 minutes; then stir well. pour into small jars and enjoy!
5. Serve with toasted bread slices!

Breakfast Enchiladas.

(Prep + Cooking Time: 1 hour 15 minutes | Servings: 9)

Ingredients:
For Tofu Scramble:

- 1 small onion; cut into large dice
- 1 (14-ounce) package firm tofu, pressed for 30 to 60 minutes
- 1 medium or large tomato; diced
- 1 bell pepper, any color; cut into large dice
- 1 jalapeño pepper; diced
- 2 garlic cloves; minced
- 1/4 cup nutritional yeast
- 1 tsp. ground cumin
- 1/2 tsp. dried oregano
- 1/2 tsp. sea salt
- 1/2 tsp. ground turmeric
- 1 to 2 tbsp. olive oil
- Few pinches red pepper flakes
- Freshly ground black pepper

For Enchiladas:

- Nonstick cooking spray; for preparing the baking dish
- 1 batch Tempeh "Sausage"
- 12 (6-inch) tortillas; or 10 (8-inch)
- About 1 ¼ cups Red Hot Enchilada Sauce; or 1 (10-ounce) can red enchilada sauce
- 4 scallions, green and light green parts, sliced

To Make Tofu Scramble:
Directions:

1. In a small bowl (or in your tofu press), use a fork to crumble the tofu. Stir in the sea salt and turmeric. Set aside.
2. Select the "Sauté" Low mode on your instant pot. When the display reads "Hot," add the oil and heat until it shimmers.
3. Add the onion, bell pepper and jalapeño. Cook for 2 to 3 minutes, stirring frequently. Turn off the Instant Pot and add the garlic
4. The inner pot will still be hot. Let the veggies cook for another minute or so. Stir in the tomatoes, tofu mixture, nutritional yeast, cumin; oregano and red pepper flakes. Season to taste with salt and pepper.
5. Lock the lid and turn the steam release handle to Sealing. Using the Manual function, set the cooker to High Pressure for 2 minutes
6. After completing the cooking time, quick release the pressure
7. Remove the lid carefully. Select Sauté Low again and cook off the remaining liquid, 3 to 5 minutes, stirring frequently. Taste and adjust the seasonings as desired.

To Make Enchiladas:

1. Preheat the oven to 375°F. Spray the bottom of a 9-by-13-inch glass baking dish with nonstick spray.

2. To build your enchiladas, add 1 spoonful of tempeh sausage to a tortilla, followed by 2 to 3 spoonfuls of tofu scramble "as needed depending on size of tortillas" and roll tightly
3. Place in the prepared baking dish, seam-side down. Repeat for the remaining tortillas
4. Spoon about two-thirds of the enchilada sauce over the top and sprinkle on the scallions
5. Cover the dish with aluminum foil and bake for 20 minutes. Top as desired before serving.

Easy Egg Muffins

(Prep + Cooking Time: 20 minutes | **Servings:** 4)

Ingredients:
- 4 eggs
- 4 bacon slices; cooked and crumbled.
- 1 green onion; chopped.
- 1 ½ cups water
- 4 tbsp. cheddar cheese; shredded.
- 1/4 tsp. lemon pepper
- A pinch of salt

Directions:
1. In a bowl, mix eggs with a pinch of salt and lemon pepper and whisk well
2. Divide green onion, bacon and cheese into muffin cups
3. Add eggs and stir a bit
4. Pour the water in your instant pot, add muffin cups in the steamer basket, seal the Instant Pot lid and cook at High for 10 minutes.
5. Quick release the pressure, divide the egg muffins among plates and serve them right away

Hard Boiled Eggs.

(Prep + Cooking Time: 10 minutes | **Servings:** 6)

Ingredients:
- 1 cup. of water
- 12 large white eggs

Directions:
1. In the Instant Pot Pour down about 1 cup. of water into the bowl.
2. Place stainless steamer basket inside the pot
3. Place the eggs in the steamer basket
4. Boil 7 minutes on manual "High" pressure.
5. Then release the pressure through the quick release valve
6. Open up the lid and take out the eggs using tongs and dunk them into a bowl of cold water.

Berry Toast Casserole

(Prep + Cooking Time: 30 minutes | **Servings:** 5)

Ingredients:
- 5 cups cubed, stale French bread
- 1 ½ cups fresh blueberries and strawberries (halve or quarter the strawberries)
- 1 cup water
- 1/2 cup applesauce
- 1 tsp. vanilla extract
- 1 tsp. ground cinnamon
- 1/4 tsp. sea salt
- 1/4 cup maple syrup, plus more for topping
- Nonstick cooking spray; for preparing the bowl
- Vegan butter; for topping

Directions:
1. Spray a 7-cup oven-safe glass bowl with nonstick spray. Pour the water into the Instant Pot and place a trivet inside the inner pot
2. In a large bowl, whisk the applesauce, maple syrup, vanilla, cinnamon and sea salt
3. Quickly toss the bread and berries in the apple mixture, making sure to get even coverage.
4. Transfer the mixture to the prepared bowl and cover tightly with aluminum foil. Place the bowl on top of the trivet in the Instant Pot

5. Lock the lid and turn the steam release handle to Sealing. Using the Manual function, set the cooker to High Pressure for 25 minutes
6. After completing the cooking time, quick release the pressure. Remove the lid carefully and serve with desired toppings.

Blackberries Jam

(Prep + Cooking Time: 30 minutes | **Servings:** 4)

Ingredients:
- 5 cups sugar
- 4 pints' blackberries
- 3 tbsp. pectin powder
- Juice of 1 small lemon

Directions:
1. Put the blackberries in your instant pot.
2. Add the sugar; then stir well and select sauté mode and cook for 3 minutes.
3. Transfer the jam to clean jars, close them and place them in the steamer basket of your instant pot.
4. Add water to cover the jars halfway, select Canning mode on your pot, close the lid and leave them for 20 minutes
5. Remove jars after 20 minutes, leave them to cool down and keep your jam in the fridge until you serve it in the morning with some toasted bread and some butter.

Delicious Poached Eggs

(Prep + Cooking Time: 20 minutes | **Servings:** 2)

Ingredients:
- 2 bell peppers; ends cut off
- 2 slices mozzarella cheese
- 2 eggs
- 1 bunch rucola leaves
- 1 cup water
- 2 slices whole wheat bread; toasted

For the sauce:
- 2/3 cup homemade mayonnaise
- 1 tbsp. white wine vinegar
- 1 ½ tsp. mustard
- 3 tbsp. orange juice
- 1 tsp. turmeric powder
- 1 tsp. lemon juice
- Salt to the taste

Directions:
1. In a bowl; mix mayo with salt, turmeric, mustard, lemon juice, orange juice and vinegar, stir well, cover the bowl and keep in the fridge for now
2. Break an egg in each bell pepper, place them in the steamer basket of your instant pot, cover the basket with tin foil, add the water to the pot and cook on Low for 5 minutes.
3. Release the pressure naturally and open the instant pot lid.
4. Divide toasted bread into 2 plates, add cheese on each, some rucola leaves and top with pepper cups.
5. Drizzle the sauce all over and serve

Spinach & Tomato Breakfast

(Prep + Cooking Time: 30 minutes | **Servings:** 6)

Ingredients:
- 3 cups baby spinach; chopped.
- 12 eggs
- 1/2 cup milk
- 3 green onions; sliced
- 4 tomatoes sliced
- 1/4 cup parmesan; grated
- 1 ½ cups water
- 1 cup tomato; diced
- Salt and black pepper to the taste

Directions:
1. Pour the water in your instant pot
2. In a bowl; mix the eggs with salt, pepper and milk and stir well.
3. Put diced tomato, spinach and green onions in a baking dish and stir them.

4. Pour the eggs mix over veggies, spread tomato slices on top and sprinkle parmesan at the end.
5. Arrange this in the steamer basket of your instant pot, seal the instant pot lid and cook everything at High for 20 minutes
6. Quick release the pressure; open the pot and introduce the baking dish in preheated broiler until the mixture is brown on top.
7. Divide among plates and serve

Banana Cake

(Prep + Cooking Time: 1 hour | **Servings:** 5)

Ingredients:
- 3 bananas, peeled and mashed
- 2 tsp. baking powder
- 1 cup water
- 2 eggs
- 1 stick butter; soft
- 1 tsp. nutmeg
- 1 ½ cups sugar
- 1 tsp. cinnamon
- 2 cups flour
- A pinch of salt

Directions:
1. In a bowl, mix eggs with butter and sugar and stir very well
2. Add salt, baking powder, cinnamon and nutmeg and stir well again.
3. Add bananas and flour and stir again
4. Grease a spring form pan with some butter, pour the batter in it and cover the pan with a paper towel and tin foil
5. Add 1 cup water to your instant pot, place the pan in the pot, close the instant pot lid and cook at High for 55 minutes
6. Quick release the pressure, remove the pot, leave banana breakfast cake to cool down, cut and serve it

Breakfast Hash

(Prep + Cooking Time: 18 minutes | **Servings:** 4)

Ingredients:
- 8 oz. sausage, ground.
- 1 package hash browns; frozen
- 1/3 cup water
- 1 yellow onion; chopped.
- 1 green bell pepper; chopped.
- 4 eggs; whisked
- 1 cup cheddar cheese; grated
- Salt and black pepper to the taste
- Salsa for serving

Directions:
1. Set your instant pot on Sauté mode; add sausage, stir and cook for 2 minutes.
2. Drain excess fat; add bell pepper and onion, stir and cook for 2 more minutes
3. Add hash browns, water, eggs, salt and cheese; then stir well and close the instant pot lid and cook on Low for 4 minutes
4. Quick release the pressure, divide hash among plates and serve with salsa

Blueberry Bliss Bowls

(Prep + Cooking Time: 22 minutes | **Servings:** 5)

Ingredients:
- 1 cup nondairy milk, plus more as needed
- 1 cup fresh blueberries
- 1 cup millet; rinsed
- 1/2 cup sliced toasted almonds
- 2 ¼ cups water
- 1 tbsp. freshly squeezed lemon juice
- 2 tbsp. maple syrup
- 1/4 tsp. ground cinnamon
- 1/4 tsp. ground nutmeg
- 1/2 tsp. salt or as your liking
- Zest of ½ lemon

Directions:

1. In the Instant Pot, stir together the millet, water, maple syrup, lemon juice, nutmeg, cinnamon and salt.
2. Lock the lid and turn the steam release handle to Sealing. Using the Manual function, set the cooker to High Pressure for 10 minutes
3. After completing the cooking time, let the pressure release naturally for 10 minutes; quick release any remaining pressure
4. Remove the lid carefully and stir in the milk, adding more if you like a creamier texture. Top with the blueberries, almonds and lemon zest before serving.

Quinoa and Granola Bowls

(Prep + Cooking Time: 20 minutes | **Servings:** 4)

Ingredients:

- 1/2 to 1 cup nondairy milk
- 1 cup quinoa; rinsed
- 2 cups granola (any variety)
- 2 cups Fresh Fruit Compote
- 1 ½ cups water
- 2 tbsp. maple syrup
- 1 tsp. vanilla extract
- 1/2 tsp. ground cinnamon
- Pinch salt
- Sliced bananas; for topping (If you like)
- Toasted walnuts; for topping (If you like)

Directions:

1. In the Instant Pot, combine the quinoa, water, maple syrup, vanilla, cinnamon and salt.
2. Lock the lid and turn the steam release handle to Sealing. Using the Manual function, set the cooker to High Pressure for 8 minutes
3. After completing the cooking time, let the pressure release naturally for 10 minutes; quick release any remaining pressure
4. Remove the lid carefully and stir the quinoa. Add enough milk to get the desired consistency.
5. Spoon the quinoa mix into bowls and top with granola, compote and any additional toppings, as desired.

Tofu and Potato Casserole

(Prep + Cooking Time: 2 hours | **Servings:** 5)

Ingredients:

- 2 cups frozen hash browns, thawed
- 1 (14-ounce) package firm tofu, pressed for 30 to 60 minutes
- ⅓ cup nutritional yeast
- 1/4 cup nondairy milk
- 1 batch Tempeh "Sausage"
- 1 cup water
- 1/4 tsp. freshly ground black pepper, plus more for seasoning
- 1 tsp. garlic powder
- 1 tsp. ground cumin
- 1 tsp. sea salt
- 1 tsp. onion powder
- 1/2 tsp. dried oregano
- Sliced scallion, green and light green parts; for serving
- Garden Salsa; for serving
- Nonstick cooking spray; for preparing the pan
- Hot sauce; for serving
- Cashew Sour Cream; for serving

Directions:

1. Lightly coat the bottom of a 7-inch springform pan with nonstick spray and set aside. In a large bowl, toss the hash browns with salt to taste and pepper and set aside.
2. In a food processor, combine the tofu, yeast, milk, sea salt, onion powder, garlic powder, cumin and oregano. Blend until smooth
3. Add the tempeh sausage to the hash browns along with one-fourth of the tofu mixture. Stir to combine.
4. Layer this mixture on the bottom of the prepared pan. Top with the remaining tofu mixture. Cover the pan with a paper towel and wrap it tightly in aluminum foil.

5. Pour the water into your Instant Pot and place a trivet inside the inner pot. Put the springform pan on the trivet.
6. Lock the lid and turn the steam release handle to Sealing. Using the Manual function, set the cooker to High Pressure for 52 minutes.
7. After completing the cooking time, quick release the pressure
8. Remove the lid carefully and remove the pan from the Instant Pot. Take off the foil and paper towel. Let cool before releasing the sides of the pan. Serve topped as desired

French Toast Casserole

(Prep + Cooking Time: 30 minutes | **Servings:** 5)

Ingredients:
- 6 cups cubed, stale French bread
- 1/4 cup maple syrup, Or more for serving
- 1/4 cup Bailey's Almande Almond Milk Liqueur
- 1 cup water
- Nonstick cooking spray; for preparing the bowl
- 1/4 tsp. sea salt
- 1 tsp. vanilla extract
- 1 large banana, plus more for topping; optional
- Vegan butter; for topping

Directions:
1. Spray a 7-cup oven-safe glass bowl with nonstick spray and set aside. Pour the water into your Instant Pot and place a trivet inside the inner pot
2. In a large bowl, mash the banana with a fork. Stir in the maple syrup, Bailey's, vanilla and sea salt, making sure the banana is completely mixed in
3. Quickly toss the bread in the banana mixture, making sure to get even coverage.
4. Transfer to the prepared bowl, cover tightly with aluminum foil and place the bowl on top of the trivet in the Instant Pot
5. Lock the lid and turn the steam release handle to Sealing. Using the Manual function, set the cooker to High Pressure for 25 minutes
6. After completing the cooking time, quick release the pressure. Remove the lid carefully. Serve with toppings as desired and enjoy!

Tomato Spinach Quiche.

(Prep + Cooking Time: 30 minutes | **Servings:** 6)

Ingredients:
- 12 large eggs
- 1/4 tsp. fresh ground black pepper
- 3 large green onions, sliced
- 1/2 tsp. salt
- 4 tomato slices, for topping the quiche
- 1/2 cup. milk
- 1 cup. tomato, seeded, diced
- 1 ½ cup. water, for the pot
- 3 cups. fresh baby spinach, roughly chopped
- 1/4 cup. Parmesan cheese, shredded.

Directions:
1. Pour the water into the Instant Pot container. In a large-sized bowl, whisk the eggs with the milk, pepper, and salt
2. Add the tomato, spinach, and the green onions into a 1 ½ quart-sized baking dish; mix well to combine
3. Pour the egg mix over the vegetables; stir until combined. Put the tomato slices gently on top
4. Sprinkle with the shredded parmesan cheese. Put the baking dish into the rack with a handle
5. Put the rack into the Instant Pot and then lock the lid. Set the pressure to "High" and the timer to 20 minutes.
6. When the timer beeps, wait for 1o minutes, then turn the steamer valve to "Venting" to release remaining pressure. Open the pot lid carefully
7. Hold the rack handles and lift the dish out from the pot

8. Broil till the top of the quiche is light brown, if desired

TIP: You can cover the baking dish with foil to prevent moisture from gathering on the quiche top. You can cook uncovered; just soak the moisture using a paper towel

Mushroom Oatmeal.

(Prep + Cooking Time: 25 minutes | **Servings:** 4)

Ingredients:

- 8 oz. mushroom; sliced
- 1 small yellow onion; chopped.
- 3 thyme springs; chopped.
- 1 cup steel cut oats
- 2 garlic cloves; minced.
- 2 tbsp. butter
- 2 tbsp. extra virgin olive oil
- 1/2 cup water
- 1/2 cup gouda; grated
- 14 oz. canned chicken stock
- Salt and black pepper to the taste

Directions:

1. Select Sauté mode on your instant pot; add butter and melt it.
2. Add onions, stir and cook for 3 minutes.
3. Add garlic, stir and cook for 1 minute more
4. Add oats, stir and cook for 1 minute.
5. Add water, salt, pepper, stock, and thyme, seal the instant pot lid and cook at High for 10 minutes.
6. Release the pressure and leave the pot aside
7. Meanwhile; heat up a pan with the olive oil over medium heat, add mushrooms and cook them for 3 minutes.
8. Add them to the instant pot; also add more salt and pepper to the taste and the gouda, stir and divide among plates.

Healthy Tasty Oats

(Prep + Cooking Time: 24 minutes | **Servings:** 5)

Ingredients:

- 2 cups steel cut oats
- 1/2 cup chia seeds
- 1 cup chopped walnuts
- 1 cup fresh blueberries
- 4 ½ cups water
- 1 cup nondairy milk
- 2 tbsp. agave; or maple syrup; optional
- 1/4 tsp. salt; optional

Directions:

1. In the Instant Pot, stir together the oats and water.
2. Lock the lid and turn the steam release handle to Sealing. Using the Manual function, set the cooker to High Pressure for 12 minutes
3. After completing the cooking time, turn off the Instant Pot. Let the pressure release naturally for 10 minutes; quick release any remaining pressure
4. Remove the lid carefully and add the milk. Stir in the agave and salt and top with the chia seeds, walnuts and blueberries.

Lemon Marmalade Recipe

(Prep + Cooking Time: 25 minutes | **Servings:** 8)

Ingredients:
- 2 lb. lemons; washed and sliced with a mandolin
- 1 tbsp. vinegar
- 4 lb. sugar

Directions:
1. Put lemon slices in your instant pot.
2. Close the instant pot lid and cook the marmalade at High for 10 minutes.
3. Quick release the pressure; add the sugar, seal the instant pot lid again and cook at High for 4 more minutes
4. Release the pressure again, stir your marmalade, pour it into jars and refrigerate until your serve it.

Tasty Sausage

(Prep + Cooking Time: 23 minutes | **Servings:** 5)

Ingredients:
- 1 (8-ounce) package unflavored tempeh
- 1 cup water
- 1 tbsp. olive oil
- 1 tsp. garlic powder
- 1 tsp. dried sage
- 1/2 tsp. dried oregano
- 2 tsp. vegan Worcestershire sauce
- 1 ½ tsp. smoked paprika
- 1 tsp. onion powder
- 1/2 tsp. salt or as your liking
- 1/4 tsp. freshly ground black pepper
- Pinch chili powder

Directions:
1. Select the "Sauté" Low mode on your instant pot. When the display reads "Hot," add the oil and heat until it begins to shimmer.
2. With your hands, crumble the tempeh into the hot oil and stir to coat
3. Add the Worcestershire sauce, paprika, onion powder, garlic powder, sage; oregano, salt, pepper and chili powder. Continue to sauté, stirring as needed, for 6 to 7 minutes more
4. Turn off the Instant Pot and add the water. Use your spoon to scrape up any bits of flavor that have stuck to the bottom of the pot. Stir well.
5. Lock the lid and turn the steam release handle to Sealing. Using the Manual function, set the cooker to High Pressure for 3 minutes
6. After completing the cooking time, quick release the pressure.
7. Remove the lid carefully. Select Sauté Low again and let the remaining liquid cook off. Taste and season with more salt, as needed.

Pecan Sweet Potatoes

(Prep + Cooking Time: 20 minutes | **Servings:** 8)

Ingredients:
- 1 cup pecans chopped
- 1 cup water
- 1/4 cup butter
- 1/4 cup maple syrup
- 1 tbsp. lemon peel
- 1/2 cup brown sugar
- 1 tbsp. cornstarch
- 1/4 tsp. salt
- 3 sweet potatoes peeled and sliced
- Whole pecans for garnish

Directions:
1. Pour the water in your instant pot; add lemon peel, brown sugar and salt and stir.
2. Add potatoes, seal the instant pot lid and cook at High for 15 minutes
3. Release the pressure and transfer the potatoes to a serving plate.
4. Select sauté mode on your instant pot; add the butter and melt it.
5. Add pecans, maple syrup, cornstarch and stir very well.
6. Pour this over the potatoes, garnish with whole pecans and serve!

Mixed Mushroom Pate

(Prep + Cooking Time: 25 minutes | **Servings:** 6)

Ingredients:
- 1 oz. dry porcini mushrooms
- 1 tbsp. extra-virgin olive oil
- 1 shallot finely chopped
- 1/4 cup white wine
- 1 lb. button mushrooms sliced
- 1 cup boiled water
- 1 bay leaf
- 1 tbsp. truffle oil
- 3 tbsp. grated parmesan cheese
- 1 tbsp. butter
- Salt and pepper to the taste

Directions:
1. Put dry mushrooms in a bowl, add 1 cup boiling water over them and leave them aside for now.
2. Set your instant pot on sauté mode; add butter and the olive oil and heat them up.
3. Add the shallot; stir and cook for 2 minutes.
4. Add dry mushrooms and their liquid, fresh mushrooms, wine, salt, pepper, and bay leaf
5. Stir; seal the instant pot lid and cook at High for 16 minutes.
6. Quick release the pressure, discard bay leaf and some of the liquid, transfer everything to your blender and pulse until you obtain a creamy spread
7. Add truffle oil and grated parmesan cheese; blend again, transfer to a bowl and serve.

Chocolate Steel Cut Oats

(Prep + Cooking Time: 25 minutes | **Servings:** 5)

Ingredients:
- 2 cups steel cut oats
- 2 ½ cups nondairy milk; divided; or more as needed
- 1/4 cup chocolate chips
- 1/4 cup peanut butter
- 2 ½ cups water
- 2 tbsp. agave; or maple syrup
- 1/4 tsp. salt or as your liking

Directions:
1. In Your Instant Pot, combine the oats, water, 2 cups of milk, the salt and chocolate chips. Stir to mix.
2. Lock the lid and turn the steam release handle to Sealing. Using the Manual function, set the cooker to High Pressure for 12 minutes.
3. After completing the cooking time, turn off the pressure cooker
4. Let the pressure release naturally for 10 minutes; quick release any remaining pressure
5. Add the remaining ½ cup of milk "more if you want the oats thinner". Stir in the peanut butter and agave and enjoy.

Note: Inner pot of your pressure cooker is never filled more than halfway when cooking oats or the foam may clog the pressure release valve.

Breakfast Quiche

(Prep + Cooking Time: 40 minutes | **Servings:** 4)

Ingredients:
- 1/2 cup ham, diced
- 1 cup sausage; already cooked and ground.
- 1 cup cheese; shredded.
- 4 bacon slices; cooked and crumbled.
- 1 ½ cups water
- 2 green onions; chopped.
- 1/2 cup milk
- 6 eggs, whisked
- Salt and black pepper to taste

Directions:

1. Put the water in your instant pot and leave it aside for now.
2. In a bowl; mix eggs with salt, pepper, milk, sausage, ham, bacon, onions and cheese and stir everything well.
3. Pour this into a baking dish, cover with some tin foil, place the dish in the steamer basket of your instant pot, cover and cook at High for 30 minutes.
4. Release the pressure naturally for 10 minutes, then release remaining pressure by turning the valve to 'Venting', and carefully open the lid, take the quiche out and leave it aside for a few minutes to cool down.
5. Cut the quiche, arrange it on plates and serve.

Eggs Breakfast

(Prep + Cooking Time: 30 minutes | **Servings:** 6)

Ingredients:

- 1 cup ham; cooked and crumbled.
- 1 cup kale leaves; chopped.
- 1 cup water
- 1 yellow onion; finely chopped
- 1/2 cup heavy cream
- 6 eggs
- 1 tsp. herbs de Provence
- 1 cup cheddar cheese; grated
- Salt and black pepper to taste

Directions:

1. In a bowl; mix eggs with salt, pepper, heavy cream, onion, kale, cheese and herbs, whisk very well and pour into a heat proof dish.
2. Put 1 cup water in your instant pot; place dish in the steamer basket, close the instant pot lid and cook at High for 20 minutes
3. Release the pressure, open the instant pot lid, remove the dish, divide eggs between plates and serve.

Chickpeas Spread

(Prep + Cooking Time: 25 minutes | **Servings:** 8)

Ingredients:

- 1 cup chickpeas soaked and drained
- 6 cups water
- 1 bay leaf
- 4 garlic cloves crushed.
- 2 tbsp. tahini paste
- Juice of 1 lemon
- 1/4 tsp. cumin
- 1/4 cup chopped parsley
- A pinch of paprika
- Extra virgin olive oil
- Salt to the taste

Directions:

1. Put chickpeas and water in your instant pot.
2. Add bay leaf, 2 garlic cloves, seal the instant pot lid and cook at High for 18 minutes
3. Quick release the pressure, discard excess liquid and bay leaf and reserve some of the cooking liquid.
4. Add tahini paste, the cooking liquid you've reserved, lemon juice, cumin, the rest of the garlic and salt to the taste
5. Transfer everything to your food processor and pulse well
6. Transfer your chickpeas spread in a serving bowl, sprinkle olive oil and paprika on top and enjoy!

Maple Millet

(Prep + Cooking Time: 22 minutes | Servings: 5)

Ingredients:

- 1/4 cup maple syrup
- 1 cup millet
- 1/2 to 1 cup nondairy milk
- 2 cups water
- 1/2 tsp. ground cinnamon
- 1/2 tsp. salt or as your liking
- Fresh berries; for topping

Directions:

1. In the Instant Pot, stir together the millet, water, cinnamon and salt.
2. Lock the lid and turn the steam release handle to Sealing. Using the Manual function, set the cooker to High Pressure for 10 minutes
3. After completing the cooking time, let the pressure release naturally for 10 minutes; quick release any remaining pressure
4. Remove the lid carefully and stir in the maple syrup and as much milk as you need to get the consistency you prefer "more milk makes it creamier"
5. You can add an extra sprinkle of salt, too. Top with the berries and serve.

Barbeque Tofu

(Prep + Cooking Time: 20 minutes | Servings: 6)

Ingredients:

- 28 oz. firm tofu; cubed
- 12 oz. BBQ sauce
- 1 red bell pepper; chopped.
- 1 yellow onion; chopped.
- 1 celery stalk; chopped.
- 1 green bell pepper; chopped.
- 2 tbsp. extra virgin olive oil
- 4 garlic cloves; minced.
- Salt to the taste
- A pinch of curry powder

Directions:

1. Set your instant pot on Sauté mode; add the oil and heat it up.
2. Add bell peppers, garlic, onion and celery and stir
3. Add salt and curry powder, stir and cook for 2 minutes.
4. Add tofu, stir and cook 4 minutes more
5. Add BBQ sauce; then stir well and seal the instant pot lid and cook at High for 5 minutes
6. Quick release the pressure, open the instant pot lid, transfer to plates and serve.

Apple Porridge

(Prep + Cooking Time: 24 minutes | Servings: 4)

Ingredients:

- 1 apple, chopped
- 1/2 to 1 cup nondairy milk
- 1 cup quinoa; rinsed
- 1 ½ cups water
- 2 tbsp. ground cinnamon
- 2 tbsp. maple syrup
- 1/2 tsp. vanilla extract
- 1/2 tsp. salt or as your liking

Directions:

1. In the Instant Pot, stir together the quinoa, water, maple syrup, cinnamon, vanilla, salt and apple.
2. Lock the lid and turn the steam release handle to Sealing. Using the Manual function, set the cooker to High Pressure for 8 minutes
3. After completing the cooking time, let the pressure release naturally for 10 minutes; quick release any remaining pressure
4. Remove the lid carefully and stir in as much milk as needed to make it creamy.
5. If you didn't cook the apples, add them now and put the cover back on for 1 to 2 minutes to warm them.

Feta Spinach Egg Cups.

(Prep + Cooking Time: 22 minutes | **Servings:** 4)

Ingredients:

- 6 eggs
- 1/2 cup. mozzarella cheese
- 1/4 cup. feta cheese
- 1 cup. water
- 1 tsp. black pepper
- 1/2 tsp. salt
- 1 cup. chopped baby spinach
- 1 chopped tomato

Directions:

1. Pour water into the Instant Pot and lower in trivet
2. Layer silicone ramekins with spinach.
3. In a bowl, mix the rest of the ingredients and pour into cups, leaving 1/4-inch of head room
4. Put in the instant pot pressure cooker [you may have to cook in batches] and adjust time to 8 minutes on "High" pressure
5. When time is up, turn off the instant pot and quick-release.

Meat Recipes

Beef and Cabbage

(Prep + Cooking Time: 1 hour and 30 minutes | **Servings:** 6)

Ingredients:

- 2 ½ lb. beef brisket
- 4 carrots; chopped
- 1 cabbage heat, cut into 6 wedges
- 6 potatoes, cut into quarters
- 4 cups water
- 2 bay leaves
- 3 garlic cloves; chopped
- 3 turnips, cut into quarters
- Horseradish sauce for serving
- Salt and black pepper to the taste

Directions:

1. Put beef brisket and water in your instant pot, add salt, pepper, garlic and bay leaves, seal the instant pot lid and cook at High for 1 hour and 15 minutes.
2. Quick release the pressure, carefully open the lid; add carrots, cabbage, potatoes, and turnips; then stir well. seal the instant pot lid again and cook at High for 6 minutes
3. Release the pressure naturally, carefully open the lid; divide among plates and serve with horseradish sauce on top

Delicious Lamb Ragout

(Prep + Cooking Time: 1 hour and 15 minutes | **Servings:** 8)

Ingredients:

- 1 ½ lb. lamb meat, bone-in
- 2 tbsp. tomato paste
- 4 tomatoes; chopped.
- 1 small yellow onion; chopped.
- 6 garlic cloves; minced.
- 1 tsp. vegetable oil
- 2 carrots, sliced
- 1/2 lb. mushrooms, sliced
- 1 tsp. oregano; dried
- A handful parsley; finely chopped
- Salt and black pepper to the taste

Directions:

1. Set your instant pot on Sauté mode; add oil and heat it up.
2. Add meat and brown it on all sides
3. Add tomato paste, tomatoes, onion, garlic, mushrooms, oregano, carrots and water to cover everything.
4. Add salt, pepper; then stir well. seal the instant pot lid and cook at High for 1 hour
5. Quick release the pressure, take meat out of the pot, discard bones and shred it
6. Return meat to pot, add parsley and stir.
7. Add more salt and pepper if needed and serve right away

Pork Chops & Smashed Potatoes

(Prep + Cooking Time: 35 minutes | **Servings:** 6)

Ingredients:

- 6 pork chops, boneless
- 2 lb. potatoes, cut into chunks
- 1 yellow onion, cut into chunks
- 1 bunch mixed rosemary, sage, oregano and thyme
- 2 tbsp. white flour
- 2 cups chicken stock
- 2 tbsp. butter
- 1 tsp. smoked paprika
- 3 garlic cloves; chopped.
- Salt and black pepper to taste

Directions:

1. Put the potatoes in your instant pot. Add garlic and half of the onion. Add herbs and stock
2. Place pork chops on top, add salt, pepper, and paprika. Cover and cook at High for 15 minutes
3. Meanwhile, heat up a pan over medium heat, add butter and heat it up
4. Add flour, stir very well, cook for 2 minutes and take off heat

5. Release the pressure quick, transfer pork to a platter and discard herbs
6. Transfer potatoes to a bowl, add some of the cooking liquid, add salt, pepper, and stir using your hand mixer.
7. Set your instant pot on Simmer mode and cook the cooking liquid for 2 minutes
8. Add butter mix and stir until it thickens. Divide pork chops on plates, add mashed potatoes on the side and drizzle the gravy from the pot all over.

Creamy Pork Chops

(Prep + Cooking Time: 30 minutes | **Servings:** 4)

Ingredients:
- 4 pork chops, boneless
- 1/2 small bunch parsley; chopped.
- 1 cup water
- 2 tbsp. extra virgin olive oil
- 2 tsp. chicken bouillon powder
- 10 oz. canned cream of mushroom soup
- 1 cup sour cream
- Salt and black pepper to taste

Directions:
1. Set your instant pot on Sauté mode; add oil and heat it up.
2. Add pork chops, salt and pepper, brown them on all sides, transfer to a plate and leave aside for now.
3. Add water and chicken bouillon powder to the pot and stir well.
4. Return pork chops, stir, cover and cook at High for 9 minutes
5. Release the pressure naturally, transfer pork chops to a platter and leave aside
6. Set the pot on Simmer mode and heat up the cooking liquid
7. Add mushroom soup, stir, cook for 2 minutes and take off heat. Add parsley and sour cream, stir and pour over pork chops

Braised Pork Recipe

(Prep + Cooking Time: 1 hour 30 minutes | **Servings:** 6)

Ingredients:
- 4 lb. pork butt; chopped.
- 16 oz. chicken stock
- 16 oz. red wine
- 4 oz. lemon juice
- 2 tbsp. extra virgin olive oil
- 1/4 cup onion; chopped.
- 1/4 cup garlic powder
- 1 tbsp. paprika
- Salt and black pepper to taste

Directions:
1. In your instant pot, mix pork with stock, wine, lemon juice, onion, garlic powder, oil, paprika, salt and pepper, stir, cover and cook on High for 45 minutes.
2. Leave the pot aside for 15 minutes, release the pressure quickly, stir braised pork, divide into bowls and serve

Lamb & Beans Dish

(Prep + Cooking Time: 50 minutes | **Servings:** 4)

Ingredients:
- 4 lamb chops
- 1 ½ cups white beans, soaked overnight and drained
- 1 cup leek; chopped.
- 2 tbsp. garlic; minced.
- 1 tsp. herbs de Provence
- 1 cup onion; chopped.
- 3 cups water
- 2 tsp. Worcestershire sauce
- 2 cups canned tomatoes; chopped.
- Salt and black pepper to the taste

Directions:

1. Put lamb chops in your instant pot
2. Add beans, onion, tomatoes, leek, garlic, salt, pepper, herbs de Provence, Worcestershire sauce and water.
3. Stir, seal the instant pot lid and cook at High for 40 minutes
4. Quick release the pressure, carefully open the lid; divide among plates and serve

Tasty Kalua Pork

(Prep + Cooking Time: 1 hour 30 minutes | **Servings:** 5)

Ingredients:

- 4 lb. pork shoulder, cut into half
- 1/2 cup water
- 2 tbsp. vegetable oil
- 1 tbsp. liquid smoke
- Steamed green beans for serving
- Salt and black pepper to taste

Directions:

1. Set your instant pot on Sauté mode; add the oil and heat it up.
2. Add pork, salt and pepper, brown for 3 minutes on each side and transfer to a plate.
3. Add water and liquid smoke to the pot and stir.
4. Return meat, stir, cover pot and cook at High for 90 minutes.
5. Release the pressure naturally for 15 minutes, then release remaining pressure by turning the valve to 'Venting', and carefully open the lid.
6. Transfer meat to a cutting board and shred it with 2 forks
7. Divide pork on plates, add some of the sauce on top and serve with steamed green beans on the side

Pork Tamales

(Prep + Cooking Time: 1 hour and 45 minutes | **Servings:** 24 pieces)

Ingredients:

- 8 oz. dried corn husks, soaked for 1 day and drained
- 3 lb. pork shoulder, boneless and chopped.
- 1 yellow onion; chopped
- 2 garlic cloves, crushed.
- 2 tbsp. chili powder
- 4 cups water
- 1 tsp. baking powder
- 1 tsp. cumin
- 4 cups masa
- 1/4 cup corn oil
- 1/4 cup shortening
- 1 tbsp. chipotle chili powder
- Salt and black pepper to taste

Directions:

1. In your instant pot, mix 2 cups water with salt, pepper, onion, garlic, chipotle powder, chili powder, and cumin.
2. Add pork, stir, close the instant pot lid and cook at High for 75 minutes
3. Release the pressure naturally for 10 minutes, carefully open the instant pot lid, transfer meat to a cutting board and shred it with 2 forks.
4. Put pork meat in a bowl, add 1 tbsp. of cooking liquid, more salt and pepper, stir and leave aside. In a bowl, mix masa with salt, pepper, baking powder, shortening and oil and stir using a mixer
5. Add cooking liquid from the instant pot and blend again well
6. Add 2 cups of water to your instant pot and place the steamer basket inside
7. Unfold 2 corn husks, place them on a work surface, add 1/4 cup masa mix near the top of the husk, press into a square and leaves 2 inches at the bottom
8. Add 1 tbsp. pork in the center of the masa, wrap the husk around the dough and place standing up in the steamer basket
9. Repeat with the rest of the husks, close the instant pot lid and cook at High for 20 minutes. Release the pressure naturally for 15 minutes, then release remaining pressure by turning the valve to 'Venting', and carefully open the lid.

Lamb Curry

(Prep + Cooking Time: 35 minutes | **Servings:** 6)

Ingredients:

- 1 ½ lb. lamb shoulder, cut into medium chunks
- 2 oz. coconut milk
- 3 tbsp. curry powder
- 2 tbsp. vegetable oil
- 3 tbsp. water
- 3 oz. dry white wine
- 1 yellow onion; chopped.
- 1 tbsp. parsley; chopped.
- 3 tbsp. pure cream
- Salt and black pepper to the taste

Directions:

1. In a bowl, mix half of the curry powder with salt, pepper and coconut milk and stir well.
2. Set your instant pot on Sauté mode; add oil and heat it up
3. Add onion, stir and cook for 4 minutes
4. Add the rest of the curry powder, stir and cook for 1 minute.
5. Add lamb pieces, brown them for 3 minutes and mix with water, salt, pepper and wine.
6. Stir, seal the instant pot lid and cook at High for 20 minutes.
7. Quick release the pressure, set the pot to Simmer mode, add coconut milk mix, stir and boil for 5 minutes.
8. Divide among plates, sprinkle parsley on top and serve

Pork Carnitas

(Prep + Cooking Time: 1 hour and 10 minutes | **Servings:** 8)

Ingredients:

- 3 lb. pork shoulder; chopped.
- 2 tbsp. extra virgin olive oil
- 1 tsp. oregano
- 3 garlic cloves; minced.
- 1 yellow onion; chopped.
- 1 lb. tomatillos, cut into quarters
- 1 tsp. cumin
- 2 cups chicken stock
- 2 bay leaves
- Salt and black pepper to taste
- 1 jalapeno pepper; chopped.
- 1 poblano pepper; chopped.
- 1 green bell pepper; chopped.
- Flour tortillas for serving
- 1 red onion; chopped for serving
- Shredded cheddar cheese, for serving

Directions:

1. Set your instant pot on Sauté mode; add oil and heat it up
2. Add pork pieces, salt and pepper and brown them for 3 minutes.
3. Add green bell pepper, jalapeno, poblano pepper, tomatillos, onion, garlic, oregano, cumin, bay leaves and stock. Stir, cover and cook at High for 55 minutes.
4. Release the pressure naturally, for 10 minutes, open the instant pot lid and transfer meat to a cutting board.
5. Puree the mix from the pot using a hand blender
6. Shred meat with a fork and mix with the puree. Divide this on flour tortillas, add red onion and cheese and serve

Feta & Lamb Meatballs.

(Prep + Cooking Time: 15 minutes | **Servings:** 6)

Ingredients:

- 1 ½ lb. ground lamb
- 4 minced garlic cloves
- 1 (28 oz.) can of crushed tomatoes
- 6 oz. can of tomato sauce
- 1 chopped onion
- 2 tbsp. chopped parsley
- 2 tbsp. olive oil
- 1 tbsp. chopped mint
- 1/2 cup. crumbled feta cheese
- 1/2 cup. breadcrumbs

- 1 tbsp. water
- 1 tsp. dried oregano
- 1 beaten egg
- 1 chopped green bell pepper
- 1/2 tsp. salt
- 1/4 tsp. black pepper

Directions:
1. In a bowl, mix lamb, egg, breadcrumbs, mint, parsley, feta, water, half of the minced garlic, pepper, and salt
2. With your hands, mold into 1-inch meatballs.
3. Turn your Instant Pot to "Sauté" and add oil.
4. When hot, toss in the bell pepper and onion. Cook for 2 minutes before adding the rest of the garlic.
5. After another minute, mix in crushed tomatoes with their liquid, the tomato sauce, and oregano. Sprinkle in salt and pepper
6. Put the meatballs in and ladle over the sauce before sealing the cooker lid
7. Select "Manual" and adjust time to 8 minutes on "High" pressure
8. When time is up, hit "Cancel" and carefully quick-release
9. Serve meatballs with parsley and more cheese!

Easy and Tasty Meatloaf

(Prep + Cooking Time: 50 minutes | **Servings:** 6)

Ingredients:
- 2 lb. ground meat
- 1/3 cup milk
- 1/4 cup ketchup
- 2 eggs, whisked
- 2 cups water
- 1/2 cup panko breadcrumbs
- 1 yellow onion, grated
- Salt and black pepper to the taste

Directions:
1. In a bowl, mix breadcrumbs with milk, stir and leave aside for 5 minutes
2. Add onion, salt, pepper and eggs and stir.
3. Add ground meat and stir very well again.
4. Place this on a greased tin foil and shape a loaf
5. Add ketchup on top.
6. Pour the water in your instant pot, arrange meatloaf in the steamer basket of the pot, seal the instant pot lid and cook at High for 35 minutes.
7. Release the pressure naturally for 10 minutes, then release remaining pressure by turning the valve to 'Venting', carefully open the lid; take meatloaf out, leave it to cool down for 5 minutes, slices and serve it.

Pork Chops & Brown Rice

(Prep + Cooking Time: 35 minutes | **Servings:** 6)

Ingredients:
- 2 lb. pork chops
- 2 cups brown rice
- 1/3 cup brown sugar
- 1 tbsp. peppercorns
- 4 garlic cloves, crushed.
- 2 cups water
- 2 bay leaves
- 1/3 cup salt
- 1 cup onion; chopped.
- 3 tbsp. butter
- 2 ½ cups beef stock
- 2 cups ice
- 2 hot peppers, crushed.
- Salt and black pepper to taste

Directions:
1. Heat up a pan over medium high heat with the water.
2. Add salt and brown sugar, stir until it dissolves, take off heat and add ice
3. Add hot peppers, garlic, peppercorns and bay leaves and stir
4. Add pork chops, toss to coat, cover and keep in the fridge for 4 hours

5. Rinse pork chops and pat dry them with paper towels.
6. Set your instant pot on Sauté mode; add butter and melt it. Add pork chops, brown them on all sides, transfer to a plate and leave aside for now.
7. Add onion to your instant pot and cook for 2 minutes. Add rice, stir and cook for 1 minute
8. Add stock, pork chops, close the instant pot lid and cook at High for 22 minutes
9. Release the pressure naturally for 10 minutes, carefully open the instant pot lid, add salt and pepper, divide pork chops and rice among plates and serve.

Beef Curry

(Prep + Cooking Time: 30 minutes | Servings: 4)

Ingredients:
- 2 lb. beef steak, cubed
- 3 potatoes, diced
- 1 tbsp. wine mustard
- 2 ½ tbsp. curry powder
- 2 yellow onions; chopped.
- 2 tbsp. extra virgin olive oil
- 2 garlic cloves; minced.
- 10 oz. canned coconut milk
- 2 tbsp. tomato sauce
- Salt and black pepper to the taste

Directions:
1. Set your instant pot on Sauté mode; add the oil and heat it up
2. Add onions and garlic, stir and cook for 4 minutes.
3. Add potatoes and mustard, stir and cook for 1 minute
4. Add beef, stir and brown on all sides.
5. Add curry powder, salt and pepper, stir and cook for 2 minutes.
6. Add coconut milk and tomato sauce; then stir well. seal the instant pot lid and cook at High for 10 minutes.
7. Quick release the pressure, carefully open the lid; divide curry among plates and serve

Meatball Delight

(Prep + Cooking Time: 20 minutes | Servings: 8)

Ingredients:
- 1 ½ lb. ground pork meat
- 2 tbsp. parsley; chopped.
- one egg
- 2 potatoes, cubed
- 1 bay leaf
- 1/4 cup white wine
- 2 garlic cloves; minced.
- 2 bread slices, soaked in water
- 1/2 tsp. paprika
- 3/4 cup beef stock
- 1/2 tsp. nutmeg
- 1/4 cup flour
- 1 tsp. Worcestershire sauce
- 2 tbsp. extra virgin olive oil
- 2 carrots; chopped.
- 3/4 cup fresh peas
- Salt and black pepper to taste

Directions:
1. In a bowl, mix ground meat with soaked bread, egg, salt, pepper, parsley, paprika, garlic and nutmeg and stir well.
2. Add 1 tbsp. stock and Worcestershire sauce and stir again
3. Shape meatballs and dust them with flour.
4. Set your instant pot on Sauté mode; add oil and heat it up
5. Add meatballs and brown them on all sides.
6. Add carrots, peas, potatoes, bay leaf, stock and wine, close the instant pot lid and cook at High for 6 minutes.
7. Release the pressure, carefully open the instant pot lid, discard bay leaf, divide meatballs mix into bowls and serve.

Red Beans & Sausage Dish

(Prep + Cooking Time: 45 minutes | **Servings:** 8)

Ingredients:

- 1 lb. smoked sausage, sliced
- 1 garlic clove; chopped.
- 2 tbsp. Cajun seasoning
- 1/2 green bell pepper; chopped.
- 1 tsp. parsley; dried
- 1 small yellow onion; chopped.
- 1 celery stalk; chopped.
- 1 lb. red beans, dried, soaked overnight and drained
- 1 bay leaf
- 5 cups water
- 1/4 tsp. cumin, ground.
- Salt and black pepper to the taste

Directions:

1. In your instant pot, mix beans with sausage, bay leaf, Cajun seasoning, celery, salt, pepper, bell pepper, parsley, cumin, garlic, onion and water; then stir well. seal the instant pot lid and cook at High for 30 minutes.
2. Quick release the pressure, carefully open the lid; divide mix into bowls and serve

Collard with Bacon.

(Prep + Cooking Time: 40 minutes | **Servings:** 6)

Ingredients:

- 1/4 lb. bacon, cut into 1-inch pieces
- 1 lb. collard greens, cleaned and then stems trimmed
- 1/2 tsp. kosher salt
- 1/2 cup. water
- Fresh ground black pepper

Directions:

1. Spread the bacon in the bottom of the Instant Pot inner pot.
2. Press the "Sauté" button and cook for about 5 minutes, occasionally stirring until the bacon is crispy and browne
3. Stir in a big handful of collard greens to coat with bacon grease until slightly wilted. Pack in the rest of the collards
4. The pot will be filled –just pack them enough to close the lid since they will quickly wilt.
5. Sprinkle the greens with salt and pour water over everything. Close and lock the lid. Turn the steam release valve to "Sealing", set the pressure to "High", and the timer to 20 minutes
6. When the timer beeps, turn the steam valve to "Venting" to quick release the pressure. Carefully open and remove the lid.
7. Pour the collard into a serving dish
8. Sprinkle with freshly ground black pepper and then serve.

Potatoes and Goat

(Prep + Cooking Time: 60 minutes | **Servings:** 5)

Ingredients:

- 2 ½ lb. goat meat, cut into small cubes
- 5 tbsp. vegetable oil
- 3 tsp. turmeric powder
- 3 cardamom pods
- 3 onions; chopped.
- 2-inch cinnamon stick
- 2 tomatoes; chopped.
- 4 garlic cloves; minced.
- 2 green chilies; chopped.
- 3/4 tsp. chili powder
- 3 potatoes, cut into halves
- 1 tsp. sugar
- 4 cloves
- A small piece of ginger, grated
- Salt and black pepper to the taste
- 2 ½ cups water
- 1 tsp. coriander; chopped.

Directions:

1. Put goat cubes in a bowl, add salt, pepper and turmeric, toss to coat and leave aside for 10 minutes.
2. Set your instant pot on Sauté mode; add the oil and half of the sugar, stir and heat up
3. Add potatoes, fry them a bit and transfer to a bowl
4. Add cloves, cinnamon stick and cardamom to pot and stir
5. Also add ginger, onion, chilies and garlic, stir and cook for 3 minutes.
6. Add tomatoes and chili powder, stir and cook for 5 minutes
7. Add meat, stir and cook for 10 minutes.
8. Add 2 cups water; then stir well. seal the instant pot lid and cook at High for 15 minutes.
9. Quick release the pressure, carefully open the lid; add more salt and pepper, the rest of the sugar, potatoes and ½ cup water, seal the instant pot lid and cook at High for 5 minutes
10. Release the pressure again, carefully open the lid; divide among plates, sprinkle coriander on top and serve.

Delicious Pork Chops

(Prep + Cooking Time: 25 minutes | Servings: 4)

Ingredients:

- 4 pork chops
- 2 tbsp. parsley; chopped.
- 1 tbsp. white flour
- 2 tbsp. extra virgin olive oil
- 1 garlic clove; minced.
- 2 tbsp. lime juice
- 2 tbsp. butter
- 2 tbsp. cornstarch mixed with 3 tbsp. water
- 1 lb. onions, sliced
- 1/2 cup milk
- 1/2 cup white wine
- Salt and black pepper to taste

Directions:

1. Set your instant pot on Sauté mode; add the oil and butter and heat it up.
2. Add pork chops, salt and pepper, brown on all sides and transfer to a bowl.
3. Add garlic and onion to pot, stir and cook for 2 minutes
4. Add wine, lime juice, milk, parsley and return pork chops to pot.
5. Stir, cover and cook at High for 15 minutes
6. Release the pressure, open the instant pot lid, add cornstarch and flour, stir well and cook on Simmer mode for 3 minutes.
7. Divide pork chops and onions on plates, drizzle cooking sauce all over and serve.

Tasty Beef Chili

(Prep + Cooking Time: 50 minutes | Servings: 6)

Ingredients:

- 16 oz. mixed beans, soaked overnight and drained
- 28 oz. canned tomatoes; chopped.
- 17 oz. beef stock
- 12 oz. pale ale
- 1 ½ lb. beef, ground.
- 1 sweet onion; chopped.
- 3 tbsp. chili powder
- 1 bay leaf
- 2 tbsp. vegetable oil
- 4 carrots; chopped.
- 1 tsp. chipotle powder
- 6 garlic cloves; chopped.
- 7 jalapeno peppers, diced
- Salt and black pepper to the taste

Directions:

1. Set your instant pot on Sauté mode; add half of the oil and heat it up.
2. Add beef; then stir well. brown for 8 minutes and transfer to a bowl
3. Add the rest of the oil to the pot and heat it up.
4. Add carrots, onion, jalapenos and garlic, stir and sauté for 4 minutes
5. Add ale and tomatoes and stir.

6. Also add beans, bay leaf, stock, chili powder, chipotle powder, salt and pepper and the beef; then stir well. seal the instant pot lid and cook at High for 25 minutes
7. Release the pressure naturally, carefully open the lid; stir chili, transfer to bowls and serve.

Pork with Orange and Honey

(Prep + Cooking Time: 1 hour 10 minutes | **Servings:** 4)

Ingredients:
- 1 ½ lb. pork shoulder; chopped
- 3 garlic cloves; minced.
- 1 cinnamon stick
- 2 cloves
- 1/2 cup water
- 1 tsp. rosemary; dried
- 2 tbsp. soy sauce
- 1 tbsp. grape seed oil
- 1 tbsp. honey
- 1 tbsp. maple syrup
- 1 tbsp. water Juice from 1 orange
- Salt and black pepper to taste
- 1 yellow onion, sliced
- 1 tbsp. ginger, sliced
- 1 ½ tbsp. cornstarch

Directions:
1. Set your instant pot on Sauté mode; add grape seed oil and heat it up.
2. Add pork, salt and pepper, stir, brown for 5 minutes on each side and transfer to a plate
3. Add onions, ginger, salt and pepper to the pot, stir and cook for 1 minute. Add garlic and cook for 30 seconds,
4. Add orange juice, water, soy sauce, honey, maple syrup, cinnamon, cloves, rosemary and pork pieces.
5. close the instant pot lid, cook at High for 50 minutes and release the pressure naturally.
6. Uncover the pot, discard cinnamon and cloves, add cornstarch mixed with water, stir, set the pot on Sauté mode again and cook until the sauce thickens.
7. Divide pork and sauce among plates and serve.

Pork Sausages and Mashed Potatoes

(Prep + Cooking Time: 30 minutes | **Servings:** 6)

Ingredients:
For the potatoes:
- 4 potatoes, peeled and cut into cubes
- 1 tbsp. butter
- 1 tsp. mustard powder
- 1 tbsp. cheddar cheese, grated
- 4 oz. milk, warm
- 6 oz. water
- Sat and black pepper to taste

For the sausages:
- 6 pork sausages
- 2 tbsp. extra virgin olive oil
- 1 tbsp. cornstarch mixed with 1 tbsp. water
- 1/2 cup onion jam
- 3 oz. red wine
- 3 oz. water
- Salt and black pepper to taste

Directions:
1. Put potatoes in your instant pot, add 6 oz. water, salt and pepper, stir, cover and cook on High for 5 minutes.
2. Release the pressure quickly, drain potatoes and put them in a bowl.
3. Add warm milk, butter, mustard and more salt and pepper, and mash well
4. Add cheese, stir again and leave aside for now
5. Set your instant pot on Sauté mode; add oil and heat it up.
6. Add sausages and brown them on all sides. Add onion jam, wine and 3 oz. water
7. Add salt and pepper to the taste, close the instant pot lid and cook at High for 8 minutes
8. Release the pressure quickly and divide sausages among plates
9. Add cornstarch mix to the pot and stir well. Drizzle the sauce over sausages and serve them with mashed potatoes.

Delicious Chili Con Carne

(Prep + Cooking Time: 40 minutes **| Servings:** 4)

Ingredients:

- 1 lb. beef, ground.
- 8 oz. canned tomatoes; chopped.
- 4 oz. kidney beans, soaked overnight and drained
- 1 tsp. tomato paste
- 5 oz. water
- 1 yellow onion; chopped.
- 4 tbsp. extra virgin olive oil
- 1 tbsp. chili powder
- 1/2 tsp. cumin, ground.
- Salt and black pepper to the taste
- 2 garlic cloves; minced.
- 1 bay leaf

Directions:

1. Set your instant pot on Sauté mode; add 1 tablespoon oil and heat it up.
2. Add meat, brown for a few minutes and transfer to a bowl
3. Add the rest of the oil to the pot and also heat it up
4. Add onion and garlic, stir and cook for 3 minutes.
5. Return beef to pot, add bay leaf, beans, tomato paste, tomatoes, chili powder, cumin, salt, pepper and water; then stir well. seal the instant pot lid and cook on High for 18 minutes
6. Quick release the pressure, carefully open the lid; discard bay leaf, divide chili among bowls and serve.

Pasta and Beef Casserole

(Prep + Cooking Time: 30 minutes **| Servings:** 4)

Ingredients:

- 17 oz. pasta
- 1 carrot; chopped.
- 1 tbsp. red wine
- 16 oz. tomato puree
- 1 celery stalk; chopped.
- 1 yellow onion; chopped.
- 2 tbsp. butter
- 1 lb. beef, ground
- 13 oz. mozzarella cheese, shredded.
- Salt and black pepper to the taste

Directions:

1. Set your instant pot on Sauté mode; add the butter and melt it.
2. Add carrot, onion, and celery, stir and cook for 5 minutes
3. Add beef, salt and pepper and cook for 10 minutes
4. Add wine, stir and cook for 1 minute more.
5. Add pasta, tomato puree and water to cover pasta; then stir well. seal the instant pot lid and cook at High for 6 minutes
6. Quick release the pressure, carefully open the lid; add cheese; then stir well. divide everything among plates and serve.

Easy Veal Dish

(Prep + Cooking Time: 45 minutes **| Servings:** 4)

Ingredients:

- 2 lb. veal shoulder, cut into medium chunks
- 3.5 oz. button mushrooms, sliced
- 3.5 oz. shiitake mushrooms, sliced
- 17 oz. potatoes; chopped.
- 16 oz. shallots; chopped.
- 9 oz. beef stock
- 2 oz. white wine
- 1 tbsp. white flour
- 1/8 tsp. thyme; dried
- 2 garlic cloves; minced.
- 2 tbsp. chives; chopped.
- 1 tsp. sage; dried
- 3 ½ tbsp. extra virgin olive oil
- Salt and black pepper to the taste

Directions:
1. Set your instant pot on Sauté mode; add 1 ½ tablespoon oil and heat it up
2. Add veal, season with salt and pepper; then stir well. brown for 5 minutes and transfer to a bowl.
3. Add the rest of the oil to the pot and heat it up
4. Add all mushrooms, stir and cook for 3 minutes.
5. Add garlic; then stir well. cook for 1 minute and transfer everything to a bowl.
6. Add wine and flour to the pot, stir and cook for 1 minute.
7. Add stock, sage, thyme and return meat to pot as well.
8. Stir, seal the instant pot lid and cook at High for 20 minutes
9. Quick release the pressure, carefully open the lid; return mushrooms and garlic and stir.
10. Also add potatoes and shallots; then stir well. seal the instant pot lid and cook at High for 4 minutes.
11. Release the pressure again, carefully open the lid; add more salt and pepper if needed, also add chives; then stir well. divide among bowls and serve.

Asian Short Ribs

(Prep + Cooking Time: 60 minutes | **Servings:** 4)

Ingredients:
- 2 green onions; chopped.
- 1 tsp. vegetable oil
- 1/4 cup pear juice
- 1/2 cup soy sauce
- 3 garlic cloves; minced.
- 3 ginger slices
- 4 lb. short ribs
- 2 tsp. sesame oil
- 1/2 cup water
- 1/4 cup rice wine

Directions:
1. Set your instant pot on Sauté mode; add the oil and heat it up.
2. Add green onions, ginger and garlic, stir and cook for 1 minute
3. Add ribs, water, wine, soy sauce, sesame oil and pear juice, stir and cook for 2 - 3 minutes.
4. Cover the pot and cook at High for 45 minutes
5. Release the pressure naturally for 15 minutes, open the instant pot lid and transfer the ribs to a plate.
6. Strain liquid from the pot, divide ribs among plates and drizzle the sauce all over

Apple Cider Pork

(Prep + Cooking Time: 35 minutes | **Servings:** 4)

Ingredients:
- 2 lb. pork loin
- 2 cups apple cider
- 2 tbsp. extra virgin olive oil
- 1 yellow onion; chopped.
- 2 apples; chopped.
- Salt and black pepper to taste
- 1 tbsp. dry onion; minced.

Directions:
1. Set your instant pot on Sauté mode; add the oil and heat it up.
2. Add pork loin, salt, pepper and dried onion, stir and brown meat on all sides and transfer to a plate.
3. Add onion to pot, stir and cook for 2 minutes.
4. Return meat to pot, add cider, apples, more salt and pepper, stir, cover and cook on High for 20 minutes.
5. Release the pressure, open the instant pot lid, transfer pork to a cutting board, slice it and divide among plates
6. Add sauce and mix from the pot on the side and serve

Pulled Pork Dish

(Prep + Cooking Time: 1 Hour 30 minutes | **Servings:** 6)

Ingredients:
- 3 lb. pork shoulder, halves
- 2 teaspoons dried mustard
- 11 oz. beer
- 3 oz. sugar
- 2 teaspoons smoked paprika
- 8 oz. water
- Salt to the taste

For the sauce:
- 12 oz. apple cider vinegar
- 2 tablespoons brown sugar
- 4 oz. hot water
- Salt and black pepper to the taste
- A pinch of cayenne pepper
- 2 teaspoons dry mustard

Directions:
1. In a bowl, mix 3 oz. sugar with smoked paprika, 2 tsp. dry mustard and salt to the taste
2. Rub pork meat with this mix and put pieces in your instant pot.
3. Add beer and 3 oz. water, stir, close the instant pot lid and cook at High for 75 minutes
4. Release the pressure quickly, carefully open the instant pot lid, transfer pork to a cutting board, shred with 2 forks and leave aside for now.
5. Discard half of the cooking liquid from the pot.
6. In a bowl, mix brown sugar with 4 oz. hot water, vinegar, cayenne, salt, pepper and 2 tsp. dry mustard and stir well.
7. Pour this over cooking sauce from the pot, stir, cover and cook at High for 3 minutes
8. Release the pressure, divide pork among plates, drizzle the sauce all over and serve

Pork Roast with Fennel

(Prep + Cooking Time: 1 hour 30 minutes | **Servings:** 4)

Ingredients:
- 2 lb. pork meat, boneless
- 2 garlic cloves; minced.
- 1 yellow onion; chopped.
- 1 lb. fennel bulbs, sliced
- 2 tbsp. extra virgin olive oil
- 5 oz. white wine
- 5 oz. chicken stock
- Salt and black pepper to taste

Directions:
1. Set your instant pot on Sauté mode; add oil and heat it up
2. Add pork, salt and pepper, stir, brown on all sides and transfer to a plate
3. Add garlic, wine and stock to the pot, stir and cook for 2 minutes.
4. Return pork to pot, cover and cook at High for 40 minutes.
5. Release the pressure, carefully open the instant pot lid, add onion and fennels, stir, cover and cook at High for 15 minutes
6. Release the pressure again, stir your mix, transfer pork to a cutting board, slice and divide among plates.
7. Serve with onion and fennel on the side and with cooking sauce all over.

Chinese BBQ Pork

(Prep + Cooking Time: 60 minutes | **Servings:** 6)

Ingredients:
- 2 lb. pork belly
- 2 tbsp. dry sherry
- 1-quart chicken stock
- 8 tbsp. char siu sauce
- 2 tsp. sesame oil
- 2 tbsp. honey
- 4 tbsp. soy sauce
- 1 tsp. peanut oil

Directions:

1. Set your instant pot on Simmer mode, add sherry, stock, soy sauce and half of char siu sauce, stir and cook for 8 minutes
2. Add pork, stir, cover and cook at High for 30 minutes.
3. Release the pressure naturally, transfer pork to a cutting board, leave aside to cool down and chop into small pieces.
4. Heat up a pan with the peanut oil over medium high heat, add pork, stir and cook for a few minutes.
5. Meanwhile, in a bowl, mix sesame oil with the rest of the char siu sauce and honey. Brush pork from the pan with this mix, stir and cook for 10 minutes.
6. Heat up another pan over medium high heat, add cooking liquid from the instant pot and bring to a boil. Simmer for 3 minutes and take off heat.
7. Divide pork on plates, drizzle the sauce over it and serve.

Spiced Pork

(Prep + Cooking Time: 1hour 25 minutes | **Servings:** 4)

Ingredients:

- 1-lb. boneless pork shoulder, cut into short ½-inch thick slices
- 1/4 cup water
- 1/4 cup sliced scallions, for garnish
- 2 yellow onions, thinly sliced
- 1 tbsp. soy sauce
- 1 tbsp. rice wine
- 1 tbsp. sesame seeds, for garnish
- 1 tbsp. minced fresh ginger
- 1 tbsp. toasted sesame oil
- 2 tbsp. gochujang (Korean red chile paste)
- 1 tbsp. minced garlic
- 1 tsp. sugar
- 1/4 to 1 tsp. cayenne pepper

Directions:

1. In your Instant Pot, combine the pork, half the sliced onions, the water, gochujang, sugar, ginger, garlic, soy sauce, rice wine, sesame oil and gochugaru. Stir until everything is well combined. Allow pork to stand at room temperature for 30 minutes.
2. Now secure the lid on the pot and close the valve. Now Press "Manual" and set the pot at "High" pressure for 20 minutes
3. After completing the cooking time, allow the pot to sit undisturbed for 10 minutes, then release any remaining pressure.
4. Heat a large cast-iron skillet over high heat. Using a slotted spoon, add the pork cubes and the remaining sliced onions to the skillet
5. When the pork and onions are very hot, add ¼ to ½ cup of the sauce from the pot and stir to combine with the pork. Cook until the sauce has thickened and the onions have softened
6. Sprinkle the meat with the sesame seeds and scallions. Serve with the remaining sauce from the pot.

Beef & Broccoli Dish

(Prep + Cooking Time: 20 minutes | **Servings:** 4)

Ingredients:

- 3 lb. chuck roast, cut into thin strips
- 1 lb. broccoli florets
- 1 tbsp. peanut oil
- 2 tsp. toasted sesame oil

For the marinade:

- 1/2 cup soy sauce
- 1/2 cup black soy sauce
- 1 tbsp. sesame oil
- 3 red peppers; dried and crushed.
- 1/2 tsp. Chinese five spice

- 2 tbsp. potato starch
- 1 yellow onion; chopped.
- 1/2 cup beef stock

- White rice, already cooked for servings
- 2 tbsp. fish sauce
- 5 garlic cloves; minced.
- Toasted sesame seeds for serving

Directions:

1. In a bowl, mix black soy sauce with soy sauce, fish sauce, 1 tablespoon sesame oil, 5 garlic cloves, five spice and crushed red peppers and stir well
2. Add beef strips, toss to coat and leave aside for 10 minutes.
3. Set your instant pot on Sauté mode; add peanut oil and heat it up.
4. Add onions, stir and cook for 4 minutes
5. Add beef and marinade, stir and cook for 2 minutes.
6. Add stock; then stir well. seal the instant pot lid and cook at High for 5 minutes
7. Release the pressure naturally for 10 minutes, then release remaining pressure by turning the valve to 'Venting', carefully open the lid; add cornstarch after you've mixed it with 1/4 cup liquid from the pot, add broccoli to the steamer basket, close the lid again and cook for 3 minutes at High
8. Release the pressure again, carefully open the lid; divide beef into bowls on top of rice, add broccoli on the side, drizzle toasted sesame oil, sprinkle sesame seeds and serve

Meatballs in Tomato Sauce

(Prep + Cooking Time: 50 minutes | **Servings:** 6)

Ingredients:
For Meatballs:

- 1 lb. ground beef
- ⅓ cup arborio rice
- 1/2 cup finely chopped yellow onion
- 1/4 cup chopped fresh parsley
- 1 large egg, slightly beaten
- Salt and black pepper to taste

For Sauce:

- 1 (14.5-ounce) can diced tomatoes; undrained
- 1/2 tsp. smoked paprika
- 1/4 tsp. ground cloves
- 1 cup water
- 1 tsp. dried oregano
- 1/2 tsp. ground cinnamon
- Salt and black pepper to taste
- Chopped fresh parsley, for garnish

Directions:

1. For meatballs: In a large bowl, combine the ground beef, egg, onion, rice and parsley and season with salt and pepper. Mix until well combined. Shape the mixture into 8 to 10 meatballs. Place in a single layer in the Instant Pot.
2. For sauce: In a medium bowl, combine the tomatoes with their juices, water, oregano, cinnamon, paprika and cloves and season with salt and pepper. Stir to combine and pour over the meatballs
3. Now secure the lid on the pot and close the valve. Now Press "Manual" and set the pot at "High" pressure for 15 minutes. After completing the cooking time, allow the pot to sit undisturbed until the pressure has released
4. Carefully transfer the meatballs to a serving bowl. Use an immersion blender to puree the sauce directly in the pot until smooth, if desired. Pour the sauce over the meatballs. Garnish with parsley, if desired and serve.

Meatloaf Dish

(Prep + Cooking Time: 35 minutes | **Servings:** 8)

Ingredients:

- 2 lb. ground beef
- 2 cups water
- 8 bacon slices
- 3 eggs, whisked
- 2 tbsp. parsley; dried
- 1/2 cup BBQ sauce
- 3 bread slices
- 1/2 cup milk
- 3/4 cup parmesan, grated
- Salt and black pepper to the taste

Directions:

1. In a bowl, mix bread slices with milk and leave aside for 5 minutes
2. Add meat, cheese, salt, pepper, eggs and parsley and stir well
3. Shape a loaf, place on a tin foil, arrange bacon slices on top, tuck them underneath and spread half of the BBQ sauce all over.
4. Put 2 cups water in the instant pot, place meatloaf in the steamer basket of the pot, seal the instant pot lid and cook on High for 20 minutes
5. Quick release the pressure, carefully open the lid; transfer meat loaf to a pan and spread the rest of the BBQ sauce over it
6. Introduce in preheated broiler for 5 minutes, transfer to a platter and slice.

Hominy Dish

(Prep + Cooking Time: 40 minutes | **Servings:** 6)

Ingredients:

- 30 oz. hominy, drained
- 1 ¼ lb. pork shoulder, boneless and cut into medium pieces
- 4 cups chicken stock
- 1/4 cup water
- 2 tbsp. cornstarch
- 2 tbsp. chili powder
- 1 white onion; chopped
- 4 garlic cloves; minced.
- Avocado slices for serving
- Lime wedges for serving
- 2 tbsp. vegetable oil
- Salt and black pepper to taste

Directions:

1. Set your instant pot on Sauté mode; add 1 tbsp. oil and heat it up
2. Add pork, salt, and pepper, brown on all sides and transfer to a bowl. Add the rest of the oil to the pot and heat it up.
3. Add garlic, onion and chili powder, stir and sauté for 4 minutes. Add half of the stock, stir and cook for 1 minute
4. Add the rest of the stock and return pork to pot, stir, cover and cook at High for 30 minutes.
5. Release the pressure naturally for 10 minutes, transfer pork to a cutting board and shred with 2 forks
6. Add cornstarch mixed with water to the pot and set on Sauté mode again. Add hominy, more salt and pepper and shredded pork, stir and cook for 2 minutes.
7. Divide among bowls and serve with avocado slices on top and lime wedges on the side

Awesome Beef Recipe

(Prep + Cooking Time: 1 hour 10 minutes | **Servings:** 4)

Ingredients:

- 1 lb. skirt steak, cut into 2-inch chunks
- 1 small jalapeño
- 1 (1.2-ounce) package rendang curry paste
- 1/2 cup water
- 1 cup full-fat coconut milk
- ¾ cup finely minced onions
- 1 tbsp. minced fresh ginger
- 1 tbsp. minced garlic
- 2 tbsp. vegetable oil
- 2 tbsp. unsweetened shredded coconut, toasted, for garnish

Directions:

1. Now Press "Sauté" on the Instant Pot. When the pot is hot, add the oil. When the oil is hot, add the onions, ginger, garlic and jalapeño, stirring to coat with the oil. Add the curry paste. Cook, stirring, until the curry paste is lightly toasted, 3 to 4 minutes.
2. Add the steak and cook, stirring to coat with the spices, for about 2 minutes. Pour in ¼ cup of the water and stir to scrape up the browned bits from the bottom of the pot. Add the remaining ¼ cup water and ½ cup of the coconut milk. Now Press "Cancel"
3. Now secure the lid on the pot and close the valve. Now Press "Manual" and set the pot at "High" pressure for 25 minutes

4. After completing the cooking time, allow the pot to sit undisturbed for 10 minutes, then release any remaining pressure
5. If you want the dish a little less saucy, select "Sauté" to cook off some of the water. Add the remaining ½ cup coconut milk and stir well to combine. Now Press "Cancel". Divide among four bowls and garnish with the shredded coconut before serving.

Rice & Beef Soup

(**Prep + Cooking Time:** 25 minutes | **Servings:** 6)

Ingredients:

- 1 lb. beef meat, ground.
- 3 garlic cloves; minced.
- 1 potato, cubed
- 1 yellow onion; chopped.
- 28 oz. canned beef stock
- 14 oz. canned tomatoes, crushed.
- 1/2 cup white rice
- 15 oz. canned garbanzo beans, rinsed
- 12 oz. spicy V8 juice
- 1/2 cup frozen peas
- 2 carrots, thinly sliced
- 1 tbsp. vegetable oil
- 1 celery rib; chopped.
- Salt and black pepper to the taste

Directions:

1. Set your instant pot on Sauté mode; add beef; then stir well. cook until it browns and transfer to a plate.
2. Add the oil to your pot and heat it up
3. Add celery and onion, stir and cook for 5 minutes.
4. Add garlic, stir and cook for 1 minute more
5. Add V8 juice, stock, tomatoes, rice, beans, carrots, potatoes, beef, salt and pepper; then stir well. seal the instant pot lid and cook at High for 5 minutes.
6. Quick release the pressure, open the instant pot lid and set it on Simmer mode
7. Add more salt and pepper if needed and peas; then stir well. bring to a simmer, transfer to bowls and serve hot.

Asian Ground Lamb

(**Prep + Cooking Time:** 45 minutes | **Servings:** 4)

Ingredients:

- 1-lb. ground lamb
- 1 cup frozen peas, thawed
- 1/2 cinnamon stick, broken into small pieces
- 1/4 cup water
- 1 cup chopped yellow onions
- 4 cardamom pods
- 1 tbsp. vegetable oil
- 1 tbsp. minced fresh ginger
- 1 tbsp. minced garlic
- 1/2 tsp. ground coriander
- 1/2 tsp. ground cumin
- 1/2 tsp. ground turmeric
- 1/2 tsp. cayenne pepper
- 1 tsp. Garam Masala
- 1 tsp. salt or as your liking

Directions:

1. Now Press "Sauté" on the Instant Pot. When the pot is hot, add the ghee. When the ghee has melted, add the cinnamon sticks and cardamom pods and let them sizzle for about 10 seconds.
2. Add the onions, garlic and ginger. Cook, stirring, for 1 to 2 minutes. Add the lamb and cook, stirring just enough to break up the clumps, for 2 to 3 minutes. Add the garam masala, salt, turmeric, cayenne, coriander, cumin and water. Now Press "Cancel"
3. Now secure the lid on the pot and close the valve. Now Press "Manual" and set the pot at "High" pressure for 10 minutes
4. After completing the cooking time, allow the pot to sit undisturbed for 10 minutes, then release any remaining pressure. Stir in the peas. Cover and allow to stand until the peas are heated through, about 5 minutes.

Hamburger Stew

(Prep + Cooking Time: 35 minutes | **Servings:** 4)

Ingredients:

- 5 ounces tomato sauce
- 1 lb. 85% lean ground beef
- 6 cups frozen mixed vegetables (corn, okra, carrots, peas and green beans)
- Juice of 1 lemon
- 1 tbsp. chicken broth base
- 2 tbsp. tomato paste
- 1 tbsp. soy sauce
- 3 tbsp. apple cider vinegar
- 1 tsp. salt or as your liking
- 2 tsp. black pepper

Directions:

1. Now Press "Sauté" on the Instant Pot. When the pot is hot, add the beef and cook, stirring just enough to break up the clumps, for 2 to 3 minutes. Stir in the frozen vegetables, tomato sauce, vinegar, tomato paste, chicken broth base, soy sauce, salt and pepper. Now Press "Cancel"
2. Now secure the lid on the pot and close the valve. Now Press "Manual" and set the pot at "High" pressure for 5 minutes
3. After completing the cooking time, allow the pot to sit undisturbed for 10 minutes, then release any remaining pressure. Stir in the lemon juice and serve.

Sausage and Kale Soup

(Prep + Cooking Time: 35 minutes | **Servings:** 4)

Ingredients:

- 1 lb. bulk hot Italian sausage meat
- 1 (12-ounce) package frozen kale
- 3 cups water
- 1/2 cup heavy cream
- 1/2 cup shredded Parmesan cheese
- 2 cups diced potatoes
- 1 cup diced yellow onions
- 6 garlic cloves; minced

Directions:

1. Now Press "Sauté" on the Instant Pot. When the pot is hot, add the sausage. Cook, stirring to break up the clumps, until it is the texture of ground beef, 3 to 4 minutes.
2. Add the onions and garlic and stir well to combine. Add the potatoes and kale and stir well to combine. Stir in the water. Now Press "Cancel".
3. Now secure the lid on the pot and close the valve. Now Press "Manual" and set the pot at "High" pressure for 6 minutes
4. After completing the cooking time, allow the pot to sit undisturbed for 5 minutes, then release any remaining pressure
5. Add the cream and stir well to combine. Divide among four bowls. Top with the Parmesan and serve.

Beef with Cracked Wheat

(Prep + Cooking Time: 1 hour 25 minutes | **Servings:** 4)

Ingredients:

For Meat:

- 1 lb. beef cut into 1-inch cubes
- 2 cups thinly sliced yellow onions
- 1/4 cup Ghee
- 4 cups water
- 1/2 cup split chana dal
- 1/2 cup cracked wheat
- 1 tbsp. minced garlic
- 1 tbsp. minced fresh ginger
- 2 tsp. Garam Masala
- 1 tsp. ground cumin
- 1 tsp. ground coriander
- 1 tsp. ground turmeric
- 1 tsp. cayenne pepper

For Serving:

- 1/2 cup chopped fresh cilantro
- 1/4 cup julienned fresh ginger

Directions:

1. For meat: Select "Sauté" on the Instant Pot. When the pot is hot, add the ghee. When the ghee has melted, add the onions and cook, stirring, until browned and crispy, about 10 minutes. Remove half the onions and set them aside for garnish. Now Press "Cancel".
2. Add the beef, water, cracked wheat, dal, ginger, garlic, 1 tsp. of the garam masala, the cumin, coriander, turmeric and cayenne to the pot
3. Now secure the lid on the pot and close the valve. Now Press "Manual" and set the pot at "High" pressure for 35 minutes. After completing the cooking time, allow the pot to sit undisturbed for 10 minutes, then release any remaining pressure
4. Using an immersion blender, puree the mixture directly in the pot until you have a smooth, thick stew. Add the remaining 1 tsp. garam masala and stir to combine
5. Divide the meat mixture among four bowls and garnish with the cilantro, ginger and reserved fried onions on top and serve.

Pulled Pork

(Prep + Cooking Time: 1 hour 15 minutes | Servings: 4)

Ingredients:

- 1 lb. boneless pork shoulder, trimmed and cut into cubes
- 1/2 cup water
- 1 onion; sliced
- 4 garlic cloves; sliced
- 2 tbsp. coconut oil
- 1/4 tsp. chipotle chile powder
- 1/4 tsp. smoked paprika
- 1/2 tsp. dried oregano
- 1/2 tsp. ground cumin
- 1/4 tsp. ancho chile powder
- Juice of 1 lemon
- 1 tsp. salt or as your liking
- 1 tsp. black pepper

Directions:

1. In your Instant Pot, combine the onion and garlic and toss to combine. Place the pork in a large bowl. In a small bowl, combine the salt, pepper, oregano, cumin, ancho chile powder, chipotle chile powder and paprika and stir to thoroughly combine. Sprinkle the seasonings over the pork. Drizzle with the lemon juice. Toss until everything is well coated.
2. Place the pork on top of the onions and garlic in the Instant Pot. Pour the water into the large bowl and swirl to rinse out the last of the spices; pour the water over the pork
3. Now secure the lid on the pot and close the valve. Now Press "Manual" and set the pot at "High" pressure for 35 minutes. After completing the cooking time, allow the pot to sit undisturbed until the pressure has released. Transfer the pork to a shallow dish.
4. Now Press "Sauté". Allow the sauce to reduce while you finish the dish
5. Using two forks, shred the meat. Heat the coconut oil in a large cast-iron pan over high heat. Lay the shredded meat in a flat layer in the pan and let it sit undisturbed
6. When it starts to brown, stir, then keep cooking until well crisped. Add a little of the concentrated sauce to the skillet. Select "Cancel". Serve the pork with guacamole, salsa, sour cream, cotija.

Corned Beef Recipe

(Prep + Cooking Time: 60 minutes | Servings: 6)

Ingredients:

- 4 lb. beef brisket
- 11 oz. celery, thinly sliced
- 17 oz. water
- 1 tbsp. dill; dried
- 3 bay leaves
- 2 oranges, sliced
- 4 cinnamon sticks, cut into halves
- 2 garlic cloves; minced.
- 2 yellow onions, thinly sliced
- Salt and black pepper to the taste

Directions:

1. Put the beef in a bowl, add some water to cover, leave aside to soak for a few hours, drain and transfer to your instant pot
2. Add celery, orange slices, onions, garlic, bay leaves, dill, cinnamon, dill, salt and pepper and 17 oz. water.
3. Stir, seal the instant pot lid and cook at High for 50 minutes
4. Quick release the pressure, leave beef aside to cool down for 5 minutes, transfer to a cutting board, slice and divide among plates
5. Drizzle the juice and veggies from the pot over beef and serve.

Chinese Steamed Ribs

(Prep + Cooking Time: 45 minutes | **Servings:** 4)

Ingredients:

- 1 ½ lbs. pork spareribs, cut into individual ribs
- 1/4 cup chopped scallions, for garnish
- 1/4 cup water
- 1 tbsp. Shaoxing wine
- 1 tbsp. dark soy sauce
- 1 tbsp. minced fresh ginger
- 2 tbsp. black bean garlic sauce
- 1 tbsp. honey
- 1 tbsp. vegetable oil
- 1 tbsp. minced garlic
- 1 tsp. toasted sesame oil; optional

Directions:

1. Now Press "Sauté" on the Instant Pot. When the pot is hot, add the oil.
2. When the oil is hot, add the garlic and ginger. Cook, stirring continuously, for 30 seconds. Add the black bean sauce, wine, soy sauce, agave and water. Stir well to combine. Now Press "Cancel".
3. Add the spareribs and stir until the ribs are well coated with the sauce
4. Now secure the lid on the pot and close the valve. Now Press "Manual" and set the pot at "High" pressure for 15 minutes
5. After completing the cooking time, allow the pot to sit undisturbed for 10 minutes, then release any remaining pressure
6. Using a slotted spoon, transfer the ribs to a serving platter. Drizzle with the sesame oil, if desired, sprinkle with the scallions and serve.

Korean Beef Dish

(Prep + Cooking Time: 35 minutes | **Servings:** 6)

Ingredients:

- 2 lb. beefsteak, cut into thin strips
- 1/4 cup Korean soybean paste
- 1 cup chicken stock
- 1/4 tsp. red pepper flakes
- 12 oz. extra firm tofu, cubed
- 1 oz. shiitake mushroom caps, cut into quarters
- 1 yellow onion, thinly sliced
- 1 zucchini, cubed
- 1 chili pepper, sliced
- 1 scallion; chopped.
- Salt and black pepper to the taste

Directions:

1. Set your instant pot on Sauté mode; add stock and soybean paste, stir and simmer for 2 minutes.
2. Add beef, salt, pepper, and pepper flakes stir, seal the instant pot lid and cook at High for 15 minutes
3. Quick release the pressure, add tofu, onion, zucchini and mushrooms; then stir well. bring to a boil, seal the instant pot lid and cook at High for 4 minutes more
4. Release the pressure again, carefully open the lid; add more salt and pepper to the taste, add chili and scallion; then stir well. divide into bowls and serve

Mexican Lamb Recipe

(Prep + Cooking Time: 60 minutes **| Servings:** 4)

Ingredients:

- 3 lb. lamb shoulder, cubed
- 19 oz. enchilada sauce
- 3 garlic cloves; minced.
- 1 yellow onion; chopped
- 2 tbsp. extra virgin olive oil
- 1/2 bunch cilantro; finely chopped
- corn tortillas, warm for serving
- lime wedges for serving
- refried beans for serving
- Salt to the taste

Directions:

1. Put enchilada sauce in a bowl, add lamb meat and marinade for 24 hours
2. Set your instant pot on Sauté mode; add the oil and heat it up.
3. Add onions and garlic, stir and cook for 5 minutes
4. Add lamb, salt and its marinade; then stir well. bring to a boil, seal the instant pot lid and cook at High for 45 minutes.
5. Quick release the pressure, take meat and put on a cutting board and leave aside to cool down for a few minutes.
6. Shred meat and put in a bowl
7. Add cooking sauce to it and stir.
8. Divide meat on tortillas, sprinkle cilantro on each, add beans, squeeze lime juice, roll and serve.

Wonton Meatballs

(Prep + Cooking Time: 45 minutes **| Servings:** 4)

Ingredients:

- 1 lb. ground pork
- 2 large eggs, lighten beaten
- 2 cups water
- 1/4 cup chopped fresh cilantro
- 1/4 cup chopped scallions
- 1 tbsp. minced garlic
- 1 tbsp. minced fresh ginger
- 1 tsp. oyster sauce
- 2 tsp. soy sauce, plus more for serving
- 1 tsp. black pepper
- 1/2 tsp. salt or as your liking

Directions:

1. In a large bowl, combine the pork, eggs, scallions, cilantro, ginger, garlic, soy sauce, oyster sauce, pepper and salt. Using your hands, gently mix until all the ingredients are thoroughly incorporated.
2. Divide the mixture into 12 equal portions. Place each in the cup of a baby food container (see headnote). Lightly cover with aluminum foil
3. Pour the water into the Instant Pot. Place a steamer rack with handles in the pot. Gently stack the baby food containers on top of the rack
4. Now secure the lid on the pot and close the valve. Now Press the STEAM setting and set to cook for 10 minutes. After completing the cooking time, allow the pot to sit undisturbed for 5 minutes, then release any remaining pressure
5. Using silicone oven mitts, carefully remove the baby food containers. Use a meat thermometer to ensure the meatballs have reached an internal temperature of 160°F. If not, re-secure the lid on the pot and close the pressure-release valve. Cook for an additional 2 to 3 minutes on the "Steam" setting
6. At the end of the second cooking time, allow the pot to sit undisturbed for 5 minutes, then release any remaining pressure. Unmold and serve the meatballs with soy sauce.

Sunday Brussels Sprouts.

(**Prep + Cooking Time:** 35 minutes | **Servings:** 6)

Ingredients:

- 6 cups. Brussels sprouts; chopped
- 5 slices bacon; chopped
- 2 tbsp. water
- 2 tbsp. balsamic reduction
- 1/4 cup. soft goat cheese, optional
- 1/4 tsp. salt
- Pepper, to taste

Directions:

1. Press the "Sauté" key of the Instant Pot. Add the bacon and sauté until desired crispiness is achieved.
2. Add the Brussels sprouts and stir to coat with the scrumptious bacon fat.
3. Add the water and sprinkle with pepper and salt. Cook for about 4 to 6 minutes, stirring occasionally, and continue sautéing until the Brussel sprouts are crisp. Transfer into a serving dish.
4. Drizzle with balsamic reduction and, if desired, sprinkle with crumbled goat cheese.

Tips: If a bit of bacon stuck in the inner pot, put 1 cup. of soapy water in the pot and PRESS SAUTÉ. The browned bits will come right off. Easy to clean up afterwards.

Tasty Beef Dish

(**Prep + Cooking Time:** 40 minutes | **Servings:** 4)

Ingredients:

- 1 ½ lb. beef stew meat, cubed
- 4 potatoes; chopped.
- 1 yellow onion; chopped.
- 2 tbsp. red wine
- 2 garlic cloves; minced.
- 2 cups water
- 2 tbsp. extra virgin olive oil
- 4 tbsp. white flour
- 2 celery stalks; chopped.
- 1 bay leaf
- 1/2 tsp. thyme; dried
- 1/2 bunch parsley; chopped.
- 2 carrots; chopped.
- 2 cups beef stock
- Salt and black pepper to the taste

Directions:

1. Season beef with salt and pepper and mix with half of the flour
2. Set your instant pot on Sauté mode; add oil and heat it up.
3. Add beef, brown for 2 minutes and transfer to a bowl.
4. Add onion to your pot, stir and cook for 3 minutes
5. Add garlic, stir and cook for 1 minute.
6. Add wine, stir well and cook for 15 seconds.
7. Add the rest of the flour and stir well for 2 minutes.
8. Return meat to pot, add stock, water, bay leaf and thyme; then stir well. seal the instant pot lid and cook on High for 12 minutes
9. Quick release the pressure, carefully open the lid; add carrots, celery and potatoes; then stir well. close the lid again and cook at High for 5 minutes
10. Release the pressure naturally for 10 minutes, then release remaining pressure by turning the valve to 'Venting', carefully open the lid; divide among plates and serve with parsley sprinkled on top

Pork Shoulder Tacos

(Prep + Cooking Time: 30 minutes | **Servings:** 4)

Ingredients:

- 1 ½ lbs. boneless pork shoulder, cut into 5 large pieces
- 1/4 cup water
- 1 tsp. ground cumin
- 1 tsp. onion powder
- 1 tsp. smoked paprika
- 1 tbsp. brown sugar
- 1 tsp. garlic powder
- 1/2 tsp. ancho chile powder
- 1 tsp. salt or as your liking
- 1/2 tsp. black pepper
- Corn tortillas, for serving

Directions:

1. In a large bowl, combine the brown sugar, garlic powder, onion powder, smoked paprika, cumin, salt, ancho chile powder and pepper. Stir well to combine. Add the pork to the bowl and toss to coat, massaging the spices into the meat. Allow to stand at room temperature for 30 minutes
2. Transfer the meat to the Instant Pot. Add the water
3. Now secure the lid on the pot and close the valve. Now Press "Manual" and set the pot at "High" pressure for 25 minutes.
4. After completing the cooking time, allow the pot to sit undisturbed for 10 minutes, then release any remaining pressure
5. Using two forks, shred the meat, making sure it's submerged under the cooking liquid until ready to serve. Serve the shredded pork in corn tortillas with any desired toppings.

Meatballs and Tomato Sauce

(Prep + Cooking Time: 20 minutes | **Servings:** 6)

Ingredients:

- 1 onion; chopped.
- 1/2 cup bread crumbs
- 1/2 tsp. oregano; dried
- 1/3 cup parmesan, grated
- 1 tbsp. extra-virgin olive oil
- 2 ¾ cups tomato puree
- 1/2 cup milk
- 1 lb. ground meat
- one egg, whisked
- 1 carrot; chopped.
- 1/2 celery stalk; chopped.
- 2 cups water
- Salt and black pepper to the taste

Directions:

1. In a bowl, mix bread crumbs with cheese, half of the onion, oregano, salt and pepper and stir
2. Add milk and meat and stir well.
3. Add the egg and stir well again.
4. Set your instant pot on Sauté mode; add oil and heat it up
5. Add onion, stir and cook for 3 minutes.
6. Add celery and carrot, tomato puree, water and salt and stir again
7. Shape meatballs and add them to the pot, toss them to coat, seal the instant pot lid and cook at High for 5 minutes
8. Release the pressure naturally for 10 minutes, then release remaining pressure by turning the valve to 'Venting', open the instant pot lid and serve with your favorite spaghetti

Pork Chile Verde

(Prep + Cooking Time: 60 minutes | **Servings:** 8)

Ingredients:
- 2 lbs. pork shoulder roast; trimmed and cut into 6 large pieces
- 2 poblano peppers
- 3 tomatillos, husked and rinsed
- 1 medium tomato; chopped
- 6 garlic cloves
- 3 jalapeños
- 1/4 cup chopped fresh cilantro
- 1 tbsp. fish sauce
- 2 tsp. ground cumin
- Salt as your liking

Directions:
1. In your Instant Pot, combine the tomatillos, tomato, garlic, jalapeños and poblanos. Place the meat on top of the vegetables. Season the meat with the cumin and salt to taste.
2. Now secure the lid on the pot and close the valve. Now Press "Manual" and set the pot at "High" pressure for 30 minutes. After completing the cooking time, allow the pot to sit undisturbed until the pressure has released
3. Using tongs, carefully transfer the pork to a platter (the meat is falling apart at this stage, so you have to be a little careful)
4. Add the cilantro and fish sauce to the pot. Using an immersion blender, puree the vegetables directly in the pot until there are no big chunks left. Return the pork to the pot and stir gently to coat with the sauce.

Korean Beef Stew

(Prep + Cooking Time: 45 minutes | **Servings:** 6)

Ingredients:
- 1 lb. beef (preferably a fatty cut), cut into 2-inch cubes
- 1/2 cup sliced scallions, for serving
- 2 cups prepared kimchi
- 2 cups water
- 1 cup chopped yellow onions
- 1 cup dried shiitake mushrooms
- 1 tbsp. toasted sesame oil
- 1 tbsp. dark soy sauce
- 1 tbsp. gochujang (Korean red chile paste)
- 1 tbsp. minced garlic
- 1 tbsp. minced fresh ginger
- 1/2 tsp. cayenne pepper
- 1/2 tsp. sugar
- Salt to taste

Directions:
1. In your Instant Pot, combine the beef, kimchi, water, onions, mushrooms, garlic, ginger, sesame oil, soy sauce, gochugaru, gochujang and sugar
2. Now secure the lid on the pot and close the valve. Now Press "Manual" and set the pot at "High" pressure for 15 minutes
3. After completing the cooking time, allow the pot to sit undisturbed until the pressure has released. Taste and season with salt. Stir in the scallions and the tofu, if desired and serve.

Pork Chops with Scallion Rice

(Prep + Cooking Time: 35 minutes | **Servings:** 4)

Ingredients:

- 4 bone-in pork chops cut into ¼ inch thick
- 1 bunch scallions; sliced
- 1 cup long-grain white rice
- 1 ¼ cups water
- 1 tsp. salted butter, vegetable oil
- 1 ½ tsp. salt or as your liking
- 1 ½ tsp. black pepper

Directions:

1. Season the pork chops with ½ tsp. each of the salt and pepper. Now Press "Sauté" on the Instant Pot. When the pot is hot, add the butter.
2. When the butter has melted, add the chops to the pot and cook until browned on each side, about 5 minutes total; when you turn the chops to brown the second side, add the scallions. Transfer the chops to a plate
3. Add the rice to the pot. Stir to coat the rice with the butter and rendered pork fat. Add the water, stirring to scrape up the browned bits at the bottom of the pot. Add the remaining 1 tsp. each salt and pepper and stir to combine. Return the pork chops to the pot. Now Press "Cancel"
4. Now secure the lid on the pot and close the valve. Now Press "Manual" and set the pot at "High" pressure for 5 minutes. After completing the cooking time, allow the pot to sit undisturbed until the pressure has released. Serve the pork chops with the rice.

Poultry Recipes

Delicious Chicken Sandwiches

(Prep + Cooking Time: 25 minutes | Servings: 8)

Ingredients:

- 20 oz. canned pineapple and its juice; chopped.
- 6 chicken breasts; skinless and boneless
- 1 tsp. soy sauce
- 1 tbsp. cornstarch
- 1/4 cup brown sugar
- 8 hamburger buns
- 12 oz. canned orange juice
- 2 tbsp. lemon juice
- 15 oz. canned peaches and their juice
- 8 grilled pineapple slices; for serving

Directions:

1. In a bowl, mix orange juice with soy sauce, lemon juice, canned pineapples pieces, peaches and sugar and stir well
2. Pour half of this mix in your instant pot; add chicken and pour the rest of the sauce over meat.
3. Cover the pot and cook at High for 12 minutes
4. Quick release the pressure, take the chicken and put on a cutting board
5. Shred meat and leave aside for now.
6. In a bowl; mix cornstarch with 1 tablespoon cooking juice and stir well.
7. Transfer the sauce to a pot, add cornstarch mix and chicken, stir and cook for a few more minutes.
8. Divide this chicken mix on hamburger buns; top with grilled pineapple pieces and serve

Simple Chicken Delight

(Prep + Cooking Time: 50 minutes | Servings: 4)

Ingredients:

- 6 chicken thighs
- 1 tsp. vegetable oil
- 15 oz. canned tomatoes; chopped.
- 1 yellow onion; chopped.
- 2 tbsp. tomato paste
- 1/2 cup white wine
- 2 cups chicken stock
- 1 ½ lb. potatoes; chopped.
- 1 celery stalk; chopped.
- 1/4 lb. baby carrots; cut into halves
- 1/2 tsp. thyme; dried
- Salt and black pepper to the taste

Directions:

1. Set your instant pot on Sauté mode; add oil and heat it up
2. Add chicken pieces; salt and pepper to the taste and brown them for 4 minutes on each side.
3. Take chicken out of the pot and leave on a plate for now.
4. Add onion, carrots, celery, thyme and tomato paste to the pot, stir and cook for 5 minutes.
5. Add white wine and salt; stir and cook for 3 minutes
6. Add chicken stock, chicken pieces and chopped tomatoes and stir.
7. Place the steamer basket in the pot; add potatoes in it, seal the instant pot lid and cook at High for 30 minutes.
8. Quick release the pressure, take potatoes out of the pot and also take chicken pieces out.
9. Shred chicken meat and return to pot.
10. Also return potatoes; more salt and pepper; then stir well. divide among plates and serve

Chickpea Chicken Masala

(**Prep + Cooking Time:** 35 minutes | **Servings:** 4)

Ingredients:

- 3 lb. chicken drumsticks and thighs
- 1 yellow onion; finely chopped
- 2 tbsp. butter
- 1/2 cup chicken stock
- 15 oz. canned tomatoes; crushed.
- 1/4 cup lemon juice
- 15 oz. canned chickpeas; drained
- 4 garlic cloves; minced.
- 1 lb. spinach; chopped.
- 1/2 cup heavy cream
- 1 tbsp. ginger; grated
- 1/2 cup cilantro; chopped.
- 1 ½ tsp. paprika
- 1 tbsp. cumin; ground.
- 1 ½ tsp. coriander; ground.
- 1 tsp. turmeric; ground.
- Salt and black pepper to the taste
- A pinch of cayenne pepper

Directions:

1. Set your instant pot on Sauté mode; add butter and melt it
2. Add ginger, onion, and garlic, stir and cook for 5 minutes.
3. Add paprika, cumin, coriander, cayenne, turmeric, salt, and pepper, stir and cook for 30 seconds.
4. Add tomatoes and spinach; stir and cook for 2 minutes
5. Add half of the cilantro, chicken pieces, and stock; then stir well. seal the instant pot lid and cook at High for 15 minutes
6. Quick release the pressure, carefully open the lid; add heavy cream, chickpeas, lemon juice, more salt, and pepper; then stir well. set the pot on Sauté mode again and simmer for 3 minutes.
7. Sprinkle the rest of the cilantro on top; then stir well. divide among plates and serve.

Delicious Chicken in Tomatillo Sauce

(**Prep + Cooking Time:** 35 minutes | **Servings:** 6)

Ingredients:

- 1 lb. chicken thighs; skinless and boneless
- 2 tbsp. extra virgin olive oil
- 5 oz. canned garbanzo beans; drained
- 1 yellow onion; thinly sliced
- 1 garlic clove; crushed.
- 4 oz. canned green chilies; chopped.
- 1 handful cilantro; finely chopped
- 15 oz. rice; already cooked
- 5 oz. tomatoes; chopped.
- 15 oz. cheddar cheese; grated
- 4 oz. black olives; pitted and chopped.
- Salt and black pepper to the taste
- 15 oz. canned tomatillos; chopped.

Directions:

1. Set your instant pot on Sauté mode; add oil and heat it up
2. Add onions, stir and cook for 5 minutes.
3. Add garlic, stir and cook 15 more seconds.
4. Add chicken, chilies, salt, pepper, cilantro, and tomatillos; then stir well. seal the instant pot lid and cook on Poultry mode for 8 minutes
5. Quick release the pressure, carefully open the lid; take the chicken out and shred it.
6. Return chicken to pot; add rice, beans, set the instant pot on Sauté mode again and cook for 1 minute.
7. Add cheese, tomatoes, and olives; then stir well. cook for 2 minutes more; divide among plates and serve

Moroccan Chicken

(**Prep + Cooking Time:** 35 minutes | **Servings:** 4)

Ingredients:

- 6 chicken thighs
- 1 tsp. cloves
- 2 tbsp. extra virgin olive oil
- 10 cardamom pods
- 1/2 tsp. cumin
- 1/2 tsp. ginger
- 1/2 cup parsley; finely chopped
- 1/2 tsp. turmeric
- 1/2 tsp. cinnamon; ground.
- 2 bay leaves
- 1/2 tsp. coriander
- 2 yellow onions; chopped.
- 2 tbsp. tomato paste
- 5 garlic cloves; chopped.
- 1/4 cup cranberries; dried
- Juice of 1 lemon
- 1 cup green olives
- 1 cup chicken stock
- 1 tsp. paprika
- 1/4 cup white wine

Directions:

1. In a bowl; mix bay leaf with cardamom, cloves, coriander, ginger, cumin, cinnamon, turmeric and paprika and stir
2. Set your instant pot on Sauté mode; add the oil and heat up
3. Add chicken thighs; brown for a few minutes and transfer to a plate.
4. Add onion to the pot, stir and cook for 4 minutes
5. Add garlic, stir and cook for 1 minute.
6. Add wine, tomato paste, spices from the bowl, stock and chicken
7. Stir; seal the Instant Pot lid and cook at High for 15 minutes.
8. Quick release the pressure, discard bay leaf, cardamom, and cloves, add olives, cranberries, lemon juice and parsley; then stir well. divide chicken mix among plates and serve

Chicken Curry

(**Prep + Cooking Time:** 40 minutes | **Servings:** 6)

Ingredients:

- 1 lb. boneless; skinless chicken thighs, cut into 3 pieces each
- 1 large potato; peeled and cut into 1-inch chunks
- 1 Scotch bonnet chile; sliced
- 1 cup chopped yellow onion
- 3 sprigs fresh thyme
- 1 cup water
- 2 tbsp. vegetable oil
- 1 tbsp. minced fresh ginger
- 1 tbsp. minced garlic
- 4 ½ tsp. Jamaican curry powder
- 1 tsp. salt or as your liking
- 1/2 tsp. ground allspice

Directions:

1. Now Press "Sauté" on the Instant Pot. When the pot is hot, add the oil. When the oil is hot, add the ginger and garlic. Cook, stirring continuously, just until fragrant, about 20 seconds.
2. Add the onion and cook, stirring, for 1 to 2 minutes. Add the curry powder, chile, thyme, salt and allspice. Stir to combine
3. If anything is browning or sticking to the bottom of the pot, add ¼ to ⅓ cup water and stir, scraping up the browned bits from the bottom and allowing the water to evaporate. Now Press "Cancel".
4. Add the chicken, potato and the 1 cup water to the pot. Stir to combine.
5. Now secure the lid on the pot and close the valve. Now Press "Manual" and set the pot at "High" pressure for 6 minutes
6. After completing the cooking time, allow the pot to sit undisturbed for 10 minutes, then release any remaining pressure.

Cheering Chicken Wings

(**Prep + Cooking Time:** 35 minutes | **Servings:** 6)

Ingredients:

- 12 chicken wings; cut into 24 pieces
- 1 cup yogurt
- 1 tbsp. parsley; finely chopped
- 4 tbsp. hot sauce
- 1 cup water
- 1/4 cup tomato puree
- 1 lb. celery; cut into thin matchsticks
- 1/4 cup honey
- Salt to the taste

Directions:

1. Put 1 cup water into your instant pot.
2. Place chicken wings in the steamer basket of your pot, seal the instant pot lid and cook at High for 19 minutes
3. Meanwhile; in a bowl, mix tomato puree with hot sauce, salt and honey and stir very well
4. Quick release the pressure, add chicken wings to honey mix and toss them to coat.
5. Arrange chicken wings on a lined baking sheet and introduce in preheated broiler for 5 minutes.
6. Arrange celery sticks on a platter and add chicken wings next to it.
7. In a bowl; mix yogurt with parsley, stir well and place next to the platter
8. Serve right away.

Delicious Duck Chili

(**Prep + Cooking Time:** 1 hour and 10 minutes | **Servings:** 4)

Ingredients:

- 1 lb. northern beans, soaked and rinsed
- 1 yellow onion; cut into half
- 1 garlic heat; top trimmed off
- 2 cloves
- 1 bay leaf
- 6 cups water
- Salt to the taste

For the duck:

- 1 lb. duck; ground.
- 15 oz. canned tomatoes and their juices; chopped.
- 4 oz. canned green chilies and their juice
- 1 tsp. brown sugar
- 1 tbsp. vegetable oil
- 1 yellow onion; minced.
- 2 carrots; chopped.
- Salt and black pepper to the taste
- A handful cilantro; chopped.

Directions:

1. Put the beans in your instant pot.
2. Add whole onion, garlic head, cloves, bay leaf, the water and salt to the taste; then stir well. seal the Instant Pot lid and cook at High for 25 minutes
3. Quick release the pressure; carefully open the lid; discard solids and transfer beans to a bowl.
4. Heat up a pan with the oil over medium high heat, add carrots and chopped onion, season with salt and pepper to the taste, stir and cook for 5 minutes
5. Add duck, stir and cook for 5 minutes.
6. Add chilies and tomatoes, bring to a simmer and take off heat.
7. Pour this into your instant pot, seal the Instant Pot lid and cook at High for 5 minutes.
8. Release pressure naturally for 15 minutes; carefully open the lid; add more salt and pepper, beans and brown sugar, stir and divide among plates.
9. Serve with cilantro on top

Chicken Salad

(Prep + Cooking Time: 60 minutes | **Servings:** 2)

Ingredients:
- 1 chicken breast, skinless and boneless
- 3 tbsp. extra virgin olive oil
- 1 tbsp. mustard
- 3 garlic cloves; minced.
- 1 tbsp. balsamic vinegar
- 1 tbsp. honey
- Mixed salad greens
- A handful cherry tomatoes; cut into halves
- 3 cups water
- Salt and black pepper to the taste

Directions:
1. In a bowl; mix 2 cups water with salt to the taste.
2. Add chicken to this mix, stir and keep in the fridge for 45 minutes.
3. Add 1 cup water to your instant pot, place chicken breast in the steamer basket of the pot, seal the instant pot lid and cook at High for 5 minutes.
4. Release the pressure naturally; leave chicken breast on a plate for 8 minutes and cut into thin strips.
5. In a bowl, mix garlic with salt and pepper to the taste, mustard, honey, vinegar and olive oil and whisk very well.
6. In a salad bowl; mix chicken strips with salad greens and tomatoes.
7. Drizzle the vinaigrette on top and serve.

Creamy Chicken Dish

(Prep + Cooking Time: 30 minutes | **Servings:** 6)

Ingredients:
- 2 lb. chicken breasts; skinless and boneless
- 4 oz. cream cheese
- 1 oz. ranch seasoning
- 2 slices bacon; chopped.
- 1 cup chicken stock
- Green onions; chopped for serving

Directions:
1. Set your instant pot on Sauté mode; add bacon and cook for 4 minutes
2. Add chicken; stock and seasoning; then stir well. seal the instant pot lid and cook at High for 12 minutes.
3. Quick release the pressure; carefully open the lid; transfer chicken to a cutting board and shred it
4. Remove 2/3 cup liquid from the pot, add cream cheese; set the pot to Sauté mode again and cook for 3 minutes.
5. Return chicken to pot; then stir well. add green onions, divide among plates and serve.

Potatoes and Chicken

(Prep + Cooking Time: 30 minutes | **Servings:** 4)

Ingredients:
- 2 lb. chicken thighs; skinless and boneless
- 3/4 cup chicken stock
- 1/4 cup lemon juice
- 2 lb. red potatoes; peeled and cut into quarters
- 2 tbsp. extra virgin olive oil
- 3 tbsp. Dijon mustard
- 2 tbsp. Italian seasoning
- Salt and black pepper to the taste

Directions:
1. Set your instant pot on sauté mode; add the oil and heat it up.
2. Add chicken thighs, salt, and pepper, stir and brown for 2 minutes
3. In a bowl; mix stock with mustard, Italian seasoning, and lemon juice and stir well.
4. Pour this over chicken, add potatoes; then stir well. seal the instant pot lid and cook at High for 15 minutes.
5. Quick release the pressure, carefully open the lid; stir chicken, divide among plates and serve

Braised Duck and Potatoes Recipe

(Prep + Cooking Time: 30 minutes | **Servings:** 4)

Ingredients:

- 1 duck, cut into small chunks
- 4 garlic cloves; minced.
- 4 tbsp. sugar
- 2 green onions; roughly chopped
- 4 tbsp. soy sauce
- 4 tbsp. sherry wine
- 1/4 cup water
- 1 potato; cut into cubes
- 1-inch ginger root; sliced
- A pinch of salt
- Black pepper to the taste

Directions:

1. Set your instant pot on Sauté mode; add duck pieces, stir and brown them for a few minutes
2. Add garlic, ginger, green onions, soy sauce, sugar, wine, a pinch of salt, black pepper and water; then stir well. close the lid; set the pot to Poultry mode and cook for 18 minutes
3. Quick release the pressure, carefully open the lid; add potatoes; then stir well. Seal the Instant Pot lid and cook at High for 5 minutes.
4. Quick release the pressure, divide braised duck among plates and serve

Barbeque Honey Chicken

(Prep + Cooking Time: 35 minutes | **Servings:** 4)

Ingredients:

- 2 lb. chicken wings
- 1/2 cup water
- 1/2 tsp. basil; dried
- 3/4 cup honey BBQ sauce
- 1/2 cup apple juice
- 1 tsp. red pepper; crushed.
- 2 tsp. paprika
- 1/2 cup brown sugar
- Salt and black pepper to the taste
- A pinch of cayenne pepper

Directions:

1. Put chicken wings in your instant pot
2. Add BBQ sauce, apple juice, salt, pepper, red pepper, paprika, basil, sugar, and water.
3. Stir, seal the Instant Pot lid and cook at High for 10 minutes
4. Quick release the pressure, carefully open the lid; transfer chicken to a baking sheet, add sauce all over, introduce in preheated broiler, broil for 7 minutes, flip chicken wings, broil for 7 more minutes, divide among plates and serve

Easy Turkey Chili

(Prep + Cooking Time: 20 minutes | **Servings:** 4)

Ingredients:

- 1 lb. turkey meat; ground.
- 15 oz. chickpeas; already cooked
- 1 ½ tsp. cumin
- 5 oz. water
- 1 yellow onion; chopped.
- 1 yellow bell pepper; chopped.
- 3 garlic cloves; chopped.
- 2 ½ tbsp. chili powder
- A pinch of cayenne pepper
- 12 oz. veggies stock
- Salt and black pepper to the taste

Directions:

1. Put turkey meat in your instant pot.
2. Add water; then stir well. seal the Instant Pot lid and cook at High for 5 minutes
3. Quick release the pressure; open the instant pot lid and add chickpeas, bell pepper, onion, garlic, chili powder, cumin, salt, pepper, cayenne and veggie stock.
4. Stir, seal the instant pot lid and cook at High for 5 minutes.
5. Release the pressure naturally for 10 minutes; then release remaining pressure by turning the valve to 'Venting', open the instant pot lid again, stir chili, divide it among plates and serve

Three Cup Chicken

(Prep + Cooking Time: 40 minutes | **Servings:** 6)

Ingredients:

- 2 lbs. boneless; skinless chicken thighs, halved
- 6 dried red chiles
- 1/4 cup soy sauce
- 1/4 cup rice wine
- 1/4 cup toasted sesame oil
- 1/4 cup chopped fresh Thai basil
- 1/4 cup crushed garlic cloves
- 1 tbsp. cornstarch mixed with 1 tbsp. water
- 2 tbsp. julienned fresh ginger
- Salt to taste

Directions:

1. Now Press "Sauté" on the Instant Pot. When the pot is hot, add the sesame oil. When the oil is hot, add the chiles, garlic and ginger
2. Cook, stirring frequently, until the ginger and garlic are just starting to crisp, about 2 minutes. Now Press "Cancel".
3. Add the chicken, soy sauce and rice wine to the pot and season with salt. Stir to combine.
4. Now secure the lid on the pot and close the valve. Now Press "Manual" and set the pot at "High" pressure for 7 minutes
5. After completing the cooking time, allow the pot to stand undisturbed for 10 minutes, then release any remaining pressure
6. Now Press "Sauté" on the Instant Pot. Add the basil and stir to combine. When the mixture comes to a boil, sprinkle over the xanthan gum and simmer until slightly thickened, 3 to 4 minutes. Now Press "Cancel". Serve.

Italian Chicken

(Prep + Cooking Time: 30 minutes | **Servings:** 6)

Ingredients:

- 2 lb. chicken breasts; skinless and boneless
- 1 tbsp. extra-virgin olive oil
- 3/4 cup marinara sauce
- 2 tbsp. pesto
- 3/4 cup mushrooms; sliced
- 1/2 cup green bell pepper; chopped.
- 1/2 cup red bell pepper; chopped.
- Salt and black pepper to the taste
- 3/4 cup yellow onion; diced
- Cheddar cheese, shredded for serving

Directions:

1. Set your instant pot on Sauté mode; add the oil and heat it up
2. Add onion, red and green bell pepper; salt and pepper to the taste, stir and cook for 4 minutes.
3. Add pesto, marinara sauce and chicken; then stir well. seal the instant pot lid and cook at High for 12 minutes
4. Quick release the pressure; carefully open the lid; remove chicken, place on a cutting board and shred,
5. Discard 2/3 cup cooking liquid, add mushrooms to the pot, set it on Sauté mode again and cook them for 3 minutes.
6. Return chicken; then stir well. divide among plates and serve with shredded cheese on top

Sesame Chicken Recipe

(**Prep + Cooking Time:** 18 minutes | **Servings:** 4)

Ingredients:

- 2 lb. chicken breasts; skinless; boneless and chopped
- 1/2 cup yellow onion; chopped.
- 1 tbsp. vegetable oil
- 3 tbsp. water
- 2 tsp. sesame oil
- 1/2 cup honey
- 2 tbsp. cornstarch
- 1/4 tsp. red pepper flakes
- 2 green onions; chopped.
- 1 tbsp. sesame seeds; toasted
- 2 garlic cloves; minced.
- 1/2 cup soy sauce
- 1/4 cup ketchup
- Salt and black pepper to the taste

Directions:

1. Set your instant pot on Sauté mode; add the oil and heat it up
2. Add garlic, onion, chicken, salt and pepper, stir and cook for 3 minutes.
3. Add pepper flakes, soy sauce and ketchup; then stir well. seal the instant pot lid and cook at High for 3 minutes
4. Quick release the pressure; carefully open the lid; add sesame oil and honey and stir.
5. In a bowl, mix cornstarch with water and stir well.
6. Add this to the pot, also add green onions and sesame seeds; stir well, divide among plates and serve

Garlic Chicken

(**Prep + Cooking Time:** 50 minutes | **Servings:** 4)

Ingredients:

- 1 lb. boneless; skinless chicken thighs
- 8 garlic cloves; chopped
- 1/4 cup heavy cream
- 1/4 cup water
- 2 tbsp. extra-virgin olive oil
- 2 tbsp. salted butter
- 1 tbsp. minced garlic
- 1 tbsp. Dijon mustard
- 1 tbsp. apple cider vinegar
- 2 tsp. herbes de Provence
- 1 tsp. salt or as your liking
- 1 tsp. black pepper

Directions:

1. In a large bowl, whisk together the mustard, vinegar; minced garlic, herbes de Provence, salt and pepper. Slowly whisk in the olive oil to emulsify and slightly thicken the mixture
2. Add the chicken and turn to coat. Allow the chicken to sit at room temperature for 30 minutes.
3. Now Press "Sauté" on the Instant Pot. When the pot is hot, add the butter. When the butter has melted, add the chicken, leaving as much marinade in the bowl as possible; set the marinade aside.
4. Cook the chicken, turning once, until lightly browned on both sides, 6 to 8 minutes. Transfer the chicken to a plate.
5. Add the chopped garlic to the pot. Cook, stirring continuously, until the garlic is fragrant and slightly softened, about 1 minute. Add the water and reserved marinade and whisk to combine. Return the chicken to the pot. Now Press "Cancel"
6. Now secure the lid on the pot and close the valve. Now Press "Manual" and set the pot at "High" pressure for 5 minutes
7. After completing the cooking time, allow the pot to sit undisturbed for 10 minutes, then release any remaining pressure. Transfer the chicken to a serving platter. Cover lightly with aluminum foil to keep warm.
8. Now Press "Sauté" on the Instant Pot. While stirring continuously, slowly add the cream in a steady stream. Cook, stirring, until the sauce starts to thicken, 5 to 8 minutes. Now Press "Cancel". Pour the sauce over the chicken and serve immediately.

Stuffed Chicken Breast

(**Prep + Cooking Time:** 40 minutes | **Servings:** 2)

Ingredients:

- 2 chicken breasts, skinless and boneless and butterflied
- 16 bacon strips
- 6 asparagus spears
- 1-piece ham; halved and cooked
- 2 cup water
- 4 mozzarella cheese slices
- Salt and black pepper to taste

Directions:

1. In a bowl; mix chicken breasts with salt and 1 cup water, stir, cover and keep in the fridge for 30 minutes
2. Pat dry chicken breasts and place them on a working surface
3. Add 2 slices of mozzarella, 1-piece ham and 3 asparagus pieces on each.
4. Add salt and pepper and roll up each chicken breast
5. Place 8 bacon strips on a working surface, add chicken and wrap it in bacon.
6. Repeat this with the rest of the bacon strips and the other chicken breast.
7. Put rolls in the steamer basket of the pot, add 1 cup water in the pot; cover and cook at High for 10 minutes.
8. Release the pressure quick, pat dry rolls with paper towels and leave them on a plate
9. Set your instant pot on Sauté mode; add chicken rolls and brown them for a few minutes. Divide among plates and serve

Chicken with Rice

(**Prep + Cooking Time:** 55 minutes | **Servings:** 4)

Ingredients:
For Rice:

- 1 cup water
- 1 cup basmati rice; rinsed and drained
- 1 tbsp. vegetable oil
- 1 tsp. salt or as your liking

For Chicken:

- 1 lb. boneless; skinless chicken thighs
- 4 ounces (½-stick) salted butter, cubed
- 1 (14.5-ounce) can diced tomatoes; undrained
- 1 tbsp. minced garlic
- 1 tbsp. minced fresh ginger
- 2 tsp. Garam Masala
- 1 tsp. ground turmeric
- 1 tsp. paprika
- 1 tsp. salt or as your liking
- 1 tsp. ground cumin
- 1 tsp. cayenne pepper
- 1/2 cup heavy cream
- ½ cup chopped fresh cilantro

Directions:

1. In a heatproof bowl 6-Inch or 7-inch, combine the rice, water, ghee and salt.
2. In your Instant Pot, combine the tomatoes and their juices, garlic, ginger, 1 tsp. of the garam masala, the turmeric, paprika, salt, cumin and cayenne
3. Stir to combine. Add the chicken. Place a tall steamer rack on top of the chicken mixture. Place the bowl of rice on the rack.
4. Now secure the lid on the pot and close the valve. Now Press "Manual" and set the pot at "High" pressure for 10 minutes
5. After completing the cooking time, allow the pot to sit undisturbed for 10 minutes, then release any remaining pressure.
6. Remove the bowl of rice and set aside. Remove the chicken and set aside on a plate.
7. Using an immersion blender, blend the sauce directly in the pot until smooth. Let the sauce cool for 5 minutes

8. Stir in the butter, cream, cilantro and remaining 1 tsp. garam masala. Remove half the sauce, transfer to a storage container and freeze or refrigerate for another use.
9. Break up the chicken into bite-size pieces and add it to the sauce in the pot. Serve the chicken with the hot rice.

Chicken Dish

(Prep + Cooking Time: 45 minutes | **Servings:** 8)

Ingredients:
- 1 whole chicken
- 1 tbsp. cumin powder
- 1 ½ tbsp. lemon zest
- 1 cup chicken stock
- 1 tbsp. thyme leaves
- 1/2 tsp. cinnamon powder
- 2 tsp. garlic powder
- 1 tbsp. coriander powder
- 1 tbsp. extra-virgin olive oil
- Salt and black pepper to the taste

Directions:
1. In a bowl, mix cinnamon with cumin; garlic, coriander, salt, pepper and lemon zest and stir well.
2. Rub chicken with half of the oil, then rub it inside and out with spices mix
3. Set your instant pot on Sauté mode; add the rest of the oil and heat it up.
4. Add chicken and brown it on all sides for 5 minutes
5. Add stock and thyme; then stir well. seal the instant pot lid and cook at High for 25 minutes.
6. Release the pressure naturally and transfer chicken to a platter.
7. Add cooking liquid over it and serve

Teriyaki Chicken Delight

(Prep + Cooking Time: 25 minutes | **Servings:** 6)

Ingredients:
- 2 lb. chicken breasts; skinless and boneless
- 2/3 cup teriyaki sauce
- 1 tbsp. honey
- 1/2 cup chicken stock
- A handful green onions; chopped.
- Salt and black pepper to the taste

Directions:
1. Set your instant pot on Sauté mode; add teriyaki sauce and honey, stir and simmer for 1 minute
2. Add stock; chicken, salt and pepper; then stir well. seal the instant pot lid and cook at High for 12 minutes
3. Quick release the pressure, take chicken breasts; place them on a cutting board and shred with 2 forks.
4. Remove 1/2 cup of cooking liquid; return shredded chicken to pot; add green onions; then stir well. divide among plates and serve

Chicken Curry

(Prep + Cooking Time: 30 minutes | **Servings:** 4)

Ingredients:
- 15 oz. chicken breast; chopped.
- 5 oz. canned coconut cream
- 1 tbsp. extra-virgin olive oil
- 1 yellow onion; thinly sliced
- 6 potatoes; cut into halves
- 1 bag chicken curry base
- 1/2 bunch coriander; chopped

Directions:
1. Set your instant pot on Sauté mode; add the oil and heat it up
2. Add chicken; stir and brown for 2 minutes. Add onion; stir and cook for 1 minute
3. In a bowl; mix curry base with coconut cream and stir.
4. Pour this over chicken; also add potatoes; then stir well. seal the instant pot lid and cook at High for 15 minutes.
5. Release pressure fast; carefully open the lid; divide curry among plates and serve with chopped coriander on top.

Chicken & Shrimp Recipe

(Prep + Cooking Time: 25 minutes | **Servings:** 4)

Ingredients:

- 8 oz. shrimp; peeled and deveined
- 8 oz. sausages; sliced
- 8 oz. chicken breasts; skinless; boneless and chopped.
- 2 tbsp. extra virgin olive oil
- 1 tsp. Creole seasoning
- 3 garlic cloves; minced.
- 1 yellow onion; chopped.
- 1 green bell pepper; chopped.
- 3 celery stalks; chopped.
- 1 cup white rice
- 1 cup chicken stock
- 2 cups canned tomatoes; chopped.
- 3 tbsp. parsley; chopped.
- 2 tsp. thyme; dried
- A pinch of cayenne pepper
- 2 tsp. Worcestershire sauce
- 1 dash Tabasco sauce

Directions:

1. In a bowl; mix Creole seasoning with thyme and cayenne and stir
2. Set your instant pot on Sauté mode; add the oil and heat it up.
3. Add chicken and brown for a few minutes
4. Add sausage slices, stir and cook for 3 minutes.
5. Add shrimp and half of the seasoning mix, stir and cook for 2 minutes.
6. Transfer everything to a bowl and leave aside for now.
7. Add garlic, onions, celery and bell peppers to your instant pot.
8. Add the rest of the seasoning mix, stir and cook for 10 minutes.
9. Add rice, stock, tomatoes, Tabasco sauce and Worcestershire sauce; then stir well. seal the Instant Pot lid and cook on High for 8 minutes
10. Quick release the pressure; return chicken, sausage and shrimp; then stir well. seal the instant pot lid and leave instant pot aside for 5 minutes.
11. Divide everything among plates and serve

Pepper Chicken Soup

(Prep + Cooking Time: 45 minutes | **Servings:** 4)

Ingredients:

- 1 ½ lbs. boneless; skinless chicken breast, cut into large chunks
- 3 poblano peppers, seeded and chopped
- 1/4 cup chopped fresh cilantro plus more for garnish
- 5 garlic cloves; chopped
- 1/2 cup dried navy beans
- 2 cups hot water
- 2 ½ cups cool water
- 1 cup chopped cauliflower
- 1 cup diced white onions
- 2 ounces cream cheese
- 1 tsp. ground cumin
- 1 tsp. salt or as your liking
- 1 tsp. ground coriander

Directions:

1. Soak the navy beans in the hot water for 1 hour; drain and transfer to the Instant Pot. Add the chicken, cool water, cauliflower, onion, poblanos, cilantro, garlic, salt, coriander and cumin.
2. Now secure the lid on the pot and close the valve. Now Press "Manual" and set the pot at "High" pressure for 15 minutes
3. After completing the cooking time, allow the pot to sit undisturbed for 10 minutes, then release any remaining pressure.
4. Using a pair of tongs, remove the chicken from the pot and set aside on a plate. Use an immersion blender to coarsely puree the soup directly in the pot
5. Now Press "Sauté" on the Instant Pot. When the soup is hot and bubbling, while whisking, add the cream cheese in chunks and whisk until melted and combined
6. Using two forks, shred the chicken and return it to the pot. Stir until heated through. Now Press "Cancel". Serve garnished with more cilantro.

Crispy Chicken

(Prep + Cooking Time: 50 minutes | **Servings:** 4)

Ingredients:

- 6 chicken thighs
- 4 garlic cloves; chopped.
- A pinch of rosemary; dried
- 1 cup cold water
- 1 tbsp. soy sauce
- 2 tbsp. extra virgin olive oil
- 2 tbsp. butter
- 1 cup white flour
- 2 eggs; whisked
- 1 yellow onion; thinly sliced
- 2 tbsp. cornstarch mixed with 2 ½ tbsp. water
- 1 ½ cups panko breadcrumbs
- Salt and black pepper to the taste

Directions:

1. In your instant pot; mix garlic with onion, rosemary and 1 cup water.
2. Place chicken things in the steamer basket and introduce in the pot
3. Cover and cook at High for 9 minutes.
4. Release the pressure naturally for 10 minutes, then release remaining pressure by turning the valve to 'Venting', and carefully open the lid
5. Heat up a pan with the butter and oil over medium high heat.
6. Add 1 ½ cups breadcrumbs; then stir well. toast them and take them off heat
7. Remove chicken thighs from the pot; pat dry them, season with salt and pepper to the taste, coat them with the flour, dip them in whisked egg and then coat them in toasted breadcrumbs.
8. Place chicken thighs on a lined baking sheet, introduce in the oven at 300 degrees F and bake for 10 minutes.
9. Meanwhile, set your instant pot on Sauté mode and heat up the cooking liquid
10. Add 1 tablespoon soy sauce, salt, pepper and cornstarch; stir and transfer to a bowl
11. Take chicken thighs out of the oven, divide them between plates and serve with the sauce from the pot on the side.

Chicken & Cabbage Dish

(Prep + Cooking Time: 40 minutes | **Servings:** 3)

Ingredients:

- 1 ½ lb. chicken thighs, boneless
- 10 oz. coconut milk
- 1 green cabbage; roughly chopped
- 1/2 cup white wine
- 1 yellow onion; chopped.
- 4 garlic cloves; chopped.
- 3 tbsp. curry paste
- 1 tbsp. fish sauce
- 1 tbsp. vegetable oil
- Salt and black pepper to the taste
- 2 chili peppers; chopped.
- A pinch of cayenne pepper

Directions:

1. Set your instant pot on Sauté mode; add oil and heat it up
2. Add chicken, season with salt and pepper; then stir well. brown for a few minutes and transfer to a bowl.
3. Add garlic, chili peppers and onions to the pot, stir and cook for 4 minutes
4. Add curry paste; stir and cook for 2 minutes more.
5. Add wine, cabbage, coconut milk, cayenne, fish sauce, chicken pieces, salt and pepper; then stir well. seal the instant pot lid and cook at High for 20 minutes.
6. Release the pressure naturally, carefully open the lid; stir your mix, divide it among plates and serve

Buffalo Chicken Recipe

(**Prep + Cooking Time:** 35 minutes | **Servings:** 6)

Ingredients:

- 1/2 cup chicken stock
- 1/2 cup celery; chopped.
- 1 small yellow onion; chopped.
- 1/2 cup buffalo sauce
- 1/4 cup bleu cheese; crumbled.
- 2 lb. chicken breasts; skinless, boneless and cut into thin strips

Directions:

1. In your instant pot; mix onion with celery; buffalo sauce, stock and chicken; then stir well. seal the instant pot lid and cook at High for 12 minutes
2. Quick release the pressure; carefully open the lid; discard 2/3 cup of cooking liquid; add crumbled cheese, stir very well, divide among plates and serve.

Lemongrass Chicken Recipe

(**Prep + Cooking Time:** 30 minutes | **Servings:** 5)

Ingredients:

- 1 bunch lemongrass; rough bottom removed and trimmed
- 1-inch piece ginger root; chopped.
- 4 garlic cloves; crushed.
- 3 tbsp. coconut aminos
- 1 tsp. Chinese five spice
- 10 chicken drumsticks
- 1 cup coconut milk
- 1/4 cup cilantro; finely chopped
- 1 yellow onion; chopped.
- 1 tbsp. lime juice
- 2 tbsp. fish sauce
- 1 tsp. ghee
- Salt and black pepper to the taste

Directions:

1. In your food processor, mix lemongrass with ginger, garlic, aminos, fish sauce and five spice and pulse well.
2. Add coconut milk and pulse again
3. Set your instant pot on Sauté mode; add ghee and melt it.
4. Add onion, stir and cook for 5 minutes.
5. Add chicken pieces, salt and pepper, stir and cook for 1 minute
6. Add coconut milk and lemongrass mix; then stir well. close the lid; set "poultry" mode and cook for 15 minutes sat High.
7. Quick release the pressure, carefully open the lid; add more salt and pepper and lime juice; then stir well. divide among plates and serve with cilantro sprinkled on top

Asian Chicken

(**Prep + Cooking Time:** 25 minutes | **Servings:** 6)

Ingredients:

- 1 ½ lbs. boneless; skinless chicken thighs, cut into 4 pieces each
- 1/2 cup grated fresh ginger
- 1/4 cup chopped fresh cilantro
- 1 (14.5-ounce) can diced tomatoes; undrained
- 2 tbsp. fresh lemon juice
- 2 tbsp. vegetable oil
- 1 tsp. ground cumin
- 2 tsp. Garam Masala
- 1 tsp. salt or as your liking
- 1/2 to 1 tsp. cayenne pepper
- Fresh ginger, cut into julienne, for serving

Directions:

1. Now Press "Sauté" on the Instant Pot. When the pot is hot, add the oil. When the oil is hot, add the minced ginger. Cook, stirring, until it starts to brown, 2 to 3 minutes
2. Now Press "Cancel". Add the chicken, tomatoes with their juices, cumin, 1 tsp. of the garam masala, the salt and the cayenne. Stir to combine

3. Now secure the lid on the pot and close the valve. Now Press "Manual" and set the pot at "High" pressure for 5 minutes.
4. After completing the cooking time, allow the pot to sit undisturbed for 10 minutes, then release any remaining pressure
5. Stir in the cilantro, lemon juice, remaining 1 tsp. garam masala and the julienned ginger and serve.

Chicken and Corn Mix

(Prep + Cooking Time: 35 minutes | **Servings:** 4)

Ingredients:

- 8 chicken drumsticks
- 8 oz. tomato sauce
- 1 tbsp. chicken bouillon
- 1/2 yellow onion; chopped.
- 1 tomato; chopped.
- 1/4 cup cilantro; chopped.
- 1 garlic clove; minced.
- 2 corn on the cob; husked and cut into halves
- 1 tsp. extra virgin olive oil
- 1/2 tsp. garlic powder
- 3 scallions; chopped.
- 2 cups water
- 1/2 tsp. cumin; ground.
- Salt and black pepper to the taste

Directions:

1. Set your instant pot on Sauté mode; add oil and heat up
2. Add onions, tomato, scallions, and garlic, stir and cook for 3 minutes.
3. Add cilantro, stir and cook for 1 minute
4. Add tomato sauce, water, bouillon, cumin, garlic powder, chicken, salt, pepper and top with the corn.
5. Cover the pot and cook at High for 20 minutes.
6. Quick release the pressure, carefully open the lid; add more salt and pepper if needed, divide chicken and corn among plates and serve

Chicken and Dumplings

(Prep + Cooking Time: 35 minutes | **Servings:** 6)

Ingredients:

- 2 lb. chicken breasts, skinless and bone-in
- 4 carrots; chopped.
- 1 yellow onion; chopped.
- 1/2 tsp. thyme; dried
- 2 eggs
- 2/3 cup milk
- 1 tbsp. chives
- 1 tbsp. baking powder
- 2 cups flour
- 3 celery stalks; chopped.
- 3/4 cup chicken stock
- Salt and black pepper to the taste

Directions:

1. In your instant pot; add chicken, onion, carrots, celery, stock, thyme, salt and pepper; then stir well. seal the instant pot lid and cook on Low for 15 minutes
2. Quick release the pressure, transfer chicken to a bowl and keep warm for now.
3. In a bowl, mix eggs with salt, milk and baking powder and stir
4. Add flour gradually and stir very well
5. Set instant pot to Simmer mode and bring the liquid inside to a boil.
6. Shape dumplings from eggs mix, drop them into stock, seal the instant pot lid and cook at High for 7 minutes.
7. Shred chicken and add to the pot after you've released the pressure; then stir well. divide everything among plates and serve with chives sprinkled on top

Turkey & Mashed Potatoes

(**Prep + Cooking Time:** 60 minutes | **Servings:** 3)

Ingredients:

- 2 turkey quarters
- 5 gold potatoes; cut into halves
- 1 yellow onion; chopped.
- 2 tbsp. parmesan cheese; grated
- 2 tbsp. extra virgin olive oil
- 3.5 oz. cream
- 2 bay leaves
- A pinch of sage; dried
- A pinch of thyme; dried
- A pinch of rosemary; dried
- 3 tbsp. cornstarch mixed with 2 tbsp. water
- 2 tbsp. butter
- 1 carrot; chopped.
- 3 garlic cloves; minced.
- 1 celery stalk; chopped.
- 1 cup chicken stock
- Salt and black pepper to the taste
- A splash of white wine

Directions:

1. Season turkey with salt and pepper.
2. Put 1 tablespoon oil in your instant pot; set the pot on Sauté mode and heat it up
3. Add turkey, brown pieces for 4 minutes, transfer them to a plate and leave aside for now.
4. Add 1/2 cup stock to the pot and stir well.
5. Add 1 tablespoon oil and heat it up.
6. Add onion; stir and cook for 1 minute
7. Add garlic, stir and cook for 20 seconds.
8. Add salt and pepper, carrot and celery, stir and cook for 7 minutes.
9. Add 2 bay leaves, thyme, sage, and rosemary, stir and cook everything 1 minute
10. Add wine, turkey and the rest of the stock.
11. Put potatoes in the steamer basket and also introduce it in the pot, seal the instant pot lid and cook for 20 minutes at High
12. Release the pressure naturally for 10 minutes, then release remaining pressure by turning the valve to 'Venting', carefully open the lid; transfer potatoes to a bowl and mash them.
13. Add salt, pepper, butter, parmesan and cream and stir well.
14. Divide turkey quarters to plates and set your instant pot on Sauté mode again.
15. Add cornstarch mix to pot; stir well and cook for 2 - 3 minutes
16. Drizzle sauce over turkey, add mashed potatoes on the side and serve.

Delicious Chicken with Cumin-Chile Sauce

(**Prep + Cooking Time:** 30 minutes | **Servings:** 8)

Ingredients:

- 2 lbs. boneless; skinless chicken thighs, cut into bite-size pieces
- 1 (5-ounce) can tomato paste
- 1 (14-ounce) can diced tomatoes; undrained
- 1 small white onion; chopped
- 1/4 cup pickled jalapeños, drained
- 3 garlic cloves; minced
- 1 tbsp. salt or as your liking
- 2 tbsp. vegetable oil
- 4 ½ tsp. ground cumin
- 4 ½ tsp. chili powder

Directions:

1. In a small bowl, combine the cumin, chili powder and salt. Place the chicken in a large bowl. Sprinkle the chicken with the spice mixture. Toss well to coat
2. Now Press "Sauté" on the Instant Pot. When the pot is hot, add the oil.
3. When the oil is hot, add the chicken. Cook, stirring, until the chicken is lightly browned, 4 to 5 minutes. Now Press "Cancel"
4. Add the diced tomatoes and their juices, onion, tomato paste, jalapeños and garlic to the pot. Stir to combine.

5. Now secure the lid on the pot and close the valve. Now Press "Manual" and set the pot at "High" pressure for 15 minutes
6. After completing the cooking time, allow the pot to sit undisturbed for 10 minutes, then release any remaining pressure. Serve with tortillas, sour cream and guacamole.

Spiced Chicken and Rice Pilaf

(**Prep + Cooking Time:** 30 minutes | **Servings:** 6)

Ingredients:
For Chicken:
- 1 lb. bone-in chicken thighs
- 1 ½ cups water
- 4 whole green cardamom pods
- 6 whole cloves
- 6 whole black peppercorns
- 1/2 cup sliced yellow onions
- 6 garlic cloves
- 3 thin slices fresh ginger
- 1/2 tsp. ground cinnamon
- 1 tsp. salt or as your liking

For Rice:
- 1 tbsp. Ghee
- 1 ½ cups basmati rice; rinsed and drained
- 2 tsp. Garam Masala
- 1 tsp. salt

Directions:
1. Place the onions, garlic, ginger, cinnamon, cardamom, cloves and peppercorns in the center of a double layer of cheesecloth. Bring up the edges to make a bundle and tie tightly with cotton kitchen string.
2. In your Instant Pot, combine the chicken, cheesecloth bundle, water and salt. Now secure the lid on the pot and close the valve
3. Now Press "Manual" and set the pot at "High" pressure for 10 minutes. After completing the cooking time, allow the pot to sit undisturbed for 10 minutes, then release any remaining pressure
4. Remove and discard the cheesecloth bundle. Transfer the chicken to a large plate and remove and discard the skin and bones.
5. Break the meat into large pieces. Measure the liquid in the pot. You'll need 1 ½ cups to cook the rice; if there is less, add water; if there is more, remove enough to make 1 ½ cups
6. Put the rice, garam masala, ghee and salt in the pot. Add the 1 ½ cups liquid and stir to combine; push the rice down to ensure it is covered by the liquid. Lay the chicken meat on top of the rice.
7. Now secure the lid on the pot and close the valve. Now Press "Manual" and set the pot at "High" pressure for 10 minutes. Stir gently before serving.

Turkey Meatballs

(**Prep + Cooking Time:** 50 minutes | **Servings:** 8)

Ingredients:
- 1 lb. turkey meat; ground.
- one egg; whisked
- 1/4 cup milk
- 1/4 cup parmesan cheese; grated
- 1/2 cup panko bread crumbs
- 1 yellow onion; minced.
- 1 cup chicken stock
- 2 tbsp. extra virgin olive oil
- 2 tsp. soy sauce
- 1 tsp. fish sauce
- 2 tbsp. butter
- 1 tsp. oregano; dried
- 12 cremini mushrooms; chopped.
- 3 dried shiitake mushrooms; soaked in water, drained and chopped.
- 2 tbsp. cornstarch mixed with 2 tbsp. water
- 4 garlic cloves; minced.
- 1/4 cup parsley; chopped.
- Salt and black pepper to the taste
- A splash of sherry wine

Directions:

1. In a bowl; mix turkey meat with parmesan cheese, salt, pepper to the taste, yellow onion, garlic, bread crumbs, parsley, oregano, egg, milk, 1 tsp. soy sauce and 1 tsp. fish sauce, stir very well and shape 16 meatballs
2. Heat up a pan with 1 tablespoon oil over medium high heat, add meatballs, brown them for 1 minutes on each side and transfer them to a plate.
3. Pour chicken stock into the pan, stir and take off heat
4. Set your instant pot on Sauté mode; add 1 tablespoon oil and 2 tablespoon butter and heat them up.
5. Add cremini mushrooms, salt, and pepper; stir and cook for 10 minutes.
6. Add dried mushrooms, sherry wine and the rest of the soy sauce and stir well.
7. Add meatballs, seal the instant pot lid and cook at High for 6 minutes
8. Quick release the pressure, carefully open the lid; add cornstarch mix, stir well, divide everything between plates and serve.

Mushroom Chicken

(Prep + Cooking Time: 45 minutes | **Servings:** 4)

Ingredients:

- 1 lb. boneless; skinless chicken thighs
- 2 cups quartered button mushrooms
- 4 sprigs fresh thyme
- 6 garlic cloves; thickly sliced
- 1 cup sliced yellow onions
- 4 cups baby spinach
- 1/2 cup heavy cream
- 1 tbsp. fresh lemon juice
- 2 tbsp. salted butter
- 2 tbsp. water
- 1 tsp. salt or as your liking
- 1 tsp. black pepper

Directions:

1. Now Press "Sauté" on the Instant Pot. When the pot is hot, add the butter. When the butter has melted, add the garlic.
2. Cook, stirring continuously, until garlic is fragrant and slightly softened, about 1 minute
3. Add the onions and mushrooms and stir to coat. Add the chicken, thyme, water, salt and pepper. Stir to combine. Place the spinach on top of the chicken mixture. Now Press "Cancel".
4. Now secure the lid on the pot and close the valve. Now Press "Manual" and set the pot at "High" pressure for 8 minutes.
5. After completing the cooking time, allow the pot to sit undisturbed for 10 minutes, then release any remaining pressure
6. Transfer the chicken to a serving platter. Cover lightly with aluminum foil to keep warm
7. Now Press "Sauté" on the Instant Pot. While stirring continuously, slowly add the cream in a steady stream.
8. Cook, stirring, until the mixture starts to thicken, 5 to 8 minutes. Stir in the lemon juice. Now Press "Cancel". Serve the chicken with the mushroom-spinach mixture.

Chicken & Broccoli Dish

(Prep + Cooking Time: 25 minutes | **Servings:** 6)

Ingredients:

- 2 chicken breasts; skinless and boneless
- 1 tbsp. butter
- 1 tbsp. extra-virgin olive oil
- 3 cups broccoli; steamed and chopped.
- 1 tbsp. parsley; dried
- 2 tbsp. water
- 2 tbsp. cornstarch
- 1 cup cheddar cheese; shredded.
- 4 oz. cream cheese; cubed
- 1/2 cup yellow onion; chopped.
- 14 oz. canned chicken stock
- Salt and black pepper to the taste
- A pinch of red pepper flakes

Directions:

1. Set your instant pot on Sauté mode; add butter and oil and heat up.
2. Add chicken breasts, salt and pepper; brown on all sides and transfer to a bowl.
3. Add onion to the pot; stir and cook for 5 minutes
4. Add more salt, pepper, stock, parsley, pepper flakes and return chicken breasts as well.
5. Stir, seal the instant pot lid and cook at High for 5 minutes.
6. Quick release the pressure, transfer chicken to a cutting board; chop it and return to pot.
7. Add cornstarch mixed with the water, shredded cheese and cream cheese and stir until all cheese dissolves.
8. Add broccoli; then stir well. set the pot on Simmer mode and cook for 5 minutes.
9. Divide among plates and serve

Easy Thai Chicken

(Prep + Cooking Time: 20 minutes | **Servings:** 4)

Ingredients:

- 2 lb. chicken thighs; boneless and skinless
- 1/2 cup fish sauce
- 1 cup lime juice
- 2 tbsp. coconut nectar
- 1 tsp. ginger; grated
- 2 tsp. cilantro; finely chopped
- 1 tsp. mint; chopped
- 1/4 cup extra virgin olive oil

Directions:

1. Put chicken thighs in your instant pot
2. In a bowl, mix lime juice with fish sauce, olive oil, coconut nectar, ginger, mint and cilantro and whisk well.
3. Pour this over chicken, seal the instant pot lid and cook at High for 10 minutes
4. Quick release the pressure; divide Thai chicken among plates and serve.

Awesome Chicken Adobo

(Prep + Cooking Time: 1 hour 10 minutes | **Servings:** 6)

Ingredients:

- 6 bone-in, skin-on chicken thighs
- 3 bay leaves
- 1/2 cup white vinegar
- 1/4 cup soy sauce
- 2 tbsp. vegetable oil
- 2 tbsp. minced garlic
- 1 tbsp. brown sugar
- 1 tsp. whole black peppercorns; crushed
- 1 tsp. red pepper flakes; optional

Directions:

1. In a large bowl, combine the vinegar, soy sauce, oil, garlic, brown sugar, peppercorns, red pepper flakes and bay leaves.
2. Stir to combine. Add the chicken thighs and toss well to coat. Allow the chicken to stand at room temperature for 30 minutes
3. Transfer the chicken and marinade to the Instant Pot. Now secure the lid on the pot and close the valve. Now Press "Manual" and set the pot at "High" pressure for 8 minutes.
4. After completing the cooking time, allow the pot to sit undisturbed for 10 minutes, then release any remaining pressure
5. Meanwhile; preheat the broiler. Line a baking sheet with aluminum foil.
6. Transfer the chicken to the prepared baking sheet. Broil until the skin crisps, 3 to 5 minutes.
7. Meanwhile; select "Sauté" on the Instant Pot and simmer the sauce until it has thickened, 3 to 5 minutes. Now Press "Cancel"
8. Transfer the chicken to a platter. Pour the sauce over the chicken and serve.

Chicken Enchilada Casserole

(Prep + Cooking Time: 35 minutes | **Servings:** 4)

Ingredients:

- 2 boneless; skinless chicken breasts
- 1 ½ cups Fire-Roasted Enchilada Sauce
- 4 corn tortillas, cut into 8 pieces each
- 1 cup diced white onions
- 1 cup shredded Mexican cheese blend
- 1 (4.5-ounce) can diced green chiles
- Vegetable oil

Directions:

1. In your Instant Pot, combine the enchilada sauce, chiles and onions. Stir to combine. Add the chicken to the pot
2. Now secure the lid on the pot and close the valve. Now Press "Manual" and set the pot at "High" pressure for 15 minutes. Meanwhile; preheat the oven to 400°F. Grease a 2-quart baking dish with oil
3. After completing the cooking time, quick release the pressure. Remove the chicken from the pot. Using two forks, shred the chicken and return it to the pot. Stir in the tortilla pieces
4. Transfer the chicken mixture to the prepared baking dish. Top evenly with the cheese. Bake until the cheese melts and is lightly browned and bubbling, about 10 minutes.

Sweet Corn Chicken Soup

(Prep + Cooking Time: 30 minutes | **Servings:** 6)

Ingredients:

- 1 lb. boneless; skinless chicken thighs, cut into bite-size pieces
- 1/4 cup water; optional
- 1/4 cup chopped scallions; Green part
- 3 cups water
- 2 (14-ounce) cans creamed corn
- 2 tbsp. cornstarch; optional
- 1 tbsp. toasted sesame oil
- 1 tbsp. apple cider vinegar
- 1 tbsp. soy sauce
- 1 tsp. salt or as your liking
- 1 tsp. white pepper

Directions:

1. In your Instant Pot, combine the chicken, water, creamed corn, vinegar, soy sauce, salt and white pepper.
2. Now secure the lid on the pot and close the valve. Now Press "Manual" and set the pot at "High" pressure for 10 minutes
3. After completing the cooking time, allow the pot to sit undisturbed for 10 minutes, then release any remaining pressure.
4. If you are using cornstarch to thicken the mixture, in a small bowl, stir together the water and cornstarch to make a slurry
5. Now Press Sauté on the Instant Pot. When the soup boils, stir in the slurry and cook, stirring continuously, until soup is slightly thickened, 2 to 3 minutes. Now Press "Cancel"
6. Stir in the sesame oil. Divide the soup among six serving bowls. Garnish with the scallions and serve.

Soups and Stews

Chicken Stew Recipe

(Prep + Cooking Time: 1 hour and 35 minutes | **Servings:** 6)

Ingredients:

- 6 chicken thighs
- 2 cups chicken stock
- 15 oz. canned tomatoes; chopped.
- 1 tsp. vegetable oil
- Salt and black pepper to the taste
- 1 yellow onion; chopped.
- 1/4 lb. baby carrots, sliced
- 1 celery stalk; chopped.
- 3/4 lb. baby carrots
- 1 ½ lb. new potatoes
- 1/2 tsp. thyme, dried
- 2 tbsp. tomato paste
- 1/2 cup white wine

Directions:

1. Set your instant pot on Sauté mode; add oil and heat it up
2. Add chicken, salt and pepper, brown for 4 minutes on each side and transfer to a plate.
3. Add celery, onion, tomato paste, carrots, thyme, salt and pepper, stir and cook for 5 minutes.
4. Add wine; then stir well. bring to a boil and simmer for 3 minutes.
5. Add stock, return chicken, add tomatoes and put potatoes in the steamer basket of your pot
6. Seal the instant pot lid and cook at High for 30 minutes.
7. Release the pressure naturally for 15 minutes, then release remaining pressure by turning the valve to 'Venting', carefully open the lid; take potatoes out of the pot and put them in a bowl
8. Transfer chicken pieces to a cutting board, leave aside to cool down for a few minutes, discard bones, shred meat and return it to the stew.
9. Add more salt and pepper if needed; then stir well. divide into bowls and serve hot

Chorizo, Kale and Chicken Soup

(Prep + Cooking Time: 30 minutes | **Servings:** 8)

Ingredients:

- 9 oz. chorizo, casings removed
- 4 cups chicken stock
- 4 chicken thighs; chopped.
- 14 oz. garbanzo beans, drained
- 15 oz. canned tomatoes; chopped.
- 4 garlic cloves; minced.
- 2 yellow onions; chopped.
- 2 tbsp. olive oil
- 3 potatoes; chopped
- 2 bay leaves
- 5 oz. baby kale
- Salt and black pepper to the taste

Directions:

1. Set your instant pot on Sauté mode; add oil and heat it up
2. Add chorizo, chicken and onion, stir and cook 5 minutes.
3. Add garlic, stir and cook for 1 minute.
4. Add stock, tomatoes and bay leaves and stir again
5. Also add, kale and potatoes, salt and pepper; then stir well. seal the instant pot lid and cook at High for 4 minutes.
6. Release the pressure naturally for 15 minutes, then release remaining pressure by turning the valve to 'Venting', carefully open the lid; add beans, more salt and pepper if needed; then stir well. divide into bowls and serve.

Tomato Soup

(**Prep + Cooking Time:** 60 minutes | **Servings:** 6)

Ingredients:
For the roasted tomatoes:
- 3 lb. cherry tomatoes, cut into halves
- 1/2 tsp. red pepper flakes
- 14 garlic cloves, crushed.
- 2 tbsp. extra virgin olive oil
- Salt and black pepper to the taste

For the soup:
- 1 yellow onion; chopped.
- 2 tbsp. olive oil
- 3 tbsp. tomato paste
- 2 celery ribs; chopped.
- 2 cups chicken stock
- 1 tsp. garlic powder
- 1 tsp. onion powder
- 1 red bell pepper; chopped.
- 1/2 tbsp. basil; dried
- 1/2 tsp. red pepper flakes
- 1 cup heavy cream
- Salt and black pepper to the taste

For serving:
- 1/2 cup parmesan, grated
- Basil leaves; chopped.

Directions:
1. Place tomatoes and garlic in a baking tray, drizzle 2 tablespoon oil, season with salt, pepper and 1/2 tsp. red pepper flakes, toss to coat, introduce in the oven at 425 degrees F and roast for 25 minutes.
2. Take tomatoes out of the oven and leave them aside for now.
3. Set your instant pot on Sauté mode; add 2 tablespoon oil and heat it up
4. Add onion, bell pepper and celery and stir
5. Also add salt, pepper, garlic powder, onion powder, dried basil and 1/2 tsp. pepper flakes, stir and cook for 3 minutes.
6. Add tomato paste, roasted tomatoes and garlic and stir
7. Add stock, close the lid and cook at High for 10 minutes
8. Release the pressure naturally, open the instant pot lid and set it on Sauté mode
9. Add heavy cream and blend everything using an immersion blender
10. Divide in bowls, add basil leaves and cheese on top and serve

Classic Cauliflower Soup

(**Prep + Cooking Time:** 30 minutes | **Servings:** 6)

Ingredients:
- 1 cauliflower head, florets separated and chopped.
- 1 cup cheddar cheese, grated
- 2 tbsp. butter
- 3 cups chicken stock
- 1 small onion; chopped.
- 1 tsp. garlic powder
- 1/2 cup half and half
- 4 oz. cream cheese, cubed
- Salt and black pepper to the taste

Directions:
1. Set your instant pot on Sauté mode; add butter and melt it.
2. Add onion, stir and cook for 3 minutes
3. Add cauliflower, stock, salt, pepper and garlic powder; then stir well. seal the instant pot lid and cook at High for 5 minutes.
4. Release the pressure naturally for 15 minutes, then release remaining pressure by turning the valve to 'Venting', carefully open the lid; blend everything using an immersion blender, add more salt and pepper if needed, cream cheese, grated cheese and half and half.
5. Stir, set the pot on Simmer mode, heat up for 2 minutes, divide into soup bowls and serve

Fish Chowder

(Prep + Cooking Time: 30 minutes | **Servings:** 4)

Ingredients:
- 1 lb. haddock fillets
- 3/4 cup bacon; chopped.
- 1 yellow onion; chopped
- 2 celery ribs; chopped.
- 3 cups potatoes, cubed
- 4 cups chicken stock
- 2 tbsp. butter
- 1 tbsp. potato starch
- 2 cups heavy cream
- 1 cup frozen corn
- 1 carrot; chopped
- 2 garlic cloves; chopped
- Salt and white pepper to the taste

Directions:
1. Set your instant pot on Sauté mode; add butter and melt it.
2. Add bacon, stir and cook until it's crispy.
3. Add garlic, celery and onion, stir and cook for 3 minutes.
4. Add salt, pepper, fish, potatoes, corn and stock; then stir well. seal the instant pot lid and cook at High for 5 minutes.
5. Release the pressure naturally, carefully open the lid; add heavy cream mixed with potato starch, stir well, set the pot on Simmer mode and cook everything for 3 minutes
6. Divide into bowls and serve

Chicken Noodle Soup

(Prep + Cooking Time: 35 minutes | **Servings:** 6)

Ingredients:
- 2 cups chicken, already cooked and shredded.
- 4 carrots, sliced
- 1 yellow onion; chopped
- 1 tbsp. butter
- 6 cups chicken stock
- 1 celery rib; chopped
- Salt and black pepper to the taste
- Egg noodles, already cooked

Directions:
1. Set your instant pot on Sauté mode; add butter and heat it up.
2. Add onion, stir and cook 2 minutes
3. Add celery and carrots, stir and cook 5 minutes
4. Add chicken, stock; then stir well. close the lid and cook at High for 5 minutes
5. Release the pressure naturally for 15 minutes, then release remaining pressure by turning the valve to 'Venting', carefully open the lid; add salt and pepper to the taste and stir
6. Divide noodles into soup bowls, add soup over them and serve.

Chicken Meatball Soup Recipe

(Prep + Cooking Time: 40 minutes | **Servings:** 6)

Ingredients:
- 1 ½ lb. chicken breast, ground.
- 2 tbsp. arrowroot powder
- 1/2 tbsp. oregano; dried
- 1/2 tsp. crushed red pepper
- 1 tsp. garlic powder
- 1/2 tbsp. basil; dried
- 1 tsp. onion powder
- 2 tbsp. nutritional yeast
- Salt and black pepper to the taste

For the soup:
- 6 cups chicken stock
- 4 celery stalks; chopped.
- 3 carrots; chopped
- 2 tsp. thyme; dried
- 2 garlic cloves; minced.
- 1/2 tsp. red pepper, crushed.
- 2 yellow onions; chopped.
- 2 eggs, whisked

- 2 tbsp. extra virgin olive oil
- 1 bunch kale; chopped

Directions:
1. Set your instant pot on Sauté mode; add oil and heat it up.
2. Add onions, celery and carrots, stir and cook for 3 minutes
3. Add garlic, salt, pepper, kale, stock, 2 tsp. thyme and 1/2 tsp. red pepper, stir and continue cooking
4. Meanwhile, in a bowl mix chicken meat with arrow powder, salt, pepper, 1/2 tsp. red pepper, garlic powder, onion powder, oregano, basil and yeast and stir well
5. Shape meatballs using your hands and drop them gently into the soup
6. Seal the instant pot lid and cook at High for 15 minutes.
7. Release the pressure naturally for 15 minutes, then release remaining pressure by turning the valve to 'Venting', open the instant pot lid and set it on Sauté mode again
8. Add eggs slowly, stir and cook for 2 minutes.
9. Divide into soup bowls and serve hot.

Endive Soup

(Prep + Cooking Time: 45 minutes | **Servings:** 4)

Ingredients:
- 6 cups veggie stock
- 1 tbsp. canola oil
- 2 tsp. sesame oil
- 1 tbsp. ginger, grated
- 1 tsp. chili sauce
- 1/2 cup uncooked rice
- 2 scallions; chopped.
- 1 ½ tbsp. soy sauce
- 3 endives, trimmed and roughly chopped
- 3 garlic cloves chopped
- Salt and white pepper to the taste

Directions:
1. Set your instant pot on Sauté mode; add canola and sesame oil and heat it up
2. Add scallions and garlic, stir and cook for 4 minutes.
3. Add chili sauce and ginger, stir and cook for 1 minute
4. Add stock and soy sauce, stir and cook for 2 minutes.
5. Add rice; then stir well. seal the instant pot lid and cook at High for 15 minutes
6. Release the pressure naturally for 15 minutes, then release remaining pressure by turning the valve to 'Venting', carefully open the lid; add salt, pepper and endives; then stir well. seal the instant pot lid and cook at High for 5 minutes.
7. Release the pressure again, carefully open the lid; stir soup, divide into bowls and serve

Sweet Potato and Turkey Soup

(Prep + Cooking Time: 35 minutes | **Servings:** 4)

Ingredients:
- 1 lb. Italian turkey sausage; chopped
- 1 yellow onion; chopped.
- 5 cups turkey stock
- 2 garlic cloves; minced.
- 1 tsp. red pepper flakes
- 1 tsp. basil; dried
- 1 tsp. oregano; dried
- 2 celery stalks; chopped
- 1 tsp. thyme; dried
- 5 oz. spinach; chopped.
- 2 bay leaves
- 2 carrots; chopped
- 1 big sweet potato, cubed
- Salt and black pepper to the taste

Directions:
1. Set your instant pot on Sauté mode; add sausage, brown it and transfer to a plate
2. Add onion, celery and carrots, stir and cook for 2 minutes
3. Add potato, stir and cook 2 minutes
4. Add stock, garlic, red pepper, salt, pepper, basil, oregano, thyme, spinach and bay leaves,
5. Stir, seal the instant pot lid and cook at High for 4 minutes.

6. Release the pressure naturally for 15 minutes, then release remaining pressure by turning the valve to 'Venting', carefully open the lid; discard bay leaves, divide soup into bowls and serve.

Beef and Mushroom Stew

(Prep + Cooking Time: 45 minutes | **Servings:** 6)

Ingredients:

- 2 lb. beef chuck, cubed
- 1 celery stalk; chopped.
- 1 oz. dried porcini mushrooms; chopped.
- 2 carrots; chopped
- 2 tbsp. butter
- 1/2 cup red wine
- 1 cup beef stock
- 2 tbsp. flour
- 1 tbsp. olive oil
- 1 red onion; chopped
- 1 tsp. rosemary; chopped
- Salt and black pepper to the taste

Directions:

1. Set your instant pot on Sauté mode; add oil and beef, stir and brown for 5 minutes
2. Add onion, celery, rosemary, salt, pepper, wine and stock and stir
3. Add carrots and mushrooms, close the lid and cook at High for 15 minutes.
4. Release the pressure naturally for 15 minutes, then release remaining pressure by turning the valve to 'Venting', open the instant pot lid and set it on Simmer mode
5. Meanwhile, heat up a pan over medium high heat, add butter and melt it
6. Add flour and 6 tablespoon of cooking liquid from the stew and stir well
7. Pour this over stew; then stir well. cook for 5 minutes, divide into bowls and serve

Chicken Chili Soup

(Prep + Cooking Time: 50 minutes | **Servings:** 4)

Ingredients:

- 1 lb. chicken breast, skinless and boneless
- 30 oz. canned cannellini beans, drained
- 4 garlic cloves; minced.
- 2 tsp. oregano, dried
- 1 tsp. cumin
- 1 white onion; chopped.
- 2 tbsp. olive oil
- 1/2 tsp. red pepper flakes, crushed.
- 3 cups chicken stock
- 1 jalapeno pepper; chopped.
- Salt and black pepper to the taste
- Cilantro; chopped for serving
- Tortilla chips, for serving
- Lime wedges for serving

Directions:

1. Set your instant pot on Sauté mode; add oil and heat it up.
2. Add jalapeno and onion, stir and cook for 3 minutes
3. Add garlic, stir and cook for 1 minute.
4. Add oregano, cumin, pepper flakes, stock, chicken, beans, salt and pepper; then stir well. seal the instant pot lid and cook on Low for 30 minutes.
5. Release the pressure naturally for 15 minutes, then release remaining pressure by turning the valve to 'Venting', carefully open the lid; shred meat with 2 forks, add more salt and pepper, stir and divide into soup bowls
6. Serve with cilantro on top and with tortilla chips and lime wedges on the side

Cheese and Potato Soup

(Prep + Cooking Time: 30 minutes | **Servings:** 6)

Ingredients:

- 6 cups potatoes, cubed
- 1 cup cheddar cheese, shredded.
- 1 cup corn
- 6 bacon slices; cooked and crumbled.
- 2 tbsp. butter
- 3 oz. cream cheese, cubed
- 2 cups half and half
- 1/2 cup yellow onion; chopped
- 28 oz. canned chicken stock
- Salt and black pepper to the taste
- 2 tbsp. parsley; dried
- 1/8 red pepper flakes
- 2 tbsp. cornstarch
- 2 tbsp. water

Directions:

1. Set your instant pot on Sauté mode; add butter and melt it
2. Add onion, stir and cook 5 minutes
3. Add half of the stock, salt, pepper, pepper flakes and parsley and stir
4. Put potatoes in the steamer basket, seal the instant pot lid and cook at High for 4 minutes
5. Release the pressure naturally for 15 minutes, then release remaining pressure by turning the valve to 'Venting', carefully open the lid and transfer potatoes to a bowl.
6. In another bowl, mix cornstarch with water and stir well.
7. Set the pot to Simmer mode, add cornstarch, cream cheese and shredded cheese and stir well.
8. Also add the rest of the stock, corn, bacon, potatoes, half and half.
9. Stir, bring to a simmer, ladle into bowls and serve.

Zuppa Toscana Delight

(Prep + Cooking Time: 40 minutes | **Servings:** 8)

Ingredients:

- 1 lb. chicken sausage, ground.
- 6 bacon slices; chopped
- 12 oz. evaporated milk
- 1 cup parmesan, shredded.
- 2 cup spinach; chopped
- 3 potatoes, cubed
- 3 tbsp. cornstarch
- 3 garlic cloves; minced.
- 1 cup yellow onion; chopped.
- 1 tbsp. butter
- 40 oz. chicken stock
- Salt and black pepper to the taste
- A pinch of red pepper flakes

Directions:

1. Set your instant pot on Sauté mode; add bacon; then stir well. cook until it's crispy and transfer to a plate
2. Add sausage to the pot; then stir well. cook until it browns on all sides and also transfer to a plate
3. Add butter to the pot and melt it
4. Add onion, stir and cook for 5 minutes
5. Add garlic, stir and cook for 1 minute
6. Add 1/3 of the stock, salt, pepper and pepper flakes and stir.
7. Place potatoes in the steamer basket of the pot, seal the instant pot lid and cook at High for 4 minutes.
8. Release the pressure naturally for 15 minutes, then release remaining pressure by turning the valve to 'Venting', carefully open the lid and transfer potatoes to a bowl.
9. Add the rest of the stock to the pot, cornstarch mixed with some evaporated milk and the milk, stir and set the pot on Simmer mode.
10. Add parmesan, sausage, bacon, potatoes, spinach, more salt and pepper if needed; then stir well. divide into bowls and serve

Delicious Okra Stew

(Prep + Cooking Time: 40 minutes | **Servings:** 4)

Ingredients:

- 1 lb. beef meat, cubed
- 14 oz. frozen okra
- 12 oz. tomato sauce
- 1 yellow onion; chopped.
- 1 garlic clove; minced.
- 1/2 cup parsley; chopped.

- A drizzle of olive oil
- 1 cardamom pod
- 2 cups chicken stock
- Juice of 1/2 lemon
- Salt and black pepper to the taste

For the marinade:

- 1 tbsp. 7- spice mix
- 1/2 tsp. onion powder

- 1/2 tsp. garlic powder
- A pinch of salt

Directions:

1. In a bowl, mix meat with 7-spice mix, a pinch of salt, onion and garlic powder, toss to coat and leave aside for now
2. Set your instant pot on Sauté mode; add some olive oil and heat it up
3. Add onion, stir and cook 2 minutes
4. Add garlic and cardamom, stir and cook for 1 minute
5. Add meat, stir and brown meat for 2 minutes.
6. Add stock, tomato sauce, okra, salt and pepper; then stir well. seal the instant pot lid and cook on Low for 20 minutes.
7. Release the pressure naturally for 15 minutes, then release remaining pressure by turning the valve to 'Venting', carefully open the lid; add more salt and pepper if needed, lemon juice and parsley; then stir well. divide into bowls and serve

Minestrone Soup

(Prep + Cooking Time: 35 minutes | **Servings:** 8)

Ingredients:

- 29 oz. canned chicken stock
- 15 oz. canned kidney beans
- 3 lb. tomatoes; peeled and chopped.
- 1 tbsp. extra-virgin olive oil
- 1 celery stalk; chopped
- 2 carrots; chopped
- 1 onion; chopped
- 1 tsp. Italian seasoning

- 2 cups baby spinach
- 1 cup corn kernels
- 1 cup asiago cheese, grated
- 2 tbsp. basil; chopped
- 1 zucchini; chopped
- 4 garlic cloves; minced.
- 1 cup uncooked pasta
- Salt and black pepper to the taste

Directions:

1. Set your instant pot on Sauté mode; add oil and heat it up.
2. Add onion, stir and cook for 5 minutes
3. Add carrots, garlic, celery, corn and zucchini, stir and cook 5 minutes.
4. Add tomatoes, stock, Italian seasoning, pasta, salt and pepper; then stir well. seal the instant pot lid and cook at High for 4 minutes.
5. Release the pressure naturally for 15 minutes, then release remaining pressure by turning the valve to 'Venting', carefully open the lid; add beans, basil and spinach
6. Add more salt and pepper if needed, divide into bowls, add cheese on top and serve

Surprising Sweet Potato Stew

(**Prep + Cooking Time:** 40 minutes | **Servings:** 4)

Ingredients:
- 1 sweet potato, cubed
- 1 big onion; chopped.
- 1/2 cup red lentils
- 3 garlic cloves; chopped.
- 1 celery stalk; chopped.
- 2 cups veggie stock
- 1/4 cup raisins
- 2 carrots; chopped
- 1 cup green lentils
- 14 oz. canned tomatoes; chopped.
- Salt and black pepper to the taste

For the spice blend:
- 1/2 tsp. cinnamon
- 1/4 tsp. ginger, grated
- 1 tsp. cumin
- 1 tsp. paprika
- 2 tsp. coriander
- 1 tsp. turmeric
- A pinch of cloves
- A pinch of chili flakes

Directions:
1. Set your instant pot on Sauté mode; add onions and brown them for 2 minutes adding some of the stock from time to time
2. Add garlic, stir and cook for 1 minute
3. Add carrots, raisins, celery, and sweet potatoes, stir and cook for 1 minute.
4. Add red and green lentils, stock, tomatoes, salt, pepper, turmeric, cinnamon, paprika, cumin, coriander, ginger, cloves and chili flakes; then stir well. seal the instant pot lid and cook at High for 15 minutes.
5. Release the pressure naturally for 15 minutes, then release remaining pressure by turning the valve to 'Venting', carefully open the lid; stir stew one more time, add more salt and pepper if needed, ladle into bowls and serve

White Bean and Swiss Chard Stew

(**Prep + Cooking Time:** 15 minutes | **Servings:** 5)

Ingredients:
- 2 cups cooked great northern beans
- 2 carrots, sliced, with thicker end cut into half-moons
- 1 small bunch Swiss chard leaves, chopped
- 1 celery stalk, sliced
- 1/2 onion; cut into large dice
- 2 or 3 garlic cloves; minced
- 3 tomatoes, chopped
- 1 tbsp. olive oil
- ¼ to ½ tsp. red pepper flakes
- 1/2 tsp. dried rosemary
- 1/2 tsp. dried oregano
- 1/4 tsp. dried basil
- 1/2 tsp. salt or as your liking
- Pinch freshly ground black pepper; or more as needed
- Nutritional yeast, for sprinkling; optional

Directions:
1. Select the "Sauté" Low mode on your instant pot. When the display reads "Hot," add the oil and heat until it shimmers.
2. Add the carrots, celery and onion. Cook for 2 to 3 minutes, stirring occasionally. Add the garlic and cook for 30 seconds more. Turn off the Instant Pot
3. Stir in the tomatoes, red pepper flakes, rosemary; oregano, basil, salt, pepper and beans. Lock the lid and turn the steam release handle to Sealing. Using the Manual function, set the cooker to High Pressure for 4 minutes.
4. After completing the cooking time, quick release the pressure.
5. Remove the lid carefully and stir in the Swiss chard. Let wilt for 2 to 3 minutes
6. Taste and season with salt and pepper, as needed and sprinkle the nutritional yeast over individual servings.

Bacon and Broccoli Soup

(**Prep + Cooking Time:** 30 minutes | **Servings:** 6)

Ingredients:

- 4 bacon slices; chopped
- 2 small broccoli heads; chopped.
- 1 tbsp. parmesan, grated
- 1 leek; chopped
- 1 celery rib; chopped
- 1-quart veggie stock
- 1 tsp. olive oil
- 2 cups spinach; chopped
- 4 tbsp. basmati rice
- Salt and black pepper to the taste

Directions:

1. Set your instant pot on Sauté mode; add oil and bacon, cook until it's crispy, transfer to a plate and leave aside
2. Add broccoli, leek, celery, spinach, rice, salt, pepper and veggie stock; then stir well. seal the instant pot lid and cook at High for 6 minutes
3. Release the pressure naturally for 15 minutes, then release remaining pressure by turning the valve to 'Venting', carefully open the lid; add more salt and pepper if needed, add bacon, divide into soup bowls and serve with parmesan on top.

Lasagna Soup

(**Prep + Cooking Time:** 25 minutes | **Servings:** 5)

Ingredients:

- 10 lasagna noodles, broken into bite-size pieces
- 1 medium onion; diced
- 1 garlic clove; diced
- 2 tomatoes, chopped
- 6 cups water
- 1 cube vegetable or "not chicken" bouillon
- 1 bay leaf
- ⅔ cup red sauce
- 2 tbsp. olive oil
- 2 tsp. dried oregano
- 1 tsp. dried rosemary
- ½ to ¾ tsp. red pepper flakes
- ½ tsp. salt or as your liking
- Fresh basil, for garnishing; optional
- Freshly ground black pepper
- Shredded vegan mozzarella cheese, for garnishing; optional

Directions:

1. Select the "Sauté" Low mode on your instant pot. When the display reads "Hot," add the oil and heat until it shimmers.
2. Add the onion. Sauté for 2 to 3 minutes until softened. Add the garlic and immediately turn off the pressure cooker. Keep stirring as the garlic cooks.
3. Add the oregano, rosemary, red pepper flakes, salt, tomatoes, bouillon cube, bay leaf, noodles, red sauce and water. Stir well to combine
4. You want the noodles to be submerged. Lock the lid and turn the steam release handle to Sealing. Using the Manual function, set the cooker to High Pressure for 4 minutes.
5. After completing the cooking time, turn off the Instant Pot and let the pressure release naturally for 10 minutes; quick release any remaining pressure
6. Remove the lid carefully and remove and discard the bay leaf. Taste and season with salt and pepper, as desired and serve with your favorite toppings!

Delicious Beef Stew

(**Prep + Cooking Time:** 50 minutes | **Servings:** 8)

Ingredients:

- 2 lb. beef stew, cubed
- 1 tbsp. vegetable oil
- 5 carrots; chopped.
- 8 potatoes, cubed
- 1 yellow onion; chopped.
- 2 tsp. cornstarch
- 2 beef bouillon cubes
- Salt and black pepper to the taste
- 2 cups water

Directions:

1. Set your instant pot on Sauté mode; add oil and heat it up
2. Add beef and onion, stir and cook until it browns on all sides.
3. Add carrots, water and bouillon; then stir well. seal the instant pot lid and cook on Medium for 20 minutes.
4. Pour water in a pot, add some salt, bring to a boil over medium high heat, add potatoes, cook for 10 minutes and drain them.
5. Release the pressure naturally for 15 minutes, then release remaining pressure by turning the valve to 'Venting', open the instant pot lid and set it on Simmer mode.
6. Add cornstarch mixed with some water, salt, pepper and potatoes; then stir well. bring to a boil, take off heat and divide stew among plates

Root and Beef Vegetables Stew

(**Prep + Cooking Time:** 55 minutes | **Servings:** 4)

Ingredients:

- 1 lb. beef meat, cubed
- 2 tbsp. olive oil
- 4 garlic cloves; minced.
- 2 cups beef stock
- 1 tbsp. tomato paste
- 4 carrots; chopped
- 1/2 cup bourbon
- 1 rutabaga, diced
- A bunch of thyme; chopped
- A bunch of rosemary; chopped
- 1 cup cipollini onions, peeled
- 1 cup peas
- 2 bay leaves
- 2 bacon slices; cooked and crumbled.
- 1/2 cup white flour
- Salt and black pepper to the taste

Directions:

1. Mix flour with salt and pepper and place on a plate
2. Dredge meat in flour mix and leave aside.
3. Set your instant pot on Sauté mode; add oil and heat up
4. Add meat, brown on all sides and transfer to a bowl
5. Add garlic, bourbon, stock, thyme, rutabaga, carrots, tomato paste, rosemary and onions, stir and cook for 2 minutes
6. Return beef to pot, seal the instant pot lid and cook at High for 10 minutes
7. Release the pressure naturally for 15 minutes, then release remaining pressure by turning the valve to 'Venting', carefully open the lid; add bay leaves, bacon, peas, more salt and pepper, stir and cook on Low for 12 minutes.
8. Release the pressure again, carefully open the lid; then stir well. discard bay leaves, divide into bowls and serve

Spinach Stew

(Prep + Cooking Time: 50 minutes **| Servings:** 4)

Ingredients:

- 6 cups baby spinach
- 1 small yellow onion; chopped.
- 2 tsp. olive oil
- 1 celery stalk; chopped.
- 1 tsp. turmeric
- 2 tsp. cumin
- 4 cups veggie stock
- 1 tsp. thyme
- 1 cup brown lentils, rinsed
- 2 carrots; chopped.
- 4 garlic cloves; minced.
- Salt and black pepper to the taste

Directions:

1. Set your instant pot on Sauté mode; add oil and heat it up
2. Add onions, celery and carrots, stir and cook for 5 minutes.
3. Add garlic, turmeric, cumin, thyme, salt and pepper, stir and cook for 1 minute more
4. Add stock and lentils; then stir well. seal the instant pot lid and cook at High for 12 minutes
5. Release the pressure naturally for 15 minutes, then release remaining pressure by turning the valve to 'Venting', carefully open the lid; add spinach, more salt and pepper; then stir well. divide into bowls and serve

Broccoli Cream

(Prep + Cooking Time: 30 minutes **| Servings:** 4)

Ingredients:

- 3 carrots; chopped.
- 1 broccoli head, florets separated and chopped.
- 1 potato; chopped
- 1 yellow onion; chopped.
- 1 tbsp. olive oil
- 2 cups chicken stock
- 5 garlic cloves; minced.
- 1 tbsp. chives; chopped.
- 2 tbsp. cream
- Salt and black pepper to the taste
- Cheddar cheese, grated for serving

Directions:

1. Set your instant pot on Sauté mode; add oil and heat it up
2. Add onion and garlic, stir and cook for 2 minutes
3. Add broccoli, carrots, potato, stock, salt and pepper; then stir well. seal the instant pot lid and cook at High for 5 minutes.
4. Release the pressure naturally for 15 minutes, then release remaining pressure by turning the valve to 'Venting', carefully open the lid; set it on Simmer mode, add cream, cheese and chives; then stir well. heat up for 2 minutes, divide into bowls and serve.

Asparagus Cream

(Prep + Cooking Time: 45 minutes **| Servings:** 4)

Ingredients:

- 2 lb. green asparagus, trimmed, tips cut off and cut into medium pieces
- 6 cups chicken stock
- 1 yellow onion; chopped
- 1/4 tsp. lemon juice
- 1/2 cup crème fraiche
- 3 tbsp. butter
- Salt and white pepper to the taste

Directions:

1. Set your instant pot on Sauté mode; add butter and melt it.
2. Add asparagus, salt and pepper, stir and cook for 5 minutes
3. Add 5 cups stock, close the lid and cook on Low for 15 minutes
4. Release the pressure naturally for 15 minutes, then release remaining pressure by turning the valve to 'Venting', open the instant pot lid and transfer soup to your blender
5. Pulse very well and return to pot

6. Set the pot on Simmer mode, add crème fraiche, the rest of the stock, salt and pepper and lemon juice, bring to a boil, divide into soup bowls and serve

Turkey Stew

(Prep + Cooking Time: 50 minutes | **Servings:** 4)

Ingredients:

- 3 cups turkey meat, already cooked and shredded.
- 1 tbsp. avocado oil
- 1 tbsp. cranberry sauce
- 1 tsp. dried garlic; minced.
- 3 celery stalks; chopped.
- 2 cups potatoes; chopped.
- 15 oz. canned tomatoes; chopped.
- 5 cups turkey stock
- 2 carrots; chopped.
- 1 yellow onion; chopped.
- Salt and black pepper to the taste

Directions:

1. Set your instant pot on Sauté mode; add oil and heat it up
2. Add carrots, celery and onions, stir and cook for 3 minutes
3. Add potatoes, tomatoes, stock, garlic, meat and cranberry sauce; then stir well. seal the instant pot lid and cook on Low for 30 minutes.
4. Release the pressure naturally for 15 minutes, then release remaining pressure by turning the valve to 'Venting', carefully open the lid; add salt and pepper; then stir well. divide into bowls and serve.

Butternut Squash Soup

(Prep + Cooking Time: 35 minutes | **Servings:** 6)

Ingredients:

- 1 ½ lb. butternut squash, baked, peeled and cubed
- 1/2 cup green onions; chopped.
- 1/8 tsp. red pepper flakes; dried
- 1 cup orzo, already cooked
- 1 cup chicken meat, already cooked and shredded.
- 3 tbsp. butter
- 1 garlic clove; minced.
- 1/2 tsp. Italian seasoning
- 15 oz. canned tomatoes and their juice; chopped.
- 1/8 tsp. nutmeg, grated
- 1 ½ cup half and half
- 1/2 cup carrots; chopped
- 1/2 cup celery; chopped
- 29 oz. canned chicken stock
- Salt and black pepper to the taste
- Some green onions; chopped for serving

Directions:

1. Set your instant pot on Sauté mode; add butter and melt it.
2. Add celery, carrots and onions, stir and cook for 3 minutes
3. Add garlic, stir and cook for 1 minute more
4. Add squash, tomatoes, stock, Italian seasoning, salt, pepper, pepper flakes and nutmeg.
5. Stir, seal the instant pot lid and cook at High for 10 minutes.
6. Release the pressure naturally for 15 minutes, then release remaining pressure by turning the valve to 'Venting', carefully open the lid and puree everything with your immersion blender
7. Set the pot on Simmer mode, add half and half, orzo and chicken, stir and cook for 3 minutes
8. Divide soup into bowls, sprinkle green onions on top and serve

Classic Lamb Stew

(Prep + Cooking Time: 45 minutes | Servings: 6)

Ingredients:

- 3 lb. lamb shoulder, cut into medium chunks
- 2 carrots; chopped.
- 2 big potatoes, roughly chopped
- 2 onions; chopped.
- 2 thyme springs; chopped.
- 1/4 cup parsley; minced.
- 6 oz. dark beer
- 2 cups water
- Salt and black pepper to the taste

Directions:

1. Put onions and lamb in your instant pot
2. Add salt, pepper, potatoes, thyme, water, beer and carrots; then stir well. seal the instant pot lid and cook at High for 15 minutes.
3. Release the pressure naturally for 15 minutes, then release remaining pressure by turning the valve to 'Venting', carefully open the lid; add parsley, more salt and pepper if needed; then stir well. divide into bowls and serve.

Simple Fennel Soup

(Prep + Cooking Time: 35 minutes | Servings: 3)

Ingredients:

- 1 fennel bulb; chopped
- 1 bay leaf
- 2 tsp. parmesan cheese, grated
- 1 tbsp. extra-virgin olive oil
- 2 cups water
- 1/2 cube vegetable bouillon
- 1 leek; chopped
- Salt and black pepper to the taste

Directions:

1. In your instant pot, mix fennel with leek, bay leaf, vegetable bouillon and water
2. Stir, seal the instant pot lid and cook at High for 15 minutes.
3. Release the pressure naturally for 15 minutes, then release remaining pressure by turning the valve to 'Venting', carefully open the lid; add cheese, oil, salt and pepper; then stir well. divide into bowls and serve.

Lamb Stew

(Prep + Cooking Time: 50 minutes | Servings: 4)

Ingredients:

- 2 lb. lamb shoulder, cubed
- 14 oz. canned tomatoes; chopped.
- 1/4 cup red wine vinegar
- 1 tbsp. garlic; minced.
- 2 yellow onions; chopped.
- 1 tbsp. olive oil
- 2 bay leaves
- 1/3 cup parsley; chopped.
- 2 tbsp. tomato paste
- 1 red bell pepper; chopped.
- 1 green bell pepper; chopped.
- 1 tsp. oregano; dried
- 1 tsp. basil; dried
- Salt and black pepper to the taste

Directions:

1. Set the pot on Sauté mode; add oil and heat it up
2. Add onions and garlic, stir and cook for 2 minutes.
3. Add vinegar, stir and cook for 2 minutes
4. Add lamb, tomatoes, tomato paste, oregano, basil, salt, pepper and bay leaves; then stir well. close the lid and cook at High for 12 minutes.
5. Release the pressure naturally for 15 minutes, then release remaining pressure by turning the valve to 'Venting', carefully open the lid; discard bay leaves, add green and red pepper, more salt and pepper if needed; then stir well. seal the instant pot lid and cook on High for 8 more minutes.
6. Release the pressure again, carefully open the lid, add parsley, stir and divide into bowls.

Celery Soup

(Prep + Cooking Time: 35 minutes | **Servings:** 2)

Ingredients:

- 3 potatoes; chopped.
- 1 yellow onion; chopped.
- 1 tbsp. curry powder
- 1 tsp. celery seeds
- 1 tsp. extra virgin olive oil
- 7 celery stalks; chopped.
- 4 cups veggie stock
- Salt and black pepper to the taste
- A handful parsley; chopped for serving

Directions:

1. Set your instant pot on Sauté mode; add oil and heat it up.
2. Add onion, celery seeds and curry powder, stir and cook for 1 minute.
3. Add celery and potatoes, stir and cook for 5 minutes.
4. Add stock, salt, pepper stir, seal the instant pot lid and cook at High for 10 minutes.
5. Release the pressure naturally for 15 minutes, then release remaining pressure by turning the valve to 'Venting', carefully open the lid; blend well using an immersion blender, add parsley; then stir well. divide into soup bowls and serve.

Cabbage Head Soup

(Prep + Cooking Time: 30 minutes | **Servings:** 4)

Ingredients:

- 1 cabbage head; chopped
- 12 oz. baby carrots
- 3 celery stalks; chopped.
- 3 tsp. garlic; minced.
- 1/4 cup cilantro; chopped.
- 4 cups chicken stock
- 1/2 onion; chopped
- 1 packet veggie soup mix
- 2 tbsp. olive oil
- 12 oz. soy burger
- Salt and black pepper to the taste

Directions:

1. In your instant pot, mix cabbage with celery, carrots, onion, veggie soup mix, soy burger, stock, olive oil and garlic; then stir well. seal the instant pot lid and cook on High for 5 minutes
2. Release the pressure naturally for 15 minutes, then release remaining pressure by turning the valve to 'Venting', carefully open the lid; add salt, pepper and cilantro, stir again well, divide into soup bowls and serve.

Corn Soup

(Prep + Cooking Time: 35 minutes | **Servings:** 4)

Ingredients:

- 6 ears of corn, kernels cut off, cobs reserved
- 2 leeks; chopped
- 1 tbsp. chives; chopped
- 1-quart chicken stock
- 2 tbsp. butter
- 2 bay leaves
- 4 tarragon sprigs; chopped.
- A drizzle of extra virgin olive oil
- 2 garlic cloves; minced.
- Salt and black pepper to the taste

Directions:

1. Set your instant pot on Sauté mode; add butter and melt it
2. Add garlic and leeks, stir and cook for 4 minutes
3. Add corn, corn cobs, bay leaves, tarragon and stock to cover everything, close the lid and cook at High for 15 minutes.
4. Release the pressure naturally for 15 minutes, then release remaining pressure by turning the valve to 'Venting', carefully open the lid; discard bay leaves and corn cobs and transfer everything to your blender

5. Pulse well obtain a smooth soup, add the rest of the stock and blend again.
6. Add salt and pepper to the taste, stir well, divide into soup bowls and serve cold with chives and olive oil on top

Double Bean Chili

(**Prep + Cooking Time:** 24 minutes | **Servings:** 5)

Ingredients:

- 1 (15-ounce) can black beans, drained and rinsed
- 1 (15-ounce) can kidney beans, drained and rinsed
- 1 (28-ounce) can fire-roasted diced tomatoes, with liquid
- 1 jalapeño pepper, seeded and diced
- 3 garlic cloves; diced
- 1 bell pepper, any color, chopped
- 1 sweet potato, peeled and chopped
- 1/4 cup barbecue sauce
- 3/4 cup water; divided; or more as needed
- 1/2 sweet onion, chopped
- 1 tsp. smoked paprika
- 1 ½ tsp. dried oregano
- 1 tsp. red pepper flakes
- 1 tsp. salt; or more as your liking
- 2 tsp. ground cumin
- 1/2 to 1 tsp. chili powder; or more as needed
- Cashew Sour Cream; for topping; optional
- Chopped avocado; for topping; optional
- Chopped onion; for topping; optional
- Fresh basil; for topping; optional
- Fresh cilantro; for topping; optional
- Crumbled tortilla chips; for topping; optional

Directions:

1. Select the "Sauté" Low mode on your instant pot. When the display reads "Hot," add ¼ cup of water, the onion, jalapeño and garlic. Cook for 2 to 3 minutes, stirring frequently.
2. Add the bell pepper and sweet potato. Cook for 2 to 3 minutes more, stirring occasionally and adding water if necessary
3. Add the salt, cumin, paprika; oregano, red pepper flakes, chili powder, black beans, kidney beans, tomatoes and remaining ½ cup of water.
4. Stir well so the spices are mixed in. Lock the lid and turn the steam release handle to Sealing. Using the Manual function, set the cooker to High Pressure for 5 minutes
5. After completing the cooking time, quick release the pressure
6. Remove the lid carefully and stir in the barbecue sauce. Taste and add salt or more chili powder, as needed, as well as your favorite toppings!

Italian Sausage Stew

(**Prep + Cooking Time:** 40 minutes | **Servings:** 6)

Ingredients:

- 1 lb. Andouille sausage, crumbled.
- 1 sweet onion; chopped.
- 1 ½ lb. gold potatoes, cubed
- 3/4 lb. collard greens, thinly sliced
- 1 cup chicken stock
- 1/2 lb. cherry tomatoes, cut into halves
- Juice of 1/2 lemon
- Salt and black pepper to the taste

Directions:

1. Set your instant pot on Sauté mode; add sausage, stir and cook for 8 minutes.
2. Add onions and tomatoes, stir and cook 4 minutes more
3. Add potatoes, stock, salt, pepper and collard greens; then stir well. close the lid and cook at High for 10 minutes.
4. Release the pressure naturally for 15 minutes, then release remaining pressure by turning the valve to 'Venting', carefully open the lid; add more salt and pepper and lemon juice; then stir well. divide into bowls and serve

Chickpeas Stew

(**Prep + Cooking Time:** 45 minutes | **Servings:** 4)

Ingredients:

- 1 lb. chickpeas, drained
- 1 yellow onion; chopped.
- 1 tsp. oregano; dried
- 2 tbsp. parmesan cheese, grated
- 3 bay leaves
- 2 tbsp. olive oil
- 2 carrots; chopped.
- 1 garlic head, halved
- 22 oz. canned tomatoes; chopped.
- 22 oz. water
- 1/2 tsp. red pepper flakes
- A drizzle of olive oil for serving
- Salt and black pepper to the taste

Directions:

1. Put onion, carrots, garlic, chickpeas, tomatoes, water, oregano, bay leaves, 2 tablespoons olive oil, salt, and pepper in your instant pot.
2. Cover, cook at High for 25 minutes and quick release the pressure
3. Ladle into bowls, add parmesan, pepper flakes and a drizzle of oil on top and serve.

Artichoke Soup

(**Prep + Cooking Time:** 40 minutes | **Servings:** 4)

Ingredients:

- 5 artichoke hearts, washed and trimmed
- 8 oz. gold potatoes; chopped.
- 12 cups chicken stock
- 1 bay leaf
- 1 leek, sliced
- 5 tbsp. butter
- 6 garlic cloves; minced.
- 1/2 cup shallots; chopped
- 4 parsley springs
- 2 thyme springs
- 1/4 cup cream
- 1/4 tsp. black peppercorns, crushed.
- Salt to the taste

Directions:

1. Set your instant pot on Sauté mode; add butter and melt it.
2. Add artichoke hearts, shallots, leek and garlic, stir and brown for 3 - 4 minutes
3. Add potatoes, stock, bay leaf, thyme, parsley, peppercorns and salt; then stir well. seal the instant pot lid and cook at High for 15 minutes.
4. Release the pressure naturally for 15 minutes, then release remaining pressure by turning the valve to 'Venting', carefully open the lid; discard herbs, blend well using an immersion blender, add salt to the taste and cream, stir well, divide into bowls and serve.

Veggie Soup

(**Prep + Cooking Time:** 25 minutes | **Servings:** 4)

Ingredients:

- 1 cup tomatoes; chopped.
- 1 zucchini; chopped.
- 4 cups veggie stock
- 6 big mushrooms, sliced
- 4 garlic cloves; minced.
- 1 brown onion; chopped
- 1 tbsp. coconut oil
- 1 bay leaf
- 1 tsp. lemon zest
- 1/2 red chili; chopped.
- 2 carrots; chopped.
- 2 celery sticks; chopped.
- 3.5 oz. kale leaves, roughly chopped
- Salt and black pepper to the taste
- A handful dried porcini mushrooms
- A handful parsley; chopped.

Directions:

1. Set your instant pot on Sauté mode; add oil and heat it up
2. Add onion, celery, carrots, salt and pepper, stir and cook for 1 minute
3. Add chili; dried mushrooms, mushrooms, garlic, stir and cook for 2 minutes

4. Add kale leaves, zucchini, tomatoes, bay leaf and stock; then stir well. seal the instant pot lid and cook at High for 10 minutes.
5. Release the pressure naturally for 10 minutes, then release remaining pressure by turning the valve to 'Venting', carefully open the lid; divide soup into bowls, add lemon zest and parsley on top and serve

Barley and Beef Soup

(**Prep + Cooking Time:** 45 minutes | **Servings:** 4)

Ingredients:

- 1 ½ lb. beef stew meat; chopped.
- 10 baby bell mushrooms, cut into quarters
- 3 cups mixed onion, carrots and celery
- 2 bay leaves
- 2/3 cup barley
- 8 garlic cloves; minced.
- 6 cups beef stock
- 2 tbsp. vegetable oil
- 1 cup water
- 1/2 tsp. thyme; dried
- 1 potato; chopped.
- Salt and black pepper to the taste

Directions:

1. Set your instant pot on Sauté mode; add oil and heat it up
2. Add meat, salt and pepper; then stir well. cook for 3 minutes and transfer to a plate
3. Add mushrooms; then stir well. brown them for 2 minutes and transfer to a plate.
4. Add mixed veggies to the pot, stir and cook for 4 minutes
5. Return meat, mushrooms to the pot and stir everything
6. Also add bay leaves, thyme, water, stock, salt and pepper; then stir well. seal the instant pot lid and cook at High for 16 minutes
7. Release the pressure naturally for 15 minutes, then release remaining pressure by turning the valve to 'Venting', carefully open the lid; add potatoes and barley; then stir well. seal the instant pot lid and cook on Low for 1 hour
8. Release the pressure again, stir soup, divide it into bowls and serve.

Curried Squash Soup

(**Prep + Cooking Time:** 40 minutes | **Servings:** 5)

Ingredients:

- 1 (2- to 3-pound) butternut squash, peeled and cubed
- 1 (14-ounce) can lite coconut milk
- 4 cups Vegetable Stock
- 1 onion, chopped
- 2 garlic cloves, chopped
- 1 tbsp. curry powder
- 1 tbsp. olive oil
- 1 tsp. salt or as your liking

Directions:

1. Select the "Sauté" Low mode on your instant pot. When the display reads "Hot," add the oil and heat until it shimmers.
2. Add the onion. Cook for 3 to 4 minutes, stirring frequently.
3. Turn off the Instant Pot and add the garlic and curry powder. Cook for 1 minute, stirring. It should start smelling delicious right about now!
4. Add the squash, stock and salt. Lock the lid and turn the steam release handle to Sealing. Using the Manual function, set the cooker to High Pressure for 30 minutes
5. After completing the cooking time, quick release the pressure
6. Remove the lid carefully. Using an immersion blender, blend the soup until completely smooth.
7. Stir in the coconut milk, saving a little bit for topping when served.

Chestnut Soup Recipe

(Prep + Cooking Time: 45 minutes | **Servings:** 4)

Ingredients:

- 1 lb. canned chestnuts, drained and rinsed
- 1 celery stalk; chopped
- 4 tbsp. butter
- 1 potato; chopped
- 1 bay leaf
- 4 cups chicken stock
- 2 tbsp. rum
- 1 yellow onion; chopped
- 1 sage spring; chopped.
- Salt and white pepper to the taste
- A pinch of nutmeg
- Whole cream for serving
- Sage leaves; chopped for serving

Directions:

1. Set your instant pot on Sauté mode; add butter and melt it
2. Add onion, sage, celery, salt and pepper, stir and cook for 5 minutes.
3. Add chestnuts, potato, bay leaf and stock; then stir well. seal the instant pot lid and cook on Low for 20 minutes.
4. Release the pressure naturally for 15 minutes, then release remaining pressure by turning the valve to 'Venting', carefully open the lid; add nutmeg and rum, discard bay leaf and blend soup using an immersion blender
5. Divide soup into bowls, add cream and sage leaves on top and serve.

Veggie Noodle Soup

(Prep + Cooking Time: 20 minutes | **Servings:** 5)

Ingredients:

- 4 celery stalks; chopped into bite-size pieces
- 1 sweet onion; chopped into bite-size pieces
- 1 cup broccoli florets
- 1 tomato; diced
- 2 garlic cloves; minced
- 1 bay leaf
- 2 sweet potatoes, peeled and chopped into bite-size pieces
- 1 cup dried pasta (I prefer a small pasta shape)
- 4 cups Vegetable Stock
- 1 to 1 ½ cups water; or more as needed
- 4 carrots; chopped into bite-size pieces
- 1 tsp. dried oregano
- 1 tsp. dried thyme
- 1 tsp. dried basil
- 2 tsp. salt or as your liking
- Pinch freshly ground black pepper
- Lemon zest, for garnishing; optional
- Chopped fresh parsley, for garnishing; optional
- Crackers; for serving; optional

Directions:

1. In the Instant Pot, combine the celery, carrots, sweet potatoes, onion, broccoli, tomato, garlic, bay leaf; oregano, thyme, basil, salt, pepper, pasta, stock and water, making sure all the good stuff is submerged "you can add more water or stock, if needed".
2. Lock the lid and turn the steam release handle to Sealing. Using the Manual function, set the cooker to High Pressure for 4 minutes
3. After completing the cooking time, let the pressure release naturally for 5 minutes; quick release any remaining pressure
4. Remove the lid carefully and stir the soup. Remove and discard the bay leaf and enjoy garnished as desired!

Chicken Soup

(Prep + Cooking Time: 40 minutes | **Servings:** 4)

Ingredients:

- 4 chicken breasts, skinless and boneless
- 16 oz. jarred chunky salsa
- 29 oz. canned tomatoes; peeled and chopped.
- 29 oz. canned chicken stock
- 2 tbsp. extra virgin olive oil
- 1 tsp. garlic powder
- 15 oz. frozen corn
- 32 oz. canned black beans, drained
- 1 onion; chopped.
- 1 tbsp. onion powder
- 2 tbsp. parsley; dried
- 1 tbsp. chili powder
- 3 garlic cloves; minced.
- Salt and black pepper to the taste

Directions:

1. Set your instant pot on Sauté mode; add oil and heat it up.
2. Add onion, stir and cook 5 minutes
3. Add garlic, stir and cook for 1 minute more.
4. Add chicken breasts, salsa, tomatoes, stock, salt, pepper, parsley, garlic powder, onion and chili powder; then stir well. seal the instant pot lid and cook at High for 8 minutes.
5. Release the pressure naturally for 15 minutes, then release remaining pressure by turning the valve to 'Venting', carefully open the lid; transfer chicken breasts to a cutting board, shred with 2 forks and return to pot
6. Add beans and corn, set the pot on Simmer mode and cook for 2 - 3 minutes more
7. Divide into soup bowls and serve

Easy Carrot Soup

(Prep + Cooking Time: 35 minutes | **Servings:** 4)

Ingredients:

- 1 lb. carrots; chopped.
- 1 tbsp. vegetable oil
- 1 tbsp. butter
- 1 garlic clove; minced.
- 1 small ginger piece, grated
- 1 onion; chopped
- 1/4 tsp. brown sugar
- 2 cups chicken stock
- 1 tbsp. Sriracha
- 14 oz. canned coconut milk
- Salt and black pepper to the taste
- Cilantro leaves; chopped for serving

Directions:

1. Set your instant pot on Sauté mode; add butter and oil and heat them up
2. Add onion, stir and cook for 3 minutes.
3. Add ginger and garlic, stir and cook for 1 minute
4. Add sugar, carrots, salt and pepper, stir and cook 2 minutes more
5. Add sriracha sauce, coconut milk, stock; then stir well. seal the instant pot lid and cook at High for 6 minutes.
6. Release the pressure naturally for 15 minutes, then release remaining pressure by turning the valve to 'Venting', carefully open the lid; blend soup with an immersion blender, add more salt and pepper if needed and divide into soup bowls. Add cilantro on top and serve.

White Bean Soup

(Prep + Cooking Time: 45 minutes | **Servings:** 5)

Ingredients:

- 1 cup dried great northern white beans; rinsed
- 3 ½ to 4 cups water; or more as needed
- 1 (14-ounce) can lite coconut milk
- 1 cube vegetable or "not chicken" bouillon
- 1 cup frozen sweet corn
- 1 small to medium tomato; diced
- 1/4 cup raw millet

- 1 ½ tsp. smoked paprika; or more as needed
- 1 tsp. salt; or as your liking

Directions:
1. In the Instant Pot, stir together the beans, tomato, millet, bouillon cube, paprika, salt, water and coconut milk.
2. Lock the lid and turn the steam release handle to Sealing. Using the Manual function, set the cooker to High Pressure for 32 minutes
3. After completing the cooking time, turn off the Instant Pot "Note: do not let it go into Keep Warm mode" and let the pressure release naturally for 10 minutes; quick release any remaining pressure.
4. Remove the lid carefully and stir in the corn. Taste and adjust the seasonings, as needed.

Ginger Carrot Soup

(Prep + Cooking Time: 20 minutes | **Servings:** 3)

Ingredients:
- 1/2 sweet onion, chopped
- 7 carrots, chopped
- 1-inch piece fresh ginger, peeled and chopped
- 1 ¼ cups Vegetable Stock
- 1/2 tsp. salt or as your liking
- 1/2 tsp. sweet paprika
- Freshly ground black pepper
- Cashew Sour Cream, for garnishing; optional
- Fresh herbs, for garnishing; optional

Directions:
1. In the Instant Pot, combine the carrots, ginger, onion, stock, salt and paprika. Season to taste with pepper.
2. Lock the lid and turn the steam release handle to Sealing. Using the Manual function, set the cooker to High Pressure for 4 minutes
3. After completing the cooking time, let the pressure release naturally for 5 minutes; quick release any remaining pressure
4. Remove the lid carefully. Using an immersion blender, blend the soup until completely smooth.
5. Taste and season with more salt and pepper, as needed. Serve with garnishes of choice.

Potato Leek Soup

(Prep + Cooking Time: 30 minutes | **Servings:** 4)

Ingredients:
- 1 pound Yukon Gold potatoes, cubed
- 2 large leeks, white and very light green parts only, cleaned well, chopped
- 2 garlic cloves; minced
- ⅔ cup soy milk
- ⅓ cup extra-virgin olive oil
- 4 cups Vegetable Stock
- 1 bay leaf
- 3 tbsp. vegan butter
- 1/2 tsp. salt or as your liking
- Freshly ground white pepper

Directions:
1. Select the "Sauté" Low mode on your instant pot. When the display reads "Hot," add the butter and leeks.
2. Cook for about 2 to 3 minutes until soft, stirring occasionally. Add the garlic. Cook for 30 to 45 seconds, stirring frequently, until fragrant.
3. Pour in the stock and add the potatoes, bay leaf and salt. Stir to combine
4. Lock the lid and turn the steam release handle to Sealing. Using the Manual function, set the cooker to High Pressure for 5 minutes.
5. After completing the cooking time, let the pressure release naturally for 15 minutes; quick release any remaining pressure
6. While waiting for the pressure to release, in a blender, combine the soy milk and olive oil. Blend until combined, about 1 minute. This is an easy dairy-free substitute for heavy cream.

7. Remove the lid carefully, remove and discard the bay leaf and stir in the "cream."
8. Using an immersion blender, purée the soup until smooth. Taste and season with salt and pepper, as desired.

Peanut Stew

(**Prep + Cooking Time:** 15 minutes | **Servings:** 5)

Ingredients:

- 1 small onion; cut into large dice
- 2 cups Vegetable Stock
- 3 garlic cloves; minced
- 3 tomatoes; cut into large dice
- 1 sweet potato; cut into large dice
- 1/2 cup creamy all-natural peanut butter; not sweetened
- 1/2 cup chopped roasted peanuts
- 1 small bunch collard green leaves, chopped
- 1 red bell pepper; cut into large dice
- 1 jalapeño pepper; diced
- 2 tbsp. minced peeled fresh ginger
- 1 tbsp. roasted walnut oil
- 1/2 tsp. chili powder
- 1 ½ tsp. ground cumin
- 1/2 tsp. salt or as your liking
- Freshly ground black pepper

Directions:

1. Select the "Sauté" Low mode on your instant pot. When the display reads "Hot," add the oil and heat until it shimmers.
2. Add the onion, bell pepper and jalapeño. Cook for 2 to 3 minutes, stirring frequently. Turn off the Instant Pot and add the garlic. Cook for 30 seconds, stirring.
3. Stir in the tomatoes, sweet potato, ginger, cumin, chili powder and salt. Let rest for a few minutes.
4. While the stew rests, in a large measuring cup, whisk the peanut butter and 1 cup of stock until smooth. Pour this into the Instant Pot
5. Use the remaining 1 cup of stock to rinse out the measuring cup, making sure you get as much of the peanut butter as possible
6. Add this to the pot. Lock the lid and turn the steam release handle to Sealing. Using the Manual function, set the cooker to High Pressure for 3 minutes.
7. After completing the cooking time, quick release the pressure
8. Remove the lid carefully and stir in the collard greens, which will wilt in 1 to 2 minutes.
9. Taste and season with salt and pepper, as needed and serve topped with chopped peanuts.

Ham and White Bean Soup

(**Prep + Cooking Time:** 25 minutes | **Servings:** 8)

Ingredients:

- 1 lb. white beans, soaked for 1 hour and drained
- 1 carrot; chopped.
- 3 garlic cloves; minced.
- 1 tomato; peeled and chopped.
- 1 lb. ham; chopped.
- 1 tbsp. extra-virgin olive oil
- 4 cups veggie stock
- 1 tsp. mint; dried
- 1 tsp. paprika
- 1 tsp. thyme; dried
- 1 yellow onion; chopped.
- Salt and black pepper to taste
- 4 cups water

Directions:

1. Set your instant pot on Sauté mode; add oil and heat it up
2. Add carrot, onion, garlic, tomato, stir and cook for 5 minutes
3. Add beans, ham, salt, pepper, water, stock, mint, paprika and thyme, stir, cover and cook at High for 15 minutes.
4. Release the pressure naturally for 15 minutes, then release remaining pressure by turning the valve to 'Venting', and carefully open the lid. Divide into soup bowls and serve

Coconut Sweet Potato Stew

(**Prep + Cooking Time:** 25 minutes | **Servings:** 5)

Ingredients:

- 2 Roma tomatoes, chopped
- 1 or 2 dashes chili powder
- 1/2 sweet onion; diced
- 2 sweet potatoes, peeled and cubed
- 2 garlic cloves; minced
- 1 (14-ounce) can lite coconut milk, shaken well
- 1 ¼ cups water; or more as needed
- 1 to 2 cups chopped kale
- 2 tbsp. avocado or olive oil
- 1 tsp. paprika
- 1/2 tsp. ground cumin
- 1/2 tsp. dried oregano
- 1 ½ tsp. salt or as your liking
- 1 tsp. ground turmeric

Directions:

1. Select the "Sauté" Low mode on your instant pot. When the display reads "Hot," add the oil and heat until it shimmers.
2. Add the onion. Cook for 2 to 3 minutes, stirring frequently. If they start to burn, hit the Cancel button and let the pot cool down a little before turning it back on
3. Stir in the sweet potatoes, garlic, salt, turmeric, paprika, cumin; oregano and chili powder. Stir, stir, stir and cook for 1 minute or so.
4. Add the tomatoes, coconut milk and water and give it one last good stir. Lock the lid and turn the steam release handle to Sealing. Using the Manual function, set the cooker to High Pressure for 5 minutes.
5. After completing the cooking time, turn off the Instant Pot. Let the pressure release naturally for 10 minutes; quick release any remaining pressure
6. Remove the lid carefully and stir in the kale, which will wilt quickly. Add more water if you want a thinner consistency.

Minestrone Soup

(**Prep + Cooking Time:** 15 minutes | **Servings:** 5)

Ingredients:

- 1 large carrot, sliced, with thicker end cut into half-moons
- 1 zucchini, roughly diced
- 1 (28-ounce) can diced tomatoes
- 1 (16-ounce) can kidney beans, drained and rinsed
- 2 celery stalks, sliced
- 1 sweet onion; diced
- 1 bay leaf
- 1 cup small dried pasta
- 6 cups Vegetable Stock
- 2 to 3 cups fresh baby spinach
- 2 garlic cloves; minced
- 2 tbsp. olive oil
- 1 tsp. dried basil
- 1 tsp. salt; or more as your liking
- 1 tsp. dried oregano
- Freshly ground black pepper

Directions:

1. Select the "Sauté" Low mode on your instant pot. When the display reads "Hot," add the oil, celery, onion and carrot.
2. Cook for 2 to 3 minutes, stirring frequently. Add the garlic and cook for another minute or so, stirring frequently.
3. Turn off the Instant Pot and add the oregano, basil, salt and bay leaf. Stir and let sit for 30 seconds to 1 minute
4. Add the zucchini, tomatoes, kidney beans, pasta and stock. Lock the lid and turn the steam release handle to Sealing. Using the Manual function, set the cooker to High Pressure for 4 minutes
5. After completing the cooking time, quick release the pressure. Remove the lid carefully and remove and discard the bay leaf

6. Stir in the spinach and let it get all nice and wilty. Taste and season with more salt, as needed and pepper. Serve hot.

Corn Chowder

(Prep + Cooking Time: 15 minutes | **Servings:** 5)

Ingredients:

- 3 large russet potatoes, peeled and cut into large dice
- 1 cup nondairy milk
- 12 ounces frozen sweet corn
- 3 celery stalks, sliced
- 3 ½ cups Vegetable Stock
- 1/2 cup all-purpose flour
- 1 carrot, grated
- 2 garlic cloves; minced

- 1 small sweet onion; diced
- 6 tbsp. vegan butter
- 1 tbsp. olive oil
- 1 tsp. dried thyme
- 1/2 tsp. ground coriander
- 1 tsp. salt or as your liking
- 1/4 tsp. freshly ground black pepper
- Sliced scallion, green and light green parts, for garnishing; optional

Directions:

1. Select the "Sauté" Low mode on your instant pot. When the display reads "Hot," add the oil and heat until it shimmers.
2. Add the onion. Cook for 2 to 3 minutes, stirring frequently. Turn off the Instant Pot and add the celery, garlic, thyme, coriander, salt and pepper. Cook for another minute or so
3. Stir in the potatoes and stock. Lock the lid and turn the steam release handle to Sealing. Using the Manual function, set the cooker to High Pressure for 6 minutes
4. While the chowder cooks, in a small pan over medium-low heat on the stovetop, melt the butter.
5. Whisk in the flour and cook for 3 to 4 minutes. Whisk in the milk, getting rid of any lumps to finish the roux.
6. After completing the cooking time, quick release the pressure. Remove the lid carefully and select Sauté Low again. Add the corn and carrot
7. Stir in the roux and let warm through and thicken. Taste and season with salt and pepper, as desired. Garnish with scallion before serving.

SERVING TIP: Make this chowder a little more fun by serving it in a bread bowl. Sourdough is my favorite, but any type of bread will do—just don't forget the vegan butter!

Split Pea Soup

(Prep + Cooking Time: 45 minutes | **Servings:** 5)

Ingredients:

- 2 carrots; diced
- 1 celery stalk; diced
- 1 bay leaf
- 1 cup green split peas
- 2 ½ cups Vegetable Stock
- 1 tbsp. roasted walnut oil

- 1 tsp. dried thyme
- 1 tsp. smoked paprika
- 1 tsp. salt; or as your liking
- 2 garlic cloves; minced
- Freshly ground black pepper

Directions:

1. Select the "Sauté" Low mode on your instant pot. When the display reads "Hot," add the oil and heat until it shimmers.
2. Add the carrots, celery, thyme, paprika, bay leaf and salt. Cook for 2 to 3 minutes, stirring frequently, until fragrant. Turn off the Instant Pot and add the garlic
3. Cook for 30 seconds. Stir in the split peas and stock. Lock the lid and turn the steam release handle to Sealing. Using the Manual function, set the cooker to High Pressure for 18 minutes.

4. After completing the cooking time, let the Instant Pot go into Keep Warm mode and let the pressure release naturally for 15 minutes; quick release any remaining pressure
5. Remove the lid carefully and remove and discard the bay leaf. Taste and season with salt and pepper, as needed.

Italian Stew

(**Prep + Cooking Time:** 28 minutes | **Servings:** 5)

Ingredients:

- 3 Yukon Gold potatoes; chopped into large bite-size pieces
- 2 cups torn kale leaves
- 1 sweet onion; cut into large dice
- 1 carrot, halved lengthwise; cut into half-moons
- 1 celery stalk, sliced
- 1 cup sliced white mushrooms
- 1 small eggplant; cut into large dice
- 3 garlic cloves; minced
- 3 Roma tomatoes; cut into large dice
- 2 leeks, white and very light green parts only, cleaned well, halved lengthwise; cut into half-moons
- 4 cups Vegetable Stock
- 2 tbsp. olive oil
- 1 tsp. dried oregano
- 1/2 tsp. salt or as your liking Freshly ground black pepper
- Fresh basil; for garnishing

Directions:

1. Select the "Sauté" Low mode on your instant pot. When the display reads "Hot," add the oil and heat until it shimmers.
2. Add the leeks, onion, carrot, celery, mushrooms and eggplant. Cook for about 2 minutes, stirring occasionally.
3. Add the garlic. Cook for 30 seconds more. Turn off the Instant Pot and add the potatoes, tomatoes, stock; oregano and salt. Lock the lid and turn the steam release handle to Sealing. Using the Manual function, set the cooker to High Pressure for 8 minutes
4. After completing the cooking time, let the pressure release naturally for 10 minutes; quick release any remaining pressure
5. Remove the lid carefully and stir in the kale. Taste and season with more salt, as needed and pepper.
6. If there's too much liquid, select Sauté Low again and cook for a few minutes to evaporate. Serve garnished with basil.

Quinoa Butternut Chili

(**Prep + Cooking Time:** 28 minutes | **Servings:** 5)

Ingredients:

- 2 carrots, sliced
- 1 sweet onion; cut into large dice
- 1 red bell pepper; cut into large dice
- 1 jalapeño pepper; diced
- 2 garlic cloves; minced
- 1 butternut squash, peeled and cut into bite-size cubes
- 1 (14-ounce) can diced tomatoes with juice
- 1 cup uncooked quinoa; rinsed
- 2 ½ cups Vegetable Stock
- 1 bay leaf
- 1 to 2 tbsp. olive oil
- 1 tsp. ground cumin
- 1 tbsp. freshly squeezed lemon juice
- 1/2 to 1 tsp. salt; or more as your liking
- 1/2 tsp. sweet paprika
- 1/2 tsp. chili powder; or more to taste
- 1/2 tsp. freshly ground black pepper; or more as needed

Directions:

1. Select the "Sauté" Low mode on your instant pot. When the display reads "Hot," add the oil and heat until it shimmers.
2. Add the carrots, onion, bell pepper and jalapeño. Cook for 2 to 3 minutes, stirring. Turn off the Instant Pot and add the garlic, stirring again so it doesn't burn
3. Add the squash, tomatoes, quinoa, stock, bay leaf, cumin, salt, paprika, chili powder and pepper.
4. Lock the lid and turn the steam release handle to Sealing. Using the Manual function, set the cooker to High Pressure for 8 minutes
5. After completing the cooking time, turn the Instant Pot off and let the pressure release naturally for 10 minutes; quick release any remaining pressure
6. Remove the lid carefully. Remove and discard the bay leaf and stir in the lemon juice.
7. Taste and season with salt and pepper, as needed. If there's too much liquid, select Sauté Low again and cook for 1 to 2 minutes, stirring frequently.

Taco Chili

(**Prep + Cooking Time:** 36 minutes | **Servings:** 7)

Ingredients:

- 1 (15-ounce) can diced tomatoes with green chilies, drained
- 1 (15-ounce) can black beans; rinsed and drained
- 1 (16-ounce) can chili beans, undrained
- 1 (8-ounce) package unflavored tempeh; cut into large dice
- 1 small onion; diced
- 1 green bell pepper; diced
- 1 jalapeño pepper; diced
- 2 tbsp. olive oil
- 1/2 tsp. garlic powder
- 1 tsp. ground cumin
- 1 tsp. smoked paprika
- 1/2 tsp. chili powder; or more as needed
- 1 tsp. salt or as your liking
- Chopped scallion, green and light green parts; for garnishing
- Chopped avocado or Cashew Sour Cream; for garnishing
- Shredded vegan cheese; for sprinkling
- Tortilla chips; for serving

Directions:

1. Select the "Sauté" Low mode on your instant pot. When the display reads "Hot," add the oil and heat until it shimmers.
2. Add the tempeh and paprika. Cook for 6 to 7 minutes, stirring frequently. The tempeh will break down a bit and that's fine
3. Add the onion, bell pepper and jalapeño. Sauté for 2 to 3 minutes more; or until soft. Add 1 to 2 tbsp. of water, if things are sticking. Turn off the Instant Pot
4. Stir in the tomatoes and green chilies, black beans, chili beans, cumin, salt, garlic powder and chili powder to taste.
5. Lock the lid and turn the steam release handle to Sealing. Using the Manual function set the cooker to High Pressure for 5 minutes
6. After completing the cooking time, let the pressure release naturally for 10 minutes; quick release any remaining pressure
7. Remove the lid carefully. If the chili is too thin, select Sauté Low again and cook until the desired consistency is reached. Serve topped as you like.

Wild Rice Soup

(**Prep + Cooking Time:** 50 minutes | **Servings:** 5)

Ingredients:

- 5 carrots, sliced, with thicker end cut into half-moons
- 5 celery stalks, sliced
- 8 ounces baby bella mushrooms, sliced
- 1 small sweet onion; diced
- 4 garlic cloves; minced
- 4 cups Vegetable Stock
- 1 cup wild rice
- 1/2 cup all-purpose flour
- 1 cup nondairy milk
- 2 bay leaves
- 8 tbsp. vegan butter; divided
- 1/2 tsp. paprika
- 1/2 tsp. dried thyme
- 1/2 tsp. salt or as your liking
- Freshly ground black pepper

Directions:

1. Select the "Sauté" Low mode on your instant pot. When the display reads "Hot," add 2 tbsp. of butter to melt.
2. Add the carrots, celery, onion, garlic, mushrooms, bay leaves, paprika, thyme and salt. Cook for 2 to 3 minutes, just until fragrant. Turn off the Instant Pot.
3. Stir in the stock and wild rice. Lock the lid and turn the steam release handle to Sealing. Using the Manual function, set the cooker to High Pressure for 35 minutes
4. When there are just a few minutes of cook time remaining, in a small pan over medium-low heat on your stovetop, melt the remaining 6 tbsp. of butter
5. Whisk in the flour and cook for 3 to 4 minutes. Whisk in the milk, getting rid of any lumps to finish the roux.
6. After completing the cooking time, quick release the pressure. Remove the lid carefully and remove and discard the bay leaves
7. Select Sauté Low again. Stir in the roux and let warm through and thicken. Taste and season with salt and pepper, as needed.

Tomato Basil Soup

(**Prep + Cooking Time:** 28 minutes | **Servings:** 5)

Ingredients:

- 3 pounds tomatoes, quartered
- 1/4 cup fresh basil, chopped, plus more for garnishing
- 2 garlic cloves; minced
- 1 large carrot, chopped
- 1 small sweet onion, chopped
- 1 celery stalk, chopped
- 3 cups Vegetable Stock
- 1/4 cup nutritional yeast
- 2 tbsp. vegan butter
- Salt as your liking
- 1/2 to 1 cup nondairy milk
- Freshly ground black pepper

Directions:

1. Select the "Sauté" Low mode on your instant pot. When the display reads "Hot," add the butter to melt. Add the onion and garlic
2. Sauté for 3 to 4 minutes, stirring frequently. Add the carrot and celery and cook for 1 to 2 minutes more. Continue to stir frequently so nothing sticks.
3. Stir in the stock (now is your chance to reincorporate any veggies stuck to the bottom).
4. Add the tomatoes, basil, yeast and a pinch or two of salt. Stir one last time
5. Lock the lid and turn the steam release handle to Sealing. Using the Manual function, set the cooker to High Pressure for 5 minutes.
6. After completing the cooking time, let the pressure release naturally for 5 to 10 minutes; quick release any remaining pressure
7. Remove the lid carefully. Using an immersion blender, blend the soup to your preferred consistency.
8. Stir in the milk. Taste and season with salt and pepper, as needed. Garnish with the remaining fresh basil.

Mushroom Cream Soup

(**Prep + Cooking Time:** 30 minutes | **Servings:** 5)

Ingredients:

- 1 ½ pounds white button mushrooms, sliced
- 1 ¾ cups Vegetable Stock
- 1/2 cup silken tofu
- 1 small sweet onion, chopped
- 2 garlic cloves; minced
- 2 tbsp. vegan butter
- 2 tsp. dried thyme
- 1 tsp. sea salt or as your liking
- Chopped fresh thyme; for garnishing

Directions:

1. Select the "Sauté" Low mode on your instant pot. When the display reads "Hot," add the butter to melt.
2. Add the onion. Sauté for 1 to 2 minutes. Add the mushrooms, garlic, dried thyme and salt. Cook for 2 minutes more and then turn off the Instant Pot
3. Stir in the stock. Lock the lid and turn the steam release handle to Sealing. Using the Manual function, set the cooker to High pressure for 6 minutes
4. While the soup cooks, place the tofu in a food processor or blender and process until smooth. Set aside.
5. After completing the cooking time, let the pressure release naturally for 10 minutes; quick release any remaining pressure.
6. Remove the lid carefully. Using an immersion blender, blend the soup until completely creamy. Stir in the tofu, garnish as desired and it's ready!

Chipotle Sweet Potato Chowder

(**Prep + Cooking Time:** 10 minutes | **Servings:** 5)

Ingredients:

- 2 large sweet potatoes, peeled and diced large
- 1 ½ cups frozen sweet corn
- 1 ¼ cups Vegetable Stock
- 1 (14-ounce) can lite coconut milk
- 2 to 4 canned chipotle peppers in adobo sauce; diced
- 1 red bell pepper; diced
- 1 small onion; diced
- 1 tsp. ground cumin
- 1 tsp. salt or as your liking
- Adobo sauce from the canned peppers, to taste

Directions:

1. In a medium bowl, whisk the stock and coconut milk, ensuring there are no solid bits of coconut milk left.
2. Pour into the Instant Pot and add the sweet potatoes, chipotles, bell pepper, onion, cumin and salt.
3. Lock the lid and turn the steam release handle to Sealing. Using the Manual function, set the cooker to High pressure for 2 minutes
4. After completing the cooking time, let the pressure release naturally for 5 minutes; quick release any remaining pressure
5. Remove the lid carefully and add the frozen corn and adobo sauce, if you want more heat. Let sit for 1 to 2 minutes while the corn warms.

Fish and Seafood

Surprising Shrimp Delight

(Prep + Cooking Time: 30 minutes | **Servings:** 4)

Ingredients:

- 18 oz. shrimp, peeled and deveined
- 1/2 tbsp. mustard seeds
- 3 oz. mustard oil
- 1 tsp. turmeric powder
- 2 onions; finely chopped
- 4 oz. curd, beaten
- 2 green chilies, cut into halves lengthwise
- 1-inch ginger; chopped.
- Salt to the taste
- Already cooked rice for serving

Directions:

1. Put mustard seeds in a bowl, add water to cover, leave aside for 10 minutes, drain and grind very well
2. Put shrimp in a bowl, add mustard oil, turmeric, mustard paste, salt, onions, chilies, curd and ginger, toss to coat and leave aside for 10 minutes.
3. Transfer everything to your instant pot, seal the instant pot lid and cook on Low for 10 minutes.
4. Quick release the pressure, divide among plates and serve with boiled rice

Tuna & Pasta Casserole.

(Prep + Cooking Time: 10 minutes | **Servings:** 2)

Ingredients:

- 1 can cream of mushroom soup
- 2 ½ cups. macaroni pasta
- 1/2 tsp. salt
- 1/2 tsp. pepper
- 1 cup. cheddar cheese, shredded.
- 1 cups. frozen peas
- 2 cans tuna
- 3 cups. water

Directions:

1. Mix the soup with the water in the Instant Pot. Except for the cheese, add the rest of the ingredients.
2. Stir to combine. Lock the lid and turn the steam valve to "Sealing". Press "Manual", set the pressure to "High", and set the timer for 4 minutes.
3. When the timer beeps, turn the steam valve to "Venting" to quickly release the pressure. Unlock and open the lid.
4. Sprinkle the cheese on top. Close the lid and let sit for 5 minutes or until the cheese is melted and the sauce is thick

Almond Cod.

(Prep + Cooking Time: 45 minutes | **Servings:** 4)

Ingredients:

- 8 oz. cod
- 3 tbsp. almond flakes
- 1 tsp. minced garlic
- 3 tbsp. soy sauce
- 1 tbsp. lime zest
- 1/4 cup. fish sauce
- 1/2 cup. almond milk
- 1 tbsp. butter

Directions:

1. Choose the roughly and transfer it to the mixing bowl
2. Add fish sauce and soy sauce. Stir the mixture.
3. Ager this, sprinkle the fish with the lime zest and minced garlic. Stir it.
4. Then add almond milk and leave the fish for 10 minutes to marinate.
5. Then toss the butter in the Instant Pot and melt it.
6. Then add the almond milk cod in the Instant Pot. Close the lid and cook the dish at the "Sauté" mode for 10 minutes
7. When the time is over - open the Instant Pot lid and add almond flakes.

8. Stir the dish gently and cook it for 3 minutes.
9. Then remove the dish from the Instant Pot. Serve it immediately. Enjoy!

Mussels and Spicy Sauce

(Prep + Cooking Time: 15 minutes | **Servings:** 4)

Ingredients:

- 2 lb. mussels, scrubbed and debearded
- 1/2 tsp. red pepper flakes
- 2 tsp. oregano; dried
- 2 tbsp. extra virgin olive oil
- 14 oz. tomatoes; chopped.
- 2 tsp. garlic; minced.
- 1/2 cup chicken stock
- 1 yellow onion; chopped.

Directions:

1. Set your instant pot on Sauté mode; add oil and heat it up.
2. Add onions, stir and cook for 3 minutes
3. Add pepper flakes and garlic, stir and cook for 1 minute
4. Add stock, oregano and tomatoes and stir well.
5. Add mussels; then stir well. seal the instant pot lid and cook on Low for 2 minutes
6. Quick release the pressure, discard unopened mussels, divide among bowls and serve

Tasty Tomato Mussels

(Prep + Cooking Time: 15 minutes | **Servings:** 3)

Ingredients:

- 28 oz. canned tomatoes, crushed.
- 2 lb. mussels, cleaned and scrubbed
- 1/4 cup extra virgin olive oil
- 1/4 cup balsamic vinegar
- 1/2 cup white onion; chopped.
- 2 jalapeno peppers; chopped.
- 2 tbsp. red pepper flakes
- 2 garlic cloves; minced.
- 1/4 cup dry white wine
- 1/2 cup basil; chopped.
- Lemon wedges for serving
- Salt to the taste

Directions:

1. Set your instant pot on Sauté mode; add tomatoes, onion, jalapenos, wine, oil, vinegar, garlic and pepper flakes, stir and bring to a boil.
2. Add mussels; then stir well. seal the instant pot lid and cook on Low for 4 minutes.
3. Quick release the pressure, carefully open the lid; discard unopened mussels, add salt and basil; then stir well. divide among bowls and serve with lemon wedges

Cheesy Tuna Dish.

(Prep + Cooking Time: 15 minutes | **Servings:** 6)

Ingredients:

- 28 oz. canned cream mushroom soup
- 3 cups. water
- 1 can (5 oz.) tuna, drained
- 1 cup. frozen peas
- 1/4 cup. bread crumbs (optional)
- 16 oz. egg noodles
- 4 oz. cheddar cheese

Directions:

1. Put the noodles in the Instant Pot. Pour in the water to cover the noodles.
2. Add the frozen peas, tuna, and the soup on top of the pasta layer. Cover and lock the lid
3. Press the "Manual" key, set the pressure to "High", and set the timer for 4 minutes. When the Instant Pot timer beeps, press the "Cancel" key and unplug the Instant Pot. Turn the steam valve to quick release the pressure.
4. Unlock and carefully open the lid. Stir in the cheese.
5. If desired, you can pour the pasta mixture in a baking dish, sprinkle the top with bread crumbs, and broil for about 2 to 3 minutes. Serve.

Poached Salmon Dish

(Prep + Cooking Time: 15 minutes | **Servings:** 4)

Ingredients:

- 16 oz. salmon fillet, skin on
- Zest from 1 lemon
- 1/2 cup dry white wine
- 1 tsp. white wine vinegar
- 2 cups chicken stock
- 1/2 tsp. fennel seeds
- 1 bay leaf
- 4 scallions; chopped.
- 3 black peppercorns
- 1/4 cup dill; chopped
- Salt and black pepper to the taste

Directions:

1. Put salmon in the steamer basket of your instant pot and season with salt and pepper.
2. Add stock, scallions, lemon zest, peppercorns, fennel, vinegar, bay leaf, wine, stock and dill to your pot.
3. Cover and cook at High for 5 minutes.
4. Quick release the pressure, carefully open the lid and divide salmon among plates
5. Set the pot on Simmer mode and cook the liquid for a few minutes more
6. Drizzle over salmon and serve

Salmon and Veggies Dish

(Prep + Cooking Time: 20 minutes | **Servings:** 2)

Ingredients:

- 2 salmon fillets, skin on
- 1 bay leaf
- 2 cups broccoli florets
- 1 cinnamon stick
- 3 cloves
- 1 tbsp. canola oil
- 1 cup water
- 1 cup baby carrots
- Salt and black pepper to the taste
- Lime wedges for serving

Directions:

1. Pour the water in your instant pot
2. Add bay leaf, cinnamon stick and cloves.
3. Place salmon fillets in the steamer basket of your pot after you've brushed them with canola oil
4. Season with salt and pepper, add broccoli and carrots, seal the instant pot lid and cook at High for 6 minutes
5. Release the pressure naturally for 4 minutes, then release remaining pressure by turning the valve to 'Venting', and carefully open the lid.
6. Divide salmon and veggies among plates.
7. Drizzle the sauce from the pot after you've discarded cinnamon, cloves and bay leaf and serve with lime wedges on the side.

Salmon Dish

(Prep + Cooking Time: 25 minutes | **Servings:** 4)

Ingredients:

- 4 salmon fillets
- 4 thyme springs
- 3 tomatoes, sliced
- 1 lemon, sliced
- 1 white onion; chopped.
- 2 cups water
- 3 tbsp. extra virgin olive oil
- 4 parsley springs
- Salt and black pepper to the taste

Directions:

1. Drizzle the oil on a parchment paper
2. Add a layer of tomatoes, salt and pepper.
3. Drizzle some oil again, add fish and season them with salt and pepper
4. Drizzle some more oil, add thyme and parsley springs, onions, lemon slices, salt and pepper

5. Fold and wrap packet, place in the steamer basket of your instant pot
6. Add 2 cups water to the pot, seal the instant pot lid and cook on Low for 15 minutes.
7. Quick release the pressure, carefully open the lid; open packet, divide fish mix among plates and serve.

Crispy Salmon Fillet

(Prep + Cooking Time: 15 minutes | Servings: 2)

Ingredients:
- 2 salmon fillets, frozen
- 2 tbsp. extra virgin olive oil
- 1 cup water
- Salt and black pepper to the taste

Directions:
1. Pour the water in your instant pot.
2. Place salmon in the steamer basket, seal the instant pot lid and cook on Low for 3 minutes.
3. Quick release the pressure, transfer salmon to paper towels and pat dry them.
4. Heat up a pan with the oil over medium high heat, add salmon fillets skin side down, season with salt and pepper to the taste and cook for 2 minutes.
5. Divide among plates and serve with your favorite salad on the side

Steamed Fish Recipe

(Prep + Cooking Time: 20 minutes | Servings: 4)

Ingredients:
- 4 white fish fillets
- 1 lb. cherry tomatoes, cut into halves
- A pinch of thyme; dried
- 1 garlic clove; minced.
- A drizzle of olive oil
- 1 cup olives, pitted and chopped.
- 1 cup water
- Salt and black pepper to the taste

Directions:
1. Pour the water in your instant pot.
2. Put fish fillets in the steamer basket of the pot.
3. Add tomatoes and olives on top
4. Also add garlic, thyme, oil, salt and pepper
5. Cover the pot and cook on Low for 10 minutes.
6. Quick release the pressure, carefully open the lid; divide fish, olives and tomatoes mix among plates and serve.

Spicy Salmon Dish

(Prep + Cooking Time: 15 minutes | Servings: 4)

Ingredients:
- 4 salmon fillets
- 2 tbsp. assorted chili pepper
- 1 lemon, sliced
- 1 cup water
- Juice of 1 lemon
- Salt and black pepper to the taste

Directions:
1. Place salmon fillets in the steamer basket of your pot, add salt, pepper, lemon juice, lemon slices and chili pepper.
2. Add 1 cup water to the pot, seal the instant pot lid and cook at High for 5 minutes.
3. Quick release the pressure, divide salmon and lemon slices among plates and serve

Tuna and Noodle

(Prep + Cooking Time: 30 minutes | **Servings:** 4)

Ingredients:

- 8 oz. egg noodles
- 1/2 cup red onion; chopped.
- 1 ¼ cups water
- 8 oz. artichoke hearts, drained and chopped.
- 1 tbsp. parsley; chopped.
- 1 tbsp. extra-virgin olive oil
- 14 oz. canned tomatoes; chopped and mixed with oregano, basil and garlic
- 14 oz. canned tuna, drained
- Salt and black pepper to the taste
- Crumbled feta cheese

Directions:

1. Set your instant pot on Sauté mode; add oil and heat it up
2. Add onion, stir and cook for 2 minutes
3. Add tomatoes, noodles, salt, pepper and water, set the pot on Simmer and cook for 10 minutes.
4. Add tuna and artichokes; then stir well. seal the instant pot lid and cook at High for 5 minutes.
5. Quick release the pressure, divide tuna and noodles among plates, sprinkle cheese and parsley on top and serve

Delicious Shrimp Paella

(Prep + Cooking Time: 15 minutes | **Servings:** 4)

Ingredients:

- 20 shrimps, deveined
- 1 ½ cups water
- 4 garlic cloves; minced.
- 1 cup jasmine rice
- 1/4 cup butter
- 1/4 cup parsley; chopped.
- A pinch of saffron
- A pinch of red pepper, crushed.
- Juice of 1 lemon
- Melted butter for serving
- Salt and black pepper to the taste
- Parsley; chopped for serving
- Hard cheese, grated for serving

Directions:

1. Put shrimp in your instant pot.
2. Add rice, butter, salt, pepper, parsley, red pepper, saffron, lemon juice, water and garlic.
3. Stir, seal the instant pot lid and cook at High for 5 minutes.
4. Quick release the pressure, carefully open the lid; takes shrimps and peel them
5. Return to pot, stir well and divide into bowls
6. Add melted butter, cheese and parsley on top and serve.

Crispy Skin Salmon Fillets.

(Prep + Cooking Time: 20 minutes | **Servings:** 2)

Ingredients:

- 2 salmon fillets, frozen (1-inch thickness)
- 2 tbsp. olive oil
- 1 cup. tap water, running cold
- Salt and pepper, to taste

Directions:

1. Pour 1 cup. water in the Instant Pot.
2. Set the steamer rack and put the salmon fillets in the rack. Lock the lid and close the steamer valve.
3. Press "Manual", set the pressure on "Low", and set the timer for 1 minute
4. When the timer beeps, turn off the pot and quick release the pressure
5. Carefully open the lid. Remove the salmon fillets and pat them dry using paper towels.
6. Over medium-high heat, preheat a skillet.
7. Grease the salmon fillet skins with 1 tablespoon olive oil and generously season with black pepper and salt.
8. When the skillet is very hot, with the skin side down, put the salmon fillet in the skillet.

9. Cook for 1 to 2 minutes until the skins are crispy.
10. Transfer the salmon fillets into serving plates and serve with your favorite side dishes.
11. This dish is great with rice and salad.

Tips: You can use a nonstick skillet to make sure the skin does not stick to the skillet. If you do not like the skin on your salmon, you can remove it after pressure cooking. Increase the cooking time to 2 minutes

Salmon Burger

(**Prep + Cooking Time:** 20 minutes | **Servings:** 4)

Ingredients:
- 1 lb. salmon meat; minced.
- 1 tsp. extra virgin olive oil
- 1/2 cup panko
- 2 tbsp. lemon zest
- Tomatoes slices for serving
- Mustard for serving
- Salt and black pepper to the taste
- Arugula leaves for serving

Directions:
- Put salmon in your food processor and blend it.
- Transfer to a bowl, add panko, salt, pepper and lemon zest and stir well.
- Shape 4 patties and place them on a working surface.
- Set your instant pot on Sauté mode; add oil and heat it up
- Add patties, cook for 3 minutes on each side and divide them on buns.
- Serve with tomatoes, arugula and mustard.

Miso Mackerel

(**Prep + Cooking Time:** 60 minutes | **Servings:** 4)

Ingredients:
- 2 lb. mackerel, cut into big pieces
- 1 cup water
- 1 garlic clove, crushed.
- 2 celery stalks, sliced
- 1/3 cup mirin
- 1/4 cup miso
- 1/3 cup sake
- 1 sweet onion, thinly sliced
- 1 tbsp. rice vinegar
- 1 tsp. Japanese hot mustard
- 1 tsp. sugar
- 1 shallot, sliced
- 1-inch ginger piece; chopped
- Salt to the taste

Directions:
1. Set your instant pot on Sauté mode; add mirin, sake, ginger, garlic and shallot, stir and boil for 2 minutes.
2. Add miso and water and stir.
3. Add mackerel, seal the instant pot lid and cook at High for 45 minutes.
4. Meanwhile, put onion and celery in a bowl and cover with ice water.
5. In another bowl, mix vinegar with salt, sugar and mustard and stir well
6. Release the pressure from the pot naturally for 10 minutes and divide mackerel among plates.
7. Drain onion and celery well and mix with mustard dressing.
8. Divide along mackerel and serve

Shrimp with Herbs and Risotto

(**Prep + Cooking Time:** 30 minutes | **Servings:** 4)

Ingredients:
- 1 lb. shrimp, peeled and deveined
- 4 tbsp. butter
- 2 garlic cloves; minced.
- 1 ½ cups Arborio rice
- 2 tbsp. dry white wine
- 4 ½ cups chicken stock
- 3/4 cup parmesan, grated
- 1/4 cup tarragon and parsley; chopped
- 1 yellow onion; chopped.
- Salt and black pepper to the taste

Directions:

1. Set your instant pot on Sauté mode; add 2 tablespoon butter and melt.
2. Add garlic and onion, stir and cook for 4 minutes
3. Add rice, stir and cook for 1 minute
4. Add wine, stir and cook 30 seconds more.
5. Add 3 cups stock, salt, and pepper; then stir well. seal the instant pot lid and cook at High for 9 minutes.
6. Quick release the pressure, carefully open the lid; add shrimp, the rest of the stock, set the pot on Sauté mode again and cook for 5 minutes stirring from time to time.
7. Add cheese, the rest of the butter, tarragon and parsley; then stir well. divide among plates and serve.

Fish with Orange Sauce

(Prep + Cooking Time: 17 minutes | **Servings:** 4)

Ingredients:

- 4 white fish fillets
- 1 cup fish stock
- Juice and zest from 1 orange
- A drizzle of extra virgin olive oil
- A small piece of ginger; chopped.
- 4 spring onions; chopped.
- Salt and black pepper to the taste

Directions:

1. Pat dry fish fillets, season with salt, pepper and rub them with the olive oil
2. Put stock, ginger, orange juice, orange zest and onions in your instant pot.
3. Put fish fillets in the steamer basket, seal the instant pot lid and cook at High for 7 minutes.
4. Quick release the pressure, divide fish among plates and drizzle the orange sauce on top.

Simple Clams

(Prep + Cooking Time: 25 minutes | **Servings:** 4)

Ingredients:

- 15 small clams
- 30 mussels, scrubbed and debearded
- 2 tbsp. parsley; chopped.
- 1 tsp. extra virgin olive oil
- 1 yellow onion; chopped.
- 10 oz. beer
- 2 chorizo links, sliced
- 1 lb. baby red potatoes
- Lemon wedges for serving

Directions:

1. Set your instant pot on Sauté mode; add oil and heat it up
2. Add chorizo and onions, stir and cook for 4 minutes.
3. Add clams, mussels, potatoes and beer; then stir well. seal the instant pot lid and cook at High for 10 minutes.
4. Quick release the pressure, carefully open the lid; add parsley; then stir well. divide among bowls and serve with lemon wedges on the side.

Crab Legs and Garlic Butter Sauce.

(Prep + Cooking Time: 15 minutes | **Servings:** 2)

Ingredients:

- 2 lb. frozen or fresh crab legs
- 1 tsp. olive oil
- 1 minced garlic clove
- 1 cup. water
- 1 halved lemon
- 4 tbsp. salted butter

Directions:

1. Pour water in your Instant Pot and lower in the steamer basket. Add the crab legs.
2. Choose the "steam" option adjust time to 3 minutes for fresh, and 4 for frozen. In the meantime, heat the oil in a skillet.
3. Cook garlic for just 1 minute, stirring so it doesn't burn

4. Add the butter and stir to melt. Squeeze the halved lemon in the butter.
5. By now, the crab will be done, so hit "cancel" and quick-release the pressure
6. Serve crabs with the garlic butter on the side

Shrimp and Potatoes Dish

(Prep + Cooking Time: 25 minutes | **Servings:** 4)

Ingredients:
- 2 lb. shrimp, peeled and deveined
- 8 potatoes, cut into quarters
- 4 tbsp. extra virgin olive oil
- 4 onions; chopped.
- 1 lb. tomatoes; peeled and chopped.
- 1 tbsp. watercress
- 1 tsp. coriander, ground.
- 1 tsp. curry powder
- Juice of 1 lemon
- Salt to the taste

Directions:
1. Put potatoes in the steamer basket of the pot, add some water to the pot, seal the instant pot lid and cook at High for 10 minutes.
2. Quick release the pressure, transfer potatoes to a bowl and clean up your pot.
3. Set the pot on Sauté mode; add oil and heat it up
4. Add onions, stir and cook for 5 minutes.
5. Add salt, coriander and curry, stir and cook for 5 minutes
6. Add tomatoes, shrimp, lemon juice and return potatoes as well.
7. Stir, seal the instant pot lid and cook at High for 3 minuets
8. Release the pressure again, divide among bowls and serve with watercress on top

Shrimp and Fish

(Prep + Cooking Time: 20 minutes | **Servings:** 4)

Ingredients:
- 1/2 lb. shrimp, cooked, peeled and deveined
- 4 lemon wedges
- 2 tbsp. butter
- 2 lb. flounder
- 1/2 cup water
- Salt and black pepper to the taste

Directions:
1. Season fish with salt and pepper and place in the steamer basket of the pot
2. Add water to the pot, seal the instant pot lid and cook at High for 10 minutes.
3. Release the pressure carefully open the lid; transfer fish to plates and leave aside
4. Discard water, clean pot and set on Sauté mode.
5. Add butter and melt it.
6. Add shrimp, salt and pepper, stir and divide among plates on top of fish and serve with lemon wedges on the side

Shrimp and Sausage Boil

(Prep + Cooking Time: 35 minutes | **Servings:** 4)

Ingredients:
- 1/2 lb. shrimp; peeled and deveined
- 4 baby red potatoes, halved
- 4 ears sweet corn, cut into thirds
- 4 shakes hot sauce
- 8 ounces smoked sausage, cut into 4 pieces each
- 1 tbsp. minced garlic
- 1 tbsp. Louisiana-style shrimp and crab boil seasoning
- 6 tbsp. (¾ stick) salted butter
- Juice of ½ lemon
- 1/4 tsp. Old Bay seasoning
- ⅛ tsp. Cajun seasoning
- ⅛ tsp. lemon-pepper seasoning
- Lemon slices

Directions:

1. In your Instant Pot, combine the sausage, corn and potatoes. Add water to cover. Add the shrimp and crab boil seasoning.
2. Now secure the lid on the pot and close the valve. Now Press "Manual" and set the pot at "High" pressure for 4 minutes
3. Meanwhile; in a small saucepan, melt the butter over medium-high heat. Add the garlic and cook, stirring continuously, until fragrant, 1 to 2 minutes
4. Add the lemon juice, Old Bay, Cajun seasoning, lemon-pepper seasoning and hot sauce. Stir until warmed through; keep warm
5. After completing the cooking time, quick release the pressure. Open the lid carefully and check to ensure the potatoes are cooked. If they are not done, you can boil them for a few minutes using the "Sauté" setting.
6. Gently stir in the shrimp. As soon as the shrimp turn pink, drizzle everything with the spiced garlic-butter sauce. Add the lemon slices to the pot. Stir gently until everything is well coated.

Tuna and Crushed Crackers Casserole.

(**Prep + Cooking Time:** 25 minutes | **Servings:** 8)

Ingredients:

- 8 oz. fresh tuna
- 3 tbsp. butter
- 3 tbsp. all-purpose flour
- 1 cup. frozen peas
- 1 cup. cheddar, shredded.
- 1 cup. celery
- 3 ½ cups. chicken stock
- 2 tsp. salt
- 2 cups. pasta (I used elbow mac)
- 1/4 cup. heavy cream
- 1 cup. onion
- 1 cup. buttery crackers, crushed.
- Fresh ground black pepper

Directions:

1. Press the "Sauté" key of the Instant Pot to preheat it. When hot, put the celery and onion
2. Sauté until the onion is translucent. Pour in the chicken stock and pasta, and season with salt and pepper.
3. Stir to combine for a bit. Put the fresh tuna on top of the pasta mix. Press "Cancel" to stop the sauté function. Close and lock the lid.
4. Press "Manual" and set the timer for 5 minutes. Meanwhile, heat the sauté pan over medium-high.
5. Put the butter in the pan and melt. Stir in the flour and cook for 2 minutes. Remove the pan from the heat and set aside.
6. When the timer of the Instant Pot beeps, turn the steam valve to "Venting" to quick release the pressure. Transfer the tuna onto a plate and set aside.
7. Pour the butter mix into the Instant Pot. Press the "Sauté" key. Stir until the mixture is thick. Turn off the Instant Pot. Stir in the heavy cream, the peas, and the tuna
8. Cover the mix with the crackers and then with the grated cheese
9. Cover and let stand for 5 minutes. Serve

Shrimp Coconut Soup

(**Prep + Cooking Time:** 21 minutes | **Servings:** 4)

Ingredients:

- 1/2 lb. medium shrimp; peeled (tails left on) and deveined
- 1/4 cup fresh lime juice
- 1 cup canned straw mushrooms; undrained
- 6 thin slices fresh ginger
- 1 (13.5-ounce) can full-fat coconut milk
- Grated zest of 1 lime
- 3 cups chicken broth
- 2 tbsp. fish sauce
- 1 tbsp. minced fresh lemongrass
- 1 tsp. honey

- 1/2 tsp. salt or as your liking
- Chopped fresh cilantro, for garnish
- Lime wedges, for serving

Directions:
1. In your Instant Pot, combine the broth, shrimp, mushrooms and their liquid, half the coconut milk, the ginger, chiles (if using), 1 tbsp. of the fish sauce, the lemongrass, honey and salt
2. Now secure the lid on the pot and close the valve. Now Press "Manual" and set the pot at "Low" pressure for 1 minute
3. After completing the cooking time, quick release the pressure. Stir in the remaining 1 tbsp. fish sauce, remaining coconut milk, the lime zest and lime juice
4. Divide the soup among four serving bowls. Garnish with cilantro and serve with lime wedges alongside for squeezing.

Shrimp Teriyaki Recipe

(Prep + Cooking Time: 15 minutes | **Servings:** 4)

Ingredients:
- 1 lb. shrimp, peeled and deveined
- 1/2 lb. pea pods
- 3/4 cup pineapple juice
- 1 cup chicken stock
- 3 tbsp. vinegar
- 3 tbsp. sugar
- 2 tbsp. soy sauce

Directions:
1. Put shrimp and pea pods in your instant pot.
2. In a bowl, mix soy sauce with vinegar, pineapple juice, stock and sugar and stir well.
3. Pour this into the pot; then stir well. seal the instant pot lid and cook at High for 3 minutes.
4. Quick release the pressure, carefully open the lid; divide among plates and serve

Instant Shrimp Boil

(Prep + Cooking Time: 15 minutes | **Servings:** 4)

Ingredients:
- 1 ½ lb. shrimp, head removed
- 1 lb. potatoes, cut into medium chunks
- 8 garlic cloves, crushed.
- 1 tbsp. old bay seasoning
- 12 oz. Andouille sausage, already cooked and chopped.
- 4 ears of corn, each cut into 3 pieces
- 1 tsp. red pepper flakes, crushed.
- 2 sweet onions, cut into wedges
- 16 oz. beer
- Salt and black pepper to the taste
- French baguettes for serving

Directions:
1. In your instant pot, mix beer with old bay seasoning, red pepper flakes, salt, black pepper, onions, garlic, potatoes, corn, sausage pieces and shrimp.
2. Cover the pot and cook at High for 5 minutes
3. Quick release the pressure, carefully open the lid; divide shrimp boil into bowls and serve with French baguettes on the side.

Cheesy Tilapia.

(Prep + Cooking Time: 35 minutes | **Servings:** 4)

Ingredients:
- 5 oz. Cheddar cheese
- 12 oz. tilapia
- 1 tbsp. butter
- 1 tsp. ground ginger
- 1 onion
- 1/3 tsp. ground black pepper
- 1/2 cup. cream

Directions:

1. Cut the tilapia into the medium fillets.
2. Then combine the ground ginger and ground black pepper together. Mix up the mixture.
3. After this, rub the tilapia fillets with the spice mixture. Leave the fish for 5 minutes
4. After this, grate Cheddar cheese.
5. Peel the onion and slice it. Toss the butter in the Instant Pot and melt it at the "Manual" mode.
6. Then add the tilapia fillets and cook them for 2 minutes from each side.
7. After this, cover the tilapia fillets with the sliced onion
8. Sprinkle the dish with the grated cheese and pour cream
9. Close the lid and cook the dish at the STEW mode for 10 minutes.
10. When the time is over - open the Instant Pot lid. Let the fish chill little
11. Serve the tilapia fillets immediately. Enjoy!

Mediterranean Fish

(Prep + Cooking Time: 20 minutes | **Servings:** 4)

Ingredients:

- 17 oz. tomatoes, cut into halves
- 4 cod fillets
- 1 cup olives, pitted and chopped.
- 2 tbsp. capers, drained and chopped.
- 1 tbsp. extra-virgin olive oil
- 1 tbsp. parsley; chopped.
- 1 garlic clove, crushed.
- Salt and black pepper to the taste

Directions:

1. Put tomatoes on the bottom of a heat proof bowl.
2. Add parsley, salt and pepper and toss to coat
3. Place fish fillets on top, add olive oil, salt, pepper, garlic, olives and capers
4. Place the bowl in the steamer basket of the pot, seal the instant pot lid and cook at High for 5 minutes.
5. Release the pressure naturally, divide among plates and serve.

Delicious Salmon and Raspberry Sauce

(Prep + Cooking Time: 2 hours and 5 minutes | **Servings:** 6)

Ingredients:

- 6 salmon steaks
- 2 tbsp. parsley; chopped.
- 1 cup clam juice
- 2 tbsp. lemon juice
- 2 tbsp. extra virgin olive oil
- 4 leeks, sliced
- 2 garlic cloves; minced
- 1 tsp. sherry
- 1/3 cup dill; finely chopped
- Salt and white pepper to the taste
- Raspberries for serving

For the raspberry vinegar:

- 1-pint cider vinegar
- 2 pints red raspberries

Directions:

1. Mix red raspberries with vinegar and stir well
2. Add salmon steaks and leave aside in the fridge for 2 hours
3. Set your instant pot on Sauté mode; add oil and heat it up.
4. Add parsley, leeks and garlic, stir and cook for 2 minutes
5. Add clam and lemon juice, sherry, salt, pepper and dill and stir
6. Add salmon steaks, seal the instant pot lid and cook at High for 3 minutes
7. Quick release the pressure, carefully open the lid; divide salmon among plates and serve with leeks and fresh raspberries

Sesame Honey Salmon

(Prep + Cooking Time: 20 minutes | **Servings:** 4)

Ingredients:

- 1 lb. salmon fillet
- 2 cups water
- 1 tbsp. dark soy sauce
- 1 tbsp. toasted sesame oil
- 2 tbsp. sesame seeds
- 1 tbsp. honey
- 2 tsp. minced fresh ginger
- 1 tsp. minced garlic
- 1/2 tsp. red pepper flakes
- Salt and black pepper to taste

Directions:

1. Place the salmon in a 6-inch round heatproof pan. In a small bowl, combine the honey, soy sauce, sesame oil, ginger, garlic and red pepper flakes and season with salt and black pepper. Whisk to combine.
2. Pour the mixture over the salmon. Allow the salmon to sit at room temperature for 15 to 30 minutes.
3. Pour the water into the Instant Pot. Place a steamer rack in the pot. Place the pan with the salmon on the rack
4. Now secure the lid on the pot and close the valve. Now Press "Manual" and set the pot at "Low" pressure for 3 minutes
5. After completing the cooking time, allow the pot to sit undisturbed for 5 minutes, then release any remaining pressure. Sprinkle with the sesame seeds. Serve the salmon immediately.

Crab Quiche

(Prep + Cooking Time: 60 minutes | **Servings:** 4)

Ingredients:

- 1 cup half-and-half
- 4 large eggs
- 2 cups water
- 8 ounces imitation crabmeat, real crabmeat
- 1 cup shredded Swiss cheese
- 1 cup chopped scallions
- Vegetable oil
- 1 tsp. smoked paprika
- 1 tsp. herbes de Provence
- 1 tsp. black pepper
- 1 tsp. salt or as your liking

Directions:

1. Grease a 6-inch or 7-inch nonstick springform pan with vegetable oil. Set the pan on a sheet of aluminum foil that is larger than the pan and crimp the foil around the bottom of the pan.
2. In a large bowl, whisk together the eggs and half-and-half. Add the cheese, scallions, pepper, paprika, herbes de Provence and salt. Stir with a fork to combine. Add the imitation crabmeat and stir to combine
3. Pour the egg mixture into the prepared pan. Cover the pan loosely with foil. Pour the water into the Instant Pot. Set a steamer rack in the pot. Place the pan on the steamer rack
4. Now secure the lid on the pot and close the valve. Now Press "Manual" and set the pot at "High" pressure for 25 minutes
5. After completing the cooking time, allow the pot to sit undisturbed for 10 minutes, then release any remaining pressure. Using silicone oven mitts, very carefully remove the pan from the pot. Using a knife, loosen the sides of the quiche from the pan, then remove the springform ring. Serve warm.

Shrimp with Tomatoes, Spinach

(Prep + Cooking Time: 31 minutes | **Servings:** 4)

Ingredients:

- 1 lb. shrimp (21 to 25 count); peeled and deveined
- 4 cups chopped baby spinach
- 1 ½ cups chopped yellow onions
- 1/4 cup shredded Parmesan cheese
- 1 (14.5-ounce) can diced tomatoes; undrained
- 1/4 cup chopped fresh basil
- 1 tbsp. minced garlic
- 2 tbsp. salted butter
- 1 tsp. dried oregano
- 1/2 tsp. red pepper flakes
- 1 tsp. salt or as your liking
- 1 tsp. black pepper

Directions:

1. Now Press "Sauté" on the Instant Pot. When the pot is hot, add the butter. When the butter has melted, add the garlic and red pepper flakes.
2. Cook, stirring, for 1 minute. Add the spinach, shrimp, onions, tomatoes and their juices, oregano, salt and pepper. Stir to combine. Now Press "Cancel"
3. Secure the lid on the pot. Close the pressure release valve. Now Press "Manual" and set the pot at "Low" pressure for 1 minute
4. After completing the cooking time, quick release the pressure. Allow the mixture to cool for 5 minutes. Stir in the basil. Divide the mixture among four shallow bowls. Top with Parmesan and serve immediately.

Seafood Stew

(Prep + Cooking Time: 43 minutes | **Servings:** 4)

Ingredients:

- 1 cup chopped carrots
- 1 cup chicken broth
- 1 cup diced yellow onions
- 1 cup water
- 1 (14.5-ounce) can fire-roasted diced tomatoes
- 2 bay leaves
- 4 cups mixed seafood, such as white fish chunks; peeled shrimp, bay scallops, shelled mussels and calamari rings
- 1 tbsp. tomato paste
- 2 tbsp. minced garlic
- 1 tbsp. fresh lemon juice
- 2 tsp. fennel seeds, toasted and ground
- 1 tsp. dried oregano
- 1 tsp. red pepper flakes, plus more for garnish
- Salt or as your liking
- Crusty bread, toasted

Directions:

1. In your Instant Pot, combine the tomatoes and their juices, onions, carrots, water, wine, garlic, fennel seeds, tomato paste, oregano, red pepper flakes and bay leaves. Season with salt. Stir to combine.
2. Now secure the lid on the pot and close the valve. Now Press "Manual" and set the pot at "High" pressure for 15 minutes
3. After completing the cooking time, allow the pot to sit undisturbed for 10 minutes, then release any remaining pressure. Remove the lid from the Instant Pot. Now Press "Sauté" and bring the soup to a boil.
4. Add the mixed seafood and cook until the fish and shellfish are cooked through, 3 to 4 minutes. Stir in the lemon juice. Now Press "Cancel"
5. Discard the bay leaves. Serve the stew garnished with red pepper flakes, with crusty bread alongside to mop up the delicious, savory broth.

Fresh Catfish with Herbs.

(**Prep + Cooking Time:** 20 minutes | **Servings:** 6)

Ingredients:
- 14 oz. catfish
- 1 tsp. fresh parsley
- 1 tsp. dill
- 2 tbsp. soy sauce
- 1 tbsp. olive oil
- 1/4 cup. fresh thyme
- 3 garlic cloves
- 1/4 cup. water
- 1 tbsp. salt

Directions:
1. Wash the fresh parsley and fresh thyme. Chop the greens.
2. Combine the chopped greens with the dill and salt. Stir the mixture.
3. After this, peel the garlic cloves and slice them. Pour the olive oil in the Instant Pot.
4. Add the sliced garlic and "Sauté" it for 1 minute
5. Then combine the catfish with the green mixture. Add soy sauce and water.
6. Stir the mixture and transfer it to the Instant Pot.
7. "Sauté" the dish for 4 minutes on each side.
8. When the dish is cooked - you will get the light golden brown color of the fish.
9. Serve the dish hot! Enjoy!

Steamed Scallion Ginger Fish

(**Prep + Cooking Time:** 32 minutes | **Servings:** 4)

Ingredients:
For Fish:
- 1 lb. firm white-fleshed fish, such as tilapia, cut into large pieces
- 2 cups water
- 2 tbsp. rice wine
- 1 tbsp. Chinese black bean paste
- 3 tbsp. soy sauce
- 1 tsp. minced fresh ginger
- 1 tsp. minced garlic

For Sauce:
- 1/4 cup chopped fresh cilantro
- 1/4 cup julienned scallions
- 2 tbsp. julienned fresh ginger
- 1 tbsp. peanut oil

Directions:
1. For fish: Place the fish pieces on a rimmed plate. In a small bowl, combine the soy sauce, rice wine, black bean paste; minced ginger and garlic. Whisk to combine. Pour over the fish, turning to coat
2. Allow the fish to stand at room temperature for 20 to 30 minutes. Pour the water into the Instant Pot. Place a steamer basket in the pot. Transfer the fish to the steamer basket, reserving the marinade
3. Now secure the lid on the pot and close the valve. Now Press "Manual" and set the pot at "Low" pressure for 2 minutes. After completing the cooking time, quick release the pressure. Transfer the fish to a serving platter.
4. Meanwhile; for the sauce: In a small saucepan, heat the peanut oil over medium-high heat. When the oil shimmers, add the julienned ginger and cook, stirring, for 10 seconds
5. Add the scallions and cilantro. Cook, stirring, until the ginger and scallions are just softened, about 2 minutes.
6. Add the reserved marinade and bring to a boil. Boil vigorously for 1 to 2 minutes. Pour the vegetable mixture over the fish and serve immediately.

Delicious Cod and Peas

(Prep + Cooking Time: 20 minutes **| Servings:** 4)

Ingredients:

- 10 oz. peas
- 9 oz. wine
- 1/2 tsp. oregano; dried
- 16 oz. cod fillets
- 1 tbsp. parsley; chopped.
- 2 garlic cloves; chopped.
- 1/2 tsp. paprika
- Salt and pepper to the taste

Directions:

1. In your food processor mix garlic with parsley, oregano and paprika and blend well.
2. Add wine, blend again and leave aside for now.
3. Place fish fillets in the steamer basket of your instant pot, add salt and pepper, seal the instant pot lid and cook at High for 2 minutes.
4. Release the pressure and divide fish among plates
5. Add peas to the steamer basket, seal the instant pot lid again and cook at High for 2 minutes.
6. Release the pressure again and arrange peas next to fish fillets.
7. Serve with herbs dressing on top

Instant Pot Steamed Mussels

(Prep + Cooking Time: 15 minutes **| Servings:** 4)

Ingredients:

- 2 lb. mussels, cleaned and scrubbed
- 1 radicchio, cut into thin strips
- 1/2 cup dry white wine
- 1 lb. baby spinach
- 1/2 cup water
- 1 garlic clove, crushed.
- 1 white onion; chopped.
- A drizzle of extra virgin olive oil

Directions:

1. Arrange baby spinach and radicchio on appetizer plates
2. Set instant pot on Sauté mode; add oil and heat it up
3. Add garlic and onion, stir and cook for 4 minutes.
4. Add wine, stir and cook for 1 minute.
5. Place mussels in the steamer basket of the pot, seal the instant pot lid and cook on Low for 1 minute.
6. Release the pressure and divide mussels on top of spinach and radicchio
7. Add cooking liquid all over and serve

Vegetable Recipes

Tomatoes and Zucchinis

(Prep + Cooking Time: 22 minutes | **Servings:** 4)

Ingredients:

- 6 zucchinis, roughly chopped
- 1 cup tomato puree
- 1 lb. cherry tomatoes, cut into halves
- A drizzle of olive oil
- 2 yellow onions; chopped.
- 1 tbsp. vegetable oil
- 2 garlic cloves; minced.
- 1 bunch basil; chopped.
- Salt and black pepper to the taste

Directions:

1. Set your instant pot on Sauté mode; add vegetable oil and heat it up
2. Add onion, stir and cook for 5 minutes
3. Add tomatoes, tomato puree, zucchinis, salt and pepper; then stir well. Seal the Instant Pot lid and cook at High for 5 minutes
4. Quick release the pressure, open the instant pot lid, add garlic and basil, stir and divide among plates.
5. Drizzle some olive oil at the end and serve

Savoy Cabbage & Cream

(Prep + Cooking Time: 20 minutes | **Servings:** 4)

Ingredients:

- 1 cup bacon; chopped.
- 1 bay leaf
- 1 yellow onion; chopped.
- 2 cups bone stock
- 1/4 tsp. nutmeg
- 1 cup coconut milk
- 2 tbsp. parsley flakes
- 1 medium Savoy cabbage head; chopped.
- Salt and black pepper to the taste

Directions:

1. Set your instant pot on Sauté mode; add bacon and onion, stir and cook until bacon is crispy
2. Add stock, cabbage, bay leaf, salt, pepper and nutmeg; then stir well. close the instant pot lid and cook on High for 5 minutes.
3. Quick release the pressure, carefully open the lid and set it on Sauté mode again.
4. Add milk, more salt and pepper if needed and parsley, stir and cook for 4 minutes.
5. Divide among plates and serve.

Maple Glazed Carrots Recipe

(Prep + Cooking Time: 15 minutes | **Servings:** 4)

Ingredients:

- 2 lb. carrots, peeled and sliced on the diagonal
- 1 tbsp. maple syrup
- 1/4 cup raisins
- 1 tbsp. butter
- 1 cup water
- Black pepper to the taste

Directions:

1. Put carrots in your instant pot
2. Add water and raisins, close the lid and cook at High for 4 minutes
3. Quick release the pressure, carefully open the lid; add butter and maple syrup; then stir well. divide carrots among plates and sprinkle black pepper before serving them.

Instant Steamed Leeks

(**Prep + Cooking Time:** 20 minutes | **Servings:** 4)

Ingredients:
- 4 leeks, washed, roots and ends cut off
- 1 tbsp. butter
- 1/3 cup water
- Salt and black pepper to the taste

Directions:
1. Put leeks in your instant pot, add water and butter, salt and pepper to the taste; then stir well. close the lid and cook at High for 5 minutes
2. Quick release the pressure, open the instant pot lid, set it on Sauté mode and cook leeks for 5 more minutes.
3. Divide among plates and serve

Wrapped Asparagus Canes

(**Prep + Cooking Time:** 10 minutes | **Servings:** 4)

Ingredients:
- 8 oz. prosciutto slices
- 1 lb. asparagus, trimmed
- 2 cups water
- A pinch of salt

Directions:
1. Wrap asparagus spears in prosciutto slices and place them on the bottom of the steamer basket in your instant pot
2. Add 2 cups water to the pot, add a pinch of salt, close the lid and cook at High for 4 minutes
3. Release the pressure naturally, carefully open the lid; transfer asparagus canes on a platter and serve at room temperature.

Braised Endives

(**Prep + Cooking Time:** 17 minutes | **Servings:** 4)

Ingredients:
- 4 endives, trimmed and cut into halves
- 1 tbsp. lemon juice
- 1 tbsp. butter
- Salt and black pepper to the taste

Directions:
1. Set your instant pot on Sauté mode
2. Add butter and melt it
3. Arrange endives in the pot, add salt and pepper and the lemon juice, Seal the Instant Pot lid and cook at High for 7 minutes.
4. Release the pressure naturally, arrange endives on a platter, add cooking juice all over them and serve.

Sausages and Cabbage

(**Prep + Cooking Time:** 15 minutes | **Servings:** 4)

Ingredients:
- 15 oz. canned tomatoes; chopped.
- 1/2 cup yellow onion; chopped.
- 3 tbsp. butter
- 1 lb. sausage links, sliced
- 2 tsp. turmeric
- 1 green cabbage head; chopped.
- Salt and black pepper to the taste

Directions:
1. Set your instant pot on Sauté mode; add sausage slices, stir and cook until they brown.
2. Drain excess grease, add butter, cabbage, tomatoes salt, pepper, onion and turmeric; then stir well. close the lid and cook at High for 2 minutes
3. Quick release the pressure, carefully open the lid; divide cabbage and sausages among plates and serve.

Turnips Dish

(Prep + Cooking Time: 30 minutes | **Servings:** 4)

Ingredients:

- 20 oz. turnips; peeled and chopped.
- 1 tsp. garlic; minced.
- 1 tsp. ginger, grated
- 1 tsp. sugar
- 1 tsp. cumin powder
- 1 tsp. coriander powder
- 2 green chilies; chopped.
- 1/2 tsp. turmeric powder
- 1 cup water
- 2 tbsp. butter
- 2 yellow onions; chopped.
- 2 tomatoes; chopped.
- Salt to the taste
- A handful coriander leaves; chopped.

Directions:

1. Set your instant pot on Sauté mode; add butter and melt it.
2. Add green chilies, garlic and ginger, stir and cook for 1 minute.
3. Add onions, stir and cook 3 minutes
4. Add salt, tomatoes, turmeric, cumin and coriander powder, stir and cook 3 minutes.
5. Add turnips and water; then stir well. Seal the Instant Pot lid and cook on Low for 15 minutes
6. Quick release the pressure, open the instant pot lid, add sugar and coriander; then stir well. divide among plates and serve

Stuffed Tomatoes Delight

(Prep + Cooking Time: 20 minutes | **Servings:** 4)

Ingredients:

- 4 tomatoes, tops cut off and pulp scooped
- 1 yellow onion; chopped.
- 2 tbsp. celery; chopped.
- 1/2 cup mushrooms; chopped.
- 1 slice of bread, crumbled.
- 1/2 cup water
- 1 cup cottage cheese
- 1 tbsp. butter
- 1/4 tsp. caraway seeds
- 1 tbsp. parsley; chopped.
- Salt and black pepper to the taste

Directions:

1. Chop tomato pulp and put it in a bowl.
2. Heat up a pan with the butter over medium high heat, add onion and celery, stir and cook for 3 minutes.
3. Add tomato pulp and mushrooms, stir and cook for 1 minute more.
4. Add salt, pepper, crumbled bread, cheese, caraway seeds and parsley, stir and cook for 4 minutes more.
5. Fill each tomato with this mix and arrange them in the steamer basket of your instant pot
6. Add the water to the pot, Seal the Instant Pot lid and cook at High for 2 minutes.
7. Quick release the pressure, open the instant pot lid, transfer stuffed potatoes to plates and serve.

Corn and Okra

(Prep + Cooking Time: 30 minutes | **Servings:** 6)

Ingredients:

- 1 lb. okra, trimmed
- 28 oz. canned tomatoes; chopped
- 6 scallions; chopped
- 3 green bell peppers; chopped.
- 2 tbsp. vegetable oil
- 1 tsp. sugar
- Salt and black pepper to the taste
- 1 cup corn kernels

Directions:

1. Set your instant pot on Sauté mode; add oil and heat it up
2. Add scallions and bell peppers, stir and cook for 5 minutes
3. Add okra, salt, pepper, sugar and tomatoes; then stir well. Seal the Instant Pot lid and cook at High for 10 minutes

4. Quick release the pressure, carefully open the lid; add corn, close the lid again and cook at High for 2 minutes.
5. Release pressure again, transfer okra mix on plates and serve

Tomato and Beet Salad

(Prep + Cooking Time: 60 minutes | **Servings:** 8)

Ingredients:

- 1-pint mixed cherry tomatoes, cut into halves
- 1 ½ cups water
- 1 cup apple cider vinegar
- 1 cup water
- 2 tsp. pickling juice
- 8 small beets, trimmed
- 1 red onion, sliced
- 2 oz. pecans
- 2 tbsp. extra virgin olive oil
- 2 tbsp. sugar
- 4 oz. goat cheese
- Salt and black pepper to the taste

Directions:

1. Put beets in the steamer basket of your instant pot, add 1 ½ cups water, close the lid and cook at High for 20 minutes
2. Quick release the pressure, open the instant pot lid, transfer beets to a cutting board, leave them to cool down, peel and chop them and put them in a bowl
3. Clean your instant pot, add 1 cup water, vinegar, sugar, pickling juice and salt to the taste; then stir well. close the lid and cook at High for 2 minutes
4. Quick release the pressure, strain liquid into a bowl, add onions, stir and leave aside for 10 minutes.
5. Add tomatoes over beets and onions and stir
6. In a bowl, mix 4 tablespoons of liquid from the onions with 2 tablespoons olive oil, salt and pepper and stir.
7. Add this to beets salad and stir.
8. Also, add goat cheese and pecans, toss to coat and serve.

Fennel Risotto Dish

(Prep + Cooking Time: 20 minutes | **Servings:** 2)

Ingredients:

- 1 ½ cups Arborio rice
- 1 yellow onion; chopped.
- 2 tbsp. butter
- 1 tbsp. extra-virgin olive oil
- 1/4 cup white wine
- 3 cups chicken stock
- 1 fennel bulb, trimmed and chopped.
- 1/2 tsp. thyme; dried
- 3 tbsp. tomato paste
- 1/3 cup parmesan cheese, grated
- Salt and black pepper to the taste

Directions:

1. Set your instant pot on Sauté mode; add butter and melt it.
2. Add fennel and onion; then stir well. sauté for 4 minutes and transfer to a bowl.
3. Add oil to your pot and heat it up
4. Add rice, stir and cook for 3 minutes
5. Add tomato paste, stock, fennel, onions, wine, salt, pepper and thyme; then stir well. close the instant pot lid and cook at High for 8 minutes.
6. Quick release the pressure, carefully open the lid; add cheese; then stir well. divide among plates and serve.

Collard Greens Delight

(Prep + Cooking Time: 30 minutes | **Servings:** 4)

Ingredients:
- 1 bunch collard greens, trimmed
- 2 tbsp. extra virgin olive oil
- 2 tbsp. tomato puree
- 1 yellow onion; chopped.
- 3 garlic cloves; minced.
- 1 tbsp. balsamic vinegar
- 1 tsp. sugar
- 1/2 cup chicken stock
- Salt and black pepper to the taste

Directions:
1. In your instant pot, mix stock with oil, garlic, vinegar, onion and tomato puree and stir.
2. Add collard greens after you've rolled them in cigar-shaped bundles
3. Add salt, pepper and sugar, close the lid and cook at High for 20 minutes
4. Quick release the pressure, carefully open the lid; divide collard greens among plates and serve.

Sweet & Spicy Cabbage

(Prep + Cooking Time: 18 minutes | **Servings:** 4)

Ingredients:
- 1 cabbage, cut into 8 wedges
- 1/4 cup apple cider vinegar
- 1 ¼ cups apple+2 tsp. water
- 1 tsp. raw sugar
- 2 tsp. cornstarch
- 1/2 tsp. cayenne pepper
- 1/2 tsp. red pepper flakes
- 1 tbsp. sesame seed oil
- 1 carrot, grated

Directions:
1. Set your instant pot on Sauté mode; add oil and heat it up
2. Add cabbage, stir and cook for 3 minutes.
3. Add carrots, 1 ¼ cups water, sugar, vinegar, cayenne and pepper flakes; then stir well. close the lid and cook at High for 5 minutes
4. Quick release the pressure, carefully open the lid and divide cabbage and carrots mix among plates
5. Add cornstarch mixed with 2 tsp. water to the pot, set the pot on Simmer mode, stir very well and bring to a boil
6. Drizzle over cabbage and serve.

Eggplant Ratatouille Dish

(Prep + Cooking Time: 22 minutes | **Servings:** 6)

Ingredients:
- 1 big eggplant, peeled and thinly sliced
- 1 red bell pepper; chopped.
- 1/2 cup water
- 2 garlic cloves; minced.
- 3 tbsp. extra virgin olive oil
- 1 cup onion; chopped.
- 1 green bell pepper; chopped.
- 1 tsp. thyme
- 14 oz. canned tomatoes; chopped.
- A pinch of sugar
- 1 cup basil; chopped.
- Salt and black pepper to the taste

Directions:
1. Set your instant pot on Sauté mode; add oil and heat it up.
2. Add green and red bell pepper, onion and garlic, stir and cook for 3 minutes
3. Add eggplant, water, salt, pepper, thyme, sugar and tomatoes, seal the instant pot lid and cook at High for 4 minutes.
4. Quick release the pressure, carefully open the lid; add basil, stir gently, divide among plates and serve

Cabbage Dish

(Prep + Cooking Time: 18 minutes | Servings: 8)

Ingredients:
- 2 cups chicken stock
- 1 green cabbage head; chopped.
- 1/4 cup butter
- 3 bacon slices; chopped
- Salt and black pepper to the taste

Directions:
1. Set your instant pot on Sauté mode; add bacon, stir and cook for 4 minutes
2. Add butter and stir until it melts.
3. Add cabbage, stock, salt and pepper; then stir well. seal the instant pot lid and cook at High for 3 minutes.
4. Quick release the pressure, carefully open the lid; transfer cabbage to plates and serve.

Artichokes with Lemon Sauce

(Prep + Cooking Time: 30 minutes | Servings: 4)

Ingredients:
- 4 artichokes
- 1 tbsp. tarragon; chopped.
- 2 cups chicken stock
- 2 lemons
- 1 celery stalk; chopped.
- 1/2 cup extra virgin olive oil
- Salt to the taste

Directions:
1. Discard stems and petal tips from artichokes.
2. Zest lemons, cut into 4 slices and place them in your instant pot
3. Place an artichoke on each lemon slices, add stock, close the lid and cook at High for 20 minutes.
4. Quick release the pressure, carefully open the lid and transfer artichokes to a platter
5. Meanwhile, in your food processor, mix tarragon with lemon zest, with the pulp from the second lemon, celery, salt and olive oil and pulse very well.
6. Drizzle this over artichokes and serve

Eggplant Surprise

(Prep + Cooking Time: 17 minutes | Servings: 4)

Ingredients:
- 1 eggplant, roughly chopped
- 3 zucchinis, roughly chopped
- 3 tbsp. extra virgin olive oil
- 3 tomatoes, sliced
- 2 tbsp. lemon juice
- 1 tsp. thyme; dried
- 1 tsp. oregano; dried
- Salt and black pepper to the taste

Directions:
1. Put eggplant pieces in your instant pot
2. Add zucchinis and tomatoes.
3. In a bowl, mix lemon juice with salt, pepper, thyme, oregano and oil and stir well
4. Pour this over veggies, toss to coat, seal the instant pot lid and cook at High for 7 minutes.
5. Quick release the pressure, carefully open the lid; divide among plates and serve.

Carrots and Turnips

(Prep + Cooking Time: 15 minutes | Servings: 4)

Ingredients:
- 2 turnips, peeled and sliced
- 1 small onion; chopped.
- 1 tsp. lemon juice
- 1 tsp. cumin, ground.
- 3 carrots, sliced
- 1 tbsp. extra-virgin olive oil
- 1 cup water
- Salt and black pepper to the taste

Directions:

1. Set your instant pot on Sauté mode; add oil and heat it up.
2. Add onion, stir and sauté for 2 minutes
3. Add turnips, carrots, cumin and lemon juice, stir and cook for 1 minute
4. Add salt, pepper, and water; then stir well. close the lid and cook at High for 6 minutes.
5. Quick release the pressure, open the instant pot lid, divide turnips and carrots among plates and serve.

Shrimp and Asparagus

(Prep + Cooking Time: 8 minutes | Servings: 4)

Ingredients:

- 1 lb. shrimp, peeled and deveined
- 1 cup water
- 1/2 tbsp. Cajun seasoning
- 1 tsp. extra virgin olive oil
- 1 bunch asparagus, trimmed

Directions:

1. Pour the water in your instant pot
2. Put asparagus in the steamer basket of the pot and add shrimp on top.
3. Drizzle olive oil, sprinkle Cajun seasoning; then stir well. close the lid and cook on Low for 2 minutes
4. Release the pressure naturally, transfer asparagus and shrimp to plates and serve

Instant Brussels Sprouts with Parmesan

(Prep + Cooking Time: 16 minutes | Servings: 4)

Ingredients:

- 1 lb. Brussels sprouts, washed
- 1 cup water
- 3 tbsp. parmesan, grated
- Juice of 1 lemon
- 2 tbsp. butter
- Salt and black pepper to the taste

Directions:

1. Put sprouts in your instant pot, add salt, pepper and water; then stir well. close the lid and cook at High for 3 minutes.
2. Quick release the pressure, transfer sprouts to a bowl, discard water and clean your pot
3. Set your pot on Sauté mode; add butter and melt it
4. Add lemon juice and stir well
5. Add sprouts, stir and transfer to plates
6. Add more salt and pepper if needed and parmesan cheese on top

Braised Fennel

(Prep + Cooking Time: 22 minutes | Servings: 4)

Ingredients:

- 2 fennel bulbs, trimmed and cut into quarters
- 3 tbsp. extra virgin olive oil
- 1/4 cup white wine
- 1/4 cup parmesan, grated
- 3/4 cup veggie stock
- Juice of 1/2 lemon
- 1 garlic clove; chopped.
- 1 dried red pepper
- Salt and black pepper to the taste

Directions:

1. Set your instant pot on Sauté mode; add oil and heat it up.
2. Add garlic and red pepper; then stir well. cook for 2 minutes and discard garlic
3. Add fennel, stir and brown it for 8 minutes.
4. Add salt, pepper, stock, wine, close the lid and cook at High for 4 minutes
5. Quick release the pressure, open the instant pot lid, add lemon juice, more salt and pepper if needed and cheese
6. Toss to coat, divide among plates and serve

Brussels Sprouts & Potatoes Dish

(Prep + Cooking Time: 15 minutes | **Servings:** 4)

Ingredients:
- 1 ½ lb. Brussels sprouts, washed and trimmed
- 1 ½ tbsp. bread crumbs
- 1/2 cup beef stock
- 1 cup new potatoes; chopped.
- 1 ½ tbsp. butter
- Salt and black pepper to the taste

Directions:
1. Put sprouts and potatoes in your instant pot
2. Add stock, salt and pepper, close the lid and cook at High for 5 minutes.
3. Quick release the pressure, carefully open the lid; set on Sauté mode; add butter and bread crumbs, toss to coat well, divide among plates and serve.

Beet and Orange Salad

(Prep + Cooking Time: 20 minutes | **Servings:** 4)

Ingredients:
- 1 ½ lb. beets
- 3 strips orange peel
- 2 tbsp. cider vinegar
- 1/2 cup orange juice
- 2 tsp. orange zest, grated
- 2 tbsp. brown sugar
- 2 scallions; chopped
- 2 tsp. mustard
- 2 cups arugula and mustard greens

Directions:
1. Scrub beets well cut them in halves and put them in a bowl.
2. In your instant pot, mix orange peel strips with vinegar and orange juice and stir
3. Add beets, seal the instant pot lid, cook at High for 7 minutes and release the pressure naturally.
4. Carefully open the lid, take beets and transfer them to a bowl
5. Discard peel strips from the pot, add mustard and sugar and stir well
6. Add scallions and grated orange zest to beets and toss them
7. Add liquid from the pot over beets, toss to coat and serve on plates on top of mixed salad greens.

Endives Dish

(Prep + Cooking Time: 30 minutes | **Servings:** 4)

Ingredients:
- 4 endives, trimmed
- 2 tbsp. butter
- 1 tbsp. white flour
- 4 slices ham
- 1/2 tsp. nutmeg
- 14 oz. milk
- Salt and black pepper to taste

Directions:
1. Put the endives in the steamer basket of your instant pot, add some water to the pot, cover and cook at High for 10 minutes.
2. Meanwhile, heat up a pan with the butter over medium heat, stir and melt it
3. Add flour, stir well and cook for 3 minutes
4. Add milk, salt, pepper and nutmeg, stir well, reduce heat to low and cook for 10 minutes
5. Release the pressure from the pot, uncover it, transfer them to a cutting board and roll each in a slice of ham.
6. Arrange endives in a pan, add milk mix over them, introduce in preheated broiler and broil for 10 minutes. Slice, arrange on plates and serve.

Roasted Potatoes

(Prep + Cooking Time: 30 minutes | **Servings:** 4)

Ingredients:

- 2 lb. baby potatoes
- 5 tbsp. vegetable oil
- 1/2 cup stock
- 1 rosemary spring
- 5 garlic cloves
- Salt and black pepper to the taste

Directions:

1. Set your instant pot on Sauté mode; add oil and heat it up.
2. Add potatoes, rosemary and garlic, stir and brown them for 10 minutes
3. Prick each potato with a knife, add stock, salt and pepper to the pot, Seal the Instant Pot lid and cook at High for 7 minutes
4. Quick release the pressure, open the instant pot lid, divide potatoes among plates and serve

Stuffed Bell Peppers

(Prep + Cooking Time: 30 minutes | **Servings:** 4)

Ingredients:

- 1 lb. turkey meat, ground.
- 5 oz. canned green chilies; chopped.
- 1 cup water
- 1 jalapeno pepper; chopped.
- 2 tsp. chili powder
- 1 tsp. garlic powder
- 1 tsp. cumin, ground.
- 2 green onions; chopped.
- 1 avocado; chopped
- Salt to the taste
- 1/2 cup whole wheat panko
- 4 bell peppers, tops, and seeds discarded
- 4 pepper jack cheese slices
- Crushed tortilla chips
- Pico de gallo

For the chipotle sauce:

- Zest from 1 lime
- Juice from 1 lime
- 1/2 cup sour cream
- 2 tbsp. chipotle in adobo sauce
- 1/8 tsp. garlic powder

Directions:

1. In a bowl, mix sour cream with chipotle in adobo sauce, lime zest and lime juice and garlic powder, stir well and keep in the fridge until you serve it
2. In a bowl, mix turkey meat with green onions, green chilies, bread crumbs, jalapeno, cumin, salt, chili powder and garlic powder, stir very well and stuff your peppers with this mix.
3. Add 1 cup water to your instant pot, add peppers in the steamer basket, close the lid and cook at High for 15 minutes
4. Release the pressure naturally for 10 minutes, then release remaining pressure by turning the valve to 'Venting', transfer bell peppers to a pan, add cheese on top, introduce in preheated broiler and broil until cheese is browned.
5. Divide bell peppers on plates, top with the chipotle sauce you've made earlier and serve

Pasta and Cauliflower Recipe

(Prep + Cooking Time: 20 minutes | **Servings:** 4)

Ingredients:

- 8 cups cauliflower florets
- 2 cups spinach; chopped
- 1 lb. fettuccine paste
- 2 garlic cloves; minced.
- 1 cup chicken stock
- 2 tbsp. butter
- 2 green onions; chopped.
- 1 tbsp. gorgonzola cheese, grated
- 3 sun-dried tomatoes; chopped.
- Salt to the taste
- A splash of balsamic vinegar

Directions:
1. Set your instant pot on Sauté mode; add butter and melt it
2. Add garlic, stir and cook for 2 minutes
3. Add stock, salt and cauliflower; then stir well. close the lid and cook at High for 6 minutes.
4. Release the pressure naturally for 10 minutes, then release remaining pressure by turning the valve to 'Venting', transfer cauliflower to your blender and pulse well.
5. Add spinach and green onions and stir gently
6. Heat up a pot with some water and a pinch of salt over medium high heat, bring to a boil, add pasta, cook according to instructions, drain and divide among plates.
7. Add cauliflower sauce, gorgonzola, sun-dried tomatoes and a splash of vinegar on top, toss to coat and serve.

Crispy Potatoes Recipe

(Prep + Cooking Time: 17 minutes | **Servings:** 4)

Ingredients:
- 1 lb. gold potatoes, cubed
- 1/4 cup parsley leaves; chopped.
- 2 tbsp. ghee
- Juice of 1/2 lemon
- 1/2 cup water
- Salt and black pepper to the taste

Directions:
1. Pour the water in your instant pot, add potatoes in the steamer basket, Seal the Instant Pot lid and cook at High for 5 minutes.
2. Release the pressure naturally, open the instant pot lid and set it on Sauté mode
3. Add ghee, lemon juice, parsley, salt and pepper, stir and cook for 2 minutes
4. Transfer to plates and serve.

Brussels Sprouts with Pomegranate

(Prep + Cooking Time: 15 minutes | **Servings:** 4)

Ingredients:
- 1 lb. Brussels sprouts
- 1/4 cup pine nuts, toasted
- 1 pomegranate, seeds separated
- Salt and black pepper to the taste
- A drizzle of extra virgin olive oil
- 1 cup water

Directions:
1. Put Brussels sprouts in the instant pot pressure cooker of your instant pot, add 1 cup water to the pot, Seal the Instant Pot lid and cook at High for 4 minutes.
2. Quick release the pressure, carefully open the lid and transfer sprouts to a bowl.
3. Add salt, pepper, pine nuts, pomegranate seeds and pine nuts and stir.
4. Add olive oil, toss to coat and serve.

Bacon and Kale

(Prep + Cooking Time: 20 minutes | **Servings:** 4)

Ingredients:
- 6 bacon slices; chopped.
- 10 oz. kale leaves; chopped.
- 1 tbsp. vegetable oil
- 1 tsp. red chili, crushed.
- 1 tsp. liquid smoke
- 1 onion, thinly sliced
- 6 garlic cloves; chopped.
- 1 ½ cups chicken stock
- 1 tbsp. brown sugar
- 2 tbsp. apple cider vinegar
- Salt and black pepper to the taste

Directions:

1. Set your instant pot on Sauté mode; add oil and heat it up.
2. Add bacon, stir and cook for 1 - 2 minutes. Add onion, stir and cook for 3 minutes
3. Add garlic, stir and cook for 1 minute
4. Add vinegar, stock, sugar, liquid smoke, red chilies, salt, pepper, kale; then stir well. close the lid and cook at High for 5 minutes
5. Quick release the pressure, carefully open the lid; divide among plates and serve

Lentil Swiss Chard Soup

(**Prep + Cooking Time:** 41 minutes | **Servings:** 4)

Ingredients:

- 1 (12-ounce) package frozen Swiss chard
- 1 cup dry brown lentils; rinsed and drained
- 1 cup diced onions
- 1/2 cup diced celery
- 1/2 cup diced carrot
- 6 cups water
- 1 tbsp. minced garlic
- 1 tbsp. chopped fresh thyme
- 1 tbsp. tomato paste
- 1 tbsp. chicken broth base
- 1 tbsp. red wine vinegar
- 1 tsp. ground cumin
- 1/2 tsp. salt or as your liking
- 1 tsp. black pepper

Directions:

1. In your Instant Pot, combine 4 cups of the water, the Swiss chard, lentils, onions, celery, carrot, garlic, thyme, tomato paste, chicken broth base, cumin, salt and pepper. Stir well to combine
2. Now secure the lid on the pot and close the valve. Now Press "Manual" and set the pot at "High" pressure for 6 minutes
3. After completing the cooking time, allow the pot to sit undisturbed for 10 minutes, then release any remaining pressure. Add the remaining 2 cups water and the vinegar. Stir well to combine.

Stuffed Bell Peppers

(**Prep + Cooking Time:** 25 minutes | **Servings:** 4)

Ingredients:

- 16 oz. beef meat, ground.
- 1 cup white rice, already cooked
- one egg
- 10 oz. canned tomato soup
- 4 bell peppers, tops and seeds removed
- 1/2 cup milk
- 2 onions; chopped
- 8 oz. water
- Salt and black pepper to the taste

Directions:

1. Put some water in a pot, bring to a boil over medium heat, add bell peppers, blanch them for 3 minutes, drain and transfer them to a working surface.
2. In a bowl, mix beef with rice, salt, pepper, egg, milk and onions and stir very well
3. Stuff bell peppers with this mix and place them in your instant pot
4. Add tomato soup mixed with water, close the lid and cook at High for 12 minutes
5. Quick release the pressure, divide bell peppers among plates, drizzle tomato sauce on top and serve

Cheesy Polenta

(Prep + Cooking Time: 42 minutes | **Servings:** 6)

Ingredients:
- 1/2 cup shredded Mexican cheese blend
- 1/4 cup half-and-half
- 4 cups chicken broth
- 1 cup polenta (coarse-ground cornmeal)
- 4 tsp. salted butter
- Salt as your liking

Directions:
1. Pour the broth into the Instant Pot. Now Press "Sauté" and bring the broth to a boil. As soon as it starts to boil, slowly whisk in the polenta. Now Press "Cancel".
2. Now secure the lid on the pot and close the valve. Now Press "Manual" and set the pot at "High" pressure for 7 minutes. After completing the cooking time, allow the pot to sit undisturbed until the pressure has released
3. Whisk the mixture to blend in any unabsorbed water. Whisk in the cheese, half-and-half and butter and season with salt. Allow the polenta to stand for 5 minutes to thicken slightly before serving.

Babaganoush

(Prep + Cooking Time: 15 minutes | **Servings:** 6)

Ingredients:
- 2 lb. eggplant, peeled and cut into medium chunks
- 1/4 cup extra virgin olive oil
- 1/2 cup water
- 1 tbsp. tahini
- A drizzle of olive oil
- 3 olives, pitted and sliced
- 4 garlic cloves
- 1/4 cup lemon juice
- 1 bunch thyme; chopped.
- Salt and black pepper to the taste

Directions:
1. Put the eggplant pieces in your instant pot, add 1/4 cup oil, set the pot on Sauté mode and heat everything up
2. Add garlic, water, salt and pepper; then stir well. Seal the Instant Pot lid and cook at High for 3 minutes
3. Quick release the pressure, carefully open the lid; transfer eggplant pieces and garlic to your blender, add lemon juice and tahini and pulse well
4. Add thyme and blend again.
5. Transfer eggplant spread to a bowl, top with olive slices and a drizzle of oil and serve.

Collard Greens Dish

(Prep + Cooking Time: 35 minutes | **Servings:** 8)

Ingredients:
- 1 sweet onion; chopped.
- 2 tbsp. extra virgin olive oil
- 1 tbsp. brown sugar
- 2 cups chicken stock
- 2 tbsp. apple cider vinegar
- 1/2 tsp. crushed red pepper
- 2 smoked turkey wings
- 3 garlic cloves, crushed.
- 2 ½ lb. collard greens; chopped.
- Salt and black pepper to the taste

Directions:
1. Set your instant pot on Sauté mode; add oil and heat it up
2. Add onions, stir and cook for 2 minutes
3. Add garlic, stir and cook for 1 minute
4. Add stock, greens, vinegar, salt, pepper, crushed red pepper and sugar and stir gently
5. Add smoked turkey, Seal the Instant Pot lid and cook at High for 20 minutes.
6. Quick release the pressure, carefully open the lid; divide greens and turkey among plates and serve

Sautéed Endives Recipe

(**Prep + Cooking Time:** 25 minutes | **Servings:** 4)

Ingredients:

- 8 endives, trimmed
- 4 tbsp. butter
- Juice of 1/2 lemon
- 1/2 cup water
- 1 tsp. sugar
- 2 tbsp. parsley; chopped.
- Salt and black pepper to the taste

Directions:

1. Put the endives in your instant pot, add 1 tablespoon butter, lemon juice, 1/2 cup water, sugar, salt and pepper, stir gently, close the lid and cook at High for 10 minutes.
2. Quick release the pressure, carefully open the lid and transfer endives to a plate
3. Heat up a pan with 3 tablespoon butter over medium high heat, add endives, more salt and pepper if needed and parsley, stir and cook for 5 minutes
4. Transfer endives to plates and serve

Bacon and Collard Greens

(**Prep + Cooking Time:** 35 minutes | **Servings:** 6)

Ingredients:

- 1/4 lb. bacon; chopped.
- 1 lb. collard greens, trimmed
- 1/2 cup water
- Salt and black pepper to the taste

Directions:

1. Set your instant pot on Sauté mode; add bacon, stir and cook for 5 minutes.
2. Add collard greens, salt, pepper and water; then stir well. close the lid and cook at High for 20 minutes
3. Quick release the pressure, carefully open the lid; divide mix among plates and serve

Artichoke Hearts Recipe

(**Prep + Cooking Time:** 50 minutes | **Servings:** 4)

Ingredients:

- 4 big artichokes, washed, stems and petal tips cut off
- 2 tbsp. lemon juice
- 2 tsp. balsamic vinegar
- 1 tsp. oregano
- 1/4 cup extra virgin olive oil
- 2 cups water
- 2 garlic cloves; minced.
- Salt and black pepper to the taste

Directions:

1. Put artichokes in the steamer basket of your instant pot
2. Add 2 cups water to the pot, close the lid and steam them for 8 minutes.
3. Meanwhile, in a bowl, mix lemon juice with vinegar, oil, salt, pepper, garlic and oregano and stir very well.
4. Quick release the pressure, transfer artichokes to a plate, cut them into halves, take out the hearts and arrange them on a platter.
5. Drizzle the vinaigrette over artichokes and leave them aside for 30 minutes
6. Heat up your kitchen grill over medium heat, add artichokes and cook for 3 minutes on each side.
7. Serve them warm

Tasty Okra Pilaf

(Prep + Cooking Time: 35 minutes | **Servings:** 4)

Ingredients:
- 2 cups okra, sliced
- 2 ¼ cups water
- 2 tsp. paprika
- 1 cup brown rice
- 4 bacon slices; chopped.
- 1 cup tomatoes; chopped
- Salt and black pepper to the taste

Directions:
1. Set your instant pot on Sauté mode; add bacon and brown it for 2 minutes.
2. Add okra, stir and cook 5 minutes
3. Add paprika and rice, stir and cook for 2 minutes.
4. Add salt, pepper, water and tomatoes; then stir well. Seal the Instant Pot lid and cook for 16 minutes.
5. Quick release the pressure, carefully open the lid; divide pilaf among plates and serve

Eggplant Marinara Sauce Dish

(Prep + Cooking Time: 18 minutes | **Servings:** 2)

Ingredients:
- 4 cups eggplant, cubed
- 1 tbsp. extra-virgin olive oil
- 3 garlic cloves; minced.
- 1 cup marinara sauce
- 1/2 cup water
- 1 tbsp. garlic powder
- Salt and black pepper to the taste

Directions:
1. Set your instant pot on Sauté mode; add the oil and heat it up
2. Add garlic, stir and cook for 2 minutes
3. Add eggplant, salt, pepper, garlic powder, marinara sauce and water, stir gently, Seal the Instant Pot lid and cook at High for 8 minutes.
4. Quick release the pressure, carefully open the lid and serve your eggplant mix right away with your favorite spaghetti

Sweet Carrots Recipe

(Prep + Cooking Time: 35 minutes | **Servings:** 4)

Ingredients:
- 2 cups baby carrots
- 1/2 tbsp. butter
- 1 tbsp. brown sugar
- 1/2 cup water
- A pinch of salt

Directions:
1. In your instant pot, mix butter with water, salt and sugar and stir well
2. Set the pot on Sauté mode and cook everything for 30 seconds
3. Add carrots; then stir well. Seal the Instant Pot lid and cook at High for 15 minutes
4. Quick release the pressure, open the instant pot lid, set it on Sauté mode again and cook everything for 1 more minute. Serve hot

Tomatoes and Okra

(Prep + Cooking Time: 25 minutes | **Servings:** 4)

Ingredients:
- 1 ½ lbs. okra, fresh
- 1 (14.5-ounce) can diced tomatoes; undrained
- 1 cup diced onions
- 1/2 cup water
- 2 tbsp. tomato paste
- 1 tbsp. minced garlic
- 1 tbsp. chicken broth
- 1 tbsp. fresh lemon juice
- 2 tbsp. apple cider vinegar

- 1/2 tsp. ground allspice
- 1 tsp. smoked paprika
- 1 tsp. salt or as your liking

Directions:

1. In your Instant Pot, combine ¼ cup of the water, the tomatoes and their juices, onions, vinegar, garlic, broth base, paprika, salt and allspice. Add the okra on top; do not stir
2. Now secure the lid on the pot and close the valve. Now Press "Manual" and set the pot at "High" pressure for 2 minutes. After completing the cooking time, allow the pot to sit undisturbed for 5 minutes, then release any remaining pressure
3. In a small bowl, dissolve the tomato paste in the remaining ¼ cup water. Gently stir the tomato paste mixture and the lemon juice into the pot.

Bacon and Brussels Sprouts

(**Prep + Cooking Time:** 10 minutes | **Servings:** 4)

Ingredients:

- 1 lb. Brussels sprouts, trimmed and cut into halves
- 2 tbsp. dill; finely chopped
- 1/2 cup bacon; chopped.
- 1 tbsp. mustard
- 1 cup chicken stock
- 1 tbsp. butter
- Salt and black pepper to the taste

Directions:

1. Set your instant pot on Sauté mode; add bacon and cook it until it's crispy
2. Add sprouts, stir and cook for 2 minutes
3. Add stock, mustard, salt and pepper; then stir well. close the lid and cook at High for 4 minutes
4. Quick release the pressure, open the instant pot lid, add butter and dill, set the pot on Sauté mode again, stir and divide among serving plates.

Braised Kale Recipe

(**Prep + Cooking Time:** 20 minutes | **Servings:** 2)

Ingredients:

- 10 oz. kale; chopped.
- 3 carrots, sliced
- 1/2 cup chicken stock
- 5 garlic cloves; chopped.
- 1 yellow onion, thinly sliced
- A splash of balsamic vinegar
- 1/4 tsp. red pepper flakes
- 1 tbsp. kale
- Salt and black pepper to the taste

Directions:

1. Set your instant pot on Sauté mode; add ghee and melt it.
2. Add carrots and onion, stir and sauté for 2 minutes
3. Add garlic, stir and cook for 1 minute more
4. Add kale, stock, salt and pepper; then stir well. Seal the Instant Pot lid and cook at High for 7 minutes
5. Quick release the pressure, open the instant pot lid, add vinegar and pepper flakes, toss to coat, divide among plates and serve.

Corn Pudding

(**Prep + Cooking Time:** 55 minutes | **Servings:** 8)

Ingredients:

- 1 (4.5-ounce) can chopped mild green chiles
- 1/2 cup whole milk
- 1 (8.5-ounce) package corn muffin mix
- 2 ¼ cups water
- Vegetable oil
- 1 (14-ounce) can creamed corn
- 1/2 tsp. unflavored powdered gelatin
- Poblanos & Corn in Cream

Directions:

1. Generously grease a 6-inch springform pan with oil. In a large bowl, combine the corn muffin mix, creamed corn, chiles, milk, ¼ cup of the water and the gelatin.
2. Stir well to combine. Pour the batter into the prepared pan. Cover the top with aluminum foil
3. Pour the remaining 2 cups water into the Instant Pot. Place a steamer rack in the pot. Set the pan on the rack.
4. Now secure the lid on the pot and close the valve. Now Press "Manual" and set the pot at "High" pressure for 25 minutes. After completing the cooking time, allow the pot to sit undisturbed until the pressure has released
5. Set the pudding on a wire rack to cool to room temperature. Run a knife around the edges to separate the pudding from the sides of the pan
6. Carefully remove the springform ring. Cut the pudding into wedges. Top with Poblanos & Corn in Cream, if you like.

Pinto Bean Stew

(Prep + Cooking Time: 2 hours | **Servings:** 8)

Ingredients:

- 1 cup dried pinto beans
- 3 cups cool water
- 1 cup finely chopped onions
- 1 (14.5-ounce) can fire-roasted diced tomatoes; undrained
- 1/2 cup chopped fresh cilantro
- 1/2 green bell pepper, finely chopped
- 4 garlic cloves; minced
- 3 cups hot water
- 2 tsp. ground cumin
- 1 tsp. salt or as your liking

Directions:

1. In a medium bowl, soak the beans in the hot water for 1 hour. Drain. In your Instant Pot, combine the beans, tomatoes and their juices, onions, cilantro, bell pepper, garlic, cumin and salt. Add the cool water.
2. Now secure the lid on the pot and close the valve. Now Press "Manual" and set the pot at "High" pressure for 30 minutes
3. After completing the cooking time, allow the pot to stand undisturbed for 10 minutes, then release any remaining pressure
4. If you'd like, blend with an immersion blender directly in the pot for 10 seconds to mash some of the beans and thicken the broth slightly.

Collard Greens

(Prep + Cooking Time: 20 minutes | **Servings:** 2)

Ingredients:

- 2 cups frozen collard greens
- 1/4 cup chopped yellow onion
- 2 cups water
- 1 tbsp. extra-virgin olive oil
- 1 tsp. paprika
- 1/2 tsp. ground turmeric
- 1 tsp. minced garlic
- 1/2 tsp. salt or as your liking
- 2 tsp. apple cider vinegar

Directions:

1. In a medium bowl, combine the collard greens, onion, garlic, paprika, turmeric and salt. Toss to combine.
2. Place on a sheet of aluminum foil. Bring the edges of the foil together and crimp tightly to seal
3. Pour the water into the Instant Pot. Place a steamer rack in the pot. Place the packet on top of the rack.
4. Now secure the lid on the pot and close the valve. Now Press "Manual" and set the pot at "High" pressure for 5 minutes. After completing the cooking time, quick release the pressure
5. In a medium skillet, heat the olive oil over medium heat until shimmering. Add the steamed vegetables to the pan and cook, stirring, for 2 minutes. Add the vinegar and toss to coat.

Mushroom Kale Stroganoff

(Prep + Cooking Time: 25 minutes | **Servings:** 5)

Ingredients:

- 1-pound baby bella mushrooms, sliced
- 1 cup Cashew Sour Cream
- 3 cups kale leaves; rinsed and torn into bite-size pieces
- 3 cups dried campanelle pasta; or similar shape
- 3 ¼ cups Vegetable Stock
- 1 sweet onion; diced
- 1 bay leaf
- 1 tomato; diced
- 2 garlic cloves; minced
- 1 tbsp. olive oil
- 1 tsp. smoked paprika
- 1/2 tsp. salt or as your liking

Directions:

1. Select the "Sauté" Low mode on your instant pot. When the display reads "Hot," add the oil and heat until it shimmers.
2. Add the onion. Sauté for 2 minutes, stirring frequently. Turn off the Instant Pot and add the garlic. Cook for 1 minute, stirring
3. Add the mushrooms, tomato, paprika, bay leaf and salt. Let sit for 2 to 3 minutes.
4. Stir in the pasta and stock. Lock the lid and turn the steam release handle to Sealing. Using the Manual function, set the cooker to High Pressure for 3 minutes.
5. After completing the cooking time, let the pressure release naturally for 5 minutes; quick release any remaining pressure
6. Remove the lid carefully and remove and discard the bay leaf. If there is excess liquid in the pot, select Sauté Low again and cook for 1 to 2 minutes, stirring frequently, to evaporate some of it.
7. Turn off the pot and stir in the sour cream and kale. Let sit for 1 to 2 minutes while the kale wilts. Taste and season with more salt, as needed.

Tuscan Stew

(Prep + Cooking Time: 65 minutes | **Servings:** 6)

Ingredients:

- 2 cups stale sourdough bread cubes
- 4 cups vegetable broth
- 1 cup dried cannellini beans
- 1 (14.5-ounce) can fire-roasted diced tomatoes; undrained
- 1/2 cup freshly grated Parmesan cheese
- 1 (12-ounce) package frozen spinach
- 1 small onion; chopped
- 1 cup coarsely chopped carrots
- 1 cup coarsely chopped celery
- 2 tbsp. tomato paste
- 1 tbsp. minced garlic
- 1 tsp. red pepper flakes
- 1 tsp. dried thyme
- 1 tsp. dried rosemary
- 1 tsp. salt or as your liking
- 1 tsp. black pepper

Directions:

1. In your Instant Pot, combine the broth, beans, tomatoes and their juices, spinach, onion, carrots, celery, tomato paste, garlic, red pepper flakes, thyme, salt, black pepper and rosemary. Stir to combine.
2. Now secure the lid on the pot and close the valve. Now Press "Manual" and set the pot at "High" pressure for 30 minutes. After completing the cooking time, allow the pot to sit undisturbed for 15 minutes, then release any remaining pressure
3. Now Press "Sauté". Using the back of a spoon, coarsely mash a few of the beans and vegetables to thicken the soup to desired consistency.
4. When the broth is boiling, add the bread cubes and cook the soup for 5 minutes more, or until the bread is completely soft
5. Add water, if needed, to create a relatively thick stew. Now Press "Cancel". Ladle the soup into serving bowls and top with the cheese.

Hearts Of Palm Soup

(**Prep + Cooking Time:** 30 minutes | **Servings:** 4)

Ingredients:

- 1 (14-ounce) can hearts of palm, drained, liquid reserved and coarsely chopped
- ¾ cup heavy cream
- 1/4 cup finely chopped scallions
- 2 ½ cups chicken broth
- 1 cup chopped yellow onion
- 1/2 tsp. freshly grated nutmeg, plus more for garnish
- 1/2 cup shredded Parmesan cheese, plus more for garnish
- 1 tbsp. minced garlic
- 1 tsp. salt or as your liking
- 1 ½ tsp. black pepper

Directions:

1. In your Instant Pot, combine the hearts of palm and their liquid, the broth, onion, garlic, salt and pepper.
2. Now secure the lid on the pot and close the valve. Now Press "Manual" and set the pot at "High" pressure for 5 minutes
3. After completing the cooking time, allow the pot to sit undisturbed for 10 minutes, then release any remaining pressure. Using an immersion blender, puree the soup directly in the pot until smooth
4. Stir in the cream, cheese and nutmeg. Pulse the soup with the immersion blender until everything is well incorporated. Garnish with the chopped scallions and additional nutmeg and cheese and serve.

Asian Coconut Rice and Veggies

(**Prep + Cooking Time:** 30 minutes | **Servings:** 5)

Ingredients:

- 8 ounces white button mushrooms, sliced
- 1 (14-ounce) can lite coconut milk
- 1 (8-ounce) can sliced water chestnuts, drained
- 1 large carrot, sliced
- 1 small onion; diced
- 1 cup jasmine rice; rinsed and drained
- 1 cup water
- 1 cup chopped bok choy
- 1 cup sugar snap peas; rinsed
- 2 garlic cloves; minced
- 1 tbsp. sesame oil
- 1/2 tsp. ground ginger
- 1 tsp. Chinese five-spice
- 1 tsp. soy sauce
- 1 tsp. salt or as your liking

Directions:

1. In the Instant Pot, combine the rice, water, salt and ginger. Lock the lid and turn the steam release handle to Sealing.
2. Using the Manual function, set the cooker to High Pressure for 4 minutes. After completing the cooking time, let the pressure release naturally for 5 minutes; quick release any remaining pressure
3. Remove the lid carefully and fluff the rice. Transfer to a bowl and set aside
4. Select the "Sauté" Low mode on your instant pot. When the display reads "Hot," add the oil and heat until it shimmers
5. Add the carrot, onion, bok choy, snap peas, garlic, mushrooms and water chestnuts. Sauté for 2 to 3 minutes.
6. Stir in the coconut milk, five-spice powder, soy sauce and cooked rice. Simmer for 5 to 6 minutes more, stirring occasionally, until the coconut milk is reduced.

Moo Goo Gai Pan

(Prep + Cooking Time: 1 hour 20 minutes | **Servings:** 4)

Ingredients:

For Marinade:

- 1 garlic clove; minced
- ½-inch piece fresh ginger, peeled and grated

For Stir-Fry:

- 1 (14-ounce) block firm tofu, pressed for least 1 hour, but overnight is best; chopped into bite-size cubes
- 1 (8-ounce) can sliced water chestnuts, drained
- 1 (8-ounce) can bamboo shoots, drained
- 1 tbsp. cornstarch
- ⅓ cup water
- 8 ounces white mushrooms, sliced
- 1 cup sugar snap peas; rinsed, tough ends removed

- 2 tbsp. lite soy sauce
- 1 tbsp. sesame oil
- 2 tbsp. Vegetable Stock

- 1 carrot, sliced into matchsticks
- 1 garlic clove; minced
- 1-inch piece fresh ginger, peeled and grated
- 1 cup Vegetable Stock
- 2 tbsp. soy sauce
- 1 tbsp. sesame oil
- Hot cooked rice or noodles; for serving; optional

Directions:

To Make Marinade:

- In a small bowl, whisk the stock, soy sauce, oil, garlic and ginger. Set aside.

To Make Stir-Fry:

1. In a shallow dish, combine the tofu cubes and marinade. Cover the dish and let sit for at least 30 minutes.
2. Select the "Sauté" Low mode on your instant pot. When the display reads "Hot," add the oil and heat until it shimmers
3. Add the marinated tofu. Cook for 8 to 10 minutes, using tongs to turn the tofu carefully.
4. Turn off the Instant Pot and add the mushrooms, snap peas, carrot, garlic, ginger, stock, soy sauce, water chestnuts and bamboo shoots. Using a large spoon, stir well
5. Select the "Sauté" Low mode on your instant pot, again. Cover the pot with a tempered glass lid and simmer for 5 minutes, stirring occasionally
6. In a small bowl, whisk the cornstarch and water. Add this slurry to the pot. Simmer, uncovered, for 5 minutes more; or until the sauce thickens. Serve over rice or noodles.

Sweet Potato and Black Bean Tacos

(Prep + Cooking Time: 20 minutes | **Servings:** 5)

Ingredients:

- 1 (15-ounce) can black beans; rinsed and drained
- 1 canned chipotle pepper in adobo sauce; diced
- 1 avocado, peeled, pitted and mashed
- 1/4 cup fresh cilantro, chopped
- 1/2 sweet onion; diced
- 1/2 cup Vegetable Stock
- 1 large sweet potato; diced
- 1 red bell pepper; diced
- 1 garlic clove; minced
- 1 tomato; diced
- 1 tbsp. freshly squeezed lime juice

- 2 tbsp. olive oil
- 2 tsp. adobo sauce from the can
- 2 tsp. chili powder
- 1/2 tsp. ground cumin
- 1/2 tsp. salt as your liking
- Zest of 1 lime
- Corn or flour tortillas; for serving
- Cashew Sour Cream; for serving; optional
- Sliced red cabbage; for serving; optional
- Sliced jalapeño peppers; for serving; optional
- Garden Salsa; for serving; optional

Directions:

1. Select the "Sauté" Low mode on your instant pot. When the display reads "Hot," add the oil and heat until it shimmers.
2. Add the onion. Cook for 1 minute, stirring. Add the sweet potato and bell pepper. Cook for 1 minute, stirring so nothing burns. Turn off the Instant Pot and add the garlic. Cook for 30 seconds to 1 minute, stirring.
3. Add the tomato, black beans, chipotle, adobo sauce, chili powder, salt, cumin, stock and lime juice.
4. Lock the lid and turn the steam release handle to Sealing. Using the Manual function, set the cooker to High Pressure for 4 minutes
5. After completing the cooking time, turn off the Instant Pot and let the pressure release naturally for 5 minutes; quick release any remaining pressure
6. Remove the lid carefully. If there is too much liquid in the inner pot, select Sauté Low again and cook for 1 to 2 minutes, stirring constantly (it gets hot fast!)
7. Stir in the lime zest. Serve in the tortillas, topped with mashed avocado and cilantro and anything else your heart desires.

Red Curry Cauliflower

(Prep + Cooking Time: 12 minutes | **Servings:** 5)

Ingredients:

- 1 (14-ounce) can full-fat coconut milk
- 1 (14-ounce) can diced tomatoes and liquid
- 1 bell pepper, any color, thinly sliced
- 1 small to medium head cauliflower; cut into bite-size pieces (3 to 4 cups)
- 1/2 to 1 cup water
- 2 tbsp. red curry paste
- 1 tsp. garlic powder
- 1/2 tsp. onion powder
- 1/4 tsp. chili powder
- 1 tsp. salt or as your liking
- 1/2 tsp. ground ginger
- Freshly ground black pepper
- Cooked rice or other grain; for serving; optional

Directions:

1. In the Instant Pot, stir together the coconut milk, water, red curry paste, garlic powder, salt, ginger, onion powder and chili powder
2. Add the bell pepper, cauliflower and tomatoes and stir again. Lock the lid and turn the steam release handle to Sealing. Using the Manual function, set the cooker to High Pressure for 2 minutes.
3. After completing the cooking time, quick release the pressure
4. Remove the lid carefully and give the whole thing a good stir. Taste and season with more salt and pepper, as needed. Serve with rice or another grain (if using).

Vegetable Salad

(Prep + Cooking Time: 20 minutes | **Servings:** 5)

Ingredients:
For Dressing:

- 1/2 cup Vegetable Stock
- 1/2 cup apple cider vinegar
- 2 tsp. Dijon mustard
- 1/2 tsp. garlic powder
- 1 tsp. salt or as your liking

For Salad:

- 1 ½ pounds red potatoes, chopped
- 1/4 cup chopped fresh parsley
- 2 cups Brussels sprouts, ends trimmed
- 1 (8-ounce) package unflavored tempeh; chopped into bite-size pieces
- 1 small red onion, sliced
- 2 bay leaves
- 1 ½ tbsp. olive oil
- 1 ½ tsp. smoked paprika
- 1/2 tsp. salt or as your liking
- 1/4 tsp. garlic powder
- Freshly ground black pepper

Directions:
To Make Dressing:
1. In a medium bowl, whisk the vinegar, stock, mustard, salt and garlic powder until well combined. Set aside.

To Make Salad:
1. Select the "Sauté" Low mode on your instant pot. When the display reads "Hot," add the oil and heat until it shimmers.
2. Add the tempeh, paprika, salt and garlic powder. Cook for 5 to 6 minutes, stirring occasionally. Transfer to a bowl and set aside
3. Now add the potatoes, Brussels sprouts, red onion and bay leaves to the Instant Pot. Pour the dressing over the vegetables.
4. Lock the lid and turn the steam release handle to Sealing. Using the Manual function, set the cooker to High Pressure for 4 minutes
5. After completing the cooking time, quick release the pressure
6. Remove the lid carefully and remove and discard the bay leaves. Stir in the tempeh and parsley.
7. Taste and season with more salt and pepper, as needed. There will be some liquid left in the bottom, which is perfect for spooning over the salad when it's served
8. If there's too much liquid for your taste, select Sauté Low again and cook for 2 to 3 minutes more.

Cabbage Rolls

(Prep + Cooking Time: 32 minutes | **Servings:** 7)

Ingredients:
For Tempeh:
- 1 (8-ounce) package unflavored tempeh, crumbled
- 2 garlic cloves; minced
- 1 bay leaf

- 1/2 onion; diced
- 1 tbsp. olive oil
- 2 tsp. vegan Worcestershire sauce
- 2 tsp. Montreal steak seasoning

For Deconstructed Cabbage Rolls:
- 1 head cabbage, thinly sliced
- 6 ounces tomato paste
- 1 ½ cups Vegetable Stock
- 1 cup basmati rice; rinsed and drained
- 1/4 cup chopped fresh parsley

- 1 cup water
- 1/2 tsp. salt as your liking
- 1/2 tsp. paprika
- 1/4 tsp. freshly ground black pepper
- Pinch cayenne pepper; or more as needed

Directions:
To Make Tempeh:
1. Select the "Sauté" Low mode on your instant pot. When the display reads "Hot," add the oil and heat until it shimmers.
2. Add the tempeh, Montreal steak seasoning, Worcestershire sauce, garlic, bay leaf and onion. Cook for 3 to 4 minutes, stirring frequently. Transfer to a bowl and set aside.

To Make Deconstructed Cabbage Rolls:
1. In the Instant Pot, combine the rice, water and salt. Lock the lid and turn the steam release handle to Sealing.
2. Using the Manual function, set the cooker to High Pressure for 8 minutes. After completing the cooking time, let the pressure release naturally for 10 minutes; quick release any remaining pressure
3. Remove the lid carefully and fluff the rice. Add the stock, cabbage, tomato paste, paprika, black pepper and cayenne

4. Select Sauté Low again and cook for 4 to 5 minutes until the cabbage softens a little. Turn off the Instant Pot, remove and discard the bay leaf and stir in the parsley. Taste and season with more salt and pepper, as needed.

Black Eyed Peas

(Prep + Cooking Time: 55 minutes | **Servings:** 5)

Ingredients:

- 1 cup dried black-eyed peas; rinsed
- 3 ¼ cups Vegetable Stock
- 2 cups cooked brown rice
- 3 cups chopped kale
- 1 cup frozen peas
- 1 red bell pepper; diced
- 2 tomatoes, chopped
- 1 sweet onion; diced
- 1 tbsp. olive oil
- 1/2 tsp. garlic powder
- 1/2 tsp. dried thyme
- 1 tsp. chili powder
- 1 tsp. vegan Worcestershire sauce
- 1/2 tsp. salt or as your liking
- 1/4 tsp. freshly ground black pepper

Directions:

1. Select the "Sauté" Low mode on your instant pot. When the display reads "Hot," add the oil and heat until it shimmers.
2. Add the onion and bell pepper. Cook for 2 to 3 minutes, stirring occasionally. Turn off the Instant Pot and add the tomatoes, chili powder, Worcestershire sauce, garlic powder, thyme, salt, pepper, black-eyed peas and stock
3. Lock the lid and turn the steam release handle to Sealing. Using the Manual function, set the cooker to High Pressure for 20 minutes
4. After completing the cooking time, let the pressure release naturally for about 20 minutes; quick release any remaining pressure
5. Remove the lid carefully and stir in the frozen peas, rice and kale. Give them a minute or two to warm and enjoy.

Mucho Burritos

(Prep + Cooking Time: 20 minutes | **Servings:** 7)

Ingredients:

- 2 canned chipotle peppers in adobo sauce
- 2 cups Cilantro Lime Brown Rice
- ¼ cup Vegetable Stock
- 1 bell pepper, any color, sliced
- 1 small onion, sliced
- 8 burrito-size tortillas
- 2 cups Poblano Cheeze Sauce
- 1 (14-ounce) container firm tofu, pressed for at least 1 hour; or overnight if possible and crumbled
- 1 (16-ounce) can chili beans, drained but not rinsed
- 1 tbsp. roasted walnut oil
- 1/2 tsp. garlic powder
- 1/2 tsp. freshly squeezed lime juice
- 2 tsp. adobo sauce from the can
- 1 tsp. ground cumin
- 1/2 tsp. salt or as your liking
- Pinch freshly ground black pepper
- Garden Salsa; or store-bought salsa of choice; for filling
- Cashew Sour Cream, for filling; optional
- Sliced avocado, for filling; optional

Directions:

1. Select the "Sauté" Low mode on your instant pot. When the display reads "Hot," add the oil and heat until it shimmers.
2. Add the tofu crumbles, chipotle peppers, adobo sauce, cumin, salt, garlic powder, lime juice and pepper. Cook for 2 to 3 minutes
3. Add the bell pepper and onion. Cook for 2 minutes more. If you need additional liquid, add 1 to 2 tbsp. of water.

4. Add the stock and simmer, stirring occasionally, for 4 to 5 minutes until the liquid is cooked out. Turn off the Instant Pot
5. To build your burritos, layer the tortillas with rice, tofu mixture, chili beans, salsa, poblano cheeze sauce and other fillings, as desired.

Barbecue Chickpea Tacos

(Prep + Cooking Time: 1 hour 20 minutes | **Servings:** 5)

Ingredients:

- 1 cup dried chickpeas; rinsed
- 2 cups pineapple chunks
- 8 taco shells
- ⅓ cup packed light brown sugar
- ⅓ cup soy sauce
- 2 cups plus 3 tbsp. water
- 3 tbsp. cornstarch

- 2 tbsp. hot chili oil
- 3 tbsp. gochujang (Korean hot pepper paste)
- 1/2 tsp. garlic powder
- 1 tsp. sriracha; or more as needed
- 2 tsp. rice wine vinegar
- 1/2 tsp. onion powder

Directions:

1. In the Instant Pot, combine the chickpeas with enough water to cover.
2. Lock the lid and turn the steam release handle to Sealing. Using the Manual function, set the cooker to High Pressure for 45 minutes
3. After completing the cooking time, let the pressure release naturally for 15 minutes; quick release any remaining pressure.
4. Remove the lid carefully and pour the contents into a colander to drain. Return the chickpeas to the inner pot.
5. In a small bowl, whisk the cornstarch and 3 tbsp. of water. Set aside. Select the "Sauté" Low mode on your instant pot
6. To the chickpeas, add the gochujang, brown sugar, soy sauce, chili oil, vinegar, onion powder and garlic powder
7. Cook until it starts to bubble. Stir in the cornstarch slurry. Simmer for 4 to 5 minutes more, stirring frequently, until the sauce thickens and the chickpeas are nice and coated
8. In a medium bowl, stir together the pineapple and sriracha. Taste before adding more sauce. Fill the taco shells with the chickpeas and top with the pineapple.

Asian Gobi Masala

(Prep + Cooking Time: 12 minutes | **Servings:** 5)

Ingredients:

- 1 garlic clove; minced
- 1 head cauliflower, chopped
- 1 white onion; diced
- 1 cup water
- 1 tbsp. ground coriander
- 1 tbsp. olive oil

- 1 tsp. cumin seeds
- 1/2 tsp. garam masala
- 1 tsp. ground cumin
- 1/2 tsp. salt or as your liking
- Hot cooked rice; for serving; optional

Directions:

1. Select the "Sauté" Low mode on your instant pot. When the display reads "Hot," add the oil and heat until it shimmers.
2. Add the cumin seeds. Cook for 30 seconds, stirring nearly constantly. Add the onion. Cook for 2 to 3 minutes, still stirring.
3. Turn off the Instant Pot and add the garlic. Cook for about 30 seconds, stirring frequently
4. Add the cauliflower, coriander, cumin, garam masala, salt and water. Lock the lid and turn the steam release handle to Sealing. Using the Manual function, set the cooker to High Pressure for 1 minute
5. After completing the cooking time, quick release the pressure
6. Remove the lid carefully and serve with hot rice.

Sloppy Janes

(**Prep + Cooking Time:** 20 minutes | **Servings:** 5)

Ingredients:

- 1 (15-ounce) can vegan refried beans
- 1 (8-ounce) package unflavored tempeh
- 1 (10-ounce) can diced tomatoes with green chilies, with liquid
- 1/4 cup quick cook oats
- 6 buns or rolls; for serving
- 1/2 cup Vegetable Stock
- 2 tbsp. vegan Worcestershire sauce
- 1 tbsp. Dijon mustard
- 1 tbsp. olive oil
- 1 tsp. smoked paprika
- 1/2 tsp. salt or as your liking
- 1/2 tsp. garlic powder
- 2 pinches chili powder
- Freshly ground black pepper
- Vegan cheese; for serving
- Barbecue sauce; for serving
- Sliced onion; for serving
- Sliced bell pepper; for serving
- Pickles; for serving

Directions:

1. Select the "Sauté" Low mode on your instant pot. When the display reads "Hot," add the oil and heat until it shimmers.
2. Crumble in the tempeh and add the paprika and salt. Cook for 4 to 5 minutes, stirring occasionally. Turn off the Instant Pot
3. Add the refried beans, tomatoes and green chilies, stock, Worcestershire sauce, mustard, garlic powder and chili powder and season to taste with pepper
4. Lock the lid and turn the steam release handle to Sealing. Using the Manual function, set the cooker to High Pressure for 2 minutes.
5. After completing the cooking time, quick release the pressure
6. Remove the lid carefully and stir in the oats. There will likely be too much liquid; if so, select Sauté Medium and cook, uncovered, for 2 to 3 minutes; or until the extra liquid evaporates. Serve on buns, topped as desired.

Polenta and Kale

(**Prep + Cooking Time:** 45 minutes | **Servings:** 5)

Ingredients:

- 1 quart Vegetable Stock
- 2 bunches kale, stemmed, leaves chopped
- 4 garlic cloves; minced
- 1 cup polenta
- 1 tbsp. olive oil
- 2 tbsp. nutritional yeast
- 3 tbsp. vegan butter
- 1 tsp. salt as your liking
- Freshly ground black pepper

Directions:

1. Select the "Sauté" Low mode on your instant pot. When the display reads "Hot," add the oil and heat until it shimmers.
2. Add the kale, garlic and ½ tsp. of salt. Cook for about 2 minutes, stirring frequently so nothing burns, until the kale is soft and the garlic is fragrant. Note: You can always turn off the Instant Pot if it gets too hot. Transfer the garlicky kale to a bowl and set aside
3. In the Instant Pot, combine the polenta, stock and remaining ½ tsp. of salt.
4. Lock the lid and turn the steam release handle to Sealing. Using the Manual function, set the cooker to High Pressure for 20 minutes
5. After completing the cooking time, let the pressure release naturally for 15 minutes; quick release any remaining pressure
6. Remove the lid carefully and stir well. Add the nutritional yeast and butter along with any additional salt and pepper. Serve in bowls topped with the kale.

Corn Chowder

(Prep + Cooking Time: 30 minutes | **Servings:** 4)

Ingredients:

- 4 slices bacon; chopped
- 2 cups diced potatoes; cut into ½-inch cubes
- 1 cup chopped yellow onions
- 3 cups chicken broth
- 1/2 cup heavy cream
- 2 cups corn kernels
- 1 tbsp. minced garlic
- 1/2 tsp. dried thyme
- 1/2 tsp. freshly grated nutmeg
- 1 tsp. salt or as your liking
- 1 tsp. black pepper

Directions:

1. In your Instant Pot, combine the broth, corn, potatoes, onions, bacon, garlic, salt, pepper and thyme. Stir to combine
2. Now secure the lid on the pot and close the valve. Now Press "Manual" and set the pot at "High" pressure for 5 minutes
3. After completing the cooking time, allow the pot to sit undisturbed for 5 minutes, then release any remaining pressure.
4. Using an immersion blender, puree some of the soup to thicken slightly, leaving some chunks of potato and corn intact. Stir in the nutmeg and cream and serve.

Vegetable Soup

(Prep + Cooking Time: 33 minutes | **Servings:** 4)

Ingredients:

- 2 cups cauliflower florets cut into 3-inch pieces
- 1 cup potatoes cut into 2-inch pieces
- 1 large onion; chopped into 2-inch pieces
- 2 cups water
- 1 cup chopped tomatoes
- 1 ½ tsp. Sambhar Spice Mix
- 1 tsp. ground turmeric
- 1 tsp. salt or as your liking

Directions:

1. In your Instant Pot, combine the cauliflower, onion, carrots, tomatoes, spice mix, salt and turmeric. Stir to combine
2. Now secure the lid on the pot and close the valve. Now Press "Manual" and set the pot at "Low" pressure for 3 minutes
3. After completing the cooking time, allow the pot to sit undisturbed for 10 minutes, then release any remaining pressure. Gradually stir in the water to thin the soup to the desired consistency.

Chickpea Kale Korma

(Prep + Cooking Time: 1 hour 20 minutes | **Servings:** 5)

Ingredients:

- 3 garlic cloves, peeled
- 2 Roma tomatoes, quartered
- ½-inch piece fresh ginger, peeled
- 1 (14-ounce) can lite coconut milk
- 1/2 cup cashews, soaked in water overnight, drained and rinsed well
- 1 cup dried chickpeas; rinsed
- 1 to 2 cups water
- 1 tsp. curry powder
- 1/2 tsp. ground cardamom
- 1 tsp. garam masala
- 1/2 tsp. ground cumin
- 1/2 tsp. ground coriander
- 1/2 tsp. ground turmeric
- 1/2 tsp. onion powder
- 1 tsp. salt or as your liking
- 1/4 tsp. freshly ground black pepper
- 1 bunch kale, leaves torn from stems and rinsed
- Hot cooked rice; for serving; optional

Directions:

1. In the Instant Pot, combine the chickpeas and enough water to cover. Lock the lid and turn the steam release handle to Sealing.
2. Using the Manual function, set the cooker to High Pressure for 45 minutes. After completing the cooking time, let the pressure release naturally for 15 minutes; quick release any remaining pressure
3. Remove the lid carefully. Drain the chickpeas and return them to the Instant Pot
4. In a high-speed blender or food processor, combine the cashews, tomatoes, garlic and ginger. Blend until smooth
5. Add the coconut milk and pulse a few more times to combine. Add this purée to the chickpeas along with the garam masala, curry powder, salt, cumin, coriander, cardamom, turmeric, onion powder, pepper and kale.
6. Select the "Sauté" Low mode on your instant pot. Simmer for 8 to 10 minutes until the kale and beans have absorbed the flavor. Serve with rice, if desired.

Butternut Mac N Cheese

(Prep + Cooking Time: 20 minutes | **Servings:** 6)

Ingredients:

- 1 cup raw cashews; soaked in water for at least 3 to 4 hours; or overnight, drained and rinsed well
- 4 ½ cups water; divided
- 1 (16-ounce) box pasta
- 1 cup nondairy milk; or more as needed
- 2 cups cooked cubed butternut squash
- ⅓ cup nutritional yeast
- 2 tbsp. freshly squeezed lemon juice
- ⅛ tsp. ground nutmeg
- 1 tsp. Dijon mustard
- 2 tsp. salt or as your liking
- Freshly ground black pepper

Directions:

1. In a high-speed blender or food processor, combine the cashews, squash, nutritional yeast, lemon juice, mustard, salt, nutmeg and 2 cups of water.
2. Blend until smooth (the longer you soaked the cashews, the quicker this will be). Pour the cashew mixture into your Instant Pot
3. Pour the remaining 2 ½ cups of water into the blender and swish it around to capture any remaining cashew mixture
4. Add that to the Instant Pot as well, along with the pasta. Lock the lid and turn the steam release handle to Sealing. Using the Manual function, set the cooker to Low Pressure for 2 minutes.
5. After completing the cooking time, turn off the Instant Pot and let the pressure release naturally for 8 minutes; quick release any remaining pressure
6. Remove the lid carefully and stir in the milk, adding as much as needed to make it nice and creamy. Taste and season with more salt and pepper, as needed.

Layered Casserole

(Prep + Cooking Time: 25 minutes | **Servings:** 5)

Ingredients:

- 2 cups mashed sweet potatoes
- 1 ¼ cups Red Hot Enchilada Sauce; or 1 (10-ounce) can; divided
- 1 (15-ounce) can black beans; rinsed and drained
- 1 (10-ounce) can diced tomatoes with green chilies, drained
- 1/2 cup sliced scallion, green and light green parts; divided
- 1/2 cup water
- 1/4 cup frozen sweet corn
- 1 tbsp. freshly squeezed lime juice
- 1 tsp. chili powder
- 1/2 tsp. garlic powder
- 1/2 tsp. onion powder
- 9 taco-size, gluten-free corn tortillas
- Nonstick cooking spray; for preparing the springform pan
- Vegan cheese shreds; for topping; optional
- Sliced avocado; for serving
- Poblano Cheeze Sauce; for serving
- Cashew Sour Cream; for serving

Directions:

1. Lightly coat the bottom and sides of a 7-inch springform pan with nonstick spray and set aside. In a medium bowl, stir together the mashed sweet potatoes, 1 cup of enchilada sauce, the lime juice, chili powder, garlic powder and onion powder.
2. In another medium bowl, stir together the black beans, tomatoes and green chilies, ¼ cup of scallion, the corn and 3 tbsp. of enchilada sauce
3. To build the casserole, spread the remaining 1 tbsp. of enchilada sauce on the bottom of the prepared pan.
4. Add a layer of tortillas, torn as needed to get full coverage. Don't be afraid to overlap. Layer on one-third of the sweet potato mixture.
5. Using a slotted spoon, top the sweet potato later with one-third of the black bean mixture. Repeat the tortilla layer, sweet potato layer and black bean layer two more times. Top with the remaining ¼ cup of scallion. If using vegan cheese shreds, add them now
6. Spray a piece of aluminum foil with nonstick spray and cover the pan tightly.
7. Pour the water into the Instant Pot and place a trivet into the inner pot.
8. Set the covered casserole on top of the trivet. Lock the lid and turn the steam release handle to Sealing. Using the Manual function, set the cooker to High Pressure for 8 minutes.
9. After completing the cooking time, let the pressure release naturally for 5 minutes; quick release any remaining pressure
10. Remove the lid carefully and the trivet and casserole from the Instant Pot. Set aside on a heat-resistant surface
11. Remove the foil and let cool for at least 5 minutes before releasing the sides of the pan. Plate and add desired toppings before serving.

Vegetable Stock

(Prep + Cooking Time: 35 minutes | **Servings:** 9)

Ingredients:

- 1 cup mushrooms
- 8 cups water
- 8 whole peppercorns
- 3 celery stalks
- 1 bay leaf
- 3 carrots
- 1 large onion

Directions:

1. In the Instant Pot, combine the celery, carrots, onion, mushrooms, peppercorns, bay leaf and water, making sure the veggies are completely covered by water.
2. Lock the lid and turn the steam release handle to Sealing. Using the Manual function, set the cooker to High Pressure for 15 minutes
3. After completing the cooking time, let the pressure release naturally for 15 minutes; quick release any remaining pressure
4. Remove the lid carefully. Strain the stock through a fine-mesh strainer into a large heatproof container.
5. Use immediately or refrigerate in an airtight container for 3 to 4 days; or keep frozen for up to a year.

Kimchi Pasta

(Prep + Cooking Time: 10 minutes | **Servings:** 5)

Ingredients:
- 8 ounces dried small pasta
- 1 ¼ cups kimchi, with any larger pieces chopped
- 1/2 cup Cashew Sour Cream
- 2⅓ cups Vegetable Stock
- 2 garlic cloves; minced
- 1/2 red onion, sliced
- 1 tsp. salt or as your liking

Directions:
1. In the Instant Pot, combine the pasta, stock, garlic, red onion and salt.
2. Lock the lid and turn the steam release handle to Sealing. Using the Manual function, set the cooker to High Pressure for 1 minute
3. After completing the cooking time, quick release the pressure. Remove the lid carefully. Select the "Sauté" Low mode on your instant pot. Stir in the kimchi. Simmer for 3 to 4 minutes. Stir in the sour cream and serve!

Tomato Basil Pasta

(Prep + Cooking Time: 5 minutes | **Servings:** 2)

Ingredients:
- 2 cups dried campanelle or similar pasta
- 12 fresh sweet basil leaves
- 2 tomatoes; cut into large dice
- 1 ¾ cups Vegetable Stock
- 1/2 tsp. salt or as your liking
- 2 pinches red pepper flakes
- 1/2 tsp. dried oregano
- 1/2 tsp. garlic powder
- Freshly ground black pepper

Directions:
1. In the Instant Pot, stir together the pasta, stock and salt. Drop the tomatoes on top "do not stir".
2. Lock the lid and turn the steam release handle to Sealing. Using the Manual function, set the cooker to High Pressure for 2 minutes
3. After completing the cooking time, quick release the pressure
4. Remove the lid carefully and stir in the red pepper flakes; oregano and garlic powder.
5. If there's more than a few tbsp. of liquid in the bottom, select Sauté Low and cook for 2 to 3 minutes until it evaporates
6. When ready to serve, chiffonade the basil and stir it in. Taste and season with more salt and pepper, as needed.

Snacks and Appetizers

Instant Chili Dip

(Prep + Cooking Time: 20 minutes | **Servings:** 8)

Ingredients:

- 5 ancho chilies; dried and chopped.
- 2 garlic cloves; minced.
- 1 ½ cups water
- 2 tbsp. balsamic vinegar
- 1/2 tsp. cumin, ground.
- 1 ½ tsp. stevia
- 1 tbsp. oregano; chopped.
- Salt and black pepper to the taste

Directions:

1. In your instant pot mix water chilies, garlic, salt, pepper, stevia, cumin and oregano; then stir well. seal the instant pot lid and cook on High for 8 minutes.
2. Blend using an immersion blender, add vinegar; then stir well. set the pot on simmer mode and cook your chili dip until it thickens
3. Serve with veggie sticks on the side as a snack.

Asian Squid Appetizer

(Prep + Cooking Time: 25 minutes | **Servings:** 4)

Ingredients:

- 4 squid, tentacles from 1 squid separated and chopped.
- 1 tbsp. mirin
- 2 tbsp. stevia
- 4 tbsp. coconut aminos
- 1 cup cauliflower rice
- 14 oz. fish stock

Directions:

1. In a bowl, mix chopped tentacles with cauliflower rice, stir well and stuff each squid with the mix.
2. Place squid in your instant pot, add stock, aminos, mirin and stevia; then stir well. seal the instant pot lid and cook on High for 15 minutes.
3. Arrange stuffed squid on a platter and serve as an appetizer

Zucchini Rolls Recipe

(Prep + Cooking Time: 18 minutes | **Servings:** 24)

Ingredients:

- 3 zucchinis, thinly sliced
- 2 tbsp. olive oil
- 24 basil leaves
- 2 tbsp. mint; chopped
- 1 ½ cups water
- 1 ⅓ cup ricotta cheese
- Salt and black pepper to the taste
- 1/4 cup basil; chopped
- Tomato sauce for serving

Directions:

1. Set your instant pot on sauté mode; add zucchini slices, drizzle the oil over them, season with salt and pepper, cook for 2 minutes on each side and transfer to a plate.
2. In a bowl, mix ricotta with chopped basil, mint, salt and pepper; then stir well. divide this into zucchini slices and roll them.
3. Add the water to your instant pot, add steamer basket, add zucchini rolls inside, seal the instant pot lid and cook on High for 3 minutes
4. Arrange on a platter and serve with tomato sauce on the side.

Delicious Shrimp Appetizer

(**Prep + Cooking Time:** 30 minutes | **Servings:** 16)

Ingredients:

- 10 oz. shrimp, cooked, peeled and deveined
- 11 prosciutto slices
- 1/3 cup blackberries, ground.
- 1/3 cup veggie stock.
- 2 tbsp. olive oil
- 1 tbsp. mint; chopped.
- 2 tbsp. erythritol

Directions:

1. Wrap each shrimp in prosciutto slices and drizzle oil over them
2. In your instant pot, mix blackberries with mint, stock and erythritol; then stir well. set on simmer mode and cook for 2 minutes
3. Add steamer basket, and wrapped shrimp, close the lid and cook on High for 2 minutes
4. Arrange wrapped shrimp on a platter, drizzle mint sauce all over and serve.

Spinach Dip Recipe

(**Prep + Cooking Time:** 30 minutes | **Servings:** 6)

Ingredients:

- 6 bacon slices; cooked and crumbled.
- 1 tbsp. garlic; minced.
- 5 oz. spinach
- 1 ½ cups water
- 1/2 cup coconut cream
- 8 oz. cream cheese, soft
- 1 ½ tbsp. parsley; chopped
- 2.5 oz. parmesan, grated
- 1 tbsp. lemon juice
- A drizzle of olive oil
- Salt and black pepper to the taste

Directions:

1. Set your instant pot on sauté mode; add oil heat it up, add spinach; then stir well. cook for 1 minute and transfer to a bowl.
2. Add cream cheese, garlic, salt, pepper, coconut cream, parsley, bacon, lemon juice and parmesan, stir well and divide this into 6 ramekins.
3. Add the water to your instant pot, add steamer basket, add ramekins inside, seal the instant pot lid and cook on High for 15 minutes
4. Introduce in a preheated broiler for 4 minutes and serve right away

Prosciutto and Asparagus Appetizer

(**Prep + Cooking Time:** 10 minutes | **Servings:** 4)

Ingredients:

- 8 asparagus spears
- 8 oz. prosciutto slices
- 2 cups water
- A pinch of salt

Directions:

1. Wrap asparagus spears in prosciutto slices and place them on a cutting board.
2. Add the water to your instant pot, add a pinch of salt, add steamer basket, place asparagus inside, seal the instant pot lid and cook on High for 4 minutes
3. Arrange asparagus on a platter and serve as an appetizer.

Tuna Patties Appetizer

(Prep + Cooking Time: 18 minutes | **Servings:** 12)

Ingredients:

- 15 oz. canned tuna, drained and flaked
- 1/2 cup red onion; chopped.
- 1 tsp. parsley; dried
- 1 tsp. garlic powder
- 1 ½ cups water
- 3 eggs
- 1/2 tsp. dill; chopped
- Salt and black pepper to the taste
- A drizzle of olive oil

Directions:

1. In a bowl, mix tuna with salt, pepper, dill, parsley, onion, garlic powder and eggs, stir and shape medium patties out of this mix.
2. Set your instant pot on sauté mode; add a drizzle of oil, heat it up, add tuna patties, cook them for 2 minutes on each side and transfer to a plate
3. Clean the pot, add the water, add steamer basket, add tuna cakes, close the lid and cook on High for 4 minutes
4. Arrange patties on a platter and serve

French Endives

(Prep + Cooking Time: 17 minutes | **Servings:** 4)

Ingredients:

- 4 endives, trimmed and halved
- 1 tbsp. ghee
- 1 tbsp. lemon juice
- Salt and black pepper to the taste

Directions:

1. Set your instant pot on Sauté mode; add ghee, heat it up, add endives, season with salt and pepper, drizzle lemon juice, close the lid and cook them on High for 7 minutes.
2. Arrange endives on a platter, drizzle some of the cooking juice over them and serve as an appetizer

Mushroom Dip

(Prep + Cooking Time: 45 minutes | **Servings:** 6)

Ingredients:

- 10 oz. shiitake mushrooms; chopped.
- 10 oz. Portobello mushrooms; chopped.
- 10 oz. cremini mushrooms; chopped.
- 1 tbsp. thyme; chopped
- 1/2 cup coconut cream
- 1 yellow onion; chopped.
- 1/4 cup olive oil
- 1 tbsp. coconut flour
- 1 oz. parmesan cheese, grated
- 1 tbsp. parsley; chopped.
- 3 garlic cloves; minced.
- 1 ¼ cup chicken stock
- Salt and black pepper to the taste

Directions:

1. Set your instant pot on Sauté mode; add oil, heat it up, add onion, salt, pepper, flour, garlic and thyme, stir well and cook for 5 minutes.
2. Add stock, shiitake, cremini and Portobello mushrooms; then stir well. seal the instant pot lid and cook on High for 25 minutes.
3. Add cream, cheese and parsley; then stir well. set the pot on Simmer mode, cook dip for 5 minutes more, transfer to bowls and serve as a dip

English Chicken Wings

(Prep + Cooking Time: 27 minutes | **Servings:** 6)

Ingredients:

- 6 lb. chicken wings, cut into halves
- one egg
- 1/2 cup parmesan cheese, grated
- 1/2 tsp. Italian seasoning
- 1 tsp. garlic powder
- 2 tbsp. ghee
- 2 cups water
- Salt and black pepper to the taste
- A pinch of red pepper flakes, crushed.

Directions:

1. Pour the water in your instant pot, add the trivet, add chicken wings, seal the instant pot lid and cook on High for 7 minutes.
2. Meanwhile, in your blender, mix ghee with cheese, egg, salt, pepper, pepper flakes, garlic powder and Italian seasoning and blend very well.
3. Arrange chicken wings on a lined baking sheet, pour cheese sauce over them, introduce in preheated broiler and broil for 5 minutes.
4. Flip and broil for 5 minutes more, arrange them all on a platter and serve.

Spicy Mussels Recipe

(Prep + Cooking Time: 15 minutes | **Servings:** 4)

Ingredients:

- 2 lb. mussels, scrubbed
- 1/2 cup chicken stock
- 1/2 tsp. red pepper flakes
- 2 tbsp. olive oil
- 2 tsp. garlic; minced.
- 2 tsp. oregano; dried
- 1 yellow onion; chopped.
- 14 oz. tomatoes; chopped.

Directions:

1. Set your instant pot on Sauté mode; add oil, heat it up, add onions, stir and sauté for 3 minutes
2. Add pepper flakes, garlic, stock, tomatoes, oregano and mussels; then stir well. seal the instant pot lid and cook on Low for 3 minutes.
3. Divide mussels into small bowls and serve as an appetizer

Sausage and Shrimp Appetizer

(Prep + Cooking Time: 15 minutes | **Servings:** 4)

Ingredients:

- 1 ½ lb. shrimp, heads removed
- 12 oz. sausage; cooked and chopped.
- 1 tsp. red pepper flakes, crushed.
- 1 tbsp. old bay seasoning
- 16 oz. chicken stock
- 2 sweet onions, cut into wedges
- 8 garlic cloves; minced.
- Salt and black pepper to the taste

Directions:

1. In your instant pot, mix stock with old bay seasoning, pepper flakes, salt, black pepper, onions, garlic, sausage and shrimp; then stir well. seal the instant pot lid and cook on High for 5 minutes.
2. Divide into small bowls and serve as an appetizer.

Cauliflower Dip Recipe

(**Prep + Cooking Time:** 20 minutes | **Servings:** 6)

Ingredients:

- 6 cups cauliflower florets
- 1/2 cup coconut milk
- 7 cups veggie stock
- 2 tbsp. ghee
- 8 garlic cloves; minced.
- Salt and black pepper to the taste

Directions:

1. Set your instant pot on Sauté mode; add ghee, heat it up, add garlic, salt and pepper, stir and cook for 2 minutes.
2. Add stock and cauliflower to the pot, heat up, seal the instant pot lid and cook on High for 7 minutes.
3. Transfer cauliflower and 1 cup stock to your blender, add milk and blend well for a few minutes
4. Transfer to a bowl and serve as a dip for veggies.

Pumpkin and Cinnamon Muffins

(**Prep + Cooking Time:** 30 minutes | **Servings:** 18)

Ingredients:

- 3/4 cup pumpkin puree
- 1/4 cup coconut flour
- 1/2 cup erythritol
- 1/2 tsp. nutmeg, ground.
- 4 tbsp. ghee
- 2 tbsp. flaxseed meal
- 1/2 tsp. baking powder
- 1/2 tsp. baking soda
- 1 ½ cups water
- one egg
- 1 tsp. cinnamon powder

Directions:

1. In a bowl, mix ghee with pumpkin puree, egg, flaxseed meal, coconut flour, erythritol, baking soda, baking powder, nutmeg and cinnamon, stir well and divide into a greased muffin pan.
2. Add the water to your instant pot, add the steamer basket, add muffin pan inside, close the lid and cook on High for 20 minutes.
3. Arrange muffins on a platter and serve as a snack.

Tomatoes Appetizer

(**Prep + Cooking Time:** 20 minutes | **Servings:** 4)

Ingredients:

- 4 tomatoes, tops cut off and pulp scooped
- 1/2 cup water
- 1 yellow onion; chopped.
- 1 tbsp. ghee
- 2 tbsp. celery; chopped.
- 1/2 cup mushrooms; chopped.
- 1 cup cottage cheese
- 1/4 tsp. caraway seeds
- Salt and black pepper to the taste
- 1 tbsp. parsley; chopped.

Directions:

1. Set your instant pot on sauté mode; add ghee, heat it up, add onion and celery, stir and cook for 3 minutes
2. Add tomato pulp, mushrooms, salt, pepper, cheese, parsley and caraway seeds; then stir well. cook for 3 minutes more and stuff tomatoes with this mix.
3. Add the water to your instant pot, add the steamer basket, and stuffed tomatoes inside, seal the instant pot lid and cook on High for 4 minutes.
4. Arrange tomatoes on a platter and serve as an appetizer.

Stuffed Clams

(Prep + Cooking Time: 14 minutes | **Servings:** 4)

Ingredients:

- 24 clams, shucked
- 1/4 cup parsley; chopped.
- 1/4 cup parmesan cheese, grated
- 2 cups water
- 3 garlic cloves; minced.
- 1 tsp. oregano; dried
- 1 cup almonds, crushed.
- 4 tbsp. ghee
- Lemon wedges

Directions:

1. In a bowl, mix crushed almonds with parmesan, oregano, parsley, butter and garlic, stir and divide this into exposed clams.
2. Add the water to your instant pot, add steamer basket, add clams inside, seal the instant pot lid and cook on High for 4 minutes
3. Arrange clams on a platter and serve them as an appetizer with lemon wedges on the side.

Stuffed Mushrooms and Shrimp

(Prep + Cooking Time: 25 minutes | **Servings:** 5)

Ingredients:

- 24 oz. white mushroom caps
- 1 tsp. curry powder
- 4 oz. cream cheese, soft
- 1 cup shrimp, cooked, peeled, deveined and chopped.
- 1/4 cup mayo
- 1 tsp. garlic powder
- 1 small yellow onion; chopped.
- 1/4 cup coconut cream
- 1/2 cup Mexican cheese, shredded.
- 1 ½ cups water
- Salt and black pepper to the taste

Directions:

1. In a bowl, mix mayo with garlic powder, onion, curry powder, cream cheese, cream, Mexican cheese, shrimp, salt and pepper, stir and stuff mushrooms with this mix.
2. Add the water to your instant pot, add steamer basket, add mushrooms inside, close the lid and cook on High for 14 minutes
3. Arrange mushrooms on a platter and serve as an appetizer

Mussels and Clams

(Prep + Cooking Time: 23 minutes | **Servings:** 4)

Ingredients:

- 30 mussels, scrubbed
- 2 chorizo links, sliced
- 1 yellow onion; chopped.
- 15 small clams
- 10 oz. veggie stock
- 2 tbsp. parsley; chopped.
- 1 tsp. olive oil
- Lemon wedges for serving

Directions:

1. Set your instant pot on Sauté mode; add oil, heat it up, add onion and chorizo, stir and cook for 3 minutes
2. Add clams, mussels and stock; then stir well. close the lid, cook on High for 10 minutes, add parsley; then stir well. divide into bowls and serve as an appetizer with lemon wedges on the side.

Chili Balls

(Prep + Cooking Time: 15 minutes | **Servings:** 3)

Ingredients:

- 3 bacon slices
- 1 cup water
- 3 oz. cream cheese
- 1/4 tsp. onion powder
- 2 jalapeno peppers; chopped.
- 1/2 tsp. parsley; dried
- 1/4 tsp. garlic powder
- Salt and black pepper to the taste

Directions:

1. Set your instant pot on sauté mode; add bacon, cook for a couple of minutes, transfer to paper towels drain grease and crumble it.
2. In a bowl, mix cream cheese with jalapenos, bacon, onion, garlic powder, parsley, salt and pepper, stir well and shape balls out of this mix
3. Clean the pot, add the water, and the steamer basket, add spicy balls inside, seal the instant pot lid and cook on High for 2 minutes.
4. Arrange balls on a platter and serve as an appetizer.

Easy Mango Dip

(Prep + Cooking Time: 23 minutes | **Servings:** 4)

Ingredients:

- 2 mangos; peeled and chopped.
- 1 shallot; chopped.
- 1 ¼ apple cider vinegar
- 1/2 tsp. cinnamon powder
- 2 red hot chilies; chopped.
- 1 tbsp. coconut oil
- 1/4 tsp. cardamom powder
- 2 tbsp. ginger; minced.
- 1/4 cup raisins
- 5 tbsp. stevia
- 1 apple, cored and chopped.

Directions:

1. Set your instant pot on Sauté mode; add oil, heat it up, add shallot and ginger, stir and cook for 3 minutes.
2. Add cinnamon, hot peppers, cardamom, mangos, apple, raisins, stevia and cider; then stir well. seal the instant pot lid and cook on High for 7 minutes.
3. Set the pot on simmer mode, cook your dip for 6 minutes more, transfer to bowls and serve cold as a snack

Zucchini Dip Recipe

(Prep + Cooking Time: 20 minutes | **Servings:** 4)

Ingredients:

- 2 lb. zucchini; chopped.
- 1 yellow onion; chopped
- 1 tbsp. olive oil
- 2 garlic cloves; minced.
- 1/2 cup water
- 1 bunch basil; chopped.
- Salt and white pepper to the taste

Directions:

1. Set your instant pot on Sauté mode; add oil, heat it up, add onion, stir and sauté for 3 minutes
2. Add zucchini, salt, pepper and water; then stir well. seal the instant pot lid and cook on High for 3 minutes.
3. Add garlic and basil, blend everything using an immersion blender, set the pot on simmer mode and cook your dip for a few more minutes until it thickens.
4. Transfer to a bowl and serve as a tasty snack.

Shrimp Appetizer

(Prep + Cooking Time: 15 minutes | Servings: 4)

Ingredients:
- 1 lb. shrimp, peeled and deveined
- 3/4 cup pineapple juice
- 2 tbsp. coconut aminos
- 3 tbsp. vinegar
- 1 cup chicken stock
- 3 tbsp. stevia

Directions:
1. Put shrimp, pineapple juice, stock, aminos and stevia in your instant pot, stir a bit, seal the instant pot lid and cook on High for 4 minutes.
2. Arrange shrimp on a platter, drizzle cooking juices all over and serve as an appetizer.

Artichoke Dip Recipe

(Prep + Cooking Time: 15 minutes | Servings: 6)

Ingredients:
- 14 oz. canned artichoke hearts
- 16 oz. parmesan cheese, grated
- 10 oz. spinach, torn
- 1 tsp. onion powder
- 8 oz. cream cheese
- 8 oz. mozzarella cheese, shredded.
- 1/2 cup chicken stock
- 1/2 cup coconut cream
- 1/2 cup mayonnaise
- 3 garlic cloves; minced.

Directions:
1. In your instant pot, mix artichokes with stock, garlic, spinach, cream cheese, coconut cream, onion powder and mayo; then stir well. seal the instant pot lid and cook on High for 5 minutes.
2. Add mozzarella and parmesan, stir well, transfer to a bowl and serve as a snack

Beet Hummus

(Prep + Cooking Time: 25 minutes | Servings: 5)

Ingredients:
- 2 beets, leafy greens (if attached) and roots trimmed
- ½-inch piece fresh ginger, peeled
- 1 (15-ounce) can chickpeas, drained, liquid reserved
- 1 cup water
- Juice of 1 lemon
- 1/2 tsp. garlic powder
- 2 tsp. tahini
- 1 tsp. salt or as your liking
- Zest of 1 lemon

Directions:
1. Scrub the beets under cold running water. The skin will be thick and bumpy in parts; just make sure all the dirt is gone. In the Instant Pot, combine the beets and water
2. Lock the lid and turn the steam release handle to Sealing. Using the Manual function, set the cooker to High Pressure for 20 minutes
3. After completing the cooking time, quick release the pressure.
4. Remove the lid carefully. Using tongs, remove the beets and run them under cold water, rubbing vigorously to remove the skins
5. Quarter 1 ½ of the beets and add them to a food processor along with the chickpeas, lemon juice, ginger, tahini, salt and garlic powder. Blend until completely smooth, adding the reserved chickpea liquid, as needed, to get a smooth, creamy texture. Transfer to a serving bowl
6. Dice the remaining ½ beet and sprinkle it over the hummus, followed by the lemon zest.

Italian Dip

(Prep + Cooking Time: 30 minutes | **Servings:** 4)

Ingredients:

- 4 oz. cream cheese, soft
- 4 black olives, pitted and chopped.
- 2 cups water
- 1/2 cup mozzarella cheese
- 1/4 cup coconut cream
- 1/4 cup mayonnaise
- 1/4 cup parmesan cheese, grated
- 1/2 cup tomato sauce
- 1 tbsp. green bell pepper; chopped.
- 6 pepperoni slices; chopped.
- 1/2 tsp. Italian seasoning
- Salt and black pepper to the taste

Directions:

1. In a bowl, mix cream cheese with mozzarella, coconut cream, mayo, salt and pepper, stir and divide this into 4 ramekins
2. Layer tomato sauce, parmesan cheese, bell pepper, pepperoni, Italian seasoning and black olives on top,
3. Add the water to your instant pot, add the steamer basket, add ramekins inside, seal the instant pot lid and cook on High for 20 minutes.
4. Serve this dip warm with veggie sticks on the side

Tasty Okra Bowls

(Prep + Cooking Time: 25 minutes | **Servings:** 6)

Ingredients:

- 28 oz. canned tomatoes; chopped.
- 1 lb. okra, trimmed
- 6 scallions; chopped.
- 3 green bell peppers; chopped.
- 2 tbsp. olive oil
- 1 tsp. stevia
- Salt and black pepper to the taste

Directions:

1. Set your instant pot on Sauté mode; add oil, heat it up, add scallions and bell peppers, stir and cook for 5 minutes
2. Add okra, salt, pepper, stevia and tomatoes; then stir well. close the lid, cook on High for 10 minutes, divide into small bowls and serve as an appetizer salad.

Instant Cod Puddings

(Prep + Cooking Time: 30 minutes | **Servings:** 4)

Ingredients:

- 1 lb. cod fillets, skinless, boneless cut into medium pieces
- 2 tbsp. parsley; chopped.
- 4 oz. coconut flour
- 2 tsp. lemon juice
- 2 eggs, whisked
- 2 oz. ghee, melted
- 1/2-pint coconut milk, hot
- 1/2-pint shrimp sauce
- 1/2-pint water
- Salt and black pepper to the taste

Directions:

1. In a bowl, mix fish with flour, lemon juice, shrimp sauce, parsley, eggs, salt and pepper and stir.
2. Add milk and melted ghee, stir well and leave aside for a couple of minutes
3. Divide this mix greased ramekins.
4. Add the water to your instant pot, add the steamer basket, add puddings inside, seal the instant pot lid and cook on High for 15 minutes.
5. Serve the warm.

Zucchini Appetizer Salad Recipe

(Prep + Cooking Time: 16 minutes | **Servings:** 4)

Ingredients:

- 1 zucchini, roughly sliced
- 1/4 cup tomato sauce
- 1 cup mozzarella, shredded.
- A pinch of cumin, ground.
- A drizzle of olive oil
- Salt and black pepper to the taste

Directions:

1. In your instant pot, mix zucchini with oil, tomato sauce, salt, pepper and cumin, toss a bit, seal the instant pot lid and cook on High for 6 minutes.
2. Divide between appetizer plates and serve right away

Turkey Meatballs

(Prep + Cooking Time: 16 minutes | **Servings:** 16 p)

Ingredients:

- 1 lb. turkey meat, ground.
- one egg
- 1/2 tsp. garlic powder
- 1/2 cup mozzarella cheese, shredded.
- 2 tbsp. olive oil
- 1/4 cup tomato paste
- 2 tbsp. basil; chopped.
- 1/4 cup coconut flour
- 2 tbsp. sun-dried tomatoes; chopped
- Salt and black pepper to the taste

Directions:

1. In a bowl, mix turkey with salt, pepper, egg, flour, garlic powder, sun-dried tomatoes, mozzarella and basil, stir well and shape 12 meatballs out of this mix.
2. Set your instant pot on sauté mode; add oil, heat it up, add meatballs, stir and brown for 2 minutes on each side
3. Add tomato paste over them, toss a bit, seal the instant pot lid and cook on High for 8 minutes.
4. Arrange meatballs on a platter and serve them right away.

Sweet Potato Slaw

(Prep + Cooking Time: 24 minutes | **Makes:** 13 to 15 cups)

Ingredients:

- 3 scallions, green and light green parts, sliced
- 2 cups sliced green cabbage
- 1 cup shredded sweet potato
- 12 to 15 dumpling wrappers
- 1 cup water
- 1/2 sweet onion, sliced
- 1 ½ tbsp. freshly squeezed lime juice
- 1 tbsp. hoisin sauce
- 2 tbsp. lite soy sauce
- 1 ½ tsp. sesame oil
- 1/2 tsp. ground ginger, plus more to taste
- Zest of 1 lime
- Nonstick cooking spray; for preparing the muffin tin

Directions:

1. Preheat the oven to 350°F. Lightly coat a muffin tin with the nonstick spray. Place one wonton wrapper in each well of the prepared tin, pressing down to create a cup shape.
2. Bake for 5 to 6 minutes; or until the cups are crispy and lightly browned. Set aside to cool
3. Pour the water into your Instant Pot. Place the cabbage, sweet potato and onion into a steamer basket and put the basket on a trivet
4. Lock the lid in place. Select Steam and set the cook time for 2 minutes. Because the Steam function doesn't seal the Instant Pot, there's no need to turn the steam release handle to Sealing or release any pressure.
5. While the veggies steam, in a medium bowl, stir together the soy sauce, hoisin sauce, lime juice, oil, lime zest and ginger

6. After completing the cooking time, carefully remove the lid and stir in the veggies, making sure all are coated with the sauce. Taste and add more ginger, if desired.
7. When ready to serve, fill the cups with the slaw and sprinkle the tops with scallion. Enjoy warm or at room temperature.

Baby Carrots

(Prep + Cooking Time: 5 minutes | **Servings:** 5)

Ingredients:

- 1 (1-pound) bag baby carrots
- 1 cup water
- 3 tbsp. packed light brown sugar
- 3 tbsp. vegan butter
- 1 tsp. salt or as your liking

Directions:

1. Put the carrots in a steamer basket and place the basket into the Instant Pot. Pour in the water.
2. Lock the lid and turn the steam release handle to Sealing. Using the Manual function, set the cooker to High Pressure for 2 minutes
3. After completing the cooking time, quick release the pressure. Remove the lid carefully and add the butter, letting it melt into the carrots for 1 minute or so
4. Add the brown sugar and salt. Stir, stir, stir until the carrots are coated. Taste and add a touch more salt, if you'd like.

Tomato Dip Recipe

(Prep + Cooking Time: 25 minutes | **Servings:** 20)

Ingredients:

- 2 lb. tomatoes; peeled and chopped.
- 1 apple, cored and chopped.
- 1 yellow onion; chopped.
- 3 oz. dates chopped
- 3 tsp. whole spice
- 1/2-pint balsamic vinegar
- 4 tbsp. stevia
- Salt to the taste

Directions:

1. Put tomatoes, apple, onion, dates, salt, whole spice and half of the vinegar in your instant pot; then stir well. seal the instant pot lid and cook on High for 10 minutes.
2. Set the pot on simmer mode, add the rest of the vinegar and stevia; then stir well. cook for a few minutes more until it thickens, transfer to bowls and serve as a snack

Squash and Beets Dip

(Prep + Cooking Time: 30 minutes | **Servings:** 8)

Ingredients:

- 4 beets; peeled and chopped.
- 1 butternut squash; peeled and chopped.
- 1 yellow onion; chopped.
- 1 bunch basil; chopped.
- 2 bay leaves
- 8 carrots; chopped.
- 2 tbsp. olive oil
- 5 celery ribs
- 8 garlic cloves; minced.
- 1 cup veggie stock
- 1/4 cup lemon juice
- Salt and black pepper to the taste

Directions:

1. Set your instant pot on Sauté mode; add oil, heat it up, add celery, carrots and onions, stir and cook for 3 minutes.
2. Add beets, squash, garlic, stock, lemon juice, basil, bay leaves, salt and pepper; then stir well. seal the instant pot lid and cook on High for 12 minutes
3. Discard bay leaves, blend dip using an immersion blender, transfer to a bowl and serve as a snack

Surprising Oysters

(**Prep + Cooking Time:** 16 minutes | **Servings:** 3)

Ingredients:
- 6 big oysters, shucked
- 2 tbsp. melted ghee
- 1 ½ cups water
- 1 lemon cut into wedges
- 1 tbsp. parsley
- 3 garlic cloves; minced.
- A pinch of sweet paprika

Directions:
1. Divide ghee, parsley, paprika and garlic in each oyster
2. Add the water to your instant pot, add steamer basket, add oysters, close the lid and cook on High for 6 minutes
3. Arrange oysters on a platter and serve with lemon wedges on the side.

Simple Baked Potatoes

(**Prep + Cooking Time:** 35 minutes | **Servings:** 4)

Ingredients:
- 4 medium russet potatoes, scrubbed well, pierced on all sides with a fork
- 1 cup water
- Toppings, as desired

Directions:
1. Add the water and a trivet to the Instant Pot. Place the potatoes on the trivet.
2. Lock the lid and turn the steam release handle to Sealing. Using the Manual function, set the cooker to High Pressure for 15 minutes
3. After completing the cooking time, let the Instant Pot go into Keep Warm mode and let the pressure release naturally for 15 minutes; quick release any remaining pressure. Add toppings and ta-da!

Crab and Cheese Dip

(**Prep + Cooking Time:** 30 minutes | **Servings:** 8)

Ingredients:
- 8 bacon strips, sliced
- 8 oz. cream cheese
- 12 oz. crab meat
- 4 garlic cloves; minced.
- 4 green onions; minced.
- 1 cup parmesan cheese, grated
- 2 poblano pepper; chopped.
- 2 tbsp. lemon juice
- 1/2 cup mayonnaise
- 1/2 cup coconut cream
- Salt and black pepper to the taste

Directions:
1. Set your instant pot on sauté mode; add bacon, cook until it's crispy, transfer to paper towels, drain grease and leave aside.
2. In a bowl, mix coconut cream with cream cheese, mayo, half of the parmesan, poblano peppers, garlic, lemon juice, green onions, salt, pepper, crab meat and bacon and stir really well.
3. Clean your instant pot, add crab mix, spread the rest of the parmesan on top, seal the instant pot lid and cook on High for 14 minutes
4. Divide into bowls and serve as a snack

Shrimp Recipe

(Prep + Cooking Time: 18 minutes | **Servings:** 2)

Ingredients:

- 1/2 lb. big shrimp, peeled and deveined
- 2 tsp. Worcestershire sauce
- 1 tsp. Creole seasoning
- 2 tsp. olive oil
- Juice of 1 lemon
- Salt and black pepper to the taste

Directions:

1. In your instant pot, mix shrimp with Worcestershire sauce, oil, lemon juice, salt, pepper and seasoning; then stir well. seal the instant pot lid and cook on High for 4 minutes.
2. Arrange shrimp on a lined baking sheet, introduce in preheated broiler and broil for 4 minutes more.
3. Arrange on a platter and serve.

Mussels Bowls

(Prep + Cooking Time: 12 minutes | **Servings:** 4)

Ingredients:

- 2 lb. mussels, scrubbed
- 12 oz. veggie stock
- 1 tbsp. olive oil
- 8 oz. spicy sausage; chopped.
- 1 tbsp. sweet paprika
- 1 yellow onion; chopped.

Directions:

1. Set your instant pot on Sauté mode; add oil, heat it up, add onion and sausages, stir and cook for 5 minutes
2. Add stock, paprika and mussels; then stir well. close the lid, cook on Low for 2 minutes, divide into bowls and serve as an appetizer.

Artichokes

(Prep + Cooking Time: 25 minutes | **Servings:** 4)

Ingredients:

- 4 big artichokes, trimmed
- 2 cups water
- 2 tsp. balsamic vinegar
- Salt and black pepper to the taste
- 2 tbsp. lemon juice
- 1/4 cup olive oil
- 2 garlic cloves; minced.
- 1 tsp. oregano; dried

Directions:

1. Add the water to your instant pot, add the steamer basket, add artichokes inside, seal the instant pot lid and cook on High for 8 minutes.
2. In a bowl, mix lemon juice with vinegar, oil, salt, pepper, garlic and oregano and stir very well.
3. Cut artichokes in halves, add them to lemon and vinegar mix, toss well, place them on preheated grill over medium high heat, cook for 3 minutes on each side, arrange them on a platter and serve as an appetizer.

Spicy Salsa

(Prep + Cooking Time: 13 minutes | **Servings:** 4)

Ingredients:

- 2 avocados, pitted; peeled and chopped.
- 1 red onion; chopped.
- 2 tbsp. lime juice
- 2 tbsp. cumin powder
- 1/2 tomato; chopped.
- 3 jalapeno pepper; chopped.
- Salt and black pepper to the taste

Directions:

1. In your instant pot, mix onion with avocados, peppers, salt, black pepper, cumin, lime juice and tomato; then stir well. seal the instant pot lid and cook on Low for 3 minutes
2. Divide into bowls and serve.

Avocado Dip Recipe

(Prep + Cooking Time: 12 minutes | **Servings:** 4)

Ingredients:
- 1/4 cup erythritol powder
- 2 avocados, pitted, peeled and halved
- Juice from 2 limes
- 1/4 tsp. stevia
- 1 cup coconut milk
- 1 cup water
- 1/2 cup cilantro; chopped
- Zest of 2 limes, grated

Directions:
1. Add the water to your instant pot, add the steamer basket, add avocado halves, seal the instant pot lid and cook on High for 2 minutes.
2. Transfer to your blender, add lime juice and cilantro and pulse well
3. Add coconut milk, lime zest, stevia and erythritol powder, pulse again, divide into bowls and serve

Mushrooms and Mustard Dip

(Prep + Cooking Time: 20 minutes | **Servings:** 4)

Ingredients:
- 6 oz. mushrooms; chopped.
- 3 tbsp. olive oil
- 1 thyme sprigs
- 1 garlic clove; minced.
- 4 oz. beef stock
- 1 tbsp. mustard
- 2 tbsp. coconut cream
- 2 tbsp. parsley; finely chopped
- 1 tbsp. balsamic vinegar

Directions:
1. Set your instant pot on Sauté mode; add oil, heat it up, add thyme, mushrooms and garlic, stir and sauté for 4 minutes.
2. Add vinegar and stock; then stir well. close the lid, cook on High for 3 minutes, discard thyme, add mustard, coconut cream and parsley; then stir well. set the pot on simmer mode and cook for 3 minutes more.
3. Divide into bowls and serve as a snack.

Roasted Garlic

(Prep + Cooking Time: 26 minutes | **Servings:** 4)

Ingredients:
- 4 large heads garlic, tops cut off to expose just the top of each clove
- 1 cup water
- Olive oil
- Crusty bread; for serving

Directions:
1. Add the water and a trivet to the Instant Pot. Place the garlic on the trivet, cut-side up.
2. Lock the lid and turn the steam release handle to Sealing. Using the Manual function, set the cooker to High Pressure for 6 minutes
3. After completing the cooking time, turn off the cooker and let the pressure release naturally until the pin drops, about 10 minutes
4. Remove the lid carefully. Using tongs, transfer the garlic to a baking sheet or other heatproof dish.
5. Generously drizzle with olive oil, making sure all the garlic gets oiled! Broil on low for about 5 minutes.
6. Watch so it doesn't burn, but you want it to be golden and caramelized. Remove from the oven and let cool for at least 10 minutes
7. Serve immediately, plated in the skins as is (that's how it's done in restaurants). Your guests can use their butter knives to scoop out the cloves for schmearing.

Italian Mussels Appetizer

(Prep + Cooking Time: 20 minutes | **Servings:** 4)

Ingredients:

- 28 oz. canned tomatoes; chopped.
- 2 jalapeno peppers; chopped
- 1/2 cup white onion; chopped.
- 1/2 cup basil; chopped.
- 1/4 cup balsamic vinegar
- 1/4 cup veggie stock
- 1/4 cup olive oil
- 2 lb. mussels, scrubbed
- 2 tbsp. red pepper flakes, crushed.
- 2 garlic cloves; minced.
- Salt to the taste

Directions:

1. Set your instant pot on Sauté mode; add oil heat it up, add tomatoes, onion, jalapenos, stock, vinegar, garlic and pepper flakes, stir and cook for 5 minutes
2. Add mussels; then stir well. close the lid, cook on Low for 4 minutes, add salt and basil; then stir well. divide everything into small bowls and serve as an appetizer.

Perfect Beets

(Prep + Cooking Time: 25 minutes | **Servings:** 5)

Ingredients:

- 6 beets, roughly 6 inches in circumference, roots trimmed
- 1 cup water

Directions:

1. Scrub the beets under cold running water. The skin will be thick and bumpy in parts; just make sure all the dirt is gone.
2. Add the water to your Instant Pot and place a steamer basket inside. Place the beets in the basket in a single layer
3. Seal and lock the lid and turn the steam release handle to Sealing. Using the Manual function, set the cooker to High Pressure for 20 minutes
4. After completing the cooking time, quick release the pressure.
5. Remove the lid carefully. Using tongs, remove the beets
6. I don't peel mine, but if you want to, simply place them in a colander and rub the skins while running them under cold water. Cut them into quarters and season as desired.

Note: If you are cooking larger beets, the rule is 2 to 3 minutes more at High Pressure for every ½-inch increase in circumference.

Appetizing Cranberry Dip

(Prep + Cooking Time: 15 minutes | **Servings:** 4)

Ingredients:

- 2 ½ tsp. lemon zest, grated
- 3 tbsp. lemon juice
- 12 oz. cranberries
- 4 tbsp. stevia

Directions:

1. In your instant pot, mix lemon juice with stevia, lemon zest and cranberries; then stir well. seal the instant pot lid and cook on High for 2 minutes.
2. Set the pot on simmer mode, stir your dip for a couple more minutes, transfer to a bowl and serve with some biscuits as a snack

Creamy Corn

(**Prep + Cooking Time:** 25 minutes | **Servings:** 5)

Ingredients:
- 20 ounces frozen sweet corn
- 1 cup raw cashews, soaked in water overnight, drained and rinsed well
- 3/4 cup nondairy milk
- 1 cup Vegetable Stock
- 1 tbsp. vegan butter
- 2 tbsp. freshly squeezed lemon juice
- 1 tbsp. sugar
- 1/2 tsp. vegetable oil
- 1/4 tsp. smoked paprika
- 1 tsp. salt or as your liking
- Freshly ground black pepper

Directions:
1. In a blender or food processor, combine the cashews, stock, lemon juice, sugar, salt and oil.
2. Blend until smooth. Pour the cashew mixture into the Instant Pot. Add the corn, milk, butter and paprika. Season to taste with salt and pepper
3. Select Slow Cooker mode and set the cook time for 20 minutes. Cover the cooker with a tempered glass lid.
4. After completing the cooking time, carefully remove the lid and stir the creamed corn
5. If there's too much liquid, select Sauté Normal and cook for 1 to 2 minutes to reduce it be careful of spatter!

Lemon Broccoli

(**Prep + Cooking Time:** 5 minutes | **Servings:** 3)

Ingredients:
- 6 cups chopped broccoli
- 4 garlic cloves, roughly chopped
- 1 cup water
- Juice of 1 lemon
- Zest of 1 lemon
- 1/2 tsp. salt or more as your liking

Directions:
1. In the Instant Pot, combine the water and garlic. Place the broccoli in a steamer basket and put the basket into the inner pot
2. Pour the lemon juice over the broccoli so it runs down into the water
3. Lock the lid and turn the steam release handle to Sealing. Using the Manual function, set the cooker to High Pressure for 0 minutes.
4. After completing the cooking time, quick release the pressure
5. Remove the lid carefully and remove the broccoli. Sprinkle the salt and lemon zest over the broccoli. Stir well.

Salmon Patties

(**Prep + Cooking Time:** 17 minutes | **Servings:** 4)

Ingredients:
- 1 lb. salmon meat; minced.
- 1 tsp. olive oil
- one egg, whisked
- 4 tbsp. coconut flour
- 2 tbsp. lemon zest, grated
- Salt and black pepper to the taste
- Arugula leaves for serving

Directions:
1. Put salmon in your food processor, blend it, transfer to a bowl, add salt, pepper, lemon zest, coconut and egg, stir well and shape small patties out of this mix
2. Set your instant pot on sauté mode; add oil, heat it up, add patties and cook them for 3 minutes on each side.
3. Arrange arugula on a platter, add salmon patties on top and serve as an appetizer.

Eggplant Spread

(Prep + Cooking Time: 20 minutes | **Servings:** 6)

Ingredients:

- 2 lb. eggplant, peeled and cut into medium chunks
- 3 olives, pitted and sliced
- 1/4 cup olive oil
- 4 garlic cloves; minced.
- 1/2 cup water
- 1/4 cup lemon juice
- 1 bunch thyme; chopped.
- 1 tbsp. sesame seed paste
- Salt and black pepper to the taste

Directions:

1. Set your instant pot on sauté mode; add oil, heat it up, add eggplant pieces, stir and cook for 5 minutes
2. Add garlic, water, salt and pepper; then stir well. close the lid, cook on High for 3 minutes, transfer to a blender, add sesame seed paste, lemon juice and thyme, stir and pulse really well.
3. Transfer to bowls, sprinkle olive slices on top and serve as an appetizer

Side Dishes

Glazed Carrots

(Prep + Cooking Time: 15 minutes **| Servings:** 4)

Ingredients:

- 1 lb. baby carrots
- 1/2 cup water
- 1 tsp. thyme; dried
- 1 tsp. dill; dried
- 1/2 cup honey
- 2 tbsp. butter
- Salt to the taste

Directions:

1. Pour the water in your instant pot, place carrots in the steamer basket, close the lid and cook at High for 3 minutes.
2. Quick release the pressure, drain carrots and put them in a bowl.
3. Set your instant pot on Sauté mode; add butter and melt it
4. Add dill, thyme, honey and salt and stir well
5. Add carrots, toss to coat, cook for 1 minute, transfer them to plates and serve hot as a side dish.

Potato Casserole

(Prep + Cooking Time: 25 minutes **| Servings:** 4)

Ingredients:

- 3 lb. sweet potatoes, scrubbed
- 2 tbsp. coconut flour
- 1 tsp. cinnamon
- 1/4 tsp. allspice
- 1/3 cup palm sugar
- 1/2 tsp. nutmeg, ground.
- 1 cup water
- 1/4 cup coconut milk
- Salt to the taste

For the topping:

- 1/2 cup almond flour
- 1/4 cup pecans, soaked, drained and ground.
- 1/4 cup shredded coconut
- 1 tbsp. chia seeds
- 1/2 cup walnuts, soaked, drained and ground.
- 1/4 cup palm sugar
- 1 tsp. cinnamon, ground.
- 5 tbsp. salted butter
- A pinch of salt

Directions:

1. Prick potatoes with a fork, place them in the steamer basket of your instant pot, add 1 cup water to the pot, close the lid and cook at High for 20 minutes.
2. Meanwhile, in a bowl, mix almond flour with pecans, walnuts, 1/4 cup coconut, 1/4 cup palm sugar, chia seeds, 1 tsp. cinnamon, a pinch of salt and the butter and stir everything.
3. Release the pressure naturally from the pot, take potatoes and peel them and add 1/2 cup water to the pot.
4. Chop potatoes and place them in a baking dish
5. Add crumble mix you've made, stir everything, spread evenly in the dish, place in the steamer basket, seal the instant pot lid again and cook at High for 10 minutes.
6. Quick release the pressure, take the dish out of the pot, leave it to cool down, cut and serve as a side dish.

Easy Veggies Dish

(Prep + Cooking Time: 16 minutes | **Servings:** 4)

Ingredients:

- 2 yellow bell peppers, thinly sliced
- 1 green bell pepper, thinly sliced
- 2 tomatoes; chopped
- 2 garlic cloves; minced.
- 1 red onion, thinly sliced
- 2 red bell peppers, thinly sliced
- 1 bunch parsley; finely chopped
- A drizzle of extra virgin olive oil
- Salt and black pepper to the taste

Directions:

1. Set your instant pot on Sauté mode; add a drizzle of oil and heat it up
2. Add onions, stir and cook for 3 minutes
3. Add red, yellow and green peppers, stir and cook for 5 minutes.
4. Add tomatoes, salt and pepper; then stir well. close the lid and cook at High for 6 minutes
5. Quick release the pressure, open the instant pot lid, transfer peppers and tomatoes to a bowl, add more salt and pepper if needed; chopped garlic, parsley and a drizzle of oil.
6. Toss to coat and serve as a side dish.

Onions & Parsnips

(Prep + Cooking Time: 40 minutes | **Servings:** 4)

Ingredients:

- 1 yellow onion, thinly sliced.
- 1 ½ cups beef stock
- 2 ½ lb. parsnips; chopped.
- 1 thyme spring
- 4 tbsp. pastured lard
- Salt and black pepper to the taste

Directions:

1. Set your instant pot on Sauté mode; add 3 tablespoon lard and heat it up
2. Add parsnips, stir and cook for 15 minutes
3. Add stock and thyme; then stir well. close the lid and cook at High for 3 minutes
4. Quick release the pressure, transfer the parsnips mix to your blender, add salt and pepper to the taste and pulse very well.
5. Set the pot on Sauté mode again, add the rest of the lard and heat it up.
6. Add onion, stir and cook for 10 minutes
7. Transfer blended parsnips to plates, top with sautéed onions and serve.

Artichokes Dish

(Prep + Cooking Time: 35 minutes | **Servings:** 4)

Ingredients:

- 2 medium artichokes, trimmed
- 1 cup water
- 1 lemon wedges
- Salt to the taste

Directions:

1. Rub artichokes with the lemon wedges, place them in the steamer basket of your instant pot, add the water in the pot, close the lid and cook at High for 20 minutes.
2. Release the pressure naturally for 10 minutes, then release remaining pressure by turning the valve to 'Venting', divide artichokes among plates add salt on top and serve them with a dipping sauce and with a steak on the side

Potatoes Au Gratin

(Prep + Cooking Time: 27 minutes | **Servings:** 6)

Ingredients:
- 6 potatoes, peeled and sliced
- 1/2 cup sour cream
- 1 cup Monterey jack cheese, shredded.
- 2 tbsp. butter
- 1 cup chicken stock
- 1/2 cup yellow onion; chopped.
- Salt and black pepper to the taste

For the topping:
- 3 tbsp. melted butter
- 1 cup bread crumbs

Directions:
1. Set your instant pot on Sauté mode; add butter and melt it
2. Add onion, stir and cook for 5 minutes.
3. Add stock, salt, pepper and put the steamer basket in the pot as well
4. Add potatoes, seal the instant pot lid and cook at High for 5 minutes.
5. In a bowl, mix 3 tablespoon butter with bread crumbs and stir well.
6. Quick release the pressure, take the steamer basket out and transfer potatoes to a baking dish.
7. Pour cream and cheese into instant pot and stir
8. Add potatoes and stir gently.
9. Spread bread crumbs mix all over, introduce in preheated broiler and broil for 7 minutes. Serve right away!

Herbed Polenta

(Prep + Cooking Time: 20 minutes | **Servings:** 6)

Ingredients:
- 1 cup polenta
- 4 cups veggie stock
- 2 tsp. oregano; finely chopped
- 1/2 cup yellow onion; chopped.
- 1/3 cup sun-dried tomatoes; chopped.
- 3 tbsp. basil; finely chopped
- 1 tsp. rosemary; finely chopped
- 2 tbsp. extra virgin olive oil
- 2 tsp. garlic; minced
- Salt to the taste
- 1 bay leaf
- 2 tbsp. parsley; finely chopped

Directions:
1. Set your instant pot on sauté mode; add the oil and heat it up
2. Add onion, stir and cook for 1 minute
3. Add garlic, stir again and cook for 1 minute
4. Add stock, salt, tomatoes, bay leaf, rosemary, oregano, half of the basil, half of the parsley and polenta
5. Do not stir, seal the instant pot lid, cook at High for 5 minutes and release pressure naturally for 10 minutes.
6. carefully open the lid, discard bay leaf, stir polenta gently, add the rest of the parsley, basil and more salt; then stir well. divide among plates and serve.

Potatoes Side Dish

(Prep + Cooking Time: 16 minutes | **Servings:** 4)

Ingredients:
- 1 lb. new potatoes, peeled and thinly sliced
- 2 garlic cloves; minced.
- 1 cup water
- 1/4 tsp. rosemary; dried
- 1 tbsp. extra-virgin olive oil
- Salt and black pepper to the taste

Directions:
1. Put the potatoes and the water in the steamer basket of your instant pot, close the lid and cook at High for 4 minutes.
2. In a heat proof dish, mix rosemary with oil and garlic, cover and microwave for 1 minute

3. Quick release the pressure, drain potatoes and spread them on a lined baking sheet
4. Add heated oil mix, salt and pepper to the taste, toss to coat, divide among plates and serve as a side dish

Poached Fennel Dish

(Prep + Cooking Time: 10 minutes | **Servings:** 3)

Ingredients:

- 2 big fennel bulbs, sliced
- 2 tbsp. butter
- 1 tbsp. white flour
- 2 cups milk
- A pinch of nutmeg, ground.
- Salt to the taste

Directions:

1. Set your instant pot on Sauté mode; add butter and melt it.
2. Add fennel slices, stir and cook until they brown a bit
3. Add flour, salt, pepper, nutmeg and milk; then stir well. close the lid and cook on Low for 6 minutes
4. Quick release the pressure, transfer fennel to plates and serve.

Mashed Squash

(Prep + Cooking Time: 30 minutes | **Servings:** 4)

Ingredients:

- 2 Acorn squash, cut into halves and seeded
- 1/4 tsp. baking soda
- 2 tbsp. butter
- 1/2 cup water
- 1/2 tsp. nutmeg, grated
- 2 tbsp. brown sugar
- Salt and black pepper to the taste

Directions:

1. Sprinkle squash halves with salt, pepper and baking soda and place them in the steamer basket of your instant pot
2. Add 1/2 cup water to the pot, close the lid and cook at High for 20 minutes.
3. Quick release the pressure, take squash and leave aside on a plate to cool down
4. Scrape flesh from the squash and put in a bowl.
5. Add salt, pepper to the taste, butter, sugar and nutmeg and mash everything with a potato mashes. Stir well and serve.

Black Beans Dish

(Prep + Cooking Time: 15 minutes | **Servings:** 8)

Ingredients:

- 1 cup black beans, soaked overnight, drained and rinsed
- 2 garlic cloves; minced.
- 1 spring epazote
- 1/2 tsp. cumin seeds
- 1-piece kombu seaweed
- 2/3 cup water
- Salt to the taste

Directions:

1. In your instant pot, mix beans with kombu, water, garlic, epazote, and cumin.
2. Stir, seal the instant pot lid and cook at High for 5 minutes
3. Quick release the pressure, discard kombu and epazote, divide beans among plates, season with salt and serve.

Cauliflower Mash Dish

(Prep + Cooking Time: 15 minutes | **Servings:** 4)

Ingredients:

- 1 cauliflower, florets separated
- 1 tbsp. butter
- 1 ½ cups water
- 1/2 tsp. turmeric
- 3 chives; finely chopped
- Salt and black pepper to the taste

Directions:

1. Pour the water in your instant pot, place cauliflower in the steamer basket, seal the instant pot lid and cook at High for 6 minutes.
2. Release the pressure naturally for 2 minutes and then release the rest quick
3. Transfer cauliflower to a bowl and mash it with a potato masher.
4. Add salt, pepper, butter and turmeric; then stir well. transfer to a blender and pulse well.
5. Serve with chives sprinkled on top

Mushrooms & Green Beans Side Dish

(Prep + Cooking Time: 18 minutes | **Servings:** 4)

Ingredients:

- 1 lb. fresh green beans, trimmed
- 8 oz. mushrooms, sliced
- 1 small yellow onion; chopped
- 6 oz. bacon; chopped.
- 1 garlic clove; minced.
- A splash of balsamic vinegar
- Salt and black pepper to the taste

Directions:

1. Put the beans in your instant pot, add water to cover them, seal the instant pot lid and cook at High for 3 minutes
2. Release the pressure naturally, drain beans and leave them aside for now.
3. Set your instant pot on Sauté mode; add bacon and brown it for 1 or 2 minutes stirring often.
4. Add garlic and onion, stir and cook 2 more minutes
5. Add mushrooms, stir and cook until they are soft.
6. Add drained beans, salt, pepper and a splash of vinegar; then stir well. take off heat, divide among plates and serve

Bok Choy Dish

(Prep + Cooking Time: 20 minutes | **Servings:** 4)

Ingredients:

- 5 bok choy bunches, end cut off
- 5 cups water
- 2 garlic cloves; minced.
- 1 tsp. ginger, grated
- 1 tbsp. coconut oil
- Salt to the taste

Directions:

1. Put bok choy in your instant pot, add the water, seal the instant pot lid and cook at High for 7 minutes
2. Quick release the pressure, drain bok choy, chop it and put them in a bowl.
3. Heat up a pan with the oil over medium heat, add bok choy, stir and cook for 3 minutes.
4. Add more salt to the taste, garlic and ginger, stir and cook for 2 more minutes
5. Divide among plates and serve with your favorite meat.

Eggplant Dish

(Prep + Cooking Time: 25 minutes | **Servings:** 4)

Ingredients:

- 2 eggplants, cubed
- 1 bunch oregano; chopped
- 2 tbsp. extra virgin olive oil
- 1 garlic clove, crushed.
- 1/2 cup water
- 2 anchovies; chopped
- Salt and black pepper to the taste
- A pinch of hot pepper flakes

Directions:

1. Sprinkle eggplant pieces with salt, place them in a strainer, press them with a plate and then drain them.
2. Set your instant pot on Sauté mode; add the oil and the garlic and heat it up.
3. Add anchovies, oregano and pepper flakes, stir and cook for 5 minutes.
4. Discard the garlic, add eggplants, salt and pepper, toss to coat and cook for 5 minutes.
5. Add the water; then stir well. seal the instant pot lid and cook at High for 3 minutes
6. Quick release the pressure, transfer eggplant mix to plates and serve

Brussels Sprouts Dish

(Prep + Cooking Time: 15 minutes | **Servings:** 8)

Ingredients:

- 2 lb. Brussels sprouts
- 2 tbsp. maple syrup
- 1 tsp. orange zest, grated
- 1/4 cup orange juice
- 1 tbsp. buttery spread
- Salt and black pepper to the taste

Directions:

1. In your instant pot, mix Brussels sprouts with orange juice, orange zest, buttery spread, maple syrup, salt and pepper to the taste; then stir well. close the lid and cook at High for 4 minutes.
2. Release the pressure naturally, transfer sprouts mix to plates and serve them.

Mashed Turnips Dish

(Prep + Cooking Time: 15 minutes | **Servings:** 4)

Ingredients:

- 4 turnips; peeled and chopped.
- 1 yellow onion; chopped.
- 1/4 cup sour cream
- 1/2 cup chicken stock
- Salt and black pepper to the taste

Directions:

1. In your instant pot, mix turnips with stock and onion
2. Stir, close the lid and cook at High for 5 minutes.
3. Release the pressure naturally, drain turnips and transfer them to a bowl.
4. Puree them using your mixer and add salt, pepper to the taste and sour cream
5. Blend again and serve right away.

Mushroom Risotto

(Prep + Cooking Time: 25 minutes | **Servings:** 4)

Ingredients:

- 2 cups risotto rice
- 4 cups chicken stock
- 4 oz. sherry vinegar
- 2 oz. extra virgin olive oil
- 1 yellow onion; chopped
- 8 oz. mushrooms, sliced
- 4 oz. heavy cream
- 2 tbsp. parmesan cheese, grated
- 1 oz. basil; finely chopped
- 2 garlic cloves, crushed.

Directions:

1. Set your instant pot on Sauté mode; add the oil and heat it up.
2. Add onions, garlic and mushrooms, stir and cook for 3 minutes
3. Add rice, stock and vinegar; then stir well. seal the instant pot lid and cook at High for 10 minutes.
4. Quick release the pressure, open the instant pot lid, add cream and parmesan and stir.
5. Divide among plates, sprinkle basil and serve.

Israeli Couscous Dish

(Prep + Cooking Time: 15 minutes | **Servings:** 10)

Ingredients:

- 16 oz. harvest grains blend
- 2 ½ cups chicken stock
- 2 tbsp. butter
- Parsley leaves; chopped for serving
- Salt and black pepper to the taste

Directions:

1. Set your instant pot on Sauté mode; add butter and melt it.
2. Add grains and stock and stir
3. Close the instant pot lid and cook at High for 5 minutes.
4. Quick release the pressure, fluff couscous with a fork, season with salt and pepper to the taste, divide among plates, sprinkle parsley on top and serve.

Quinoa Pilaf

(Prep + Cooking Time: 12 minutes | **Servings:** 4)

Ingredients:

- 2 cups quinoa
- 2 garlic cloves; minced.
- 3 cups water
- 2 tsp. turmeric
- 1 handful parsley; chopped.
- 2 tsp. cumin, ground.
- 2 tbsp. extra virgin olive oil
- Salt to the taste

Directions:

1. Set your instant pot on Sauté mode; add oil and heat it up.
2. Add garlic, stir and cook for 30 seconds.
3. Add water, quinoa, cumin, turmeric and salt; then stir well. close the lid and cook at High for 1 minute
4. Release the pressure naturally for 10 minutes, then release remaining pressure by turning the valve to 'Venting', fluff quinoa with a fork, transfer to plates, season with more salt if needed, sprinkle parsley on top and serve as a side dish.

Green Beans Dish

(Prep + Cooking Time: 15 minutes | **Servings:** 4)

Ingredients:

- 1 lb. green beans, trimmed
- 1 tsp. extra virgin olive oil
- 2 cups tomatoes; chopped.
- 1 basil spring
- 1 tbsp. extra-virgin olive oil
- 1 garlic clove crushed.
- Salt to the taste

Directions:

1. Set your instant pot on Sauté mode; add 1 tablespoon oil and heat it up
2. Add garlic, stir and cook for 1 minute.
3. Add tomatoes, stir and cook for 1minute.
4. Place green beans in the steamer basket and introduce it in the pot
5. Add salt to the taste, seal the instant pot lid and cook at High for 5 minutes
6. Quick release the pressure, transfer green beans from the basket into the pot and toss to coat
7. Transfer to plates, sprinkle with basil and drizzle 1 tsp. oil over them.

Fava Bean Sauté

(**Prep + Cooking Time:** 18 minutes | **Servings:** 4)

Ingredients:

- 3 lb. fava beans, shelled
- 1/2 cup white wine
- 3 parsley springs; chopped.
- 4 oz. bacon; chopped.
- 3/4 cup water
- 1 tsp. extra virgin olive oil
- Salt and black pepper to the taste

Directions:

1. Set your instant pot on Sauté mode; add the oil and heat up.
2. Add bacon, stir and cook until it browns.
3. Add wine, stir and cook for 2 minutes
4. Add water and fava beans; then stir well. close the lid and cook at High for 7 minutes
5. Quick release the pressure, transfer beans to plates, add parsley, salt and pepper, stir and serve.

Flavored Mashed Sweet Potatoes

(**Prep + Cooking Time:** 20 minutes | **Servings:** 8)

Ingredients:

- 3 lb. sweet potatoes; peeled and chopped.
- 2 garlic cloves
- 1/4 cup milk
- 1/4 tsp. sage; dried
- 1/2 tsp. rosemary; dried
- 1/2 tsp. thyme dried
- 1/2 cup parmesan, grated
- 2 tbsp. butter
- Salt and black pepper to the taste
- 1/2 tsp. parsley; dried
- 1 ½ cups water

Directions:

1. Put potatoes and garlic in the steamer basket of your instant pot, add 1 ½ cups water in the pot, close the lid and cook at High for 10 minutes.
2. Quick release the pressure, drain water, transfer the potatoes and garlic to a bowl and mash them using your kitchen mixer
3. Add butter, parmesan, milk, salt, pepper, parsley, sage, rosemary and thyme and blend everything well.
4. Divide among plates and serve

Pumpkin Risotto

(**Prep + Cooking Time:** 15 minutes | **Servings:** 4)

Ingredients:

- 6 oz. pumpkin puree
- 2 oz. extra virgin olive oil
- 1 small yellow onion; chopped.
- 1/2 tsp. nutmeg
- 1 tsp. thyme; chopped.
- 1/2 tsp. ginger, grated
- 4 oz. heavy cream
- 1/2 tsp. cinnamon
- 1/2 tsp. allspice
- 2 garlic cloves; minced.
- 12 oz. risotto rice
- 4 cups chicken stock

Directions:

1. Set your instant pot on Sauté mode; add oil and heat it up
2. Add onion and garlic, stir and cook for 1 - 2 minutes
3. Also add risotto, chicken stock, pumpkin puree, thyme, nutmeg, cinnamon, ginger and allspice and stir.
4. Close the instant pot lid and cook at High for 10 minutes.
5. Quick release the pressure, add cream, stir very well and serve as a side dish.

Special Side Dish

(Prep + Cooking Time: 30 minutes | **Servings:** 4)

Ingredients:

- 1 bread loaf, cubed and toasted
- 1 cup celery; chopped.
- ½ cup butter
- 1 ¼ cup turkey stock
- 1 yellow onion; chopped.
- 1 tsp. sage
- 1 tsp. poultry seasoning
- 1 ½ cups water
- Salt and black pepper to the taste

Directions:

1. Set your instant pot on Sauté mode; add butter and melt it.
2. Add stock, onion, celery, salt, pepper, sage and poultry seasoning and stir well
3. Add bread cubes, stir and cook for 1 minute
4. Transfer this to a Bundt pan and close the lid it with tin foil
5. Clean your instant pot, add the water and place the pan in the steamer basket, seal the instant pot lid and cook at High for 15 minutes.
6. Quick release the pressure, take out the pan, introduce it in the oven at 350 degrees F and bake for 5 minutes. Serve hot.

Refried Beans

(Prep + Cooking Time: 30 minutes | **Servings:** 4)

Ingredients:

- 3 cups pinto beans, soaked for 4 hours and drained
- 1 jalapeno; chopped
- 2 tbsp. garlic; minced.
- 9 cups vegetable stock
- 1/8 tsp. cumin, ground.
- 1 yellow onion, cut into halves
- Salt and black pepper to the taste

Directions:

1. In your instant pot, mix beans with salt, pepper, stock, onion, jalapeno, garlic and cumin.
2. Stir, close the lid and cook at High for 20 minutes
3. Release the pressure naturally, discard onion halves, strain beans, transfer them to your blender and reserve cooking liquid
4. Blend very well adding some of the liquid, transfer to a bowl and serve them as a side dish

Tomato & Calamari Dish

(Prep + Cooking Time: 40 minutes | **Servings:** 4)

Ingredients:

- 1 ½ lb. calamari, washed, tentacles separated and cut into strips
- 1 garlic clove, crushed.
- 1/2 cup white wine
- 1 cup water
- 2 anchovies
- Juice of 1 lemon
- 14 oz. canned tomatoes; chopped.
- 1 bunch parsley; chopped
- 2 tbsp. extra virgin olive oil
- Salt and black pepper to the taste
- A pinch of red pepper flakes

Directions:

1. Set your instant pot on Sauté mode; add oil, pepper flakes, garlic and anchovies, stir and cook for 3 minutes.
2. Add calamari, stir and cook for 5 minutes
3. Add wine, stir and cook 3 minutes.
4. Add tomatoes, 1 cup water, half of the parsley, salt, and pepper
5. Stir, seal the instant pot lid and cook at High for 20 minutes.
6. Quick release the pressure, add the rest of the parsley, the lemon juice, salt, and pepper; then stir well. divide among plates and serve with rice.

Parmesan & Garlic Asparagus

(Prep + Cooking Time: 12 minutes | **Servings:** 4)

Ingredients:

- 1 bunch asparagus, trimmed
- 3 tbsp. butter
- 3 tbsp. parmesan cheese, grated
- 3 garlic cloves; minced.
- 1 cup water

Directions:

1. Pour the water in your instant pot.
2. Place asparagus on a tin foil, add garlic and butter and curve the edges of the foil
3. Place this in your pot, close the lid it and cook at High for 8 minutes.
4. Quick release the pressure, arrange asparagus on plates, sprinkle parmesan and serve

Sweet Carrot Puree

(Prep + Cooking Time: 10 minutes | **Servings:** 4)

Ingredients:

- 1 ½ lb. carrots; peeled and chopped.
- 1 tsp. brown sugar
- 1 tbsp. soft butter
- 1 tbsp. honey
- 1 cup water
- Salt to the taste

Directions:

1. Put carrots in your instant pot, add the water, close the lid and cook at High for 4 minutes.
2. Release the pressure naturally, drain carrots and place them in a bowl.
3. Mash them using a hand blender, add butter salt and honey
4. Blend again well, add sugar on top and serve right away

Lemon Peas & Parmesan Risotto

(Prep + Cooking Time: 27 minutes | **Servings:** 6)

Ingredients:

- 1 ½ cup peas
- 3 ½ cups chicken stock
- 2 tbsp. parmesan, finely grated
- 2 tbsp. parsley; finely chopped
- 1 ½ cup rice
- 2 tbsp. butter
- 1 yellow onion; chopped.
- 1 tbsp. extra-virgin olive oil
- 2 tbsp. lemon juice
- 1 tsp. lemon zest, grated
- Salt and black pepper to the taste

Directions:

1. Set your instant pot on sauté mode; add 1 tablespoon butter and the oil and heat them up.
2. Add onions, stir and cook for 5 minutes.
3. Add rice, stir and cook for 3 more minutes.
4. Add 3 cups stock and the lemon juice; then stir well. close the lid and cook at High for 5 minutes
5. Quick release the pressure, set the pot on Simmer, add peas and the rest of the stock, stir and cook for 2 minutes.
6. Add parmesan, parsley, the rest of the butter, lemon zest, salt and pepper to the taste and stir. Divide among plates and serve.

Apple and Butternut Mash

(Prep + Cooking Time: 25 minutes | **Servings:** 4)

Ingredients:
- 1 butternut squash, peeled and cut into medium chunks
- 1/2 tsp. apple pie spice
- 2 tbsp. brown butter
- 2 apples, sliced
- 1 cup water
- 1 yellow onion, thinly sliced
- Salt to the taste

Directions:
1. Put squash, onion and apple pieces in the steamer basket of your instant pot, put the water in the pot, close the lid and cook at High for 8 minutes.
2. Quick release the pressure and transfer squash, onion and apple pieces to a bowl.
3. Mash using a potato masher, add salt, apple pie spice and brown butter, stir well and serve warm

Barley & Cauliflower Risotto

(Prep + Cooking Time: 1 hour and 10 minutes | **Servings:** 4)

Ingredients:
- 1 cauliflower head, florets separated
- 4 tbsp. extra virgin olive oil
- 3 cups chicken stock
- 1 tbsp. butter
- 2 thyme springs
- 2 tbsp. parsley; chopped.
- 1/2 cup parmesan, grated
- 2 garlic cloves; minced.
- 1 cup pearl barley
- 1 yellow onion; chopped.
- Salt and black pepper to the taste

Directions:
1. Spread cauliflower florets on a lined baking dish, add 3 tablespoon of oil, and salt and pepper, toss to coat, introduce in the oven at 425 degrees F and bake for 20 minutes, turning them every 10 minutes.
2. Take cauliflower out of the oven, sprinkle 1/4 cup parmesan and bake for 5 minutes more
3. Meanwhile, set your instant pot on Sauté mode; add 1 tablespoon oil and heat it up
4. Add onion, stir and cook for 5 minutes.
5. Add garlic, stir and cook for 1 minute
6. Add stock, thyme, and barley; then stir well. seal the instant pot lid and cook at High for 25 minutes.
7. Quick release the pressure, carefully open the lid; the pot, stir the barley, discard thyme, add butter, the rest of the parmesan, roasted cauliflower, salt, pepper to the taste and parsley.
8. Stir the risotto well, divide among plates and serve

Saffron Risotto

(Prep + Cooking Time: 20 minutes | **Servings:** 10)

Ingredients:
- 1/3 cup almonds; chopped.
- 1/3 cup currants; dried
- 1 tbsp. honey
- 1 cinnamon stick
- 1/2 cup onion; chopped.
- 2 tbsp. extra virgin olive oil
- 1/2 tsp. saffron threads, crushed.
- 2 tbsp. hot milk
- 1 ½ cups Arborio rice
- 3 ½ cups veggie stock
- A pinch of salt

Directions:
1. In a bowl, mix hot milk with saffron, stir and leave aside
2. Set your instant pot on Sauté mode; add oil and heat it up
3. Add onions, stir and cook for 5 minutes
4. Add rice, veggie stock, saffron and milk, honey, salt, almonds, cinnamon stick and currants.
5. Stir, seal the instant pot lid and cook at High for 5 minutes.
6. Quick release the pressure, fluff the rice a bit, discard cinnamon, divide it among plates and serve

Citrus and Cauliflower Dish

(Prep + Cooking Time: 15 minutes | **Servings:** 4)

Ingredients:

- 1 cauliflower, florets separated
- 1 Romanesco cauliflower, florets separated.
- 4 tbsp. extra virgin olive oil
- 1 cup water
- 2 oranges, peeled and sliced
- 4 anchovies
- 1 tbsp. capers; chopped.
- 1 lb. broccoli, florets separated.
- Zest from 1 orange
- Juice from 1 orange
- A pinch of hot pepper flakes
- Salt and black pepper to the taste

Directions:

1. In a bowl, mix orange zest with orange juice, pepper flakes, anchovies, capers salt, pepper and olive oil, stir well and leave aside for now.
2. Place cauliflower and broccoli florets in the steamer basket of you instant pot, add 1 cup water to the pot, close the lid and cook on Low for 6 minutes
3. Quick release the pressure, open the instant pot lid, transfer florets to a bowl and mix with orange slices
4. Add the orange vinaigrette you've made earlier, toss to coat and divide among plates.
5. Serve with some chicken!

Broccoli dish

(Prep + Cooking Time: 20 minutes | **Servings:** 6)

Ingredients:

- 31 oz. broccoli, florets separated
- 1 cup water
- 5 lemon slices
- Salt and black pepper to the taste

Directions:

1. Pour the water in your instant pot.
2. Season broccoli with salt and pepper to the taste and add it to the pot
3. Also, add lemon slices and stir gently.
4. Close the instant pot lid and cook at High for 15 minutes
5. Release the pressure and divide broccoli among plates
6. Serve with a tasty meat-based the main course!

Mixed Beans Side Dish

(Prep + Cooking Time: 25 minutes | **Servings:** 4)

Ingredients:

- 1 cup garbanzo beans, soaked overnight and drained.
- 2 celery stalks; chopped.
- 1 bunch parsley; chopped.
- 1 tbsp. sugar
- 5 tbsp. apple cider vinegar
- 4 tbsp. extra virgin olive oil
- 1 cup cranberry beans, soaked overnight and drained.
- 1 ½ cups green beans
- 1 small red onion; chopped.
- 1 garlic clove, crushed.
- 1 bay leaf
- 4 cups water
- Salt and black pepper to the taste

Directions:

1. Pour the water in your instant pot
2. Add bay leaf, garlic and garbanzo beans
3. Put the steamer basket in your pot as well and put cranberry beans in it.
4. Wrap green beans in tin foil and also place in the steamer basket
5. Close the instant pot lid and cook at High for 15 minutes.

6. Release the pressure naturally for 10 minutes, then release remaining pressure by turning the valve to 'Venting', open the instant pot lid, drain beans, unwrap green beans and put them all in a bowl
7. In another bowl, mix onion with vinegar and sugar, stir well and leave aside for a few minutes.
8. Add onions to beans and toss to coat.
9. Also add celery, olive oil, salt, pepper to the taste and parsley, toss to coat and divide among plates.
10. Serve right away as a side dish

Garlic and Beet Dish

(Prep + Cooking Time: 25 minutes | **Servings:** 4)

Ingredients:
- 3 beets, greens cut off and washed.
- 1 tbsp. extra-virgin olive oil
- 2 garlic cloves; minced.
- 1 tsp. lemon juice
- Water to cover
- Salt to the taste

Directions:
1. Put beets in your instant pot, add water to cover, also add salt to the taste, seal the instant pot lid and cook at High for 15 minutes.
2. Release the pressure naturally for 10 minutes, then release remaining pressure by turning the valve to 'Venting', strain beets, peel them and roughly chop.
3. Heat up a pan with the oil over medium high heat, add beets, stir and cook for 3 minutes.
4. Add garlic, lemon juice, and more salt; then stir well. take off heat and divide among plates

Delicious Almonds & Quinoa Side Dish

(Prep + Cooking Time: 20 minutes | **Servings:** 4)

Ingredients:
- 1 ½ cups quinoa, rinsed
- 1/2 cup almonds, toasted and sliced
- 2 tbsp. parsley; chopped.
- 1 celery stalk; chopped.
- 14 oz. chicken stock
- 1/2 cup yellow onion; finely chopped
- 1 tbsp. butter
- 1/4 cup water
- Salt and black pepper to the taste

Directions:
1. Set your instant pot on Sauté mode; add butter and melt it
2. Add onion and celery, stir and cook for 5 minutes
3. Add quinoa, water, stock, salt and pepper; then stir well. close the lid and cook at High for 3 minutes.
4. Release the pressure naturally for 5 minutes, then release remaining pressure by turning the valve to 'Venting', and carefully open the lid
5. Fluff with a fork, add almonds and parsley; then stir. divide among plates and serve as a side dish.

Goat Cheese & Spinach Risotto

(**Prep + Cooking Time:** 20 minutes | **Servings:** 6)

Ingredients:

- 4 oz. goat cheese, soft and crumbled.
- 1/3 cup pecans, toasted and chopped.
- 1/2 cup white wine
- 12 oz. spinach; chopped.
- 3 ½ cups hot veggie stock
- 2 garlic cloves; minced.
- 2 tbsp. extra virgin olive oil
- 3/4 cup yellow onion; chopped.
- 1 ½ cups Arborio rice
- 2 tbsp. lemon juice
- Salt and black pepper to the taste

Directions:

1. Set your instant pot on sauté mode; add the oil and heat it up
2. Add garlic and onions, stir and cook for 5 minutes
3. Add rice, stir and cook for 1 minute more
4. Add wine, stir and cook until it's absorbed.
5. Add 3 cups stock, seal the instant pot lid and cook at High for 4 minutes.
6. Quick release the pressure, open the instant pot lid, add spinach, stir and cook on Simmer mode for 3 minutes
7. Add salt, pepper, the rest of the stock, lemon juice and goat cheese and stir.
8. Divide among plates, garnish with pecans and serve

Farro Side Dish

(**Prep + Cooking Time:** 50 minutes | **Servings:** 6)

Ingredients:

- 1 cup whole grain farro
- 1 tbsp. apple cider vinegar
- 1/2 cup cherries; dried and chopped.
- 1/4 cup green onions; chopped.
- 10 mint leaves; chopped.
- 1 tsp. lemon juice
- 3 cups water
- 1 tbsp. extra-virgin olive oil
- 2 cups cherries, pitted and cut into halves
- Salt to the taste

Directions:

1. Pour the water in your instant pot, add rinsed farro; then stir well. close the lid and cook at High for 40 minutes
2. Quick release the pressure, drain farro, transfer to a bowl and mix with salt, oil, lemon juice, vinegar; dried cherries, fresh cherries, green onions, and mint
3. Stir well, divide among plates and serve

Rice Recipes

Mexican Rice

(Prep + Cooking Time: 15 minutes | **Servings:** 8)

Ingredients:
- 1 cup long grain rice
- 1/2 cup cilantro; chopped
- 1/2 avocado, pitted; peeled and chopped.
- 1/4 cup green hot sauce
- 1 ¼ cups veggie stock
- Salt and black pepper to the taste

Directions:
1. Put the rice in your instant pot, add stock; then stir well. close the lid and cook at High for 4 minutes
2. Release the pressure naturally for 10 minutes, then release remaining pressure by turning the valve to 'Venting', open the instant pot lid, fluff it with a fork and transfer to a bowl
3. Meanwhile, in your food processor, mix avocado with hot sauce and cilantro and blend well.
4. Pour this over rice, stir well, add salt and pepper to the taste, stir again, divide among plates and serve

Chipotle Rice.

(Prep + Cooking Time: 35 minutes | **Servings:** 4)

Ingredients:
- 2 cups. brown rice, rinsed
- 1 ½ tbsp. olive oil
- 1 tsp. salt
- 1/2 cup. chopped cilantro
- 2 ¾ cups. water, hot
- 1 lime, juiced
- 4 small bay leaves

Directions:
1. In a 6-quarts Instant Pot place rice, then add bay leaves and water.
2. Plug in and switch on the pot, select RICE option and secure pot with lid. Then position pressure indicator and let cook on default time.
3. When the timer beeps, switch off the Instant Pot and let pressure release naturally for 10 minutes and then do quick pressure release.
4. Carefully open the lid, add salt, oil, lime juice and cilantro and mix until combined. Serve warm and enjoy!

Fried Basmati Rice.

(Prep + Cooking Time: 15 minutes | **Servings:** 4)

Ingredients:
- 1 cup. basmati rice, uncooked
- 1/2 cups. peas, frozen OR your preferred vegetable
- 1/4 cup. soy sauce
- 1 ½ cups. chicken stock
- 1 tbsp. butter (or oil)
- 1 medium onion, diced
- 2 cloves garlic; minced.
- one egg

Directions:
1. Heat the Instant Pot to more "Sauté" mode. Put the oil in the pot
2. Add the garlic and the onion. Sauté for 1 minute.
3. Add the egg, scramble with the garlic mix for about 1 to 2 minutes
4. Add the rice, stock, and soy sauce in the pot. Press "Cancel". Close and lock the lid. Press RICE and set the time for 10 minutes
5. When the timer beeps, quick release the pressure. Carefully open the lid. Stir in the frozen peas or veggies.
6. Let sit until the peas/ veggies are warmed through.

Wild Rice and Chicken Soup

(Prep + Cooking Time: 25 minutes | **Servings:** 6)

Ingredients:

- 2 chicken breasts, skinless and boneless and chopped.
- 1 cup yellow onion; chopped.
- 28 oz. chicken stock
- 4 oz. cream cheese, cubed.
- 6 oz. wild rice
- 2 tbsp. butter
- 1 cup celery; chopped.
- 1 cup milk
- 1 cup half and half
- 1 tbsp. parsley; dried
- 2 tbsp. cornstarch mixed with 2 tbsp. water
- 1 cup carrots; chopped.
- A pinch of red pepper flakes
- Salt and black pepper to the taste

Directions:

1. Set your instant pot on Sauté mode; add butter and melt it
2. Add carrot, onion and celery, stir and cook for 5 minutes.
3. Add rice, chicken, stock, parsley, salt and pepper; then stir well. close the lid and cook at High for 5 minutes.
4. Quick release the pressure, carefully open the lid; add cornstarch mixed with water, stir and set the pot on Simmer mode.
5. Add cheese, milk and half and half; then stir well. heat up, transfer to bowls and serve.

Cajun Rice

(Prep + Cooking Time: 34 minutes | **Servings:** 4)

Ingredients:

- 1 lb. 85% lean ground beef
- 1/2 cup diced yellow onion, 1/2 cup diced bell pepper and 1/2 cup diced celery
- 1 cup water
- 1 cup basmati rice; rinsed and drained
- 1 bay leaf
- 2 tbsp. vegetable oil
- 1 tbsp. salt-free Cajun seasoning
- 1 tsp. dried oregano
- 2 tsp. hot sauce
- 1 tsp. salt or as your liking

Directions:

1. Now Press "Sauté" on the Instant Pot. When the pot is hot, add the oil. When the oil is hot, add the mirepoix and ground beef. Cook 2 to 3 minutes, stirring to break up the clumps of meat.
2. Add the rice, Cajun seasoning, hot sauce, oregano, salt and bay leaf. Stir well to combine. Now Press "Cancel". Stir in the water
3. Now secure the lid on the pot and close the valve. Now Press "Manual" and set the pot at "High" pressure for 4 minutes
4. After completing the cooking time, allow the pot to sit undisturbed for 10 minutes, then release any remaining pressure. Stir gently to fluff up the rice, discard the bay leaf and serve.

Mix-Fruit Wild Rice.

(Prep + Cooking Time: 50 minutes | **Servings:** 6)

Ingredients:

- 2 peeled and chopped small apples
- 1 chopped pear
- 1 tbsp. maple syrup
- 1/2 cup. slivered almonds
- 2 tbsp. apple juice
- 1 tsp. veggie oil
- 1 tsp. cinnamon
- 1/2 tsp. ground nutmeg
- 3 ½ cups. water
- 1 ½ cups. wild rice
- 1 cup. dried, mixed fruit
- Salt and pepper to taste

Directions:

1. Pour water into your Instant Pot along the rice
2. Close and seal the lid. Select "Manual" and cook for 30 minutes on "High" pressure.
3. While that cooks, soak the dried fruit in just enough apple juice to cover everything.
4. After 30 minutes, drain the fruit. By now, the rice should be done, so hit "Cancel" and wait for the pressure to come down on its own. Drain the rice and move rice to a bowl
5. Turn your instant pot to "Sauté" and add veggie oil. Cook the apples, pears, and almonds for about 2 minutes.
6. Pour in 2 tablespoon apple juice and keep cooking for a few minutes more
7. Add syrup, the cooked rice, soaked fruit, and seasonings. Keep stirring for 2 to 3 minutes. Serve.

Pink Rice

(Prep + Cooking Time: 15 minutes | **Servings:** 8)

Ingredients:

- 2 cups pink rice
- 2 ½ cups water
- 1 tsp. salt

Directions:

1. Put the rice in your instant pot
2. Add the water and salt; then stir everything well. close the lid and cook at High for 5 minutes
3. Release the pressure naturally for 10 minutes, then release remaining pressure by turning the valve to 'Venting', open the instant pot lid, fluff rice with a fork, divide among plates and serve

Mexican Brown Rice Casserole.

(Prep + Cooking Time: 35 minutes | **Servings:** 4)

Ingredients:

- 2 cups. uncooked brown rice
- 5 cups. water
- 1 cup. soaked black beans
- 6 oz. tomato paste
- 2 tsp. chili powder
- 2 tsp. onion powder
- 1 tsp. garlic
- 1 tsp. salt

Directions:

1. A few hours before dinner, put your dry beans in a bowl with enough water to cover them.
2. Soak on the countertop for at least two hours and drain.
3. Put everything in your Instant Pot. Close and seal the pressure cooker. Select "Manual" and then cook on "High" pressure for 28 minutes.
4. When time is up, hit "Cancel" and quick-release
5. Taste and season more if necessary

Mexican Basmati Rice.

(Prep + Cooking Time: 30 minutes | **Servings:** 6)

Ingredients:

- 2 cups. rice, long-grain, such as Lundberg Farms Brown Basmati.
- 1/2 cup. tomato paste
- 2 tsp. salt
- 1/2 white onion; chopped.
- 3 cloves garlic; minced
- 1 small jalapeño, optional
- 2 cups. water

Directions:

1. Set the Instant Pot to normal "Sauté". Heat the olive oil.
2. Add the garlic, onion, rice, and salt. Sauté for about 3 - 4 minutes or until fragrant
3. Mix the tomato paste with the water until well combined. Pour into the pot. Add the whole jalapeno pepper.
4. Press "Cancel". Close and lock the lid. Press "Pressure", set to "High", and the timer for 3 minutes is using white rice or for 22 minutes if using brown rice

5. When the timer beeps, release the pressure naturally for about 15 minutes. Turn the steam valve to "Venting". Carefully open the lid
6. Using a fork, fluff the rice and serve hot

Rice Bowl

(Prep + Cooking Time: 12 minutes | **Servings:** 4)

Ingredients:
- 1 cup brown rice
- 1 cup coconut milk
- 2 cups water
- 1/2 cup maple syrup
- 1/2 cup coconut chips
- 1/4 cup raisins
- 1/4 cup almonds
- A pinch of cinnamon powder
- A pinch of salt

Directions:
1. Put the rice in a pot, add the water, place on stove over medium high heat, cook according to instructions, drain and transfer it to your instant pot.
2. Add milk, coconut chips, almonds, raisins, salt, cinnamon and maple syrup, stir well, seal the instant pot lid and cook at High for 5 minutes
3. Quick release the pressure, transfer rice to breakfast bowls and serve right away.

Lentil & Rice.

(Prep + Cooking Time: 55 minutes | **Servings:** 4)

Ingredients:
For the sauté:
- 2 cloves garlic; minced.
- 1/2 cup. onion; chopped.
- 1 tbsp. oil, OR dry sauté (or add a little water/vegetable broth)

For the porridge:
- 1 ½ cups. brown rice
- 2-inch sprig fresh rosemary
- 1 cup. brown lentils
- 1 tbsp. dried marjoram (or thyme)
- 3 ½ cups. water
- 1 cup. rutabaga, peeled and diced, OR potato OR turnip
- Salt and pepper, to taste

Directions:
1. Press the "Sauté" key of the Instant Pot and select the Normal option.
2. Put the oil/ broth in the pot and, if using oil, heat. When the oil is hot, add the onion and sauté for 5 minutes or until transparent
3. Add the garlic and sauté for 1 minute
4. Add the lentils, brown rice, rutabaga, marjoram, rosemary, and pour in the water into the pot and stir to combine. Press the "Cancel" key to stop the sauté function
5. Press the "Manual" key, set the pressure to "High", and set the timer for 23 minutes
6. When the Instant Pot timer beeps, press the "Cancel" key. Let the pressure release naturally for 10 - 15 minutes or until the valve drops. Release remaining pressure. Unlock and carefully open the lid
7. Taste and, if needed, season with pepper and salt to taste.
8. If needed, add more ground rosemary and more marjoram.

Rice & Beef Soup

(Prep + Cooking Time: 25 minutes | **Servings:** 6)

Ingredients:

- 1 lb. beef meat, ground.
- 3 garlic cloves; minced.
- 1 yellow onion; chopped
- 15 oz. canned garbanzo beans, rinsed.
- 1 potato, cubed
- 1/2 cup frozen peas
- 14 oz. canned tomatoes, crushed.
- 1/2 cup white rice
- 12 oz. spicy V8 juice
- 2 carrots, thinly sliced
- 1 tbsp. vegetable oil
- 1 celery rib; chopped
- 28 oz. canned beef stock
- Salt and black pepper to the taste

Directions:

8. Set your instant pot on Sauté mode; add beef; then stir well. cook until it browns and transfer to a plate
9. Add the oil to your pot and heat it up.
10. Add celery and onion, stir and cook for 5 minutes
11. Add garlic, stir and cook for 1 minute more.
12. Add V8 juice, stock, tomatoes, rice, beans, carrots, potatoes, beef, salt and pepper; then stir well. close the lid and cook at High for 5 minutes
13. Quick release the pressure, remove the instant pot lid and set it on Simmer mode
14. Add more salt and pepper if needed and peas; then stir well. bring to a simmer, transfer to bowls and serve hot.

Pineapple Rice.

(Prep + Cooking Time: 12 minutes | **Servings:** 4)

Ingredients:

- 8 oz. crushed pineapple
- 1 cup. brown rice
- 1/4 cup. pineapple juice
- 1 tbsp. butter

Directions:

1. Put everything in your instant pot pressure cooker and seal the lid
2. Hit "Manual" and adjust time to 7 minutes
3. When time is up, wait 1 to 2 minutes before quick-releasing.
4. Stir and serve!

French Butter Rice.

(Prep + Cooking Time: 30 minutes | **Servings:** 4)

Ingredients:

- 1 ¼ cups. vegetable stock
- 2 cups. brown rice
- 1 stick (1/2 cup) butter
- 1 ¼ cups. French Onion soup

Directions:

1. Put all of the ingredients in the Instant Pot. Stir to incorporate.
2. Close and lock the lid. Press "Manual". Set to "High" pressure and the time for 22 minutes
3. When the timer beeps, let the pressure release naturally.
4. Serve warm. If desired, garnish with parsley

Simple White Rice.

(**Prep + Cooking Time:** 15 minutes | **Servings:** 4)

Ingredients:
- 1 cup. white basmati rice
- 1 cup. water

Directions:
1. Put the rice in a colander. Rinse until the water is clear
2. Transfer into the Instant Pot and then add the water.
3. Set the pot to "Manual", set the pressure to "Low", and the timer to 8 minutes.
4. When the timer beeps, quick release the pressure.
5. Fluff the rice using a fork and serve

Rice and Peas

(**Prep + Cooking Time:** 20 minutes | **Servings:** 6)

Ingredients:
- 1 cup canned kidney beans, drained and rinsed
- 1/2 cup full-fat coconut milk
- 1 cup jasmine rice; rinsed and drained
- 3 sprigs fresh thyme
- 1 cup water
- 1 Scotch bonnet chile
- 1 tbsp. melted Ghee, vegetable oil
- 1 tsp. salt or as your liking
- 1/2 tsp. ground allspice

Directions:
1. In your Instant Pot, combine the rice, water, whole chile, thyme, salt and allspice. Stir to combine. Add the ghee and stir to combine. Gently add the kidney beans on the top of the rice; do not stir.
2. Now secure the lid on the pot and close the valve. Now Press "Manual" and set the pot at "High" pressure for 4 minutes
3. After completing the cooking time, allow the pot to sit undisturbed for 10 minutes, then release any remaining pressure
4. Stir in the coconut milk. Place the lid back on the pot and allow to stand for about 10 minutes for the coconut milk to be absorbed. Remove the thyme sprigs and the chile and serve.

Chickpea & Rice Stew.

(**Prep + Cooking Time:** 35 minutes | **Servings:** 6)

Ingredients:
- 3 medium-sized onions, peeled and sliced.
- 6 oz. brown basmati rice, rinsed
- 30 oz. cooked chickpeas
- 8 fluid-ounce orange juice
- 1 tbsp. olive oil
- 4 cups. vegetable broth
- 4 oz. chopped cilantro
- 1 lb. sweet potato, peeled and diced.
- 1/4 tsp. salt
- 1/4 tsp. ground black pepper
- 2 tsp. ground cumin
- 2 tsp. ground coriander

Directions:
1. Plug in and switch on a 6-quarts Instant Pot, select "Sauté" option, add oil and onion and let cook for 10 - 12 minutes or until browned.
2. Stir in coriander and cumin and continue cooking for 15 seconds or until fragrant.
3. Add remaining ingredients into the pot except for black pepper and cilantro and stir until just mixed
4. Press "Cancel" and secure pot with lid. Then position pressure indicator, select "Manual" option and adjust cooking time on timer pad to 5 minutes and let cook on "High" pressure
5. Instant Pot will take 10 minutes to build pressure before cooking timer starts.
6. When the timer beeps, switch off the Instant Pot and let pressure release naturally for 10 minutes and then do quick pressure release.
7. Then remove the instant pot lid and stir in pepper until mixed. Garnish with cilantro and serve

Dolma Casserole

(Prep + Cooking Time: 40 minutes | **Servings:** 4)

Ingredients:

- 1 cup chopped yellow onions
- 1 lb. 85% lean ground beef
- 8 ounces brined grape leaves, drained and chopped
- ⅓ cup fresh lemon juice
- 1/4 cup chopped fresh mint
- 1 cup basmati rice; rinsed and drained
- 1 cup water
- 2 tbsp. extra-virgin olive oil
- 1 tbsp. minced garlic
- 1/4 cup chopped fresh parsley
- 1 tsp. ground allspice
- 1 tsp. salt or as your liking
- 1 tsp. black pepper

Directions:

1. Press "Sauté" on the Instant Pot. When the pot is hot, add the olive oil. When the oil is hot, add the garlic and onions.
2. Stir to combine. Add the beef and cook, stirring just enough to break up the clumps, for 2 to 3 minutes (don't worry about it being fully cooked at this point). Add the water, rice, grape leaves, parsley, allspice, salt and pepper. Stir well to combine. Now Press "Cancel"
3. Now secure the lid on the pot and close the valve. Now Press "Manual" and set the pot at "High" pressure for 4 minutes
4. After completing the cooking time, let the pot sit undisturbed for 10 minutes, then release any remaining pressure. Gently stir in the lemon juice and mint. Serve with tzatziki on the side.

Rice Pudding

(Prep + Cooking Time: 20 minutes | **Servings:** 6)

Ingredients:

- 7 oz. long grain rice
- 1 tbsp. butter
- 4 oz. water
- 16 oz. milk
- 3 oz. sugar
- one egg
- 1 tbsp. cream
- 1 tsp. vanilla
- A pinch of salt
- Cinnamon to the taste

Directions:

1. Put the butter in your instant pot, set it on Sauté mode; melt it, add rice and stir.
2. Add water and milk and stir again
3. Add salt and sugar, stir again, close the lid and cook at High for 8 minutes.
4. Meanwhile, in a bowl, mix cream with vanilla and eggs and stir well
5. Quick release the pressure, carefully open the lid; and pour some of the liquid from the pot over egg mixture and stir very well.
6. Pour this into the pot and whisk well
7. Seal the instant pot lid, cook at High for 10 minutes, release pressure, open the instant pot lid, pour pudding into bowls, sprinkle cinnamon on top and serve

Salmon and Rice

(Prep + Cooking Time: 10 minutes | **Servings:** 2)

Ingredients:

- 2 wild salmon fillets, frozen
- 1/2 cup jasmine rice
- 1/4 cup vegetable soup mix; dried
- 1 cup chicken stock
- 1 tbsp. butter
- A pinch of saffron
- Salt and black pepper to the taste

Directions:

1. In your instant pot, mix stock with rice, soup mix, butter and saffron and stir.
2. Season salmon with salt and pepper, place in the steamer basket of your pot, close the lid and cook on High for 5 minutes.
3. Quick release the pressure, divide salmon among plates, add rice mix on the side and serve.

Rice and Chicken

(Prep + Cooking Time: 50 minutes **| Servings:** 2)

Ingredients:

- 3 chicken quarters cut into small pieces
- 2 carrots, cut into chunks
- 1 yellow onion, sliced
- 1 tsp. cumin, ground
- 1 tbsp. soy sauce
- 1 tbsp. peanut oil
- 2 potatoes, cut into quarters
- 1 shallot, sliced

- 1 ½ tbsp. cornstarch mixed with 2 tbsp. water
- 1 ½ tsp. turmeric powder
- 1 green bell pepper; chopped
- 7 oz. coconut milk
- 2 bay leaves
- 3 garlic cloves; minced.
- Salt and black pepper to the taste

For the marinade:

- 1 ½ cups water
- 1 ½ cups rice
- 1 tbsp. white wine

- 1 tbsp. soy sauce
- 1/2 tsp. sugar
- A pinch of white pepper

Directions:

1. In a bowl, mix chicken with sugar, white pepper, 1 tablespoon soy sauce and 1 tablespoon white wine, stir and keep in the fridge for 20 minutes.
2. Set your instant pot on Sauté mode; add peanut oil and heat it up
3. Add onion and shallot, stir and cook for 3 minutes
4. Add garlic, salt, and pepper, stir and cook for 2 minutes more.
5. Add chicken, stir and brown for 2 minutes
6. Add turmeric and cumin, stir and cook for 1 minute.
7. Add bay leaves, carrots, potatoes, bell pepper, coconut milk and 1 tablespoon soy sauce
8. Stir everything, place steamer basket in the pot, place the rice in a bowl and the basket
9. Add 1 ½ cups water in the bowl, seal the instant pot lid and cook at High for 4 minutes.
10. Release the pressure naturally, take the rice out of the pot and divide among plates, add cornstarch to pot and stir
11. Add chicken next to rice and serve.

Steamed Eggs with Rice

(Prep + Cooking Time: 15 minutes **| Servings:** 2)

Ingredients:

- 2 eggs
- 1 ⅓ cup water
- 2 scallions; finely chopped
- Salt and black pepper to the taste

- A pinch of sesame seeds
- A pinch of garlic powder
- Hot rice for serving

Directions:

1. In a bowl, mix the eggs with 1/3 cup water and whisk well.
2. Strain this into a heat proof dish
3. Add salt, pepper to the taste, sesame seeds, garlic powder and scallions and whisk very well.
4. Put 1 cup water in your instant pot, place the dish in the steamer basket, seal the instant pot lid and cook at High for 5 minutes
5. Quick release the pressure, open the instant pot lid, divide the rice among plates and add eggs mix on the side.

Instant Brown Rice.

(**Prep + Cooking Time:** 30 minutes | **Servings:** 6)

Ingredients:
- 2 cups. brown rice
- 2 ½ cups. any kind vegetable broth or water
- 1/2 tsp. of sea salt

Directions:
1. Put the rice into the Instant Pot
2. Pour in the broth or water and salt. Close and lock the lid. Press the "Manual" and set the timer to 22 minutes pressure cooking.
3. When the timer beeps, Release the pressure naturally for 10 minutes, then release remaining pressure by turning the valve to 'Venting'
4. Carefully open the lid and Serve hot.

Coconut Sweet Rice.

(**Prep + Cooking Time:** 25 minutes | **Servings:** 4)

Ingredients:
- 1 cup. Thai sweet rice
- 1/2 can Full-Fat: coconut milk
- 1 ½ cups. water
- 2 tbsp. sugar Dash of salt

Directions:
1. Mix rice and water in your Instant Pot
2. Select "Manual" and cook for just 3 minutes on "High" pressure
3. When time is up, hit "Cancel" and wait 10 minutes for a natural release
4. In the meanwhile, heat coconut milk, sugar, and salt in a saucepan.
5. When the sugar has melted, remove from the heat.
6. When the cooker has released its pressure, mix the coconut milk mixture into your rice and stir
7. Put the lid back on and let it rest 5 - 10 minutes, without returning it to pressure. Serve and enjoy!

Black Beans and Rice.

(**Prep + Cooking Time:** 35 minutes | **Servings:** 4)

Ingredients:
- 1 cup. onion, diced
- 2 cups. brown rice
- 2 cups. dry black beans
- 4 cloves garlic, crushed and then minced.
- 9 cups. water
- 1 tsp. salt
- 1 to 2 limes, optional
- Avocado, optional

Directions:
1. Put garlic and onion in your Instant Pot
2. Add the black beans and the brown rice. Pour in the water and sprinkle the salt. Close the lid. Press "Manual" and set the time to 28 minutes.
3. When the timer is up, press "Cancel" or unplug the pot. Let the pressure release naturally. You can let it sit for 20 minutes
4. Scoop into a serving bowl and squeeze a lime wedge over the bowl
5. Serve with a couple of avocado slices for garnishing.

Arroz Con Pollo

(Prep + Cooking Time: 46 minutes | **Servings:** 6)

Ingredients:

- 1 lb. boneless; skinless chicken thighs, cut into bite-size chunks
- 2 tomatoes, quartered
- 1/2 cup coarsely chopped fresh cilantro
- 3 garlic cloves; crushed
- 1/2 jalapeño
- 1 cup basmati rice; rinsed and drained
- 1/2 yellow onion, quartered
- 1 ½ cups water
- 2 tbsp. vegetable oil
- 2 tsp. ground cumin
- 1 tsp. salt or as your liking
- Tomatillo salsa, for serving

Directions:

1. In a blender, combine the onion, tomatoes, cilantro, garlic and jalapeño. Blend until smooth.
2. Now Press "Sauté" on the Instant Pot. When the pot is hot, add the oil. When the oil is hot, add the rice and cook, stirring frequently, until the rice is translucent, 3 to 4 minutes. Add the chicken, cumin, and salt. Cook, stirring, for 1 to 2 minutes. Now Press "Cancel"
3. Add the blended vegetables and the water. Stir well to combine.
4. Now secure the lid on the pot and close the valve. Now Press "Manual" and set the pot at "High" pressure for 6 minutes
5. After completing the cooking time, allow the pot to sit undisturbed for 10 minutes, then release any remaining pressure. Serve with tomatillo salsa, if desired.

Rice & Veggies Dish

(Prep + Cooking Time: 20 minutes | **Servings:** 4)

Ingredients:

- 2 cups basmati rice
- 3 garlic cloves; minced.
- 2 tbsp. butter
- 1 cinnamon stick
- 1 tbsp. cumin seeds
- 2 bay leaves
- 3 whole cloves
- 1/2 tsp. ginger, grated
- 1 cup mixed frozen carrots, peas, corn, green beans
- 2 cups water
- 1/2 tsp. green chili; minced.
- 5 black peppercorns
- 2 whole cardamoms
- 1 tbsp. sugar
- Salt to the taste

Directions:

1. Pour the water in your instant pot.
2. Add rice, mixed frozen veggies, green chili, grated ginger, garlic cloves, cinnamon stick, whole cloves and butter
3. Also add cumin seeds, bay leaves, cardamoms, black peppercorns, salt and sugar.
4. Stir, close the lid and cook at High for 15 minutes.
5. Quick release the pressure, divide among plates and serve with your favorite steaks

Cauliflower & Pineapple Rice

(Prep + Cooking Time: 30 minutes | **Servings:** 6)

Ingredients:

- 2 cups rice
- 2 tsp. extra virgin olive oil
- 1 cauliflower, florets separated and chopped.
- 1/2 pineapple; peeled and chopped.
- 4 cups water
- Salt and black pepper to the taste

Directions:

1. In your instant pot, mix rice with pineapple, cauliflower, water, oil, salt and pepper; then stir well. close the lid and cook for 20 minutes on Low.

2. Release the pressure naturally for 10 minutes, then release remaining pressure by turning the valve to 'Venting', open the instant pot lid, fluff with a fork, add more salt and pepper to the taste, divide among plates and serve.

Grain Rice Millet Blend.

(**Prep + Cooking Time:** 15 minutes | **Servings:** 8)

Ingredients:
- 2 cups. jasmine rice OR long-grain white rice
- 1/2 tsp. sea salt (optional)
- 3 ¼ cups. water
- 1/2 cup. millet

Directions:
1. Put all the ingredients in the Instant Pot and stir
2. Cover and lock the lid.
3. Press the RICE button and let the pot do all the cooking, about 10 minutes

Veggie Rice Acorn Squash.

(**Prep + Cooking Time:** 20 minutes | **Servings:** 4)

Ingredients:
- 3 ¾ cups. veggie stock
- 2 medium-sized, halved acorn squash
- 1/2 cup. quinoa
- 1/2 cup. vegan cheese
- 2 minced garlic cloves
- 1 tbsp. Earth Balance spread
- 1 cup. white rice
- 1 tsp. chopped rosemary
- 1 tsp. chopped thyme
- 1 tsp. chopped sage
- 1 cup. diced onion

Directions:
1. Turn your Instant Pot to "Sauté" and melt the Earth Balance. Add onion and salt, and cook for 2 minutes.
2. Toss in the garlic and cook for another minute or so. Add rice, quinoa, herbs, and pour in the broth. Stir.
3. Put your de-seeded squash halves with the cut-side UP in a steamer basket
4. Put the trivet in the cooker, and place the basket on top. Close and seal the lid.
5. Hit "Manual" and cook for 6 minutes on "High" pressure
6. When the timer beeps, carefully quick-release the pressure after hitting "Cancel"
7. Take out the steamer basket and drain any liquid that's hanging around in the squash.
8. Add vegan cheese to the pot and stir. Wait 5 minutes or so for the stuffing to thicken
9. Fill the squash and sprinkle on some extra cheese. Serve!

Pumpkin Rice Pudding

(**Prep + Cooking Time:** 1 hour | **Servings:** 6)

Ingredients:
- 3 cups cashew milk
- 1/2 cup dates; chopped
- 1 cup brown rice
- 1 cinnamon stick
- 1 cup pumpkin puree
- 1/2 cup maple syrup
- 1/2 cup water
- 1 tsp. vanilla extract
- 1 tsp. pumpkin spice mix
- A pinch of salt

Directions:
1. Put the rice in your instant pot, add boiling water to cover, leave aside for 10 minutes and drain
2. Pour the water in milk in your instant pot, add rice, cinnamon stick, dates and salt; then stir well. close the lid and cook at High for 20 minutes.
3. Quick release the pressure, carefully open the lid; add maple syrup, pumpkin pie spice and pumpkin puree; then stir well. set the pot on Simmer mode and cook for 5 minutes.

4. Discard cinnamon stick, add vanilla; then stir well. transfer pudding to bowls, leave aside for 30 minutes to cool down and serve

Delicious Rice Pudding

(Prep + Cooking Time: 45 minutes | **Servings:** 4)

Ingredients:

- 2 cups black rice, washed and rinsed
- 6 ½ cups water
- 3/4 cup sugar
- 5 cardamom pods, crushed.
- 3 cloves
- 1/2 cup coconut, grated
- Chopped mango for serving
- 2 cinnamon sticks
- A pinch of salt

Directions:

1. Put the rice in your instant pot, add a pinch of salt and the water and stir
2. In a cheesecloth bag, mix cardamom with cinnamon and cloves and tie it.
3. Place this in the pot with the rice, close the lid and cook on Low for 35 minutes
4. Release the pressure naturally, open the instant pot lid, stir the rice, add coconut and set your pot to sauté mode
5. Cook for 10 minutes, discard spices bag, transfer to breakfast bowls and serve with chopped mango on top.

Tasty Green Rice.

(Prep + Cooking Time: 50 minutes | **Servings:** 6)

Ingredients:

- 2 cups. rice basmati.
- 1 cup. dill
- 3 oz. butter
- 1 tbsp. salt
- 4 cups. beef broth
- 1 cup. spinach
- 1 tsp. olive oil
- 1 tsp. dried oregano
- 1 tbsp. minced garlic

Directions:

1. Pour the olive oil in the Instant Pot. Add rice, butter, and minced garlic
2. "Sauté" the mixture for 5 minutes. Stir it frequently
3. After this, add beef broth.
4. Wash the spinach and dill carefully. Chop the greens
5. Transfer the chopped greens in the blender and blend them well
6. Then add the blended greens in the rice mixture
7. Add butter, salt, and dried oregano
8. Mix up the mixture carefully with the help of the wooden spoon. After this, close the lid and set the Instant Pot mode RICE
9. Cook the dish for 20 minutes.
10. When the time is over - release the remaining pressure and transfer the green rice in the serving bowl.

Mix Rice Medley.

(Prep + Cooking Time: 35 minutes | **Servings:** 4)

Ingredients:

- 3/8 to 1/2 tsp. sea salt, optional
- 3/4 cup. (or more) short grain brown rice.
- 2 to 4 tbsp. red, wild or black rice
- 1 tbsp. water
- 1 ½ cups. water

Directions:

1. Put as much as 2 to 4 tablespoons of red, wild, or black rice or use all three kinds in 1-cup measuring cup.
2. Add brown rice to make 1 cup. total of rice. Put the rice in a strainer and wash. Put the rice in the Instant Pot
3. Add 1 ½ cup. plus 1 tablespoon water in the pot. If desired, add salt.
4. Stir and then check the sides of the pot to make sure the rice is pushed down into the water. Close and lock the lid. Press MULTIGRAIN and set the time to 23 minutes.
5. When the timer beeps, let the pressure release naturally for 5 minutes, then turn the steam valve and release the pressure slowly
6. If you have time, let the pressure release naturally for 15 minutes. Stir and serve.

Easy Risotto.

(Prep + Cooking Time: 25 minutes | **Servings:** 6)

Ingredients:

- 28 oz. chicken stock
- 12 oz. Arborio rice
- 1 ½ tbsp. olive oil
- 3 tbsp. Romano or Parmesan cheese
- 1 finely chopped medium onion
- Salt and pepper to taste

Directions:

1. Press sauté button and Heat the oil in your instant pot
2. Add onion and Sauté until soft and nearly translucent
3. Add the rice and chicken stock.
4. Close the lid and select the RICE function. Set a timer for 15 minutes
5. Wait for the cycle to end and for the pressure to naturally drop
6. Open the lid and stir in a little bit of black pepper
7. Add the Romano or Parmesan cheese.
8. Serve warm and enjoy!

Wild Rice & Farro Pilaf

(Prep + Cooking Time: 45 minutes | **Servings:** 12)

Ingredients:

- 1 ½ cups whole grain faro
- 1 tbsp. parsley and sage; finely chopped
- 1/2 cup hazelnuts, toasted and chopped.
- 3/4 cup wild rice
- 1 shallot; finely chopped
- 1 tsp. garlic; minced.
- 6 cups chicken stock
- 3/4 cup cherries; dried
- Some chopped chives for serving
- A drizzle of extra virgin olive oil
- Salt and black pepper to the taste

Directions:

1. Set your instant pot on Sauté mode; add a drizzle of oil and heat it up.
2. Add onion and garlic, stir and cook for 2 - 3 minutes.
3. Add farro, rice, salt, pepper, stock and 1 tablespoon mixed sage and parsley; then stir well. seal the instant pot lid and cook on High for 25 minutes.
4. Meanwhile, put cherries in a pot, add hot water to cover, leave aside for 10 minutes and drain them
5. Release the pressure naturally for 5 minutes, then release remaining pressure by turning the valve to 'Venting', now open the instant pot lid, drain excess liquid, add hazelnuts and cherries, stir gently, divide among plates and garnish with chopped chives

Artichokes Rice and Side Dish

(Prep + Cooking Time: 30 minutes | **Servings:** 4)

Ingredients:

- 15 oz. canned artichoke hearts chopped
- 5 oz. Arborio rice
- 16 oz. cream cheese
- 1 tbsp. extra-virgin olive oil
- 1 tbsp. grated parmesan cheese
- 1 tbsp. white wine
- 6 oz. graham cracker crumbs
- 1 ¼ cups water
- 1 ½ tbsp. thyme chopped
- 2 garlic cloves crushed.
- 1 ¼ cups chicken broth
- Salt and black pepper to the taste

Directions:

1. Set your instant pot on Sauté mode; add the oil, heat up, add rice and cook for 2 minutes.
2. Add garlic, stir and cook for 1 minute
3. Transfer this to a heat proof dish.
4. Add stock, crumbs, salt, pepper and wine, stir and cover the with tin foil.
5. Place the dish in the steamer basket of the pot, add water, close the lid and cook at High for 8 minutes
6. Quick release the pressure, take the dish out, uncover, add cream cheese, parmesan, artichoke hearts, and thyme.
7. Mix well and serve while it's hot!

Ground Beef and Rice

(Prep + Cooking Time: minutes | **Servings:** 6)

Ingredients:

- 1 lb. 85% lean ground beef
- 5 cardamom pods,
- 2 cups water
- 1 cup basmati rice; rinsed and drained
- 1 cup sliced yellow onions
- 1/2 cup pine nuts
- 1/2 cup chopped fresh cilantro
- 1 tbsp. minced garlic
- 2 tbsp. vegetable oil
- 1 tsp. ground cinnamon
- 1/2 tsp. freshly grated nutmeg
- 1 ½ tsp. ground allspice
- 1 tsp. salt or as your liking
- 1 tsp. black pepper
- Tzatziki, for serving; optional

Directions:

1. Press "Sauté" on the Instant Pot. When the pot is hot, add the oil. When the oil is hot, add the pine nuts. Cook, stirring, for 1 to 2 minutes.
2. Add the onions and garlic and stir to combine. Add the ground beef and cook, stirring just enough to break up the clumps of meat, for 2 to 3 minutes.
3. Add the rice, cardamom, allspice, cinnamon, nutmeg, salt and pepper. Stir well to combine. Stir in the water. Now Press "Cancel"
4. Now secure the lid on the pot and close the valve. Now Press "Manual" and set the pot at "High" pressure for 4 minutes
5. After completing the cooking time, allow the pot to sit undisturbed for 10 minutes, then release any remaining pressure.
6. Stir gently to fluff up the rice. Sprinkle with the chopped fresh herbs. Serve hot, with a side of tzatziki if you like.

(Prep + Cooking Time: 45 minutes | **Servings:** 6)

Ingredients:

- 1 cup basmati rice; rinsed and drained
- 2 cups thinly sliced yellow onions
- ⅓ cup brown lentils
- 2 cups water
- 2 tbsp. Ghee
- 1/2 tsp. ground cumin
- 1/2 tsp. ground coriander
- Salt to taste

Directions:

1. Place the lentils in a small bowl. Cover with hot water and let soak while you get everything else going.
2. Now Press "Sauté" on the Instant Pot. When the pot is hot, add the ghee. When the ghee has melted, add the onions.
3. Season with a little salt and cook, stirring, until the onions begin to crisp around the edges but are not burned, 5 to 10 minutes. Remove half the onions from the pot and reserve for garnish. Now Press "Cancel".
4. Drain the lentils. Add the lentils, water, rice, cumin and coriander to the pot and season with salt. Stir well to combine
5. Now secure the lid on the pot and close the valve. Now Press "Manual" and set the pot at "High" pressure for 6 minutes. After completing the cooking time, allow the pot to sit undisturbed for 10 minutes, then release any remaining pressure
6. Very gently stir and place the lid halfway on the pot. Let the rice and lentils rest for 5 to 10 minutes. Transfer the rice and lentils to a serving dish. Sprinkle with the reserved onions and serve.

Sauce Recipes

Carrot Sauce Recipe

(Prep + Cooking Time: 25 minutes | **Servings:** 6)

Ingredients:
- 2 cups carrot juice
- 4 tbsp. butter
- 1 tbsp. mixed chervil, chives and tarragon
- Salt and black pepper to the taste
- A pinch of cayenne pepper
- A pinch of cinnamon

Directions:
1. Put carrot juice in your instant pot, set the pot on Simmer mode and bring to a boil.
2. Add butter, salt, pepper, cayenne and cinnamon; then stir well. seal the instant pot lid and cook at High for 5 minutes.
3. Quick release the pressure, carefully open the lid; add mixed herbs, stir and serve

Fennel Sauce Recipe

(Prep + Cooking Time: 20 minutes | **Servings:** 6)

Ingredients:
- 1 fennel bulb, cut into pieces
- 1/4 cup dry white wine
- 5 thyme springs
- 3 tbsp. olive oil
- 2 pints' grape tomatoes, cut into halves
- A pinch of sugar
- Salt and black pepper to the taste

Directions:
1. Set your instant pot in Sauté mode; add oil and heat it up.
2. Add fennel, tomatoes, thyme, sugar, salt and pepper, stir and sauté for 5 minutes.
3. Add white wine, close the lid and cook for 4 minutes more.
4. Quick release the pressure, carefully open the lid; discard thyme, stir sauce well and serve.

Apple sauce

(Prep + Cooking Time: 18 minutes | **Servings:** 4)

Ingredients:
- 8 apples, cored and chopped.
- 1 tsp. cinnamon powder
- 2 drops cinnamon oil
- 1 cup water

Directions:
1. Put apples in your instant pot, add the water, close the lid and cook at High for 8 minutes
2. Quick release the pressure, carefully open the lid; add oil and cinnamon and puree using an immersion blender. serve cold.

Asian Tomato Chutney

(Prep + Cooking Time: 20 minutes | **Servings:** 6)

Ingredients:
- 3 lb. tomatoes; peeled and chopped.
- 3/4 tsp. cinnamon, ground.
- 1/4 tsp. cloves
- 1/2 tsp. coriander, ground.
- 1 tsp. chili powder
- 1 cup red wine vinegar
- 1 ¾ cups sugar
- 1/4 tsp. nutmeg
- 1/4 tsp. ginger, ground.
- 1 pinch paprika
- 1-inch ginger piece, grated
- 3 garlic cloves; minced.
- 2 onions; chopped.
- 1/4 cup raisins

Directions:
1. Mix tomatoes and grated ginger in your blender, pulse well and transfer to your instant pot.
2. Add vinegar, sugar, garlic, onions, raisins, cinnamon, cloves, coriander, nutmeg, ground ginger, paprika and chili powder; then stir well. seal the instant pot lid and cook at High for 10 minutes
3. Quick release the pressure, carefully open the lid; transfer to jars and serve when needed

Quince Sauce Recipe

(Prep + Cooking Time: 25 minutes | Servings: 6)

Ingredients:
- 2 lb. grated quince
- 2 lb. sugar
- 1/4 cup water
- Juice of 1 lemon
- 10 cloves

Directions:
1. In your instant pot, mix quince with sugar and stir well
2. Add water and stir again
3. Tie cloves in a cheesecloth and add to the pot as well
4. Cover and cook at High for 10 minutes.
5. Release pressure for 10 minutes, carefully open the lid; stir sauce again and transfer to jars.
6. Serve on top of cakes

Rhubarb Sauce Recipe

(Prep + Cooking Time: 25 minutes | Servings: 6)

Ingredients:
- 8 oz. rhubarb, trimmed and chopped.
- 1/4 cup raisins
- 1/4 cup water
- 1/3 cup honey
- 1 tbsp. cider vinegar
- 1 small onion; chopped.
- 2 jalapeno peppers; chopped.
- A pinch of cardamom, ground.
- 1 garlic clove; minced.

Directions:
1. In your instant pot, mix rhubarb with vinegar, onion, cardamom, garlic, jalapenos, honey, water, and raisins; then stir well. seal the instant pot lid and cook at High for 7 minutes.
2. Quick release the pressure, carefully open the lid; set it on Simmer mode and cook for 3 more minutes.
3. Serve when needed.

Leeks Sauce Recipe

(Prep + Cooking Time: 12 minutes | Servings: 8)

Ingredients:
- 2 leeks, thinly sliced
- 2 tbsp. butter
- 1 cup whipping cream
- 3 tbsp. lemon juice
- Salt and pepper to the taste

Directions:
1. Set your instant pot on Sauté mode; add butter and melt it.
2. Add leeks, stir and cook for 2 minutes.
3. Add lemon juice; then stir well. seal the instant pot lid and cook at High for 3 minutes
4. Quick release the pressure, carefully open the lid; transfer sauce to your blender, add whipping cream and blend everything.
5. Return sauce to the pot, set on Simmer mode, add salt and pepper to the taste, stir and cook for 2 minutes.
6. Serve with fish

Corn Sauce Recipe

(**Prep + Cooking Time:** 16 minutes | **Servings:** 4)

Ingredients:
- 2 cups corn kernels
- 1 ¾ cups chicken stock
- 1/4 cup white wine
- 1 thyme spring
- 1 tsp. white flour
- 2 tsp. butter
- 1 yellow onion; chopped.
- 1 tbsp. olive oil
- 1 tsp. thyme; finely chopped
- Salt and black pepper to the taste

Directions:
1. Set your instant pot on Sauté mode; add oil and heat it up
2. Add onion, stir and cook for 3 minutes.
3. Add flour, stir well and cook for 1 minute more.
4. Add wine, stir and cook for 1 minute.
5. Add thyme spring, stock and corn; then stir well. seal the instant pot lid and cook at High for 1 minute.
6. Quick release the pressure, carefully open the lid; discard thyme spring, transfer corn sauce to a blender, add salt, pepper, butter and chopped thyme and blend well.
7. Return to pot set it on Sauté mode again and cook 1 - 2 minutes more.
8. Serve when needed

Orange Sauce

(**Prep + Cooking Time:** 17 minutes | **Servings:** 6)

Ingredients:
- 1 cup orange juice
- 1/4 cup white wine vinegar
- 2 tbsp. agave nectar
- 1/4 cup veggie stock
- 2 tbsp. cornstarch
- 1 tsp. ginger paste
- 2 tbsp. tomato paste
- 3 tbsp. sugar
- 1 tsp. sesame oil
- 1 tsp. chili sauce
- 2 tbsp. soy sauce
- 1 tsp. garlic; finely chopped

Directions:
1. Set your instant pot on Sauté mode; add oil and heat it up
2. Add garlic and ginger paste, stir and cook for 2 minutes.
3. Add tomato paste, sugar, orange juice, vinegar, agave nectar, soy and chili sauce; then stir well. seal the instant pot lid and cook at High for 3 minutes more.
4. Quick release the pressure, carefully open the lid; add stock and cornstarch; then stir well. seal the instant pot lid again and cook at High for 4 minutes
5. Release pressure again and serve your sauce

Cranberry Sauce

(**Prep + Cooking Time:** 25 minutes | **Servings:** 4)

Ingredients:
- 12 oz. cranberries
- 1/4 cup orange juice
- 2 ½ tsp. orange zest
- 2 tbsp. maple syrup
- A pinch of salt
- 1 cup sugar

Directions:
1. In your instant pot, mix orange juice with maple syrup and stir well
2. Add orange zest and almost all cranberries; then stir well. seal the instant pot lid and cook at High for 2 minutes
3. Quick release the pressure, open the instant pot lid and set it on Sauté mode.
4. Add the rest of the cranberries, a pinch of salt and the sugar, stir and cook until sugar dissolves. Serve cold.

Cherry Sauce Recipe

(Prep + Cooking Time: 15 minutes | **Servings:** 4)

Ingredients:

- 2 cups cherries
- 1 tbsp. lemon juice
- 1 tbsp. sugar
- 1/4 cup water
- 1 tsp. kirsch
- 2 tbsp. cornstarch
- A pinch of salt

Directions:

1. In your instant pot, mix water with lemon juice, salt, sugar, kirsch and cornstarch
2. Add cherries; then stir well. seal the instant pot lid and cook at High for 5 minutes.
3. Quick release the pressure, carefully open the lid; transfer sauce to a bowl and serve after it's cold.

Apricot Sauce Recipe

(Prep + Cooking Time: 30 minutes | **Servings:** 6)

Ingredients:

- 3 oz. apricots; dried and cut into halves
- 2 cups water
- 1 tsp. vanilla extract
- 2/3 cup sugar

Directions:

1. In your instant pot mix apricots with water, sugar and vanilla; then stir well. seal the instant pot lid and cook on Medium for 20 minutes
2. Quick release the pressure, carefully open the lid; transfer sauce to your blender and pulse well.
3. Divide into jars and serve with a poultry dish.

Bread Sauce recipe

(Prep + Cooking Time: 20 minutes | **Servings:** 12)

Ingredients:

- 26 oz. milk
- 6 bread slices, torn
- 2 bay leaves
- 2 tbsp. butter
- 2 garlic cloves, crushed.
- 1 yellow onion; chopped.
- 6 cloves
- Salt to the taste
- A splash of double cream

Directions:

1. Set your instant pot on Simmer mode, add milk and heat it up.
2. Add garlic, cloves, onion, bay leaves and salt, stir well and cook for 3 minutes.
3. Add bread; then stir well. seal the instant pot lid and cook at High for 4 minutes.
4. Quick release the pressure, carefully open the lid; transfer sauce to a blender, add butter and cream, discard bay leaf and blend well
5. Return sauce to the pot set it on Simmer mode and simmer sauce for 3 minutes more.

Pineapple Sauce

(Prep + Cooking Time: 13 minutes | **Servings:** 4)

Ingredients:

- 3 cups pineapple tidbits
- 3 tbsp. rum
- 1 tsp. cinnamon
- 1 tsp. ginger
- 1 tsp. allspice
- 1 tsp. nutmeg
- 3 tbsp. butter
- 4 tbsp. brown sugar

Directions:

1. Set your instant pot on sauté mode; add butter and melt it.
2. Add sugar, pineapple tidbits, rum, allspice, nutmeg, cinnamon and ginger; then stir well. seal the instant pot lid and cook at High for 3 minutes.
3. Quick release the pressure, carefully open the lid; stir sauce one more time and serve.

Elderberry Sauce Recipe

(Prep + Cooking Time: 20 minutes | **Servings:** 20)

Ingredients:

- 1 cup elderberries
- 1-inch ginger piece, grated
- 5 cloves
- 4 cups water
- 1 cinnamon stick
- 1 cup honey
- 1 vanilla bean, split

Directions:

1. In your instant pot, mix elderberries with water, ginger, cinnamon, vanilla and cloves; then stir well. seal the instant pot lid and cook at High for 10 minutes.
2. Quick release the pressure, strain sauce and keep in jars.

Green Tomato Sauce

(Prep + Cooking Time: 15 minutes | **Servings:** 12)

Ingredients:

- 2 lb. green tomatoes; chopped.
- 4 red chili peppers; chopped.
- 1 Anaheim chili pepper; chopped.
- 3/4 cup brown sugar
- 3/4 cup white vinegar
- 2 tbsp. ginger, grated
- 1 white onion; chopped.
- 1/4 cup currants

Directions:

1. In your instant pot, mix green tomatoes with onion, currants, Anaheim pepper, chili pepper, ginger, sugar, and vinegar; then stir well. seal the instant pot lid and cook at High for 10 minutes.
2. Release the pressure naturally for 5 minutes, then release remaining pressure by turning the valve to 'Venting', and carefully open the lid.
3. Transfer sauce to jars and serve.

Chili Jam

(Prep + Cooking Time: 50 minutes | **Servings:** 12)

Ingredients:

- 17 oz. cranberries
- 4 oz. sugar
- 4 red chili peppers, seeded and chopped.
- 4 garlic cloves; minced.
- 2 red onions; finely chopped
- 2 tbsp. red wine vinegar
- 3 tbsp. water
- A drizzle of olive oil
- Salt and black pepper to the taste

Directions:

1. Set your instant pot on Sauté mode; add oil and heat it up
2. Add onions, garlic and chilies, stir and cook for 8 minutes.
3. Add cranberries, vinegar, water and sugar; then stir well. close the lid and cook at High for 14 minutes.
4. Quick release the pressure, carefully open the lid; mash sauce using an immersion blender, set the pot on Simmer mode and cook the sauce for 15 minutes.
5. Add salt and pepper to the taste, transfer to jars and serve when needed

Sauce Recipe

(Prep + Cooking Time: 30 minutes | **Servings:** 8)

Ingredients:

- 1 yellow onion; chopped.
- 1 butternut squash; chopped.
- 8 garlic cloves; minced.
- 2 bay leaves
- 2 tbsp. olive oil
- 1 cup veggie stock
- 1/4 cup lemon juice
- 1 bunch basil; chopped.
- 5 celery ribs
- 8 carrots; chopped
- 4 beets; chopped
- Salt and black pepper to the taste

Directions:

1. Set your instant pot on Sauté mode; add oil and heat it up
2. Add celery, onion and carrots, stir and cook for 4 minutes.
3. Add beets, squash, garlic, stock, lemon juice, basil, bay leaves, salt and pepper; then stir well. seal the instant pot lid and cook for 12 minutes at High.
4. Quick release the pressure, carefully open the lid; discard bay leaves, puree sauce using an immersion blender, transfer to a bowl and serve

Grapes Sauce Recipe

(Prep + Cooking Time: 20 minutes | **Servings:** 6)

Ingredients:

- 6 oz. black grapes
- 1/2 cup water
- 2 ½ tbsp. sugar
- 1 cup corn flour
- A splash of lemon juice

Directions:

1. Put grapes in your instant pot, add water to cover, cook at High for 7 minutes, release pressure, leave mix aside to cool down, blend using an immersion blender, strain sauce and leave aside for now.
2. Heat up a pan over medium heat, add grapes mix, sugar, the water and corn flour, stir and boil until it thickens
3. Add lemon juice; then stir well. take off heat and serve.

Sriracha Sauce

(Prep + Cooking Time: 25 minutes | **Servings:** 6)

Ingredients:

- 4 oz. red chilies, seeded and chopped.
- 3 tbsp. palm sugar
- 3 oz. bird's eye chilies
- 12 garlic cloves; minced.
- 5 oz. distilled vinegar
- 5 oz. water

Directions:

1. In your instant pot, mix water with palm sugar and stir
2. Add all chilies and garlic; then stir well. seal the instant pot lid and cook at High for 7 minutes
3. Quick release the pressure, carefully open the lid; blend sauce using an immersion blender, add vinegar; then stir well. set the pot on Simmer mode and cook the sauce for 10 minutes
4. Serve when needed

Mushroom Gravy

(**Prep + Cooking Time:** 40 minutes | **Servings:** 5)

Ingredients:

- 8 ounces baby bella mushrooms; diced
- 1 ¼ cups Vegetable Stock
- 1/4 cup red wine
- 1/2 small sweet onion; diced
- 2 garlic cloves; minced
- 1 tbsp. cornstarch
- 2 tbsp. vegan Worcestershire sauce
- 1 tbsp. olive oil
- 1 tsp. Montreal chicken seasoning
- 1 tsp. Dijon mustard
- 1 tsp. rubbed sage

Directions:

1. Select the "Sauté" Low mode on your instant pot. When the display reads "Hot," add the oil and heat until it shimmers
2. Add the mushrooms and onion. Sauté for 2 to 3 minutes, stirring frequently. Turn off the Instant Pot and add the garlic. Cook, stirring so it doesn't burn, for 30 seconds more
3. Add the Worcestershire sauce, mustard, sage, Montreal chicken seasoning, ¾ cup of stock and the red wine.
4. Lock the lid and turn the steam release handle to Sealing. Using the Manual function, set the cooker to High Pressure for 20 minutes
5. After completing the cooking time, let the pressure release naturally for 10 minutes; quick release any remaining pressure.
6. In a small bowl, whisk the remaining ½ cup of stock and cornstarch.
7. Remove the lid carefully and stir this slurry into the gravy. Select Sauté Low again and simmer the gravy for 2 to 3 minutes until thickened

Mustard Sauce Recipe

(**Prep + Cooking Time:** 18 minutes | **Servings:** 4)

Ingredients:

- 6 oz. mushrooms; chopped.
- 3.5 oz. beef stock
- 3.5 oz. dry sherry
- 1 thyme spring
- 1 garlic clove; minced.
- 2 tbsp. parsley; finely chopped
- 3 tbsp. olive oil
- 1 tbsp. balsamic vinegar
- 1 tbsp. mustard
- 2 tbsp. crème fraiche

Directions:

1. Set your instant pot on Sauté mode; add oil and heat it up.
2. Add garlic, thyme and mushrooms, stir and cook for 5 minutes.
3. Add sherry, vinegar and stock; then stir well. seal the instant pot lid and cook at High for 3 minutes.
4. Quick release the pressure, carefully open the lid; discard thyme, add crème fraiche, mustard, and parsley; then stir well. set the pot on Simmer mode and cook the sauce for 3 minutes
5. Serve right away

Clementine Sauce Recipe

(**Prep + Cooking Time:** 16 minutes | **Servings:** 4)

Ingredients:

- 12 oz. cranberries
- Juice and peel from 1 clementine
- 1 cup water
- 1 cup sugar

Directions:

1. In your instant pot, mix cranberries with clementine juice and peel, water and sugar; then stir well. seal the instant pot lid and cook at High for 6 minutes.
2. Quick release the pressure, open the instant pot lid and serve your sauce

Eggplant Sauce

(**Prep + Cooking Time:** 30 minutes | **Servings:** 6)

Ingredients:

- 1 eggplant; chopped.
- 5 oz. canned tomato paste
- 1 lb. ground meat
- 28 oz. canned tomatoes; chopped.
- 5 garlic cloves; minced.
- 1/4 cup parsley; chopped.
- 1 sweet onion; chopped.
- 1 tbsp. apple cider vinegar
- 1/2 tsp. turmeric
- 1 cup bone stock
- 1/2 tsp. dill; dried
- 1/2 cup olive oil
- Salt and black pepper to the taste

Directions:

1. Set your instant pot on Sauté mode; add meat, brown for a few minutes and transfer to a bowl.
2. Heat up the oil in your instant pot, add onion and some salt and cook for 2 minutes.
3. Add eggplant and garlic, stir and cook for 1 minute.
4. Add vinegar, stir and cook for 2 minutes
5. Add tomato paste, tomatoes, meat, salt, pepper, parsley, dill, turmeric and stock; then stir well. seal the instant pot lid and cook at High for 15 minutes.
6. Quick release the pressure, carefully open the lid; add more salt and pepper and a splash of lemon juice, stir well and serve.

Basil Red Sauce

(**Prep + Cooking Time:** 45 minutes | **Makes:** 4 Cups)

Ingredients:

- 2 medium tomatoes, quartered
- 4 ounces tomato paste
- 2 garlic cloves, peeled
- 3 cups butternut squash, peeled and cubed
- ¼ to ½ cup water; if necessary
- 1/2 cup fresh sweet basil leaves, torn
- 1 bay leaf
- Pinch red pepper flakes
- 2 tbsp. fresh Italian parsley leaves
- 1/4 tsp. baking soda
- 1 tsp. salt or as your liking
- 1/2 tsp. freshly ground black pepper

Directions:

1. In the Instant Pot, combine the squash, tomatoes, garlic and water (if using). Top with the tomato paste, bay leaf, salt, pepper, baking soda and red pepper flakes
2. There is no need to stir. Lock the lid and turn the steam release handle to Sealing. Using the Manual function, set the cooker to High Pressure for 20 minutes
3. After completing the cooking time, let the pressure release naturally for 10 to 15 minutes; quick release any remaining pressure
4. Remove the lid carefully, Let the sauce cool for a few minutes. Discard the bay leaf and add the basil and parsley. Using an immersion blender, blend the sauce until smooth.

Peach Sauce Recipe

(**Prep + Cooking Time:** 8 minutes | **Servings:** 6)

Ingredients:

- 10 oz. peaches, stoned and chopped.
- 2 tbsp. cornstarch
- 3 tbsp. sugar
- 1/2 cup water
- 1/8 tsp. almond extract
- 1/8 tsp. nutmeg, ground.
- 1/8 tsp. cinnamon
- A pinch of salt

Directions:

1. In your instant pot, mix peaches with nutmeg, cornstarch, sugar, cinnamon and salt; then stir well. seal the instant pot lid and cook at High for 3 minutes.
2. Quick release the pressure, carefully open the lid; add almond extract, stir and serve sauce.

Ginger and Orange Sauce

(**Prep + Cooking Time:** 12 minutes | **Servings:** 4)

Ingredients:

- 1-inch ginger piece; chopped
- 1 tbsp. olive oil
- 1 cup fish stock
- 4 spring onions; chopped.
- Salt and black pepper to the taste
- Zest and juice from 1 orange

Directions:

1. In your instant pot, mix fish stock with salt, pepper, olive oil, spring onions, ginger, orange juice and zest and stir well
2. Seal the instant pot lid and cook at High for 7 minutes.
3. Quick release the pressure, open the instant pot lid and serve your sauce

Plum Sauce Recipe

(**Prep + Cooking Time:** 25 minutes | **Servings:** 20)

Ingredients:

- 3 lb. plumps, pitted and chopped.
- 2 apples, cored and chopped.
- 4 tbsp. ginger, ground.
- 1 ½ tbsp. salt
- 2 onions; chopped.
- 4 tbsp. cinnamon
- 4 tbsp. allspice
- 1-pint vinegar
- 3/4 lb. sugar

Directions:

1. Put plumps, apples, and onions in your instant pot
2. Add ginger, cinnamon, allspice, salt and almost all the vinegar; then stir well. seal the instant pot lid and cook at High for 10 minutes.
3. Quick release the pressure, carefully open the lid; set it on Simmer mode, add the rest of the vinegar and the sugar, stir and cook until sugar dissolves.

Tomato Sauce

(**Prep + Cooking Time:** 25 minutes | **Servings:** 20)

Ingredients:

- 2 lb. tomatoes; peeled and chopped.
- 1 apple, cored and chopped.
- 3 tsp. whole spice
- 1/2 lb. brown sugar
- 1/2-pint vinegar
- 1 yellow onion; chopped.
- 6 oz. sultanas; chopped.
- 3 oz. dates chopped
- Salt to the taste

Directions:

1. Put tomatoes in your instant pot
2. Add apple, onion, sultanas, dates, salt, whole spice and half of the vinegar; then stir well. seal the instant pot lid and cook at High for 10 minutes.
3. Quick release the pressure, carefully open the lid; set it on Simmer mode, add the rest of the vinegar and sugar, stir and simmer until sugar dissolves
4. Transfer to jars and serve when needed

Guava Sauce Recipe

(**Prep + Cooking Time:** 30 minutes | **Servings:** 6)

Ingredients:

- 1 can guava shells and syrup
- 2 onions; chopped.
- 2 garlic cloves; chopped.
- 1/2 tsp. nutmeg
- 2 bird chilies; chopped.
- 1-inch ginger piece; minced.
- 1/4 cup vegetable oil
- Juice from 2 lemons

Directions:

1. Put guava shells and syrup in your blender, pulse well and leave aside.
2. Set your instant pot on Sauté mode; add oil and heat it up
3. Add onion and garlic, stir and cook for 4 minutes
4. Add guava mix, ginger, lemon juice, chilies and nutmeg; then stir well. seal the instant pot lid and cook on High for 15 minutes.
5. Quick release the pressure, open the instant pot lid and serve sauce with fish

Garden Salsa

(**Prep + Cooking Time:** 20 minutes | **Makes:** 7 Cups)

Ingredients:

- 8 large tomatoes, roughly chopped
- 6 garlic cloves, finely diced
- 1/4 cup tomato paste
- 2 jalapeño peppers, seeded and diced
- 1 bell pepper, any color; diced
- 1 small red onion; diced
- 1 small yellow onion; diced
- 1 tbsp. ground cumin
- 2 tbsp. freshly squeezed lime juice
- 1/2 tsp. baking soda
- 1/2 tsp. freshly ground black pepper
- 4 tsp. salt or as your liking
- Chopped fresh cilantro leaves, to taste

Directions:

1. In the Instant Pot, stir together the tomatoes, garlic, jalapeños, bell pepper, red onion, yellow onion, cumin, salt, pepper and baking soda
2. Lock the lid and turn the steam release handle to Sealing. Using the Manual function, set the cooker to High Pressure for 5 minutes.
3. After completing the cooking time, let the pressure release naturally for 10 minutes; quick release any remaining pressure
4. Remove the lid carefully and stir in the tomato paste, lime juice and cilantro. Let cool completely before serving.

Cilantro Sauce Recipe

(**Prep + Cooking Time:** 12 minutes | **Servings:** 6)

Ingredients:

- 3 garlic cloves; minced.
- 1 tbsp. olive oil
- 3 scallions; chopped.
- 3 tomatoes; chopped.
- 2 red chilies; minced.
- 3 shallots; minced.
- 2 tbsp. cilantro; chopped.
- 1/4 cup water
- Salt and black pepper to the taste

Directions:

1. Set your instant pot on Sauté mode; add oil and heat it up
2. Add garlic, shallots and chilies, stir and cook for 3 minutes.
3. Add scallions, tomatoes, water, salt, pepper and cilantro; then stir well. seal the instant pot lid and cook on High for 3 minutes.
4. Quick release the pressure, carefully open the lid; blend using an immersion blender and serve.

Garlic Red Sauce

(Prep + Cooking Time: 40 minutes | **Makes:** 2 ½ Cups)

Ingredients:

- 1 pound tomatoes, quartered
- 4 ounces tomato paste
- 1 small sweet onion, peeled and quartered
- 1/2 cup water; or more as needed
- ⅓ cup strong hearty wine
- 5 garlic cloves; or to taste, peeled

- 1 ½ tsp. dried oregano
- 1/4 tsp. baking soda
- 1 tsp. dried basil
- 1 tsp. salt or as your liking
- Pinch red pepper flakes

Directions:

1. Drop the tomatoes and onion into the Instant Pot. Add the wine, water and tomato paste. Cover the veggies with the garlic; oregano, basil, salt, baking soda and red pepper flakes.
2. There is no need to stir; it's better to have everything mostly on top of the tomatoes than at the bottom of the pot
3. Lock the lid and turn the steam release handle to Sealing. Using the Manual function, set the cooker to High Pressure for 20 minutes.
4. After completing the cooking time, turn off the Instant Pot and let the pressure release naturally for 15 minutes; quick release any remaining pressure
5. Remove the lid carefully. Using an immersion blender, create the red sauce of your dreams. Add a bit more water (or wine!) if you need to thin it.

Poblano Sauce

(Prep + Cooking Time: 20 minutes | **Makes:** 3 Cups)

Ingredients:

- 2 poblano peppers, roasted
- 1 medium sweet potato, peeled and chopped
- 1 cup raw cashews, soaked in water overnight, drained and rinsed well
- 1 cup unsweetened nondairy milk
- 1 cup water

- 1/4 cup nutritional yeast
- 1 tbsp. apple cider vinegar
- 2 tsp. salt or as your liking
- 1/4 tsp. garlic powder
- Pinch freshly ground black pepper
- Chili powder, to taste; optional

Directions:

1. In the Instant Pot, combine the sweet potato and water. Lock the lid and turn the steam release handle to Sealing
2. Using the Manual function, set the cooker to High Pressure for 5 minutes
3. After completing the cooking time, quick release the pressure. Remove the lid carefully and drain the water from the pot
4. In a high-speed blender or food processor, combine the cashews, milk, nutritional yeast, vinegar, salt, garlic powder and pepper
5. Blend until completely smooth. Add the sweet potatoes and blend again. Finally, add the poblanos and pulse just until there are green specks throughout
6. Pour the blended mixture back into the Instant Pot. Using a rubber spatula, make sure you get as much as possible.
7. Select Sauté Low. When the sauce is hot, turn off the Instant Pot. Taste and adjust the seasonings. If you want more heat, add chili powder to taste

Strawberry Sauce

(**Prep + Cooking Time:** 12 minutes | **Servings:** 8)

Ingredients:
- 1 lb. strawberries, cut into halves
- 1/8 cup sugar
- 1/2 tsp. vanilla extract
- 1 oz. orange juice
- A pinch of ginger, ground.

Directions:
1. In your instant pot, mix strawberries with sugar, stir and leave them aside for 10 minutes
2. Add orange juice; then stir well. seal the instant pot lid and cook at High for 2 minutes.
3. Release the pressure naturally for 15 minutes, then release remaining pressure by turning the valve to 'Venting', carefully open the lid; add vanilla extract and ginger, puree a but using an immersion blender and leave aside until it's cold enough.
4. Serve your strawberry sauce with some tasty pancakes

Red Enchilada Sauce

(**Prep + Cooking Time:** 20 minutes | **Makes:** 3 Cups)

Ingredients:
- 2 canned chipotle peppers in adobo sauce
- 2 tomatoes, chopped
- 6 garlic cloves, peeled
- 1/2 red onion, chopped
- 1/2 cup Vegetable Stock
- 2 poblano peppers, chopped
- 8 ounces tomato paste
- 1 tbsp. adobo sauce from the can
- 1 tsp. chili powder; or more as needed
- 1 tsp. apple cider vinegar
- 1/2 tsp. smoked paprika
- 1 tsp. ground cumin
- 1 tsp. salt or as your liking

Directions:
1. In the Instant Pot, combine the garlic, poblanos, tomatoes, chipotles, red onion, stock, adobo sauce, chili powder, cumin, salt, vinegar and paprika. Stir well
2. Spoon the tomato paste on top, without mixing it in. Lock the lid and turn the steam release handle to Sealing. Using the Manual function, set the cooker to High Pressure for 10 minutes
3. After completing the cooking time, turn off the Instant Pot and let the pressure release naturally until the pin drops
4. Remove the lid carefully. Using an immersion blender. There may still be a few small intact pieces of basil—I like it that way.

Melon Sauce Recipe

(**Prep + Cooking Time:** 15 minutes | **Servings:** 6)

Ingredients:
- 1 oz. sugar
- 1 tbsp. butter
- 1 tsp. starch
- 1 cup sweet wine
- Flesh from 1 small melon
- Juice of 1 lemon

Directions:
1. Put melon and sweet wine in your instant pot, seal the instant pot lid and cook at High for 7 minutes
2. Quick release the pressure, transfer sauce to a blender, add lemon juice, sugar, butter and starch and blend very well.
3. Return this sauce to your instant pot, set it on Simmer mode and cook sauce until it thickens for 3 minutes.
4. Serve right away

Mango Sauce

(Prep + Cooking Time: 40 minutes **| Servings:** 4)

Ingredients:

- 2 mangos; chopped
- 1 shallot; chopped
- 1 tbsp. vegetable oil
- 2 tsp. salt
- 1 ¼ cup raw sugar
- 1 ¼ apple cider vinegar
- 1/4 cup raisins
- 1/4 tsp. cardamom powder
- 2 tbsp. ginger; minced.
- 1/2 tsp. cinnamon
- 2 red hot chilies; chopped.
- 1 apple, cored and chopped.

Directions:

1. Set your instant pot on Sauté mode; add oil and heat it up
2. Add ginger and shallot, stir and cook for 5 minutes
3. Add cinnamon, hot peppers and cardamom, stir and cook for 2 minutes.
4. Add mangos, apple, raisins, sugar and cider, stir and cook until sugar melts.
5. Cover the pot and cook at High for 7 minutes.
6. Quick release the pressure, carefully open the lid; transfer to a pan and simmer on medium heat for 15 minutes more, stirring from time to time
7. Transfer to jars and serve when needed

Barbeque Sauce

(Prep + Cooking Time: 20 minutes **| Servings:** 8)

Ingredients:

- 5 oz. plums; dried and seedless
- 1 tbsp. sesame seed oil
- 1/2 cup tomato puree
- 1 yellow onion; chopped.
- 4 tbsp. honey
- 4 tbsp. white wine vinegar
- 1 tsp. salt
- 1/2 tsp. granulated garlic
- 1/8 tsp. cumin powder
- 1 tsp. liquid smoke
- 1 tsp. Tabasco sauce
- 1/8 tsp. clove powder
- 1/2 cup water

Directions:

1. Set your instant pot on Sauté mode; add oil and heat it up
2. Add onion, stir and cook for 5 minutes.
3. Add tomato puree, honey, water, vinegar, salt, garlic, Tabasco sauce, liquid smoke, cumin and clove powder and stir everything very well.
4. Add plums and stir again well.
5. Seal the instant pot lid and cook at High for 10 minutes
6. Quick release the pressure, carefully open the lid; blend everything with an immersion blender, transfer sauce to a bowl and serve

Cashew Sour Cream

(Prep + Cooking Time: 5 minutes | **Servings:** 5)

Ingredients:

- 1/4 cup nondairy milk; or more as needed
- 1 cup raw cashews, soaked in water overnight, drained and rinsed well
- Juice of 1 lemon; or more as needed
- 1 ½ tsp. apple cider vinegar
- 1/2 tsp. salt or as your liking

Directions:

1. In a blender, combine the cashews, lemon juice, milk, vinegar and salt. Blend until completely smooth.
2. Taste and add more salt or lemon juice as desired
3. If you want a thinner cream, add a little more milk. Keep refrigerated in an airtight container for 4 to 6 days.

Beans and Grains

Mexican Cranberry Beans

(Prep + Cooking Time: 30 minutes | **Servings:** 6)

Ingredients:

- 1 lb. cranberry beans, soaked for 8 hours and drained
- 1 yellow onion; chopped.
- 1 ½ tsp. cumin
- 1/3 cup cilantro; chopped.
- 3 ¼ cups water
- 4 garlic cloves; minced.
- 1 tbsp. chili powder
- 1 tsp. oregano; dried
- Salt and black pepper to the taste
- Cooked rice for serving

Directions:

1. Put beans in your instant pot; add the water, garlic and onion, close the lid and cook at High for 20 minutes.
2. Quick release the pressure, open the instant pot lid; add cumin, cilantro, oregano, chili powder, salt and pepper; stir well, mash a bit using a potato mashes, divide among plates on top of rice and serve

Cheesy Barley Dish

(Prep + Cooking Time: 35 minutes | **Servings:** 4)

Ingredients:

- 1 ½ cups pearl barley, rinsed
- 1 tbsp. extra-virgin olive oil
- 1 tbsp. butter
- 1/3 cup mushrooms; chopped.
- 4 cups veggie stock
- 2 ¼ cups water
- 1 white onion; chopped.
- 3 tbsp. parsley; chopped.
- 1 cup parmesan cheese; grated
- 1 garlic clove; minced.
- 1 celery stalk; chopped.
- Salt and black pepper to the taste

Directions:

1. Set your instant pot on Sauté mode; add oil and butter and heat them up
2. Add onion and garlic; stir and cook for 4 minutes.
3. Add celery and barley and toss to coat
4. Add mushrooms, water, stock, salt and pepper; then stir well. close the lid and cook at High for 18 minutes.
5. Quick release the pressure, open the instant pot lid; add cheese and parsley and more salt and pepper if needed, stir for 2 minutes; divide into bowls and serve

Kidney Beans Curry Recipe

(Prep + Cooking Time: 1 hour and 10 minutes | **Servings:** 8)

Ingredients:

- 2 cups red kidney beans, soaked for 8 hours and drained
- 1-inch piece ginger; chopped
- 1 tsp. turmeric; ground.
- 2 tbsp. vegetable oil
- 2 tsp. ghee
- 2 red chili peppers; dried and crushed.
- Salt and black pepper to the taste
- 6 cloves
- 1 tsp. cumin; ground.
- 1 tsp. coriander; ground.
- 1 yellow onion; chopped.
- 2 cups water
- 1 tsp. sugar
- 1 tsp. red pepper; ground.
- 2 tsp. garam masala
- 4 garlic cloves; chopped.
- 1 tsp. cumin seeds
- 2 tomatoes chopped
- 1/4 cup cilantro; chopped.

Directions:
1. Grind ginger, garlic and onion using a mortar and pestle and transfer paste to a bowl.
2. Set your instant pot on Sauté mode; add ghee and oil and heat it up.
3. Add red chili pepper, cloves and cumin seeds, stir and fry for 3 minutes
4. Add onion paste, stir and cook for 3 more minutes
5. Add coriander, cumin and turmeric, stir and cook for 30 seconds.
6. Add tomatoes, stir and cook 5 minutes.
7. Add beans, 2 cups water, salt, pepper and sugar; then stir well. close the lid and cook at High for 40 minutes.
8. Switch instant pot to Low and cook for 10 minutes more.
9. Quick release the pressure, open the instant pot lid; add red pepper, garam masala and cilantro; then stir well. divide among plates and serve

Asian Lentils Recipe

(**Prep + Cooking Time:** 30 minutes | **Servings:** 4)

Ingredients:
- 1 cup red lentils
- 1/4 tsp. red pepper flakes
- 1 yellow onion; chopped.
- 2 tsp. cumin
- 1/4 tsp. coriander
- 1/4 tsp. garlic powder
- 3 tsp. butter
- 1 tsp. extra virgin olive oil
- 1/4 tsp. turmeric
- 1/4 tsp. Aleppo pepper
- Salt and black pepper to the taste
- 3 cups chicken stock

Directions:
1. Set your instant pot on Sauté mode; add butter and oil and heat up
2. Add onions; stir and cook for 4 minutes
3. Add cumin, coriander, garlic powder, turmeric, Aleppo pepper and pepper flakes, stir and cook for 2 minutes.
4. Add lentils and stock; then stir well. close the lid and cook at High for 15 minutes
5. Quick release the pressure, carefully open the lid; divide into bowls and serve

Classic Cranberry Bean Chili

(**Prep + Cooking Time:** 50 minutes | **Servings:** 8)

Ingredients:
- 1 lb. cranberry beans, soaked in water for 7 hours and drained
- 14 oz. canned tomatoes and green chilies; chopped.
- 5 cups water
- 1 ½ tsp. cumin; ground.
- 2 tbsp. tomato paste
- 1 tsp. chili powder
- 1/2 tsp. ancho chili powder
- 1/4 cup millet
- 1/2 cup bulgur
- 1 tsp. garlic; minced.
- 1/2 tsp. liquid smoke
- 1 tsp. oregano; dried
- Salt and black pepper to the taste
- Hot sauce for serving
- Pickled jalapenos for serving

Directions:
1. Put beans and 3 cups water in your instant pot, close the lid and cook at High for 25 minutes
2. Quick release the pressure, add the rest of the water, tomatoes and chilies, millet, bulgur, cumin, tomato paste, chili powder, garlic, liquid smoke, oregano, ancho chili powder, salt and pepper; then stir well. close the lid and cook on High for 10 minutes more
3. Release the pressure again, carefully open the lid; divide into bowls and serve with hot sauce on top and pickled jalapenos on the side.

Lentils and Tomato Sauce

(**Prep + Cooking Time:** 30 minutes | **Servings:** 4)

Ingredients:

- 1 ½ cups lentils
- 1 yellow onion; chopped.
- 1 celery stalk; chopped.
- 1 ½ cups tomatoes; chopped.
- 1 tbsp. olive oil
- 1 green bell pepper; chopped.
- 1 tsp. curry powder
- 2 cups water
- Salt and black pepper to the taste

Directions:

1. Set your instant pot on Sauté mode; add the oil and heat it up.
2. Add celery, bell pepper, onion and tomatoes, stir and cook for 4 minutes
3. Add curry, salt, pepper, lentils and water; then stir well. close the lid and cook at High for 15 minutes
4. Quick release the pressure, open the instant pot lid; divide lentils among bowls and serve

Creamy White Beans

(**Prep + Cooking Time:** 45 minutes | **Servings:** 8)

Ingredients:

- 1 lb. white beans
- 1 yellow onion; chopped.
- 1 green bell pepper; chopped.
- 5 cups water
- 2 celery ribs; chopped.
- 2 bay leaves
- 1 tsp. oregano
- 1 tsp. thyme
- 1 tbsp. soy sauce
- 1 tbsp. Tabasco sauce
- 4 garlic cloves; minced.
- Salt and white pepper to the taste

Directions:

1. Put beans and water in your instant pot
2. Add onion; celery, garlic, bell pepper, oregano, thyme, salt, white pepper and soy sauce; then stir well. close the lid and cook at High for 15 minutes
3. Release the pressure naturally for 15 minutes, carefully open the lid and set it on Simmer mode
4. Add more salt and pepper to the taste and Tabasco sauce; stir and cook for 20 minutes.
5. Divide into bowls and serve.

Black Eyed Peas with Peanuts

(**Prep + Cooking Time:** 45 minutes | **Servings:** 6)

Ingredients:

- 1 cup dried black-eyed peas
- 1 cup chopped yellow onions
- 1 cup drained canned diced tomatoes
- 2 ½ cups water
- 1/2 cup peanut butter
- 2 cups frozen Swiss chard
- 1 tsp. salt or as your liking
- 1 tsp. black pepper

Directions:

1. In your Instant Pot, combine the water, Swiss chard, onions, tomatoes, black-eyed peas, salt and pepper. Stir to combine.
2. Add the peanut butter to the top of the mixture; do not stir in. Be sure that everything, including the peanut butter, is submerged under the liquid. (This is to prevent the peanut butter from sticking to the pot and burning)
3. Now secure the lid on the pot and close the valve. Now Press "Manual" and set the pot at "High" pressure for 15 minutes
4. After completing the cooking time, allow the pot to sit undisturbed for 10 minutes, then release any remaining pressure. Stir thoroughly before serving.

Marrow Beans & Lemon Dish

(Prep + Cooking Time: 55 minutes | **Servings:** 4)

Ingredients:

- 2 cups marrow beans, soaked for 8 hours and drained
- 1 tbsp. rosemary; chopped.
- 4 garlic cloves; minced.
- 1 carrot; chopped
- 4 cups water
- 1 bay leaf
- 2 tbsp. lemon juice
- 1 cup yellow onion; chopped.
- 1 tbsp. extra-virgin olive oil
- Salt and black pepper to the taste
- Already cooked quinoa for serving

Directions:

1. Set your instant pot on Sauté mode; add oil and heat it up.
2. Add onion; carrot, garlic and rosemary, stir and cook for 3 minutes
3. Add water, bay leaf, beans and some salt; then stir well. close the lid and cook at High for 45 minutes.
4. Release the pressure naturally, open the instant pot lid, discard bay leaf, add salt and pepper to the taste and lemon juice; stir well and divide into bowls over already cooked quinoa

Garlic and Chickpeas

(Prep + Cooking Time: 45 minutes | **Servings:** 4)

Ingredients:

- 2 cups chickpeas, rinsed
- 2 tomatoes; chopped.
- 2 small cucumbers; chopped
- 2 bay leaves
- 4 garlic cloves
- Water
- 1 tsp. olive oil
- Salt and black pepper to the taste

Directions:

1. Put chickpeas in your instant pot
2. Add water, garlic and bay leaves; then stir well. close the lid and cook at High for 35 minutes.
3. Release the pressure naturally for 10 minutes, then release remaining pressure by turning the valve to 'Venting', carefully open the lid; drain water and put chickpeas and garlic in a bowl
4. Add cucumber, tomatoes, salt, pepper and oil, toss to coat and serve

Veggie Risotto

(Prep + Cooking Time: 16 minutes | **Servings:** 5)

Ingredients:

- 1 cup Arborio rice; rinsed and drained
- 1 bunch asparagus tips; cut into 1-inch pieces
- 2 ¾ cups Vegetable Stock
- 2 cups fresh baby spinach
- 1 cup sugar snap peas; rinsed, tough ends removed
- 1/2 sweet onion; diced
- 1 garlic clove; minced
- 2 tbsp. vegan butter
- 2 tbsp. olive oil
- 1 tsp. dried thyme
- 1/2 tsp. salt; or as your liking
- 1/4 tsp. freshly ground black pepper
- Pinch red pepper flakes
- Juice of 1/2 lemon

Directions:

1. Select the "Sauté" Low mode on your instant pot. When the display reads "Hot," add the oil and heat until it shimmers
2. Add the onion. Cook for about 2 minutes, stirring frequently. Turn off the Instant Pot and stir in the garlic and asparagus, cooking for 30 seconds.
3. Add the stock, rice, peas, thyme, salt, black pepper and red pepper flakes, stirring well
4. Lock the lid and turn the steam release handle to Sealing. Using the Manual function, set the cooker to High Pressure for 8 minutes.

5. After completing the cooking time, quick release the pressure
6. Remove the lid carefully and stir in the butter, lemon juice and spinach, being gentle so as not to tear the snap peas. Taste and season with more salt, as needed.

Cracked Wheat and Jaggery

(Prep + Cooking Time: 22 minutes | **Servings:** 2)

Ingredients:

- 2 cups cracked wheat
- 2 cups jaggery
- 3 cloves
- 1 cup milk
- 1 tsp. fennel seeds
- 2 ½ cups clarified butter
- 3 cups water
- A pinch of salt
- A few almonds; chopped.

Directions:

1. Set your instant pot on Sauté mode; add butter and heat it up
2. Add cracked wheat, stir and cook for 5 minutes
3. Add cloves and fennel seeds, stir and cook for 2 minutes
4. Add jaggery, a pinch of salt, milk and water; then stir well. close the lid and cook at High for 10 minutes.
5. Quick release the pressure, open the instant pot lid, divide into bowls and serve with chopped almonds on top

Delicious Frijoles

(Prep + Cooking Time: 1 hour 45 minutes | **Servings:** 4)

Ingredients:

- 1 cup finely chopped white onions
- 1/2 cup finely chopped fresh cilantro
- 1/2 cup finely chopped green bell pepper
- 1 cup dried pinto beans
- 3 cups cool water
- 4 garlic cloves; minced
- 1 (14.5-ounce) can fire-roasted diced tomatoes; undrained
- 6 slices bacon; chopped
- 1 ½ tsp. ground cumin
- 1 ½ tsp. salt or as your liking

Directions:

1. Place the pinto beans in a medium bowl. Cover with hot water. Soak for 1-hour drain. Place the pinto beans in the Instant Pot. Add the cool water, tomatoes and their juices, onions, cilantro, bell pepper, bacon, garlic, cumin and salt
2. Now secure the lid on the pot and close the valve. Now Press "Manual" and set the pot at "High" pressure for 30 minutes
3. After completing the cooking time, allow the pot to sit undisturbed for 10 minutes, then release any remaining pressure. If you like, use an immersion blender to puree some of the beans to thicken the broth.

Cold Quinoa Salad with Pecans and Fruit

(Prep + Cooking Time: 25 minutes | **Servings:** 5)

Ingredients:

- 1/2 cup fresh cilantro, chopped
- 1 cup pecans, chopped
- 1/2 bunch scallions, green and light green parts, sliced
- 2 celery stalks, halved lengthwise and chopped
- 2 apples, unpeeled; cut into large dice
- 1 cup quinoa; rinsed
- 1 cup dried cranberries, white raisins and regular raisins
- 1 cup water
- 2 tbsp. freshly squeezed lemon juice
- 1 tbsp. white rice vinegar
- 2 tbsp. avocado oil; or walnut oil
- 1 tsp. chili powder
- 1/4 tsp. salt; or more as your liking
- Pinch freshly ground black pepper

Directions:

1. In the Instant Pot, combine the quinoa, water and salt and stir.
2. Lock the lid and turn the steam release handle to Sealing. Using the Manual function, set the cooker to High Pressure for 8 minutes
3. After completing the cooking time, let the pressure release naturally for 10 minutes; quick release any remaining pressure.
4. Remove the lid carefully and transfer the quinoa to a large bowl. Refrigerate for 5 minutes to cool.
5. In a small resealable container, combine the apples, lemon juice and vinegar. Cover and shake lightly to coat the apples, then refrigerate
6. Remove the cooled quinoa from the refrigerator and stir in the scallions, celery, cranberry-raisin mix, chili powder and oil
7. Taste and season with more salt and pepper, as needed. Stir the apples and whatever lemon-vinegar juice is in the container into the salad. Add the cilantro and pecans immediately before serving.

Orange & Bulgur Salad

(Prep + Cooking Time: 25 minutes | **Servings:** 4)

Ingredients:

- 1 cup bulgur; rinsed
- 1 tbsp. soy sauce
- 2/3 cup scallions; chopped.
- 2 tsp. brown sugar
- Zest from 1 orange
- Juice from 2 oranges
- 1/2 cups water
- 1/3 cup almonds; chopped.
- 2 garlic cloves; minced.
- 2 tsp. canola oil
- 2 tbsp. ginger; grated
- Salt to the taste

Directions:

1. Set your instant pot on Sauté mode; add oil and heat it up
2. Add ginger and garlic; stir and cook for 1 minutes.
3. Add bulgur; sugar, water, and orange juice; then stir well. close the lid and cook at High for 5 minutes.
4. Release the pressure naturally, remove the instant pot lid and leave bulgur aside for now.
5. Heat up a pan over medium heat, add almonds, stir them for 3 minutes
6. Add orange zest, salt, soy sauce and scallions; stir and cook for 1 minute
7. Add this to bulgur mix; stir with a fork, transfer to a bowl and serve.

Healthy Barley Salad

(Prep + Cooking Time: 30 minutes | **Servings:** 4)

Ingredients:

- 1 cup hulled barley, rinsed
- 3/4 cup jarred spinach pesto
- 1 green apple; chopped.
- 2 ½ cups water
- 1/4 cup celery; chopped.
- Salt and white pepper to the taste

Directions:

1. Put barley, water, salt and pepper in your instant pot; then stir well. close the lid and cook at High for 20 minutes
2. Quick release the pressure, carefully open the lid; strain barley and put in a bowl
3. Add celery, apple, spinach pesto and more salt and pepper, toss to coat and serve right away.

Bacon Butter Beans

(Prep + Cooking Time: 1 hour and 10 minutes | **Servings:** 8)

Ingredients:

- 1 lb. butter beans, soaked for 8 hours and drained
- 1/2 tsp. cumin; ground.
- 1 garlic clove; minced.
- 12 oz. beer
- 1 lb. bacon; chopped.
- 1 jalapeno pepper; chopped.
- 4 cups water
- Salt and black pepper to the taste

Directions:

1. Set your instant pot on Sauté mode; add bacon and brown it for 10 minutes
2. Transfer bacon to paper towels, drain grease, put in a bowl and leave aside.
3. Add the water, cumin and beer to your pot and stir
4. Add beans; then stir well. close the lid and cook at High for 30 minutes.
5. Quick release the pressure, open the instant pot lid, add garlic, bacon, jalapeno, salt and pepper; then stir well. close the lid again and cook at High for 3 minutes more.
6. Release pressure again, carefully open the lid; transfer to bowls and serve

Chickpeas Curry

(Prep + Cooking Time: 30 minutes | **Servings:** 6)

Ingredients:

- 28 oz. canned tomatoes; chopped.
- 3 potatoes; cubed
- 3 cups chickpeas; already cooked; drained and rinsed
- 1 yellow onion; finely chopped
- 2 tsp. garam masala
- 2 tsp. coriander; ground.
- 2 tsp. turmeric; ground.
- 4 tsp. cumin seeds
- 1/2 cup water
- 8 tsp. olive oil
- 4 tsp. garlic; minced.
- Salt and black pepper to the taste
- Basmati rice; already cooked for serving
- Some cilantro; chopped for serving

Directions:

1. Set your instant pot on Sauté mode; add oil and heat it up.
2. Add cumin seeds; stir and cook for 30 seconds
3. Add onion; stir and cook for 5 minutes
4. Add garlic, garam masala, coriander, turmeric, tomatoes, potatoes, chickpeas, water, salt and pepper; then stir well. close the lid and cook at High for 15 minutes.
5. Quick release the pressure; open the instant pot lid, divide chickpeas curry on plates and serve with rice on the side and cilantro on top

Cranberry Beans Mix

(Prep + Cooking Time: 25 minutes | **Servings:** 6)

Ingredients:

- 1 ½ cups cranberry beans; soaked for 8 hours and drained
- 8 cups kale; chopped.
- 4 oz. shiitake mushrooms; chopped.
- 4-inch kombu piece; sliced
- 4 bacon slices; chopped
- 1/2 tsp. garlic powder
- 1 tsp. extra virgin olive oil
- Salt and black pepper to the taste

Directions:

1. Put beans in your instant pot, add 2 inches' water, salt, pepper, kombu, close the lid and cook at High for 8 minutes.
2. Release the pressure open the instant pot lid, transfer beans and cooking liquid to a pot and leave aside for now
3. Set your pot on Sauté mode; add oil and heat it up
4. Add garlic powder, bacon, mushrooms, salt, pepper and 3/4 cup cooking liquid from the pot, stir well and cook for 1 minute.
5. Seal the instant pot lid; cook at High for 3 minutes and Quick release the pressure.
6. Add beans and kale, stir and divide into bowls

Cabbage & Navy Beans

(Prep + Cooking Time: 50 minutes | **Servings:** 8)

Ingredients:

- 1 ½ cups navy beans; soaked for 8 hours and drained
- 6 bacon slices; chopped.
- 1 cabbage head; chopped.
- 3 tbsp. white wine vinegar
- 1/4 tsp. cloves
- 1 yellow onion; chopped.
- 3 tbsp. honey
- 1 bay leaf
- 3 cups chicken stock
- Salt and black pepper to the taste

Directions:

1. Set your instant pot on Sauté mode; add bacon, stir and brown it for 4 minutes.
2. Add onions, stir and cook for 4 minutes
3. Add stock, beans, clove and bay leaf; then stir well. close the lid and cook at High for 35 minutes.
4. Quick release the pressure, carefully open the lid; add vinegar, honey and cabbage; then stir well. close the lid and cook at High for 12 minutes more
5. Release pressure again, carefully open the lid; add salt and pepper; then stir well. divide into bowls and serve.

Mushroom & Barley Risotto

(Prep + Cooking Time: 40 minutes | **Servings:** 4)

Ingredients:

- 1.5 oz. dried mushrooms
- 2 cups yellow onions; chopped
- 1/3 cup dry sherry
- 1 cup pearl barley
- 1 tsp. fennel seeds
- 1 ½ cups water
- 1 tbsp. olive oil
- 2 tbsp. black barley
- 3 cups chicken stock
- Salt and black pepper to the taste
- 1/4 cup parmesan; grated

Directions:

1. Set your instant pot on Sauté mode; add oil and heat it up.
2. Add fennel and onions, stir and cook for 4 minutes
3. Add barley and black barley, sherry, mushrooms, stock, water, salt and pepper and stir well.
4. Close the instant pot lid, cook at High for 18 minutes; Quick release the pressure, open the instant pot lid and set it on Simmer mode
5. Add more salt and pepper of needed, stir and cook for 5 more minutes.
6. Divide into bowls; add parmesan on top and serve

Hummus

(Prep + Cooking Time: 1 hour 45 minutes | **Servings:** 8)

Ingredients:

- 1/2 cup dried chickpeas
- 4 garlic cloves
- 2 tbsp. tahini
- Juice of 1 lemon
- Salt to taste

Directions:

1. Place the chickpeas in a medium bowl and cover with hot water. Soak for 1 hour; drain. Place the chickpeas in the Instant Pot with enough water to cover and a little salt
2. Now secure the lid on the pot and close the valve. Now Press "Manual" and set the pot at "High" pressure for 20 minutes
3. After completing the cooking time, allow the pot to sit undisturbed until the pressure has released. Drain the chickpeas, reserving about ½ cup of the water

4. In a food processor, combine the chickpeas, the reserved ½ water, the garlic, tahini, lemon juice and salt to taste. Process until smooth. Transfer the hummus to a serving bowl.

Mung Beans

(Prep + Cooking Time: 27 minutes | Servings: 4)

Ingredients:

- 3/4 cup mung beans, soaked for 15 minutes and drained
- 28 oz. canned tomatoes; crushed.
- 1/2 cup brown rice; soaked for 15 minutes and drained
- 1 small red onion; chopped.
- 1/2 tsp. cumin seeds
- 1 tsp. coriander; ground.
- 1 tsp. turmeric
- 1/2 tsp. garam masala
- 1/2 tsp. coconut oil
- 1 tsp. lemon juice
- 4 cups water
- 5 garlic cloves; minced.
- 1-inch ginger piece; chopped
- A pinch of cayenne
- Salt and black pepper to the taste

Directions:

1. In your food processor, mix tomatoes with onions, ginger, garlic, coriander, turmeric, cayenne, salt, pepper and garam masala and blend well
2. Set your instant pot on Sauté mode; add oil and heat up.
3. Add cumin seeds; stir and fry for 2 minutes.
4. Add tomatoes mix; stir and cook for 15 minutes
5. Add beans; rice, water, salt, pepper and lemon juice; then stir well. close the instant pot lid and cook at High for 15 minutes.
6. Release the pressure naturally for 10 minutes, then release remaining pressure by turning the valve to 'Venting', open the instant pot lid; stir again, divide into bowls and serve

Classic Chili Lime Black Beans

(Prep + Cooking Time: 50 minutes | Servings: 4)

Ingredients:

- 2 cups black beans, soaked for 8 hours and drained
- 4 garlic cloves; minced.
- 3 cups water
- 1 tsp. smoked paprika
- 2 tsp. red palm oil
- 1 tbsp. chili powder
- 1 yellow onion; chopped.
- Salt to the taste
- Juice from 1 lime

Directions:

1. Set your instant pot on Sauté mode; add oil and heat it up
2. Add garlic and onion, stir and cook for 2 minutes
3. Add beans, chili powder, paprika, salt and water; then stir well. close the lid and cook on High for 40 minutes.
4. Release the pressure naturally, open the instant pot lid, add lime juice and more salt; then stir well. divide into bowls and serve

Instant Wheat Berry Salad

(Prep + Cooking Time: 45 minutes | **Servings:** 6)

Ingredients:
- 1 ½ cups wheat berries
- 1 tbsp. extra-virgin olive oil

For the salad:
- 2 oz. feta cheese; crumbled.
- 1/2 cup Kalamata olives; pitted and chopped.
- 1 handful basil leaves; chopped.
- 1 tbsp. balsamic vinegar

- 4 cups water
- Salt and black pepper to the taste

- 1 tbsp. olive oil
- 2 green onions; chopped.
- 1 handful parsley leaves; chopped.
- 1 cup cherry tomatoes, cut into halves

Directions:
1. Set your instant pot on Sauté mode; add 1 tablespoon oil and heat it up.
2. Add wheat berries; stir and cook for 5 minutes
3. Add water, salt and pepper to the taste, close the lid and cook on High for 30 minutes.
4. Release the pressure naturally for 10 minutes, then release remaining pressure by turning the valve to 'Venting', open the instant pot lid, drain wheat berries and put them in a salad bowl
5. Add salt and pepper, 1 tablespoon oil, balsamic vinegar, tomatoes, green onions, olives, cheese, basil and parsley, toss to coat and serve right away

Pasta & Cranberry Beans

(Prep + Cooking Time: 30 minutes | **Servings:** 8)

Ingredients:
- 26 oz. canned tomatoes; chopped.
- 3 tsp. basil; dried
- 1/2 tsp. smoked paprika
- 2 tsp. oregano; dried
- 2 cups dried cranberry beans; soaked for 8 hours and drained.
- 7 garlic cloves; minced.
- 6 cups water

- 2 celery ribs; chopped.
- 1 yellow onion; chopped.
- 2 cups small pasta
- 3 tbsp. nutritional yeast
- 1 tsp. rosemary; chopped.
- 1/4 tsp. red pepper flakes
- Salt and black pepper to the taste
- 10 oz. kale leaves

Directions:
1. Set your instant pot on Sauté mode; add onion, celery, garlic, pepper flakes, rosemary and a pinch of salt, stir and brown for 2 minutes
2. Add tomatoes, basil, oregano and paprika, stir and cook for 1 minute
3. Add beans; 6 cups water, close the lid and cook at High for 10 minutes
4. Quick release the pressure; open the instant pot lid, add pasta, yeast, kale, salt and pepper, stir and set the pot on Sauté mode again
5. Cook for 5 minutes more, divide into bowls and serve.

Kidney Beans Dish

(Prep + Cooking Time: 35 minutes | **Servings:** 8)

Ingredients:
- 1 lb. red kidney beans, soaked for 8 hours and drained
- 8 oz. smoked Cajun Tasso; chopped.
- 1 celery rib; chopped.
- 2 tbsp. garlic; minced.
- 1 green bell pepper; chopped.
- 2 tsp. thyme; dried

- 4 green onions; chopped.
- 2 yellow onions; chopped.
- 3 tbsp. extra virgin olive oil
- 2 bay leaves
- Cajun seasoning to the taste
- Hot sauce to the taste

Directions:

1. Set your instant pot on Sauté mode; add oil and heat it up
2. Add Tasso; then stir well. cook for 5 minutes and transfer to a bowl
3. Add onions and Cajun seasoning to the pot; stir and cook for 10 minutes
4. Add garlic, stir and cook 5 minutes.
5. Add bell pepper and celery; stir and cook 5 minutes.
6. Add beans, water to cover everything, bay leaves, thyme, close the lid and cook at High for 15 minutes.
7. Quick release the pressure, open the instant pot lid, add Tasso and leave aside for 5 minutes
8. Divide beans and Tasso mix on plates, garnish with green onions and serve with hot sauce to the taste.

Lentils Tacos

(Prep + Cooking Time: 25 minutes | **Servings:** 4)

Ingredients:

- 2 cups brown lentils
- 4 cups water
- 1 tsp. salt
- 1 tsp. garlic powder
- 4 oz. tomato sauce
- 1/2 tsp. cumin
- 1 tsp. chili powder
- 1 tsp. onion powder
- Taco shells for serving

Directions:

1. In your instant pot, mix lentils with water, tomato sauce, cumin, garlic powder, chili powder and onion powder; then stir well. close the lid and cook at High for 15 minutes
2. Quick release the pressure, open the instant pot lid; divide lentils mix into taco shells and serve.

Couscous with Veggies and Chicken

(Prep + Cooking Time: 25 minutes | **Servings:** 4)

Ingredients:

- 8 chicken thighs; skinless
- 15 oz. canned stewed tomatoes; chopped.
- 3/4 cup couscous
- 1 zucchini; chopped
- 1 ½ cups mushrooms; cut into halves
- 1 ½ cups carrots; chopped.
- 1/2 cup chicken stock
- 1 green bell pepper; chopped.
- 1 yellow onion; chopped
- 2 garlic cloves; minced.
- Salt and black pepper to the taste
- A handful parsley; chopped.

Directions:

1. In your instant pot; mix chicken with mushrooms, carrots, bell pepper, onion, garlic, tomatoes and stock; then stir well. close the lid and cook at High for 8 minutes
2. Quick release the pressure, open the instant pot lid, add couscous, zucchini, salt and pepper; then stir well. close the lid again and cook on Low for 6 minutes
3. Release the pressure again, open the instant pot lid; add parsley, stir gently, divide into bowls and serve.

Mediterranean Lentils

(Prep + Cooking Time: 40 minutes | **Servings:** 3)

Ingredients:

- 1 cup brown or green lentils
- 1 tomato; diced
- 2 ½ cups Vegetable Stock
- 1 bay leaf
- 1 small sweet or yellow onion; diced
- 1 garlic clove; diced
- 1 tbsp. olive oil
- 1 tsp. dried oregano
- 1/2 tsp. ground cumin
- 1/2 tsp. dried parsley
- 1/2 tsp. salt or as your liking
- 1/4 tsp. freshly ground black pepper; or more as needed

Directions:

1. Select the "Sauté" Low mode on your instant pot. When the display reads "Hot," add the oil and heat until it shimmers.
2. Add the onion. Cook for 3 to 4 minutes until soft. Turn off the Instant Pot and add the garlic; oregano, cumin, parsley, salt and pepper. Cook until fragrant, about 1 minute
3. Stir in the tomato, lentils, stock and bay leaf. Lock the lid and turn the steam release handle to Sealing.
4. Using the Manual function, set the cooker to High Pressure for 18 minutes
5. After completing the cooking time, let the pressure release naturally for 10 minutes; quick release any remaining pressure
6. Remove the lid carefully and remove and discard the bay leaf.
7. Taste and season with more salt and pepper, as needed. If there's too much liquid remaining, select Sauté Medium or High and cook until it evaporates.

Asian Rice

(Prep + Cooking Time: 22 minutes | **Servings:** 5)

Ingredients:

- 2 cups basmati rice; rinsed well, drained and dried
- 2 ½ cups water
- 1 tbsp. chili oil
- 1/2 tsp. ground cardamom
- 2 tsp. cumin seeds
- 1 tsp. salt as your liking

Directions:

1. Select the "Sauté" Low mode on your instant pot. When the display reads "Hot," add the oil and heat until it shimmers.
2. Add the cumin seeds and cardamom. Cook until fragrant, stirring frequently. Add the salt, rice and water and stir well
3. Lock the lid and turn the steam release handle to Sealing. Using the Manual function, set the cooker to High Pressure for 6 minutes
4. After completing the cooking time, let the pressure release naturally for 10 minutes; quick release any remaining pressure. Remove the lid carefully and fluff the rice.

Black Beans

(Prep + Cooking Time: 1 hour 5 minutes | **Servings:** 7)

Ingredients:

- 2 cups dried black beans; rinsed but not soaked
- 4 garlic cloves; diced
- 1 small onion; diced
- 3 cups Vegetable Stock
- 1/4 cup fresh cilantro leaves, chopped
- 1 cup diced roasted green chiles
- 2 tbsp. freshly squeezed lime juice
- 1 to 2 tbsp. olive oil
- 1 tbsp. ground cumin
- 1 tsp. dried oregano
- 1 tsp. chili powder
- 1 tsp. salt; or more as your liking

Directions:

1. Select the "Sauté" Low mode on your instant pot. When the display reads "Hot," add the oil and onion. Sauté for 1 to 2 minutes, turning off the Instant Pot after about 1 minute
2. Add the garlic. Sauté for 30 seconds. Stir in the cumin; oregano and chili powder and cook for another 30 seconds or so until the spices "bloom"
3. Add the green chiles, stock and black beans, stirring well. Lock the lid and turn the steam release handle to Sealing.
4. Using the Manual function, set the cooker to High Pressure for 35 minutes
5. After completing the cooking time, let the pressure release naturally for 20 minutes; or until the pin drops.
6. Remove the lid carefully and stir. Add the salt, lime juice and cilantro. Stir again and serve.

Cilantro Lime Brown Rice

(**Prep + Cooking Time:** 34 minutes | **Servings:** 5)

Ingredients:

- 2 cups brown rice; rinsed and drained
- ⅓ cup fresh cilantro, chopped
- 2 ½ cups water
- Juice of 1 lime
- Zest of 1 lime
- Dash ground cumin
- Salt as your liking

Directions:

1. In the Instant Pot, combine the rice and water.
2. Lock the lid and turn the steam release handle to Sealing. Using the Manual function, set the cooker to High Pressure for 22 minutes
3. After completing the cooking time, let the pressure release naturally for 10 minutes while the Instant Pot goes into Keep Warm mode; quick release any remaining pressure
4. Remove the lid carefully and stir in the cilantro, lime juice and zest and cumin. Season to taste with salt.

Black Beans and Chorizo

(**Prep + Cooking Time:** 55 minutes | **Servings:** 6)

Ingredients:

- 1 lb. black beans, soaked for 8 hours and drained
- 6 oz. chorizo; chopped
- 1 yellow onion; cut into half
- 6 garlic cloves; minced.
- 1 tbsp. vegetable oil
- 2 bay leaves
- 1 orange; cut into half
- 2 quarts' chicken stock
- Salt to the taste
- Chopped cilantro; chopped. For serving

Directions:

1. Set your instant pot on Sauté mode; add oil and heat it up.
2. Add chorizo, stir and cook for 2 minutes
3. Add onion, beans, garlic, bay leaves, orange, salt and stock; then stir well. close the lid and cook at High for 40 minutes.
4. Release the pressure naturally, carefully open the lid; discard bay leaves, onion and orange, add more salt and cilantro; then stir well. divide into bowls and serve

Green Chile and Baked Beans

(**Prep + Cooking Time:** 1 hour 25 minutes | **Servings:** 5)

Ingredients:

- 1 pound dried navy beans, soaked in water overnight; rinsed and drained
- 1/4 cup maple syrup
- 1 ½ cups diced roasted green chiles
- 1/4 cup blackstrap molasses
- 1/4 cup packed light brown sugar
- 1 small sweet onion; cut into large dice
- 3 garlic cloves; minced
- 2 tbsp. ketchup
- 1 tbsp. vegan Worcestershire sauce
- 1 tbsp. olive oil
- 1 tsp. salt or as your liking
- 1 tsp. apple cider vinegar

Directions:

1. In a small bowl, whisk the molasses, maple syrup, brown sugar, ketchup and Worcestershire sauce. Set aside.
2. Select the "Sauté" Low mode on your instant pot. When the display reads "Hot," add the oil and heat until it shimmers.
3. Add the onion and garlic. Turn off the Instant Pot and sauté the veggies for 1 to 2 minutes, stirring frequently. Add the salt, beans and molasses mix, stirring well

4. Lock the lid and turn the steam release handle to Sealing. Using the Manual function, set the cooker to High Pressure for 35 minutes
5. After completing the cooking time, let the pressure release naturally for 20 minutes; or until the pin drops.
6. Remove the lid carefully and stir. Select Sauté Medium. Stir in the green chiles and simmer the beans for 5 to 10 minutes; or until the sauce thickens. Stir in the vinegar and serve.

Green Chile Chickpeas

(Prep + Cooking Time: 1 hour 15 minutes | **Servings:** 5)

Ingredients:
- 2 cups dried chickpeas; rinsed
- 1 small tomato; diced
- 6 cups water
- 1 cup diced roasted green chiles or from a can
- 2 tsp. freshly squeezed lemon juice
- 1 tsp. ground cumin
- 1/2 tsp. chili powder; or more as your liking
- 1/2 tsp. onion powder
- 1/4 tsp. dried oregano
- 1/2 tsp. garlic powder
- 1/2 tsp. red pepper flakes
- 1/2 tsp. smoked paprika
- 1/4 tsp. freshly ground black pepper
- 1 tsp. salt or as your liking

Directions:
1. In the Instant Pot, combine the chickpeas and water.
2. Lock the lid and turn the steam release handle to Sealing. Using the Manual function, set the cooker to High Pressure for 45 minutes
3. After completing the cooking time, let the pressure release naturally for 20 minutes; quick release any remaining pressure.
4. Remove the lid carefully and drain the chickpeas, reserving 1 to 2 tbsp. of the cooking water. Return the chickpeas to the Instant Pot
5. Stir in the tomato, green chiles, lemon juice, cumin, chili powder, salt, garlic powder, red pepper flakes, paprika, onion powder; oregano and black pepper. If they're too dry, add the reserved cooking water.
6. Select the "Sauté" Low mode on your instant pot and cook for 3 to 4 minutes. You may need to turn the Instant Pot off if anything starts to burn at the bottom
7. Put the lid back on and turn on the Keep Warm function. Let the chickpeas sit in all that goodness for 5 minutes, then they're ready.

Red Beans and Rice

(Prep + Cooking Time: 1 hour 15 minutes | **Servings:** 5)

Ingredients:
- 5 cups cooked white rice
- 2 celery stalks, sliced
- 5 garlic cloves; minced
- 2 cups dried red beans
- 4 cups Vegetable Stock
- 2 bay leaves
- 1 red onion; diced
- 1 bell pepper, any color; diced
- 1 tbsp. olive oil
- 2 tsp. Cajun seasoning
- 1/2 tsp. dried oregano
- 1/2 tsp. dried parsley
- Salt as your liking
- Freshly ground black pepper
- Chopped fresh parsley; for garnishing
- Hot sauce; for serving

217 | P a g e

Directions:

1. Select the "Sauté" Low mode on your instant pot. When the display reads "Hot," add the oil and heat until it shimmers.
2. Add the red onion, bell pepper and celery. Cook for 3 to 4 minutes, stirring frequently.
3. Turn off the Instant Pot and add the garlic, bay leaves, Cajun seasoning; oregano and dried parsley. Continue to cook for 1 minute more, stirring
4. Stir in the beans and stock. Lock the lid and turn the steam release handle to Sealing. Using the Manual function, set the cooker to High Pressure for 40 minutes
5. After completing the cooking time, let the pressure release naturally for about 25 minutes; or until the pin drops.
6. Remove the lid carefully and remove and discard the bay leaves
7. Taste and season with salt and pepper, as needed. Serve with rice and top with parsley and hot sauce.

Spicy Lentils

(**Prep + Cooking Time:** 34 minutes | **Servings:** 5)

Ingredients:

- 2 Roma tomatoes; diced
- 2 cups Vegetable Stock
- 1 cup green; rinsed and drained
- 1 cup well chopped kale
- 1 small onion; diced
- 1 or 2 garlic cloves, finely diced
- 1 bell pepper, any color; diced
- 1 tbsp. olive oil
- 1 tsp. smoked paprika
- 1 tsp. chili powder
- 1 tsp. ground cumin
- 1 tsp. salt; or more as your liking
- Freshly ground black pepper

Directions:

1. Select the "Sauté" Low mode on your instant pot. When the display reads "Hot," add the oil and heat until it shimmers.
2. Add the onion. Sauté for 1 to 2 minutes and then turn off the Instant Pot. Add the garlic. Cook for about 30 seconds, stirring (don't let it burn)
3. Add the bell pepper, tomatoes, stock, lentils, salt, cumin, chili powder and paprika.
4. Lock the lid and turn the steam release handle to Sealing. Using the Manual function, set the cooker to High Pressure for 15 minutes
5. After completing the cooking time, let the Instant Pot go into Keep Warm mode and let the pressure release naturally for 10 minutes; quick release any remaining pressure
6. Remove the lid carefully and stir in the kale, which will wilt after 1 to 2 minutes. Taste and season with salt and pepper, as needed.

Butternut Lentils

(**Prep + Cooking Time:** 30 minutes | **Servings:** 5)

Ingredients:

- 3 cups butternut squash, peeled and cubed
- 1 ¾ cups water; or Vegetable Stock,
- 1/2 onion; diced
- 1 cup red lentils; rinsed
- 1 tbsp. olive oil
- 1 garlic clove; minced
- 1 tsp. smoked paprika
- 1/2 tsp. salt or as your liking
- 1/2 tsp. ground cumin
- Pinch chili powder

Directions:

1. Select the "Sauté" Low mode on your instant pot. When the display reads "Hot," add the oil and heat until it shimmers.
2. Add the onion. Cook for 2 to 3 minutes, stirring frequently. Turn off the Instant Pot and add the garlic. Cook for 30 seconds, stirring
3. Stir in the squash, water, lentils, paprika, salt, cumin and chili powder.

4. Lock the lid and turn the steam release handle to Sealing. Using the Manual function, set the cooker to High Pressure for 10 minutes
5. After completing the cooking time, let the pressure release naturally for 10 minutes; quick release any remaining pressure
6. Remove the lid carefully and stir. The lentils and butternut will break down quickly, no need to mash. Just stir and, when they're smooth, taste and adjust the seasonings, as needed.

Shrimp and White Beans

(Prep + Cooking Time: 45 minutes | **Servings:** 8)

Ingredients:
- 1 lb. white beans; soaked for 8 hours and drained
- 1 garlic clove; minced.
- 1 green bell pepper; chopped.
- 1 celery rib; chopped
- 4 parsley springs; chopped.
- 2 yellow onions; chopped.
- 2 cups seafood stock
- 1 lb. shrimp; peeled and deveined
- 2 bay leaves
- 3 tbsp. canola oil
- Creole seasoning to the taste
- Cooked rice for serving
- Hot sauce for serving

Directions:
1. Set your instant pot on Sauté mode; add oil and heat it up
2. Add onions and Creole seasoning to the taste; stir and cook for 5 minutes
3. Add garlic; stir and cook 5 minutes more
4. Add bell pepper and celery; stir and cook for 5 minutes
5. Add beans, stock and some water to cover everything in the pot.
6. Add bay leaves and parsley; then stir well. close the lid and cook at High for 15 minutes.
7. Quick release the pressure, open the instant pot lid, add shrimp, close the lid and leave it aside for 10 minutes
8. Divide beans and shrimp among plates on top of cooked rice and serve with hot sauce

Mushroom and Leek Risotto

(Prep + Cooking Time: 20 minutes | **Servings:** 5)

Ingredients:
- 12 ounces baby bella mushrooms, sliced
- 1 leek, white and lightest green parts only, halved and sliced
- 2 garlic cloves; minced
- 1 cup Arborio rice; rinsed and drained
- 2 ¾ cups Vegetable Stock
- 4 tbsp. vegan butter; divided
- 1 tsp. dried thyme
- 1/2 tsp. salt; or as your liking
- Juice of 1/2 lemon
- Freshly ground black pepper
- Chopped fresh parsley; for garnishing

Directions:
1. Select the "Sauté" Low mode on your instant pot. When the display reads "Hot," add 2 tbsp. of butter to melt.
2. Add the leek and mushrooms. Sauté for about 2 minutes, stirring frequently
3. Add the garlic. Cook for about 30 seconds, stirring, turn off the Instant Pot if it starts to burn. Add the rice and toast it for 1 minute. Turn off the Instant Pot
4. Stir in the stock, thyme and salt. Lock the lid and turn the steam release handle to Sealing. Using the Manual function, set the cooker to High Pressure for 8 minutes.
5. After completing the cooking time, quick release the pressure
6. Remove the lid carefully and stir in the lemon juice and remaining 2 tbsp. of vegan butter. Taste and season with more salt and pepper, as needed. Garnish with fresh parsley.

Italian Lentils Dinner

(Prep + Cooking Time: 25 minutes | **Servings:** 4)

Ingredients:

- 3/4 cup green lentils; soaked overnight and drained
- 1/2 cup brown rice; soaked overnight and drained
- 1 cup mozzarella cheese; shredded.
- 1 cup green and red bell pepper; chopped.
- 2 cups chicken; already cooked and shredded.
- 3 carrots; chopped.
- 2 ½ cups chicken stock
- 1 cup tomato sauce
- 3/4 cup onion; chopped.
- 3 tsp. Italian seasoning
- 2 garlic cloves; crushed.
- A handful greens
- Salt and black pepper to the taste

Directions:

1. In your instant pot; mix lentils with rice, salt, pepper, stock, tomato sauce, onion, red and green pepper, chicken, carrots, greens, Italian seasoning and garlic; then stir well. close the lid and cook on High for 15 minutes
2. Quick release the pressure, carefully open the lid; add cheese; then stir well. divide among bowls and serve.

Veggies Rice Pilaf

(Prep + Cooking Time: 28 minutes | **Servings:** 5)

Ingredients:

- 1/2 cup frozen peas
- 1/2 cup sliced almonds
- 1/2 sweet onion, chopped
- 1 carrot, halved lengthwise and sliced
- 1 celery stalk, sliced
- 1 cup basmati rice; rinsed and drained
- 1 cup Vegetable Stock
- 1 cup broccoli florets
- 1/2 cup sliced white mushrooms
- 2 garlic cloves; minced
- 1 tbsp. olive oil; or avocado oil
- Salt as your liking
- Freshly ground black pepper

Directions:

1. Select the "Sauté" Low mode on your instant pot. When the display reads "Hot," add the oil and heat until it shimmers.
2. Add the onion, carrot, celery, broccoli and mushrooms. Sauté for 2 to 3 minutes, stirring frequently. Add the garlic and turn off the Instant Pot. Sauté the garlic for 30 seconds, stirring frequently
3. Stir in the rice and stock and season to taste with salt and pepper
4. Lock the lid and turn the steam release handle to Sealing. Using the Manual function, set the cooker to High Pressure for 3 minutes.
5. After completing the cooking time, let the pressure release naturally for 15 minutes; quick release any remaining pressure
6. Remove the lid carefully and stir in the frozen peas. Replace the cover (no need to seal it) and let sit for a few minutes. When ready to serve, stir in the almonds.

Black Bean Soup

(Prep + Cooking Time: 1 hour 25 minutes | **Servings:** 4)

Ingredients:

- 1/2 cup chopped scallions, for garnish
- 4 slices bacon, diced
- 1 green bell pepper; chopped
- 1 jalapeño; chopped
- 4 garlic cloves; minced
- 1/2 bunch fresh cilantro, finely chopped
- 1 yellow onion, diced
- 1 cup dried black beans
- 3 cups chicken broth
- 2 bay leaves
- 1 tsp. dried thyme
- 2 tsp. dried oregano
- 2 tsp. ground cumin
- 2 tsp. salt or as your liking

Directions:
1. In your Instant Pot, combine the beans, broth, bacon, onion, bell pepper, jalapeño, garlic, cilantro, salt, oregano, thyme, cumin and bay leaves. Stir well to combine
2. Now secure the lid on the pot and close the valve. Now Press "Manual" and set the pot at "High" pressure for 45 minutes.
3. After completing the cooking time, allow the pot to sit undisturbed for 10 minutes, then release any remaining pressure
4. Using an immersion blender, puree some of the soup to thicken it while leaving some beans intact. Garnish with the scallions and serve.

Chickpea Basil Salad

(Prep + Cooking Time: 1 hour 10 minutes **| Servings:** 3)

Ingredients:
- 1 cup dried chickpeas; rinsed
- 1 cup fresh basil leaves; chopped or sliced
- 1 ½ cups grape tomatoes, halved
- water, enough to cover the chickpeas by 3 to 4 inches
- 3 tbsp. balsamic vinegar
- 1/2 tsp. garlic powder
- 1/2 tsp. salt; or more as your liking

Directions:
1. In the Instant Pot, combine the chickpeas and water. Lock the lid and turn the steam release handle to Sealing. Using the Manual function, set the cooker to High Pressure for 45 minutes.
2. After completing the cooking time, let the pressure release naturally for 20 minutes; quick release any remaining pressure
3. Remove the lid carefully and drain the chickpeas. Refrigerate to cool (unless you want to serve this warm, which is good, too)
4. While the chickpeas cool, in a large bowl, stir together the basil, tomatoes, vinegar, garlic powder and salt. Add the beans, stir to combine and serve.

Texas Roma Caviar

(Prep + Cooking Time: 25 minutes **| Servings:** 8)

Ingredients:
- 1 cup diced yellow onions
- 1 cup dried black-eyed peas
- 1/2 cup extra-virgin olive oil
- 2 Roma (plum) tomatoes; chopped
- 1/2 cup chopped fresh cilantro
- 2 cups water
- 3 tbsp. apple cider vinegar
- 1 tbsp. minced jalapeño
- 2 tbsp. fresh lemon juice
- 1 tsp. ground cumin
- 2 tsp. salt or as your liking

Directions:
1. In your Instant Pot, combine the water and black-eyed peas. Now secure the lid on the pot and close the valve. Now Press "Manual" and set pot at "High" pressure for 10 minutes
2. After completing the cooking time, allow the pot to sit undisturbed until the pressure has released. Drain any excess water. Allow the peas to cool slightly
3. Meanwhile; in a large bowl, whisk together the olive oil, vinegar, cumin, lemon juice, salt and ancho chile powder (if using). Add the black-eyed peas, onions, tomatoes, cilantro and jalapeño to the bowl. Stir gently to combine
4. Taste and adjust the lemon juice, vinegar and salt as needed. (Resist the urge to oversalt at this point, as the salad will get saltier as it sits.) Allow the salad to rest for 1 hour before serving.

Re-fried Pinto Beans

(Prep + Cooking Time: 1 hour | **Servings:** 7)

Ingredients:

- 1 pound dried pinto beans; rinsed
- 2 quarts Vegetable Stock
- 1 onion, quartered
- 3 garlic cloves, peeled
- 1 tbsp. freshly squeezed lime juice
- 1 tbsp. olive oil
- 1 tbsp. salt or as your liking
- 1/2 tsp. chili powder
- 1 tsp. ground cumin
- 1 tsp. dried Mexican oregano
- 1/4 tsp. freshly ground black pepper

Directions:

1. In the Instant Pot, combine the oil, onion, garlic, beans, stock, cumin; oregano, chili powder and pepper.
2. Lock the lid and turn the steam release handle to Sealing. Using the Manual function, set the cooker to High Pressure for 38 minutes
3. After completing the cooking time, let the pressure release naturally for about 20 minutes; or until the pin drops
4. Remove the lid carefully and use a ladle to remove most of the remaining liquid, saving it.
5. Using an immersion blender, blend the beans until smooth, adding the cooking water back in as needed. Stir in the lime juice and salt.

Coconut Jasmine Rice

(Prep + Cooking Time: 20 minutes | **Servings:** 5)

Ingredients:

- 1 (14-ounce) can lite coconut milk
- 2 cups jasmine rice; rinsed and drained
- 1/2 cup water
- 1/2 tsp. sea salt or as your liking

Directions:

1. In the Instant Pot, combine the rice, coconut milk, water and salt.
2. Lock the lid and turn the steam release handle to Sealing. Using the Manual function, set the cooker to High Pressure for 4 minutes
3. After completing the cooking time, let the pressure release naturally for 10 minutes; quick release any remaining pressure
4. Remove the lid carefully and fluff the rice. Taste and season with more salt, as needed.

Pepper Lemon Quinoa

(Prep + Cooking Time: 20 minutes | **Servings:** 5)

Ingredients:

- 1 ½ cups quinoa; rinsed
- 1 ½ cups water
- 1 tbsp. vegan butter
- 1/4 tsp. garlic powder
- 1/4 tsp. dried basil
- 1 tsp. salt; or more as your liking
- 1/2 tsp. freshly ground black pepper
- Juice of 1 lemon
- Zest of 1 lemon

Directions:

1. In the Instant Pot, combine the quinoa, water, salt, pepper, garlic powder and basil.
2. Lock the lid and turn the steam release handle to Sealing. Using the Manual function, set the cooker to High Pressure for 8 minutes
3. After completing the cooking time, let the pressure release naturally for 10 minutes; quick release any remaining pressure.
4. Remove the lid carefully and stir in the butter, lemon juice and zest. Taste and season with more salt and pepper, as needed

Chinese Fried Rice

(Prep + Cooking Time: 22 minutes | **Servings:** 5)

Ingredients:

- 1 small onion; diced
- 1 ¾ cups jasmine rice; rinsed and drained
- 1/4 cup lite soy sauce
- 1 ¾ cups water
- 2 cups frozen mixed vegetable; peas, carrots, corn
- 1 tbsp. sesame oil
- 3/4 tsp. garlic powder
- 3/4 tsp. ground ginger

Directions:

1. Select the "Sauté" Low mode on your instant pot. When the display reads "Hot," add the oil and heat until it shimmers.
2. Add the onion. Cook for 1 minute, stirring frequently. Turn off the Instant Pot and add the rice, ginger, garlic powder, soy sauce and water
3. Lock the lid and turn the steam release handle to Sealing. Using the Manual function, set the cooker to High Pressure for 5 minutes
4. After completing the cooking time, turn off the Instant Pot and let the pressure release naturally for 10 minutes; quick release any remaining pressure.
5. Remove the lid carefully and stir in the frozen vegetables
6. Rest the lid back on "no need to lock it" and select the Keep Warm function. Let the veggies warm for 3 to 4 minutes before serving.

Yogurt Recipes

Raspberry Yogurt.

(Prep + Cooking Time: 20 minutes | **Servings:** 6)

Ingredients:

- 1 cup raspberry puree
- 4 capsules high-quality probiotic
- 2 tbsp. gelatin powder
- 1 tsp. vanilla paste
- 1 tbsp. raw honey
- 2 cans full cream milk

Directions:

1. Pour the milk in instant pot
2. Lock the lid and select the yogurt button; then press the adjust button till the display states boil
3. When the Instant Pot beeps; turn off the pot, remove the lid and take out the metal bowl.
4. Using a candy thermometer measure the temperature of the milk till it reaches 115 C.
5. Once the milk is cooled below 115 C; empty the contents of probiotic capsules in the milk.
6. Return the metal bowl to the pot; close the lid and seal it and press the yogurt button again.
7. Use the (+) button to adjust the time to 14hours. When the Instant pot beeps; taste the yogurt to make sure it is tart.
8. Transfer the yogurt to the blender or food processor, sprinkle gelatin powder and add remaining ingredients.
9. Blending the yogurt in a food blender until smooth.
10. Pour the yogurt into glasses or bowls and refrigerate the same for 2 - 3 hours

Pumpkin Spice Yogurt.

(Prep + Cooking Time: 20 minutes | **Servings:** 4)

Ingredients:

- 4 capsules high-quality probiotic
- 2 cans full cream milk
- 1 tbsp. raw honey
- 1 tbsp. pumpkin spice
- 2 tbsp. gelatin powder
- 1 tsp. vanilla paste

Directions:

1. Pour the milk in instant pot
2. Lock the lid and select the yogurt button; then press the adjust button till the display states boil
3. When the Instant Pot beeps; turn off the pot, remove the lid and take out the metal bowl
4. Using a candy thermometer measure the temperature of the milk till it reaches 115 C.
5. Once the milk is cooled below 115 C; empty the contents of probiotic capsules in the milk
6. Return the metal bowl to the pot; close the lid and seal it and press the yogurt button again.
7. Use the (+) button to adjust the time to 14hours. When the Instant pot beeps; taste the yogurt to make sure it is tart
8. Transfer the yogurt to the blender or food processor, sprinkle gelatin powder and add remaining ingredients.
9. Blending the yogurt in a food blender until smooth
10. Pour the yogurt into glasses or bowls and refrigerate the same for 2 - 3 hours

Chocolate Yogurt.

(Prep + Cooking Time: 20 minutes | **Servings:** 4)

Ingredients:

- 4 capsules high-quality probiotic
- 2 tbsp. cocoa powder
- 1 cup melted dark chocolate
- 1 tbsp. raw honey
- 2 tbsp. gelatin powder
- 2 cans full cream milk
- 1 tsp. vanilla paste

Directions:

1. Pour the milk in instant pot. Add cocoa powder.
2. Lock the lid and select the yogurt button; then press the adjust button until the display states boil
3. When the Instant Pot beeps; turn off the pot, remove the lid and take out the metal bowl
4. Using a candy thermometer measure the temperature of the milk till it reaches 115 C.
5. Once the milk is cooled below 115 C; empty the contents of probiotic capsules in the milk
6. Return the metal bowl to the pot; close the lid and seal it and press the yogurt button again.
7. Use the (+) button to adjust the time to 14hours. When the Instant pot beeps; taste the yogurt to make sure it is tart
8. Transfer the yogurt to the blender or food processor, sprinkle gelatin powder and add remaining ingredients.
9. Blending the yogurt in a food blender until smooth.
10. Pour the yogurt into glasses or bowls and refrigerate the same for 2 - 3 hours

White Chocolate Yogurt.

(**Prep + Cooking Time:** 20 minutes | **Servings:** 4)

Ingredients:

- 1 cup melted white chocolate
- 2 tbsp. gelatin powder
- 1 tbsp. raw honey
- 2 cans full cream milk
- 4 capsules high-quality probiotic
- 1 tsp. vanilla paste

Directions:

1. Pour the milk in instant pot
2. Lock the lid and select the yogurt button; then press the adjust button till the display states boil.
3. When the Instant Pot beeps; turn off the pot, remove the lid and take out the metal bowl
4. Using a candy thermometer measure the temperature of the milk till it reaches 115 C
5. Once the milk is cooled below 115 C; empty the contents of probiotic capsules in the milk
6. Return the metal bowl to the pot; close the lid and seal it and press the yogurt button again
7. Use the (+) button to adjust the time to 14hours. When the Instant pot beeps; taste the yogurt to make sure it is tart
8. Transfer the yogurt to the blender or food processor, sprinkle gelatin powder and add remaining ingredients, including white chocolate.
9. Blending the yogurt in a food blender until smooth
10. Pour the yogurt into glasses or bowls and refrigerate the same for 2 - 3 hours

Vanilla Yogurt.

(**Prep + Cooking Time:** 20 minutes | **Servings:** 4)

Ingredients:

- 4 capsules high-quality probiotic
- 2 cans full cream milk
- 3 tsp. vanilla paste
- 2 tbsp. gelatin powder
- 1 tbsp. raw honey

Directions:

1. Pour the milk in instant pot.
2. Lock the lid and select the yogurt button; then press the adjust button till the display states boil.
3. When the Instant Pot beeps; turn off the pot, remove the lid and take out the metal bowl
4. Using a candy thermometer measure the temperature of the milk till it reaches 115 C
5. Once the milk is cooled below 115 C; empty the contents of probiotic capsules in the milk
6. Return the metal bowl to the pot; close the lid and seal it and press the yogurt button again
7. Use the (+) button to adjust the time to 14hours. When the Instant pot beeps; taste the yogurt to make sure it is tart.
8. Transfer the yogurt to the blender or food processor, sprinkle gelatin powder and add remaining ingredients.

9. Blending the yogurt in a food blender until smooth
10. Pour the yogurt into glasses or bowls and refrigerate the same for 2 - 3 hours.

Strawberry Yogurt.

(**Prep + Cooking Time:** 20 minutes | **Servings:** 4)

Ingredients:

- 1 cup strawberry puree
- 4 capsules high-quality probiotic
- 1 tbsp. raw honey
- 1 tsp. vanilla paste
- 2 tbsp. gelatin powder
- 2 cans full cream milk

Directions:

1. Pour the milk in instant pot.
2. Lock the lid and select the yogurt button; then press the adjust button till the display states boil.
3. When the Instant Pot beeps; turn off the pot, remove the lid and take out the metal bowl
4. Using a candy thermometer measure the temperature of the milk till it reaches 115 C.
5. Once the milk is cooled below 115 C; empty the contents of probiotic capsules in the milk
6. Return the metal bowl to the pot; close the lid and seal it and press the yogurt button again
7. Use the (+) button to adjust the time to 14hours. When the Instant pot beeps; taste the yogurt to make sure it is tart.
8. Transfer the yogurt to the blender or food processor, sprinkle gelatin powder and add remaining ingredients.
9. Blending the yogurt in a food blender until smooth
10. Pour the yogurt into glasses or bowls and refrigerate the same for 2 - 3 hours

Blueberry Oats Yogurt.

(**Prep + Cooking Time:** 20 minutes | **Servings:** 6)

Ingredients:

- 4 capsules high-quality probiotic
- 2 cans full cream milk
- 1/2 cup roasted oats
- 2 tbsp. gelatin powder
- 1 tbsp. raw honey
- 1 tsp. vanilla paste
- 1 cup blueberry puree or pulp

Directions:

1. Pour the milk in instant pot.
2. Lock the lid and select the yogurt button; then press the adjust button till the display states boil
3. When the Instant Pot beeps; turn off the pot, remove the lid and take out the metal bowl
4. Using a candy thermometer measure the temperature of the milk till it reaches 115 C
5. Once the milk is cooled below 115 C; empty the contents of probiotic capsules in the milk
6. Return the metal bowl to the pot; close the lid and seal it and press the yogurt button again.
7. Use the (+) button to adjust the time to 14hours. When the Instant pot beeps; taste the yogurt to make sure it is tart.
8. Transfer the yogurt to the blender or food processor, sprinkle gelatin powder and add remaining ingredients.
9. Blending the yogurt in a food blender until smooth
10. Pour the yogurt into glasses or bowls and refrigerate the same for 2 - 3 hours

Slow Cooked Fruity Yogurt.

(Prep + Cooking Time: 12 hours | **Servings:** 4)

Ingredients:
- 5 ⅔ cups. milk; organic, reduced fat or whole
- 4 tbsp. yogurt culture; plain; divided
- 4 tbsp. dry milk powder; non-fat; divided
- 1 ½ cup. water; for the pot
- 4 tbsp. sugar; all natural; divided
- 2 cups. fresh fruit; chopped

Equipment:
- 4 wide mouth pint jars

Directions:
1. Pour the water into the Instant Pot and then put a rack or a grate in the pot.
2. Pour 1 and 1/3 cup. Milk into each jar and the cover the jar loosely with their lids. Put the jars onto the rack/ grate
3. Set the Instant Pot to Pressure Cycle and set the timer to 2 minutes; this will heat the milk and kill any pathogens that might be in the milk.
4. When the cycle is done; turn the steam valve to quick release the pressure
5. Open the pot lid and with a jar lifter, remove the jars from the pot. Put the jars into cool water and carefully remove the jar lids.
6. Once the milk is below 100F; add 1 tbsp. yogurt culture, 1 tbsp. dry milk powder; and 1 tbsp. sugar into each jar; stir until well mixed.
7. Carefully add about 1/2 cup. of fresh fruits into each jar; do not over fill them and leave at least 1/ 8-inch clear from the top each jar. Return the jar lids back
8. Check and make sure that there is still 1 ½ cup. of water in the bottom of the Instant Pot
9. Put the jars back onto the rack/ grate. Press the yogurt cycle and set the timer for 8 - 12 hours.
10. When the cycle is complete; put the jars in the refrigerator; this will cool them down and stop the cooking process

Tips: Making the yogurt in jars enables you to make plain or different flavored yogurt at the same time

Mango Yogurt.

(Prep + Cooking Time: 30 minutes | **Servings:** 4)

Ingredients:
- 2 cans full cream milk
- 2 tbsp. gelatine
- 1 tsp. vanilla extract
- 4 capsules high-quality probiotic
- 1 tbsp. raw honey
- 1 cup mango puree or pulp

Directions:
1. Pour the milk in instant pot
2. Lock the lid and select the yogurt button; then press the adjust button till the display states boil.
3. When the Instant Pot beeps; turn off the pot, remove the lid and take out the metal bowl
4. Using a candy thermometer measure the temperature of the milk till it reaches 115 C.
5. Once the milk is cooled below 115 C; empty the contents of probiotic capsules in the milk
6. Stir in mango puree as well
7. Return the metal bowl to the pot, close the lid and seal it and press the yogurt button again
8. Use the (+) button to adjust the time to 14hours. When the Instant pot beeps; taste the yogurt to make sure it is tart
9. Transfer the yogurt to the blender or food processor, sprinkle gelatin powder, add honey and vanilla extract
10. Blending the yogurt until smooth.
11. Pour the yogurt into glasses or bowls and refrigerate the same for 2 - 3 hours.

Passionfruit Yogurt.

(Prep + Cooking Time: 20 minutes | **Servings:** 4)

Ingredients:
- 4 capsules high-quality probiotic
- 2 cans full cream milk
- 2 tbsp. gelatin powder
- 1 ½ cups passionfruit pulp
- 1 tbsp. raw honey
- 1 tsp. vanilla paste

Directions:
1. Pour the milk in instant pot
2. Lock the lid and select the yogurt button; then press the adjust button till the display states boil
3. When the Instant Pot beeps; turn off the pot, remove the lid and take out the metal bowl
4. Using a candy thermometer measure the temperature of the milk till it reaches 115 C
5. Once the milk is cooled below 115 C; empty the contents of probiotic capsules in the milk.
6. Return the metal bowl to the pot; close the lid and seal it and press the yogurt button again
7. Use the (+) button to adjust the time to 14hours. When the Instant pot beeps; taste the yogurt to make sure it is tart.
8. Transfer the yogurt to the blender or food processor, sprinkle gelatin powder and add remaining ingredients, including pulp.
9. Blending the yogurt in a food blender until smooth
10. Pour the yogurt into glasses or bowls and refrigerate the same for 2 - 3 hours

Vegan Soy Yogurt.

(Prep + Cooking Time: 12 hours | **Servings:** 4)

Ingredients:
- 1 packet vegan yogurt culture
- 1-quart soy milk (use only made soybeans and water; no vitamins or sugar added)
- Sweetener; if desired

Directions:
1. Pour the soymilk into a wide mouth; 1-quart Mason jar with lid or into multiple heatproof containers with a lids.
2. Add the vegan yogurt culture. Close the lid and shake to mix. Remove the lid from the jar; you don't need it at this point.
3. Put the Mason jar directly into the Instant Pot container. Close and lock the Instant Pot lid. You can leave the steam valve to "Sealing" or "Releasing"; it won't affect the cooking. Press the YOGURT button and the timer to 12 hours.
4. When the timer beeps at the end of the cooking cycle, carefully remove the Mason jar from the pot, cover with its lid and refrigerate for at least 6 hours
5. Sweeten and/ or flavor, if desired. This will keep for up to 6 days in the refrigerator.

Tips: This thick, creamy, unsweetened, tart soy yogurt can be used as a sour cream substitute or in recipes. You can enjoy it topped with pears and cinnamons; with bananas, shredded coconut and pecans, with jam or sweetened with coconut sugar. You can also strain it overnight to make yogurt cheese

Cinnamon Yogurt.

(Prep + Cooking Time: 20 minutes **| Servings:** 6)

Ingredients:
- 2 cans full cream milk
- 4 capsules high-quality probiotic
- 1 tsp. vanilla paste
- 2 tbsp. gelatin powder
- 1 tbsp. raw honey
- 2 tsp. Ceylon cinnamon

Directions:
1. Pour the milk in instant pot.
2. Lock the lid and select the yogurt button; then press the adjust button till the display states boil.
3. When the Instant Pot beeps; turn off the pot, remove the lid and take out the metal bowl.
4. Using a candy thermometer measure the temperature of the milk till it reaches 115 C
5. Once the milk is cooled below 115 C; empty the contents of probiotic capsules in the milk.
6. Return the metal bowl to the pot; close the lid and seal it and press the yogurt button again.
7. Use the (+) button to adjust the time to 14hours. When the Instant pot beeps; taste the yogurt to make sure it is tart.
8. Transfer the yogurt to the blender or food processor, sprinkle gelatin powder and add remaining ingredients.
9. Blending the yogurt in a food blender until smooth
10. Pour the yogurt into glasses or bowls and refrigerate the same for 2 - 3 hours

Kiwi Yogurt.

(Prep + Cooking Time: 20 minutes **| Servings:** 4)

Ingredients:
- 4 capsules high-quality probiotic
- 1 tsp. vanilla paste
- 3/4 cup kiwi puree
- 2 tbsp. gelatin powder
- 1 tbsp. raw honey
- 2 cans full cream milk

Directions:
1. Pour the milk in instant pot.
2. Lock the lid and select the yogurt button; then press the adjust button till the display states boil
3. When the Instant Pot beeps; turn off the pot, remove the lid and take out the metal bowl.
4. Using a candy thermometer measure the temperature of the milk till it reaches 115 C
5. Once the milk is cooled below 115 C; empty the contents of probiotic capsules in the milk
6. Return the metal bowl to the pot; close the lid and seal it and press the yogurt button again
7. Use the (+) button to adjust the time to 14hours. When the Instant pot beeps; taste the yogurt to make sure it is tart
8. Transfer the yogurt to the blender or food processor, sprinkle gelatin powder and add remaining ingredients.
9. Blending the yogurt in a food blender until smooth
10. Pour the yogurt into glasses or bowls and refrigerate the same for 2 - 3 hours.

Desserts

Ricotta Cake Recipe

(Prep + Cooking Time: 60 minutes | **Servings:** 6)

Ingredients:

- 6 oz. dates, soaked for 15 minutes and drained
- 1 lb. ricotta
- 2 oz. honey softened
- 4 eggs
- 2 oz. sugar
- 17 oz. water
- Orange juice and zest from ½ orange
- Some vanilla extract

Directions:

1. In a bowl, whisk ricotta until it softens.
2. In another bowl, whisk eggs well.
3. Combine the 2 mixtures and stir very well.
4. Add honey, vanilla, dates, orange zest and juice to the ricotta mixture and stir again
5. Pour the batter into a heatproof dish and cover with tin foil
6. Place dish in the steamer basket of your instant pot, add water to the pot, seal the instant pot lid and cook at High for 20 minutes
7. Quick release the pressure, carefully open the lid; allow cake to cool down, transfer to a platter, slice and serve.

Ginger and Pineapple Risotto

(Prep + Cooking Time: 22 minutes | **Servings:** 4)

Ingredients:

- 1/4 cup candied ginger; chopped.
- 1 ¾ cups risotto rice
- 20 oz. canned pineapple; chopped.
- 4 cups milk
- 1/2 cup coconut, shredded.

Directions:

1. In your instant pot, mix milk with rice, coconut, pineapple and ginger; then stir well. seal the instant pot lid and cook at High for 12 minutes.
2. Release the pressure naturally, carefully open the lid and serve your dessert

Instant Pot Key Lime Pie

(Prep + Cooking Time: 25 minutes | **Servings:** 6)

Ingredients:

For the crust:

- 5 graham crackers, crumbled.
- 3 tbsp. butter, melted
- 1 tbsp. sugar

For the filling:

- 4 egg yolks
- 1/2 cup key lime juice
- 1/3 cup sour cream
- 14 oz. canned condensed milk
- 2 tbsp. key lime zest, grated
- Cooking spray
- 1 cup water

Directions:

1. In a bowl, whisk egg yolks very well
2. Add milk gradually and stir again well.
3. Add lime juice, sour cream and lime zest and stir again
4. In a bowl, whisk butter with crackers and sugar, stir well and spread on the bottom of a spring form greased with some cooking spray.
5. Cover pan with some tin foil and place it in the steamer basket of your instant pot.

6. Add 1 cup water to the pot, seal the instant pot lid and cook at High for 15 minutes.
7. Release the pressure naturally for 10 minutes, then release remaining pressure by turning the valve to 'Venting', carefully open the lid; take pie out, leave aside to cool down and keep in the fridge for 4 hours before slicing and serving it.

Zucchini Nut Bread Recipe

(Prep + Cooking Time: 30 minutes | **Servings:** 6)

Ingredients:
- 2 cups zucchini, grated
- 1/2 cup baking cocoa
- 1 tsp. baking soda
- 1/4 tsp. baking powder
- 1 cup applesauce
- 3 eggs, whisked
- 1 tbsp. vanilla extract
- 2 cups sugar
- 1/2 cup walnuts; chopped.
- 1/2 cup chocolate chips
- 1 tsp. salt
- 2 ½ cups white flour
- 1 tsp. cinnamon
- 1 ½ cups water

Directions:
1. In a bowl, mix zucchini with sugar, vanilla, eggs and applesauce and stir well
2. In another bowl, mix flour with salt, cocoa, baking soda, baking powder, cinnamon, chocolate chips and walnuts and stir.
3. Combine the 2 mixtures; then stir well. pour into a Bundt pan, place pan in the steamer basket of your instant pot, add the water to the pot, seal the instant pot lid and cook at High for 25 minutes.
4. Release the pressure naturally, carefully open the lid; transfer bread to a plate, cut and serve it.

Instant Pot Sweet Carrots

(Prep + Cooking Time: 25 minutes | **Servings:** 4)

Ingredients:
- 2 cups baby carrots
- 1/2 cup water
- 1/2 tbsp. butter
- 1 tbsp. brown sugar
- A pinch of salt

Directions:
1. Set your instant pot on Sauté mode; add butter and melt it.
2. Add sugar, water and salt, stir and cook for 1 minute.
3. Add carrots, toss to coat, seal the instant pot lid and cook at High for 15 minutes. Quick release the pressure, carefully open the lid;
4. Transfer carrots to plates and serve

Mix Berries Compote

(Prep + Cooking Time: 15 minutes | **Servings:** 8)

Ingredients:
- 1 cup blueberries
- 2 tbsp. lemon juice
- 3/4 cup sugar
- 1 tbsp. cornstarch
- 1 tbsp. water
- 2 cups strawberries, sliced

Directions:
1. In your instant pot, mix blueberries with lemon juice and sugar; then stir well.
2. Seal the instant pot lid and cook at High for 3 minutes.
3. Release pressure naturally for 10 minutes and carefully open the lid
4. In a bowl, mix cornstarch with water, stir well and add to the pot.
5. Stir, set the pot on Sauté mode and cook compote for 2 minutes more
6. Divide into jars and keep in the fridge until you serve it.

Poached Pears with Caramel Sauce

(**Prep + Cooking Time:** 12 minutes | **Servings:** 4)

Ingredients:

- 1 whole vanilla bean, split and scraped
- 4 Bosc pears, ripe but not soft
- 1 batch Easy Caramel Sauce, warmed
- 1 lemon, halved
- 2 cups sugar
- 3 cups water
- 2 cups white wine
- 1 cinnamon stick

Directions:

1. Select the "Sauté" Low mode on your instant pot. When the display reads "Hot," add the water, white wine, sugar, vanilla bean and seeds and cinnamon stick, stirring well
2. Cook for 1 to 2 minutes; or until the sugar dissolves completely. Cancel Saute and select Keep Warm.
3. Gently peel the pears. If presentation is important, keep the stems intact. Rub the pears with the lemon halves to prevent browning and add the pears to the Instant Pot.
4. Lock the lid and turn the steam release handle to Sealing. Using the Manual function, set the cooker to High Pressure for 3 minutes
5. After completing the cooking time, quick release the pressure. Remove the lid carefully and remove the pears. Set aside to cool
6. Save the sauce and pour it over the pears once cooled. Serve, warm or at room temperature, topped with caramel sauce.

Instant Pot Baked Apples

(**Prep + Cooking Time:** 20 minutes | **Servings:** 6)

Ingredients:

- 6 apples, cored
- 1 cup red wine
- 1/4 cup raisins
- 1/2 cup raw sugar
- 1 tsp. cinnamon powder

Directions:

1. Put the apples in your instant pot
2. Add wine, raisins, sugar and cinnamon, close the lid and cook at High for 10 minutes.
3. Release pressure naturally, carefully open the lid; transfer apples and their cooking juice to plates and serve.

Stuffed Peaches

(**Prep + Cooking Time:** 15 minutes | **Servings:** 6)

Ingredients:

- 6 peaches, insides removed
- 2 tbsp. coconut butter
- 1 tsp. almond extract
- 1/4 cup coconut flour
- 1/2 tsp. cinnamon powder
- 1/4 cup maple syrup
- 1 cup water
- A pinch of salt

Directions:

1. In a bowl, mix flour with salt, syrup, butter, cinnamon and half of the almond extract and stir well.
2. Fill peaches with this mix, place them in the steamer basket of your instant pot, add the water and the rest of the almond extract to the pot, seal the instant pot lid and cook at High for 4 minutes.
3. Release pressure naturally, divide stuffed peaches on servings plates and serve warm

Berry Jam Recipe

(Prep + Cooking Time: 50 minutes | **Servings:** 12)

Ingredients:
- 2 lb. sugar
- 1 lb. strawberries
- 1/2 lb. blueberries
- Zest from 1 lemon
- 1 lb. cranberries
- 2 tbsp. water
- 3.5 oz. black currant
- A pinch of salt

Directions:
1. In your instant pot, mix strawberries with cranberries, blueberries, currants, lemon zest and sugar.
2. Stir and leave aside for 1 hour.
3. Add salt and water, set the pot on Simmer mode and bring to a boil
4. Seal the instant pot lid, cook on Low for 10 minutes and release pressure for 10 minutes
5. Carefully open the lid, set it on Simmer mode again, bring to a boil and simmer for 4 minutes. Divide into jars and keep in the fridge until you need it.

Banana Bread

(Prep + Cooking Time: 40 minutes | **Servings:** 6)

Ingredients:
- 2 bananas, mashed
- 3/4 cup coconut sugar
- 1/3 cup ghee, soft
- 1 tsp. vanilla
- 1/2 tsp. baking soda
- 1/3 cup cashew milk
- one egg
- 1 ½ tsp. cream of tartar
- 2 cups water
- 1 tsp. baking powder
- 1 ½ cups flour
- A pinch of salt
- Cooking spray

Directions:
1. In a bowl, mix milk with cream of tartar and stir well.
2. Add sugar, ghee, egg, vanilla and bananas and stir everything.
3. In another bowl, mix flour with salt, baking powder and soda
4. Combine the 2 mixtures, stir well, pour this into a cake pan which you've greased with some cooking spray and arrange pan in the steamer basket of your instant pot
5. Add the water to your pot, seal the instant pot lid and cook at High for 30 minutes
6. Quick release the pressure, carefully open the lid; take bread out, leave aside to cool down, slice and serve it.

Delicious Cobbler Recipe

(Prep + Cooking Time: 22 minutes | **Servings:** 4)

Ingredients:
- 3 apples, cored and cut into chunks
- 1 tsp. cinnamon
- 1 ½ cup hot water
- 1/4 cup date syrup
- 2 pears, cored and cut into chunks
- 1 cup steel cut oats
- ice cream for serving

Directions:
1. Put apples and pears in your instant pot and mix with hot water, date syrup, oats and cinnamon
2. Stir, seal the instant pot lid and cook at High for 12 minutes.
3. Release pressure naturally, transfer cobbler to bowls and serve it with ice cream on top.

Chocolate Cheese cake

(Prep + Cooking Time: 2 hours **| Servings:** 12)

Ingredients:
For the crust:
- 1 ½ cups chocolate cookie crumbs
- 4 tbsp. melted butter

For the filling:
- 24 oz. cream cheese, soft
- 2 tbsp. cornstarch
- 4 oz. bittersweet chocolate
- 4 oz. white chocolate
- 4 oz. milk chocolate
- 1 cup water
- 1/2 cup Greek yogurt
- 1 cup sugar
- 3 eggs
- 1 tbsp. vanilla extract
- Cooking spray

Directions:
1. In a bowl mix cookie crumbs with butter and stir well.
2. Spray a spring form pan with some cooking oil, line with parchment paper, press crumbs and butter mix on the bottom and keep in the freezer for now.
3. In a bowl, mix cream cheese with cornstarch and sugar and stir using your mixer.
4. Add eggs, yogurt, and vanilla, stir again to combine everything and divide into 3 bowls.
5. Put milk chocolate in a heatproof bowl and heat up in the microwave for 30 seconds
6. Add this into one of the bowls with the batter you've made earlier and stir well
7. Put dark and white chocolate in 2 heatproof bowls and heat them up in the microwave for 30 seconds.
8. Add these to the other 2 bowls with cheesecake batter, stir and introduce them all in the fridge for 30 minutes
9. Take bowls out of the fridge and layer your cheesecake
10. Pour the dark chocolate batter in the center of the crust.
11. Add white chocolate batter on top and spread evenly and end with milk chocolate batter
12. Put the pan in the steamer basket of your pot, add 1 cup water in the pot, seal the instant pot lid and cook at High for 45 minutes
13. Release pressure for 10 minutes, take the cake out of the pot, leave aside to cool down and serve.

Crème Brule

(Prep + Cooking Time: 1 hour 15 minutes **| Servings:** 6)

Ingredients:
- 2 cups fresh cream
- 2 cups water
- 5 tbsp. white sugar
- 1 tsp. cinnamon powder
- 6 egg yolks
- 4 tbsp. raw sugar
- Zest from 1 orange
- A pinch of nutmeg for serving

Directions:
1. In a pan, mix cream with cinnamon and orange zest, stir and bring to a boil over medium high heat.
2. Take the pan off heat and leave it aside for 30 minutes.
3. In a bowl, mix egg yolks with white sugar and whisk well. Add this to cooled cream and whisk well again.
4. Strain this mix and then divide it into ramekins
5. Cover with foil, place them in the steamer basket of your instant pot, add 2 cups water to the pot, seal the instant pot lid and cook on Low for 10 minutes.
6. Release the pressure naturally, carefully open the lid; take ramekins out and leave them aside for 30 minutes.
7. Sprinkle nutmeg and raw sugar on top of each and melt this with a culinary torch. Serve right away.

Pears Jam Recipe

(**Prep + Cooking Time:** 15 minutes | **Servings:** 12)

Ingredients:
- 8 pears, cored and cut into quarters
- 2 apples, peeled, cored and cut into quarters
- 1/4 cup apple juice
- 1 tsp. cinnamon, ground.

Directions:
1. In your instant pot, mix pears with apples, cinnamon and apple juice; then stir well. seal the instant pot lid and cook at High for 4 minutes.
2. Release the pressure naturally, carefully open the lid;
3. blend using an immersion blender, divide jam into jars and keep in a cold place until you serve it

Instant pot Banana Cake

(**Prep + Cooking Time:** 60 minutes | **Servings:** 5)

Ingredients:
- 3 bananas, peeled and mashed
- 1 cup water
- 1 ½ cups sugar
- 1 tsp. cinnamon
- 1 stick butter, soft
- 1 tsp. nutmeg
- 2 cups flour
- 2 tsp. baking powder
- A pinch of salt
- 2 eggs

Directions:
7. In a bowl, mix eggs with butter and sugar and stir very well
8. Add salt, baking powder, cinnamon and nutmeg and stir well again.
9. Add bananas and flour and stir again.
10. Grease a spring form pan with some butter, pour the batter in it and cover the pan with a paper towel and tin foil.
11. Add 1 cup water to your instant pot, place the pan in the pot, seal the instant pot lid and cook at High for 55 minutes
12. Quick release the pressure, remove the pot, leave banana breakfast cake to cool down, cut and serve it.

Apple Bread

(**Prep + Cooking Time:** 1 hour and 20 minutes | **Servings:** 6)

Ingredients:
- 3 cups apples, cored and cubed
- 1 cup sugar
- 2 eggs
- 1 tbsp. baking powder
- 1 tbsp. apple pie spice
- 2 cups white flour
- 1 stick butter
- 1 tbsp. vanilla
- 1 cup water

Directions:
1. In a bowl mix egg with 1 butter stick, apple pie spice and sugar and stir using your mixer.
2. Add apples and stir again well.
3. In another bowl, mix baking powder with flour and stir.
4. Combine the 2 mixtures, stir and pour into a spring form pan.
5. Place in the steamer basket of your instant pot, add 1 cup water to the pot, seal the instant pot lid and cook at High for 1 hour and 10 minutes.
6. Quick release the pressure, leave bread to cool down, cut and serve it.

Holiday Pudding

(Prep + Cooking Time: 50 minutes | Servings: 4)

Ingredients:

- 4 oz. dried cranberries, soaked in hot water for 30 minutes, drained and chopped.
- 1 cup white flour
- 3 tsp. baking powder
- 1 cup raw sugar
- 15 tbsp. butter
- 3 tbsp. maple syrup
- 1 tsp. ginger powder
- 2 cups water
- 4 eggs
- 1 carrot, grated
- 4 oz. dried apricots; chopped.
- A pinch of cinnamon powder
- A pinch of salt
- A drizzle of olive oil

Directions:

1. Grease a heatproof pudding mould with a drizzle of oil and leave aside for now
2. In a blender, mix flour with baking powder, sugar, cinnamon, salt and ginger and pulse a few times.
3. Add butter and pulse again.
4. Add maple syrup and eggs and pulse again.
5. Add dried fruits and carrot and fold them into the batter
6. Spread this mix into the pudding mold, place this in the steamer basket of your instant pot and add 2 cups water in the pot as well
7. Set the pot on Sauté mode and steam your pudding for 10 minutes.
8. Cover your pot, cook pudding at High for 30 minutes.
9. Release the pressure naturally for 10 minutes, then release remaining pressure by turning the valve to 'Venting', carefully open the lid; take pudding out and leave it aside to cool down before serving it

Pina Colada Pudding

(Prep + Cooking Time: 15 minutes | Servings: 8)

Ingredients:

- 8 oz. canned pineapple tidbits, drained and halved
- 14 oz. canned coconut milk
- 1 tbsp. coconut oil
- 2 eggs
- 1/2 tsp. vanilla extract
- 1/2 cup milk
- 1/2 cup sugar
- 1 ½ cups water
- 1 cup Arborio rice
- A pinch of salt

Directions:

1. In your instant pot, mix oil, water, rice and salt; then stir well. seal the instant pot lid and cook at High for 3 minutes.
2. Release the pressure naturally for 10 minutes, then release remaining pressure by turning the valve to 'Venting', carefully open the lid; add sugar and coconut milk and stir well.
3. In a bowl, mix eggs with milk and vanilla, stir and pour over rice.
4. Stir, set the pot on Sauté mode and bring to a boil
5. Add pineapple tidbits; then stir well. divide into dessert bowls and serve

Pumpkin Chocolate Cake Recipe

(Prep + Cooking Time: 55 minutes | **Servings:** 12)

Ingredients:
- 3/4 tsp. pumpkin pie spice
- 3/4 cup white flour
- 3/4 cup whole wheat flour
- 1/2 tsp. vanilla extract
- 2/3 cup chocolate chips
- 1 tsp. baking soda
- one egg
- 3/4 cup sugar
- 1/2 tsp. baking powder
- 1/2 cup Greek yogurt
- 1 banana, mashed
- 2 tbsp. canola oil
- 8 oz. canned pumpkin puree
- 1-quart water
- Cooking spray
- A pinch of salt

Directions:
1. In a bowl, mix white flour with whole wheat flour, salt, baking soda and powder and pumpkin spice and stir.
2. In another bowl, mix sugar with oil, banana, yogurt, pumpkin puree, vanilla and egg and stir using a mixer.
3. Combine the 2 mixtures, add chocolate chips and mix everything.
4. Pour this into a greased Bundt pan, cover pan with paper towels and foil and place in the steamer basket of your instant pot.
5. Add 1-quart water to the pot, seal the instant pot lid and cook at High for 35 minutes.
6. Release the pressure naturally for 10 minutes, then release remaining pressure by turning the valve to 'Venting', carefully open the lid; leave the cake to cool down, before cutting and serving it.

Carrot Cake Recipe

(Prep + Cooking Time: 40 minutes | **Servings:** 6)

Ingredients:
- 1/3 cup carrots, grated
- 1/2 cup sugar
- 1/4 cup pineapple juice
- 4 tbsp. coconut oil, melted
- 1/2 tsp. baking soda
- 1/2 tsp. cinnamon powder
- 3/4 tsp. baking powder
- 1/4 tsp. nutmeg, ground.
- 1/2 tsp. allspice
- 1/3 cup pecans, toasted and chopped.
- 1/3 cup coconut flakes
- one egg
- 5 oz. flour
- A pinch of salt
- 3 tbsp. yogurt
- 2 cups water
- Cooking spray

Directions:
1. In a bowl, mix flour with baking soda and powder, salt, allspice, cinnamon and nutmeg and stir.
2. In another bowl, mix egg with yogurt, sugar, pineapple juice, oil, carrots, pecans and coconut flakes and stir well.
3. Combine the two mixtures and stir very well everything.
4. Pour this into a spring form greased with some cooking spray, add 2 cups water in your instant pot and place the form into the steamer basket.
5. Cover the instant pot and cook at High for 32 minutes.
6. Release pressure for 10 minutes, remove cake from the pot, leave it to cool down, then cut and serve it

Sticky Rice and Fruit

(Prep + Cooking Time: 31 minutes | **Servings:** 4)

Ingredients:

- 1 cup full-fat coconut milk
- 1/4 cup sugar
- 1 cup sweet rice; rinsed and drained
- 2 ¼ cups water; divided
- 1/2 tsp. salt or as your liking
- Sliced fresh fruit; for serving

Directions:

1. In a small saucepan over low heat, make the coconut sauce by combining the coconut milk, sugar and salt.
2. Cook for 2 to 3 minutes, stirring frequently, don't let it boil-until the sugar dissolves. Remove from the heat
3. Pour 1 cup of water into the Instant Pot and place a trivet into the inner pot. In a medium glass or stainless steel bowl, combine the remaining 1 ¼ cups water and the rice, ensuring the rice is completely covered.
4. Place the bowl atop the trivet. Lock the lid and turn the steam release handle to Sealing. Using the Manual function, set the cooker to High Pressure for 14 minutes
5. After completing the cooking time, let the pressure release naturally for 10 to 12 minutes; quick release any remaining pressure
6. Remove the lid carefully and add half the coconut sauce. Cover the cooker and let sit for at least 5 minutes so the rice absorbs the liquid. Top each serving with fruit and additional coconut sauce

Delicious Apple Crisp

(Prep + Cooking Time: 18 minutes | **Servings:** 4)

Ingredients:

- 5 apples, cored and cut into chunks
- 2 tsp. cinnamon
- 1/2 tsp. nutmeg
- 1/4 cup brown sugar
- 1/4 cup flour
- 3/4 cup old fashioned rolled oats
- 1/2 cup water
- 1 tbsp. maple syrup
- 4 tbsp. butter
- A pinch of salt

Directions:

1. Put the apples in your instant pot.
2. Add cinnamon, nutmeg, maple syrup and water.
3. In a bowl, mix butter with oats, sugar, salt and flour and stir well.
4. Drop spoonfuls of oats mix on top of apples, close the lid and cook at High for 8 minutes.
5. Release the pressure and serve warm

Quick Raspberry Curd

(Prep + Cooking Time: 25 minutes | **Servings:** 4)

Ingredients:

- 12 oz. raspberries
- 2 tbsp. butter
- 2 egg yolks
- 1 cup sugar
- 2 tbsp. lemon juice

Directions:

1. Put raspberries in your instant pot.
2. Add sugar and lemon juice; then stir well. seal the instant pot lid and cook at High for 2 minutes.
3. Release pressure for 5 minutes, carefully open the lid; strain raspberries and discard seeds
4. In a bowl, mix egg yolks with raspberries and stir well.
5. Return this to your instant pot, set it on Sauté mode; simmer for 2 minutes, add butter, stir and transfer to a container. Serve cold.

Candied Lemon Peel

(Prep + Cooking Time: 40 minutes | Servings: 80 pieces)

Ingredients:
- 5 big lemons
- 2 ¼ cups white sugar
- 5 cups water

Directions:
1. Wash lemons, slice them in half, reserve juice for another use, slice each half into quarters, take out the pulp and cut peel into thin strips
2. Put strips in your instant pot, add 4 cups water, seal the instant pot lid and cook at High for 3 minutes.
3. Release pressure fast, carefully open the lid; strain peel, rinse and put in a bowl.
4. Clean your instant pot and add 2 cups sugar and 1 cup water in it.
5. Add lemon strips; then stir well. set pot on Simmer mode and cook for 5 minutes.
6. Seal the instant pot lid, cook at High for 10 more minutes and release pressure naturally for 20 minutes
7. Strain peels again, spread them on a cutting board and leave them to cool down for 10 minutes. Keep them in jars until you serve them.

Coconut Rice Pudding

(Prep + Cooking Time: 35 minutes | Servings: 5)

Ingredients:
- 1 cup jasmine rice; rinsed and drained
- 1 (14-ounce) can full-fat coconut milk
- 1/4 cup sugar
- 2 cups water
- 2 tsp. ground cinnamon
- 1 ½ tsp. vanilla extract
- 1/2 tsp. ground nutmeg
- 1 tsp. salt or as your liking
- Nondairy milk, to thin after cooking
- Coconut flakes; for topping
- Raisins; for topping
- Maple syrup; for topping

Directions:
1. In the Instant Pot, combine the rice, coconut milk, water, cinnamon, vanilla, nutmeg, salt and sugar. If needed, whisk to break down any chunks from the canned coconut milk
2. Lock the lid and turn the steam release handle to Sealing. Select the Porridge function. This will automatically cook for 20 minutes
3. After completing the cooking time, let the pressure release naturally for 10 minutes; quick release any remaining pressure
4. Remove the lid carefully and stir in the milk if you want a thinner pudding. Keep in mind it will thicken as it cools, so if you're planning to reheat it later you'll likely need more milk.

Peach Jam Recipe

(Prep + Cooking Time: 15 minutes | Servings: 6)

Ingredients:
- 4 ½ cups peaches, peeled and cubed
- 1 box fruit pectin
- 6 cups sugar
- 1/4 cup crystallized ginger; chopped.

Directions:
1. Set your instant pot on Simmer mode, add peaches, ginger, and pectin, stir and bring to a boil
2. Add sugar; then stir well. seal the instant pot lid and cook at High for 5 minutes.
3. Quick release the pressure, carefully open the lid, divide jam into jars and serve.

Peach Compote

(Prep + Cooking Time: 13 minutes **| Servings:** 6)

Ingredients:

- 8 peaches; chopped.
- 6 tbsp. sugar
- 1 tsp. cinnamon, ground.
- 1 tsp. vanilla extract
- 1 vanilla bean, scraped
- 2 tbsp. grape nuts cereal

Directions:

1. Put peaches in your instant pot and mix with sugar, cinnamon, vanilla bean and vanilla extract. Stir well, close the lid and cook at High for 3 minutes.
2. Release pressure for 10 minutes, add grape nuts, stir well, transfer the compote to bowls and serve

Ruby Pears Delight

(Prep + Cooking Time: 20 minutes **| Servings:** 4)

Ingredients:

- 4 pears
- 26 oz. grape juice
- 11 oz. currant jelly
- 4 garlic cloves
- Juice and zest of 1 lemon
- 4 peppercorns
- 2 rosemary springs
- 1/2 vanilla bean

Directions:

1. Pour the jelly and grape juice in your instant pot and mix with lemon zest and juice
2. Dip each pear in this mix, wrap them in tin foil and arrange them in the steamer basket of your pot
3. Add garlic cloves, peppercorns, rosemary and vanilla bean to the juice mixture,
4. close the lid and cook at High for 10 minutes.
5. Quick release the pressure, carefully open the lid; take the pears out, unwrap them, arrange them on plates and serve cold with cooking juice on top.

Brownie Cake Recipe

(Prep + Cooking Time: 60 minutes **| Servings:** 6)

Ingredients:

- 1 cup borlotti beans, soaked for 8 hours and drained
- 4 cups water

For the cake:

- 1/4 cup almonds, sliced
- 1/2 cup cocoa powder
- 1/8 tsp. almond extract
- 1/2 cup raw sugar
- 3 tbsp. extra virgin olive oil
- 2 eggs
- 2 tsp. baking powder
- A pinch of salt

Directions:

1. Put beans and water in your instant pot, close the lid, cook at High for 12 minutes, release pressure, carefully open the lid; strain beans, transfer them to a blender and puree them.
2. Discard water from the pot and keep 1 cup
3. Grease a heatproof bowl with some olive oil and leave it aside for now.
4. Add cocoa powder, almond extract, honey, salt, eggs and oil to your blender with the beans and puree everything for 1 minute.
5. Transfer mix to greased bowl, spread, place bowl in the steamer basket of your pot, add reserved water from cooking the beans,
6. Seal the instant pot lid and cook at High for 20 minutes.
7. Quick release the pressure, take cake out of the pot, leave it aside for 15 minutes,
8. Transfer to a plate, sprinkle almonds on top, slice and serve.

Lemon Crème Pots

(Prep + Cooking Time: 35 minutes | **Servings:** 4)

Ingredients:
- 1 cup whole milk
- 2/3 cup sugar
- 6 egg yolks
- 1 cup fresh cream
- 1/2 cup fresh blackberries
- Zest from 1 lemon
- 1 cup water
- Blackberry syrup for serving

Directions:
1. Heat up a pan over medium heat, add milk, lemon zest and cream; then stir well. bring to a boil, take off heat and leave aside for 30 minutes
2. In a bowl, mix egg yolks with sugar and cold cream mix and stir well
3. Pour this into ramekins, cover them with tin foil, place them in the steamer basket of your instant pot, add 1 cup water to the pot, seal the instant pot lid and cook at High for 5 minutes.
4. Release the pressure naturally for 10 minutes, then release remaining pressure by turning the valve to 'Venting', carefully open the lid; take ramekins out
5. leave them to cool down and serve with blackberries and blackberry syrup on top

Fruit Compote

(Prep + Cooking Time: 20 minutes | **Makes:** 4 cups)

Ingredients:
- 1/4 cup freshly squeezed orange juice
- 1 ½ cups sugar
- 6 cups mixed berries

Directions:
1. In the Instant Pot, combine the berries, sugar and orange juice.
2. Lock the lid and turn the steam release handle to Sealing. Using the Manual function, set the cooker to High Pressure for 3 minutes
3. After completing the cooking time, turn off the Instant Pot and let the pressure release naturally for 10 minutes; quick release any remaining pressure
4. Remove the lid carefully. Select Sauté Medium. Stir the berry mixture and cook for 5 to 10 minutes (depending on how much liquid there is) so some of the excess liquid evaporates
5. Switch to Low if it's spattering too much. When you've reached the desired consistency, let the compote cool a bit before enjoying.

Samoa Cheese Cake Recipe

(Prep + Cooking Time: 1 hour 15 minutes | **Servings:** 6)

Ingredients:
For the crust:
- 1/2 cup chocolate graham crackers, crumbled.
- 2 tbsp. butter, melted

For the filling:
- 1 ½ tsp. vanilla extract
- 1/4 cup sour cream
- 1 tbsp. flour
- one egg yolk
- 2 eggs
- 1/4 cup heavy cream
- 1/2 cup sugar
- 12 oz. cream cheese, soft
- 1 cup water
- Cooking spray

For the topping:
- 1/4 cup chocolate; chopped.
- 12 caramels
- 3 tbsp. heavy cream
- 1 ½ cups coconut, sweet and shredded.

Directions:
1. Grease a spring form pan with some cooking spray and leave it aside

2. In a bowl, mix crackers with butter; then stir well. spread in the bottom of the pan and keep in the freezer for 10 minutes.
3. Meanwhile, in another bowl, mix cheese with sugar, heavy cream, vanilla, flour, sour cream and eggs and stir very well using a mixer.
4. Pour this into the pan on top of crust, cover with tin foil and place in the steamer basket of your instant pot.
5. Add 1 cup water to the pot, seal the instant pot lid and cook at High for 35 minutes
6. Release the pressure naturally for 10 minutes, then release remaining pressure by turning the valve to 'Venting', carefully open the lid; take the pan, remove tin foil and leave cake to cool down in the fridge for 4 hours.
7. Spread coconut on a lined baking sheet, introduce in the oven at 300 degrees F and bake for 20 minutes, stirring often
8. Put caramels in a heatproof bowl, introduce in the microwave for 2 minutes, stir every 20 seconds and then mix with toasted coconut
9. Spread this on your cheesecake and leave aside for now.
10. Put chocolate in another heatproof bowl, introduce in your microwave for a few seconds until it melts and drizzles over your cake. Serve right away

Delicious Apple Cake

(Prep + Cooking Time: 30 minutes | **Servings:** 8)

Ingredients:

- 1 apple, sliced
- 1 cup white flour
- 2 tsp. baking powder
- 1 tbsp. lemon juice
- 1/4 cup raw sugar
- 1/8 tsp. cinnamon powder
- one egg
- 1 tsp. vanilla extract
- 3 tbsp. olive oil
- 1 apple; chopped.
- 2 cup water
- 1 cup ricotta cheese
- 1 tsp. baking soda

Directions:

1. Put chopped and sliced apple in a bowl, add lemon juice, toss to coat and leave aside for now.
2. Line a heatproof dish with some parchment paper, grease with some oil and dust with some flour.
3. Sprinkle some sugar on the bottom and arrange sliced apple on top.
4. In a bowl, mix the egg with cheese, sugar, vanilla extract and oil and stir well.
5. Add flour, baking powder and soda and cinnamon and stir again.
6. Add chopped apple, toss to coat and pour everything into the pan.
7. Place the pan in the steamer basket of your instant pot, add the water to the pot, seal the instant pot lid and cook at High for 20 minutes
8. Quick release the pressure, carefully open the lid; turn cake on a plate and serve warm.

Chocolate Lava Cake Recipe

(Prep + Cooking Time: 15 minutes | **Servings:** 3)

Ingredients:

- 1 tbsp. cocoa powder
- 1/2 tsp. baking powder
- 1/2 tsp. orange zest
- 4 tbsp. milk
- 4 tbsp. flour
- one egg
- 4 tbsp. sugar
- 2 tbsp. olive oil
- A pinch of salt
- 1 cup water

Directions:

1. In a bowl, mix the egg with sugar, oil, milk, flour, salt, cocoa powder, baking powder and orange zest and stir very well.
2. Pour this into greased ramekins and place them in the steamer basket of your instant pot.

3. Add 1 cup water to the pot, seal the instant pot lid and cook at High for 6 minutes.
4. Quick release the pressure, carefully open the lid; take lava cakes out and serve them after they cool down a bit.

Tomato Jam Recipe

(Prep + Cooking Time: 40 minutes | **Servings:** 12)

Ingredients:
- 1 ½ lb. tomatoes, cored and chopped.
- 2 tbsp. lime juice
- 1 tsp. cinnamon
- 1 tsp. cumin
- 1/8 tsp. cloves, ground.
- 1 cup white sugar
- 1 tbsp. ginger, grated
- A pinch of salt
- 1 jalapeno pepper; minced.

Directions:
1. In your instant pot mix tomatoes with sugar, lime juice, ginger, cumin, cinnamon, cloves, salt and jalapeno pepper; then stir well.
2. Seal the instant pot lid and cook at High for 30 minutes.
3. Quick release the pressure, carefully open the lid; divide jam into jars and serve when needed

Caramel Sauce

(Prep + Cooking Time: 1 hour 10 minutes | **Servings:** 5)

Ingredients:
- 1 cup water
- 1 (11-ounce) can sweetened condensed coconut milk
- 1 tsp. coarse sea salt; optional

Directions:
1. Peel the label off the can and place the can on a trivet and into your Instant Pot. Pour in the water.
2. Lock the lid and turn the steam release handle to Sealing. Using the Manual function, set the cooker to High Pressure for 45 minutes
3. After completing the cooking time, let the pressure release naturally for about 20 minutes; or until the pin drops.
4. Remove the lid carefully. Wearing oven mitts, carefully remove the can and trivet. Set aside until cool enough to handle
5. Once cooled, open the can and pour the caramel sauce into a glass jar for storage. If separation occurs, whisk for 1 minute or so. For a salted caramel, stir in the sea salt

Lemon Marmalade Recipe

(Prep + Cooking Time: 25 minutes | **Servings:** 8)

Ingredients:
- 2 lb. lemons, washed, sliced and cut into quarters
- 4 lb. sugar
- 2 cups water

Directions:
1. Put lemon pieces in your instant pot, add 2 cups water, seal the instant pot lid and cook at High for 10 minutes.
2. Release the pressure naturally, carefully open the lid; add sugar; then stir well. set pot in Simmer mode and cook for 6 minutes, stirring all the time
3. Divide into jars and serve when needed.

Dulce De Leche

(**Prep + Cooking Time:** 35 minutes | **Servings:** 6)

Ingredients:
- 16 oz. canned sweet condensed milk.
- Water to cover

Directions:
1. Put condensed milk can in the steamer basket of your instant pot, add water in the pot to seal the instant pot lid and cook at High for 20 minutes.
2. Release the pressure naturally, carefully open the lid; take can out of the pot and leave it aside to cool down.

Bourbon Apple Crisp

(**Prep + Cooking Time:** 25 minutes | **Servings:** 4)

Ingredients:
- 5 apples, peeled and cut into thick slices
- 1/4 cup all-purpose flour
- 3/4 cup old-fashioned oats
- 1/4 cup bourbon
- 1/2 cup packed light brown sugar
- 1/4 cup water
- 4 tbsp. vegan butter
- 2 tbsp. maple syrup
- 2 tbsp. ground cinnamon
- 1/2 tsp. ground nutmeg
- Salt as your liking

Directions:
1. In the Instant Pot, stir together the apples, maple syrup, cinnamon, nutmeg and pinch of salt. Cover the apples with the water and bourbon.
2. In a medium microwave-safe bowl, microwave the butter until just barely melted. Add the oats, flour, brown sugar and ½ tsp. of salt. Stir to combine
3. Spoon the oat mixture over the apples, getting as much coverage as possible. Lock the lid and turn the steam release handle to Sealing
4. Using the Manual function, set the cooker to High Pressure for 8 minutes.
5. After completing the cooking time, let the pressure release naturally for 10 to 12 minutes; quick release any remaining pressure. Turn off the Instant Pot
6. Remove the lid carefully and let the crisp rest for a few minutes to thicken before serving.

Poached Figs

(**Prep + Cooking Time:** 17 minutes | **Servings:** 4)

Ingredients:
- 1 lb. figs
- 1 cup red wine

For the yogurt crème:
- 2 lb. plain yogurt
- 1/2 cup pine nuts, toasted
- 1/2 cup sugar

Directions:
1. Put the yogurt in a strainer, press well, transfer to a container and keep in the fridge overnight.
2. Put the wine in your instant pot, place figs in the steamer basket, seal the instant pot lid and cook on Low for 4 minutes.
3. Quick release the pressure, carefully open the lid; take figs out and arrange them on plates.
4. Set the pot on Simmer mode, add sugar and stir
5. Cook until sugar melts and then drizzle this sauce over figs
6. Add yogurt crème on top or the side and serve right away.

Classic Rhubarb Compote

(Prep + Cooking Time: 40 minutes | **Servings:** 8)

Ingredients:

- 1 lb. strawberries; chopped.
- 1/3 cup water
- 3 tbsp. honey
- 2 lb. rhubarb; chopped.
- Some fresh mint, torn

Directions:

1. Put rhubarb and water in your instant pot, close the lid, cook at High for 10 minutes, release pressure and carefully open the lid.
2. Add strawberries and honey; then stir well.
3. Set the pot on Simmer mode and cook compote for 20 minutes.
4. Add mint; then stir well. divide into jars and serve.

Vanilla Applesauce

(Prep + Cooking Time: 25 minutes | **Servings:** 7)

Ingredients:

- 3 pounds apples, cored and quartered, no need to peel
- ⅓ cup water
- 1 tsp. ground cinnamon; or more as needed
- 1 tsp. freshly squeezed lemon juice
- 1 tsp. vanilla extract
- 1/2 tsp. salt or as your liking

Directions:

1. In the Instant Pot, combine the apples, water, vanilla, cinnamon, lemon juice and salt.
2. Lock the lid and turn the steam release handle to Sealing. Using the Manual function, set the cooker to High Pressure for 5 minutes
3. After completing the cooking time, let the pressure release naturally for 10 minutes; quick release any remaining pressure
4. Remove the lid carefully. Using an immersion blender, blend the applesauce until smooth. Taste and add more cinnamon, as desired.

Tapioca Pudding

(Prep + Cooking Time: 18 minutes | **Servings:** 6)

Ingredients:

- 1/3 cup tapioca pearls, rinsed
- 1/2 cup sugar
- 1 ¼ cups milk
- 1 cup water
- 1/2 cup water
- Zest from 1/2 lemon

Directions:

1. In a heat proof bowl mix tapioca with milk, sugar, 1/2 cup water and lemon zest and stir well.
2. Put this in the steamer basket of your instant pot, add 1 cup water to the pot, seal the instant pot lid and cook at High for 8 minutes.
3. Quick release the pressure, leave it aside for 5 minutes more, carefully open the lid; take pudding out and serve it warm

Chocolate Pudding

(Prep + Cooking Time: 30 minutes | **Servings:** 4)

Ingredients:

- 6 oz. bittersweet chocolate; chopped.
- Chocolate shavings for serving
- 2 tsp. vanilla extract
- 1 ½ cups water
- 1/4 tsp. cardamom, ground.
- 1/2 cup milk
- 1 ½ cups heavy cream
- 5 egg yolks
- 1/3 cup brown sugar
- Crème fraiche for serving
- A pinch of salt

Directions:

1. Put cream and milk in a pot, bring to a simmer over medium heat, take off heat, add chocolate and whisk well.
2. In a bowl, mix egg yolks with vanilla, sugar, cardamom and a pinch of salt; then stir well. strain and mix with chocolate mix.
3. Pour this into a soufflé dish, cover with tin foil, place in the steamer basket of your instant pot, add water to the pot, close the lid, cook on Low for 18 minutes, release pressure naturally.
4. Take pudding out of the instant pot, leave aside to cool down and keep in the fridge for 3 hours before you serve it with crème fraiche and chocolate shavings on top

Chocolate Fondue Recipe

(Prep + Cooking Time: 12 minutes | **Servings:** 4)

Ingredients:

- 3.5 oz. dark chocolate, cut into chunks
- 2 cups water
- 1 tsp. liquor
- 1 tsp. sugar
- 3.5 oz. crème fraiche

Directions:

1. In a heat proof container, mix chocolate chunks with sugar, crème fraiche and liquor.
2. Pour the water in your instant pot, add the container in the steamer basket, close the lid and cook at High for 2 minutes.
3. Release the pressure naturally, carefully open the lid; take container out, stir well your fondue and serve it right away with some fresh fruits.

Made in the USA
Columbia, SC
30 November 2019

84073992R00141